D0983441

Jonah & Micah

REFORMED EXPOSITORY COMMENTARY

A Series

Series Editors

Richard D. Phillips
Philip Graham Ryken

Testament Editors

Iain M. Duguid, Old Testament
Daniel M. Doriani, New Testament

Jonah & Micah

RICHARD D. PHILLIPS

P&R
PUBLISHING
P.O. BOX 817 • PHILLIPSBURG • NEW JERSEY 08865-0817

Unless otherwise indicated, all Scripture quotations are from The Holy Bible, English Standard Version® (ESV®), copyright © 2001 by Crossway, a publishing ministry of Good News Publishers. Used by permission. All rights reserved.

Italics within Scripture quotations indicate emphasis added.

Page design by Lakeside Design Plus

Printed in the United States of America

Library of Congress Cataloging-in-Publication Data

Phillips, Richard D. (Richard Davis), 1960-
  Jonah & Micah / Richard D. Phillips.
      p. cm. -- (Reformed expository commentary)
  Includes bibliographical references and indexes.
  ISBN 978-1-59638-114-8 (cloth)
  1. Bible. O.T. Jonah--Commentaries. 2. Bible. O.T. Micah--Commentaries. I. Title. II. Title: Jonah and Micah.
  BS1605.53.P45 2010
  224'.92077--dc22
                    2010009423

To the board of directors of the Alliance of Confessing Evangelicals,
who have lovingly directed and supported
the preaching of God's Word for over fifty years

and

to our incomparable God,
who delights in showing mercy (Mic. 7:18)

Contents

Contents

Series Introduction

In every generation there is a fresh need for the faithful exposition of God's Word in the church. At the same time, the church must constantly do the work of theology: reflecting on the teaching of Scripture, confessing its doctrines of the Christian faith, and applying them to contemporary culture. We believe that these two tasks—the expositional and the theological—are interdependent. Our doctrine must derive from the biblical text, and our understanding of any particular passage of Scripture must arise from the doctrine taught in Scripture as a whole.

We further believe that these interdependent tasks of biblical exposition and theological reflection are best undertaken in the church, and most specifically in the pulpits of the church. This is all the more true since the study of Scripture properly results in doxology and praxis—that is, in praise to God and practical application in the lives of believers. In pursuit of these ends, we are pleased to present the Reformed Expository Commentary as a fresh exposition of Scripture for our generation in the church. We hope and pray that pastors, teachers, Bible study leaders, and many others will find this series to be a faithful, inspiring, and useful resource for the study of God's infallible, inerrant Word.

The Reformed Expository Commentary has four fundamental commitments. First, these commentaries aim to be *biblical*, presenting a comprehensive exposition characterized by careful attention to the details of the text. They are not exegetical commentaries—commenting word by word or even verse by verse—but integrated expositions of whole passages of Scripture. Each commentary will thus present a sequential, systematic treatment of an entire book of the Bible, passage by passage. Second, these commentaries are unashamedly *doctrinal*. We are committed to the Westminster Confession of Faith and Catechisms as containing the system of doctrine taught in the Scriptures of the Old and New Testaments. Each volume will teach, promote, and defend the doctrines of the Reformed faith as they are found in the Bible. Third, these commentaries are *redemptive-historical* in their orientation. We believe in the unity of the Bible and its central message of salvation in Christ. We are thus committed to a Christ-centered view of the Old Testament, in which its characters, events, regulations, and institutions are properly understood as pointing us to Christ and his gospel, as well as giving us examples to follow in living by faith. Fourth, these commentaries are *practical*, applying the text of Scripture to contemporary challenges of life—both public and private—with appropriate illustrations.

The contributors to the Reformed Expository Commentary are all pastor-scholars. As pastor, each author will first present his expositions in the pulpit ministry of his church. This means that these commentaries are rooted in the teaching of Scripture to real people in the church. While aiming to be scholarly, these expositions are not academic. Our intent is to be faithful, clear, and helpful to Christians who possess various levels of biblical and theological training—as should be true in any effective pulpit ministry. Inevitably this means that some issues of academic interest will not be covered. Nevertheless, we aim to achieve a responsible level of scholarship, seeking to promote and model this for pastors and other teachers in the church. Significant exegetical and theological difficulties, along with such historical and cultural background as is relevant to the text, will be treated with care.

We strive for a high standard of enduring excellence. This begins with the selection of the authors, all of whom have proven to be outstanding communicators of God's Word. But this pursuit of excellence is also reflected in a disciplined editorial process. Each volume is edited by both a series editor and a testament editor. The testament editors, Iain Duguid for the Old Testament and Daniel Doriani for the New Testament, are accomplished pastors and respected scholars who have taught at the seminary level. Their job is to ensure that each volume is sufficiently conversant with up-to-date scholarship and is faithful and accurate in its exposition of the text. As series editors, we oversee each volume to ensure its overall quality—including excellence of writing, soundness of teaching, and usefulness in application. Working together as an editorial team, along with the publisher, we are devoted to ensuring that these are the best commentaries our gifted authors can provide, so that the church will be served with trustworthy and exemplary expositions of God's Word.

It is our goal and prayer that the Reformed Expository Commentary will serve the church by renewing confidence in the clarity and power of Scripture and by upholding the great doctrinal heritage of the Reformed faith. We hope that pastors who read these commentaries will be encouraged in their own expository preaching ministries, which we believe to be the best and most biblical pattern for teaching God's Word in the church. We hope that lay teachers will find these commentaries among the most useful resources they rely upon for understanding and presenting the text of the Bible. And we hope that the devotional quality of these studies of Scripture will instruct and inspire each Christian who reads them in joyful, obedient discipleship to Jesus Christ.

May the Lord bless all who read the Reformed Expository Commentary. We commit these volumes to the Lord Jesus Christ, praying that the Holy Spirit will use them for the instruction and edification of the church, with thanksgiving to God the Father for his unceasing faithfulness in building his church through the ministry of his Word.

Richard D. Phillips
Philip Graham Ryken
Series Editors

PREFACE

I will not be the first Bible teacher to point out our great need to recover the Old Testament today. The New Testament is of course indispensable to Christians and justly loved by us all. But the Old Testament presents the same God, the same gospel, and the same issues of sin and redemption in the form of historical events that powerfully connect with us today. This is especially true of the so-called Minor Prophets, the twelve books at the end of the Old Testament that deliver God's prophetic Word in settings that are often very much like our own.

I have the privilege in this volume of presenting expositions on two of the Minor Prophets, Jonah and Micah. Jonah is a figure of such contemporary features that he could walk out of one of our churches just as easily as he once walked (or, more likely, crawled!) out of the belly of the great fish. The book of Jonah challenges us to consider not only what it means to *believe* the gospel of God's grace, but also what it means to *live* the gospel of grace. Moreover, Jonah reminds us that the chief characteristic of redeemed people is not that they never sin, for sadly we still do, but that they are ready to repent of their sin when they are reminded of God's grace. If readers find that they are still learning the grace of our Lord Jesus, then Jonah is an ideal companion, and God's dealings with his ancient prophet may well help us to understand God's challenge to us as well.

The prophet Micah lived several generations later than Jonah, and his ministry took place in a very different setting. God called Jonah to cry out to the wicked idolaters in Nineveh, but God called Micah to cry out against the wicked sinners of Jerusalem. Unlike the earlier prophet, who wrestled against God's gospel message for pagan unbelievers, Micah was brokenhearted in his fervent desire for Jerusalem to repent and believe. If Jonah connects with our mission to the world today, Micah informs our challenge to today's church. This contemporary of Isaiah, with whom Micah shared many sermons, faced not only the external threats of neighboring powers (Sennacherib's invasion in 701 B.C.) but the far more alarming threat of divine judgment for Jerusalem's corruption and injustice. Like Isaiah, however, the darkness of Micah's prophetic denunciation was rivaled only by the bright gospel light that shone through God's promises to him of comfort and hope. Studying Micah will remind Christians today that ours is a holy God who responds angrily to the presumption of his people, but also a faithful God of matchless grace to whom we may ever appeal for saving mercy. The God whom Micah presents to us truly is an incomparable God: sovereign, holy, and abounding in grace.

These expositions on Jonah were first preached to the congregation of First Presbyterian Church, Coral Springs/Margate, Florida, and then again, along with the studies in Micah, during the evening services of Second Presbyterian Church in Greenville, South Carolina. I thank these beloved congregations, with special thanks for the encouragement I have received from both Sessions and the congregations for my commitment to study and writing. I also am appreciative to Drs. Philip Ryken and Iain Duguid, whose editorial labors have measurably improved the quality of this book, as well as to Marvin Padgett and my many friends at P&R Publishing. This commentary is dedicated to the board of directors of the Alliance of Confessing Evangelicals, with praise to God for their support and oversight of over fifty years of expository preaching in radio broadcasts, as well as for their loving friendship to me over many years.

Additionally, I give praise to God for the devoted ministry of my dear wife, Sharon, both for her unflagging support and her companionship in ministry, as well as for our five dearly beloved children. Lastly, I give thanks to the God of grace: Father, Son, and Holy Spirit. Truly, who is a God like him, who pardons our sins and delights in showing mercy? To him be glory forever.

Jonah

LEARNING THE GRACE OF GOD

1

MESSENGER OF GRACE

Jonah 1:1–3

*Now the word of the LORD came to Jonah the son of Amittai, say-
ing, "Arise, go to Nineveh, that great city, and call out against it,
for their evil has come up before me." But Jonah rose to flee to Tarshish from the presence of the LORD. (Jonah 1:1–3)*

*I*t is one thing to know the doctrine of salvation by grace, and
quite another to know the grace of the doctrine of salvation.
This is the lesson of Jonah, the prophet who knew God's grace
but was challenged by God inwardly to embrace it. Sinclair Ferguson has
expressed Jonah's story in these terms: "It is really a book about . . . how one
man came, through painful experience, to discover the true character of the
God whom he had already served in the earlier years of his life. He was to
find the doctrine about God (with which he had long been familiar) come
alive in his experience."[1]

When most people think of Jonah, they think only of the famous fish
that swallowed him. Their first question is, Did this really happen? Or,
What kind of fish was it? But these questions are incidental to the book.

---

1. Sinclair B. Ferguson, *Man Overboard! The Story of Jonah* (Edinburgh: Banner of Truth, 2008), xi.

Far more importantly, Jonah brings us face to face with such important issues as God's grace for the wicked, God's sovereignty over his servants, and the intense human struggle involved with forgiveness and repentance. Ferguson summarizes, "The Book of Jonah is not so much about this great fish that appears in the middle of the book . . . [but] in order to teach Jonah that he has a gracious God."[2]

THE PROPHECY OF JONAH

When approaching a book of prophecy, we usually think of future predictions or divine pronouncements for God's people. But the book of Jonah mainly recounts a story from the life of the prophet himself. The closest parallels are the accounts of Elijah and Elisha in 1 and 2 Kings. Indeed, since Jonah begins his ministry shortly after the time of Elijah and Elisha, he likely was one of their immediate successors, and may have been a personal disciple of the latter.

The Bible does not name the author of the book of Jonah, although Jonah may well have written it about his own experience. Some scholars argue that the Hebrew language found in this book is typical of a later period in history, perhaps the time of the Jews' exile in Babylon. But this is not conclusive, especially since Jonah's northern dialect may account for differences in language and style. In short, there is no compelling reason to doubt that this book of Scripture dates from the time frame it describes, the eighth century B.C.

It is helpful to know something about the world in which Jonah lived. According to 2 Kings 14:25, Jonah served as a prophet in the time of King Jeroboam II, one of the many wicked kings of the northern kingdom of Israel. It was now about 150 years since the death of King Solomon, and the nation had long been divided. Ten of Israel's twelve tribes were united as this northern kingdom, while only Judah and Benjamin held to the Davidic throne in Jerusalem and worshiped at the temple that Solomon built.

The northern kingdom had many problems, beginning with constant idolatry and rebellion against the Lord. This was the main issue with which the prophets contended. However, there were political and military problems as well, for just north of them was the Assyrian Empire, the superpower of

2. Sinclair B. Ferguson, "What Jonah Learned," in *The Doctrines of Grace, 2006 Philadelphia Conference on Reformed Theology* (Philadelphia: Alliance of Confessing Evangelicals, 2006), audio recording.

the time. Israel's constant concern was to maintain her independence and power against this ominous threat.

The prophets of the northern kingdom engaged in two main tasks. The first was to call the kings and the nation to repentance. We find men like Elijah facing down the priests of Baal and confronting the king over idolatry. But the prophets were also messengers of grace. Over and again, God showed mercy to his wayward people, often through the ministry of these prophets.

It is in this connection that Jonah is mentioned in 2 Kings. For a while, Assyria was divided and suffered from famine, so that Israel's former boundaries were restored. This was by God's hand, to demonstrate his grace to Israel, renew their hope, and encourage their repentance. Jonah himself had delivered the good news:

> [The king] restored the border of Israel from Lebo-hamath as far as the Sea of the Arabah, according to the word of the LORD, the God of Israel, which he spoke by his servant Jonah the son of Amittai, the prophet, who was from Gath-hepher. For the LORD saw that the affliction of Israel was very bitter, for there was none left, bond or free, and there was none to help Israel. But the LORD had not said that he would blot out the name of Israel from under heaven, so he saved them by the hand of Jeroboam the son of Joash (2 Kings 14:25–27).

This shows that Jonah was in a remarkable position to view the grace and mercy of God. Israel had done nothing to merit God's favor; instead, their wickedness deserved God's wrath. Yet God was merciful. He reached out a hand of favor to woo his wayward people. In this, Jonah had a front-row seat. But as this book records, Jonah still had much to learn about the grace of God, just as we do today.

GOD'S REDEMPTIVE CONCERN FOR THE WORLD

Jonah's struggle with God's grace is displayed from the very start of this book. The cause was a most unexpected call from God that shocked and repulsed the prophet. "Arise," said the Lord, "go to Nineveh, that great city, and call out against it, for their evil has come up before me" (Jonah 1:2). This is the kind of command a prophet might expect to receive: a summons to confront the wicked with their sin. So what bothered Jonah so much? Simply this: his knowledge of the grace of God. Jonah had learned what most people do not know, that when God calls us to face our sin his purpose is to show his mercy and thereby to save. Knowing the grace of God as he did, from the very start Jonah suspected God's purposes toward hated Nineveh.

This reminds us that God is aware of all that is happening in the world. Most people think that if they ignore God, he will ignore them. They like to think of God—if they think of God at all—like the blind watchmaker who winds things up and lets them run pretty much as they will. But, says Frank Page, "This text portrays God as one who notices, as a God who is active, and as a God who takes sin seriously."[3] Nineveh was a city that seems to have known little of the true God and was completely given over to evil. However, this does not mean that God knew nothing of Nineveh or that he had yet given over Nineveh to final judgment. The same is true today: people may deny God, but God does not deny them, does not ignore their sin, and does not fail to extend his mercy for their salvation.

This is a truth that many of God's people have struggled to accept. They are all too happy for God's mercy to be extended to them—but not to others! This was very much the case of the ancient Israelites, who prided themselves as God's chosen people. The Israelites possessed the word of the prophets and God's covenant of grace. Yet they forgot that these were held not solely for themselves, but in trust for all the world. The psalmist sang, "May God be gracious to us and bless us and make his face to shine upon us, that your way may be known on earth, your saving power among all nations" (Ps. 67:1–2). In fact, Israel's call to bless the nations goes back to their very beginning, in God's promise to the patriarch Abraham: "I will make of you a great nation, and I will bless you and make your name great, so that you will be a blessing" (Gen. 12:2).

Jonah is in this respect a figure depicting all of Israel. He resented the idea of Israel's God sending Israel's grace to non-Israelites—especially to the hated Ninevites. The name Nineveh dominated their minds the way Babylon would later strike fear into Jewish hearts. Nineveh was the military capital of Assyria, a place of unbounded violence and evil. The best parallels today would be the most violent terrorist organizations or narcotics cartels, who

---

3. Billy K. Smith and Frank S. Page, *Amos, Obadiah, Jonah*, New American Commentary 19B (Nashville: Broadman & Holman, 1995), 226.

strike their victims with a bloodthirsty glee. A visit to the British Museum in London, which contains a fantastic collection of Assyrian artifacts, discovers their own self-depiction as sadistic, genocidal oppressors. Northern Israelites like Jonah—his hometown of Gath-hepher seems to have been in the northernmost region—suffered most from Assyrian depredations. So Jonah was like Christians today who want God's grace for themselves but God's judgment against other wicked sinners, especially those who have hurt them. How easy it is for us to ask God's blessing for ourselves while we pray for him to cure the coworker who slandered our reputation, the thief who broke into our house, or the family member who never had a good word for us. Jonah did not want Nineveh to be blessed because of what Nineveh had done before and what Nineveh might do again. His quarrel with God's grace was born at least in part of revulsion, hatred, and fear.

But Jonah's resentment was not directed merely against his national enemies. He seems to have disdained God's grace for all unworthy sinners. At the end of the book, Jonah explains why he rejected God's summons to preach at Nineveh: "For I knew that you are a gracious God and merciful, slow to anger and abounding in steadfast love, and relenting from disaster" (Jonah 4:2). Jonah might have learned this from Exodus 34:6, in which the Lord reveals himself as "a God merciful and gracious, slow to anger, and abounding in steadfast love and faithfulness." This truth was reinforced by Jonah's own dealings with Israel's wicked king. Despite Jeroboam's gross sins against God—many of which must have brought affliction to the faithful—God had shown him mercy. By this point, Jonah had had enough of God's forgiving mercy for the wicked.

God had extended grace to Jeroboam and the idolatrous Israelites, and Jonah had borne this good news. Yet it was not good news to him. He understood why God might show favor to people like himself—was he not faithful?—but he resented God's grace for the wicked. This self-righteousness lives on today, and it accounts for the failure of many Christians to proclaim the good news of salvation in Jesus Christ joyfully to people they consider unworthy. If Jonah felt this way toward idolatrous Israelites, how much greater must his contempt have been for the idolatrous Ninevites! As each of us looks into the mirror, it would be good to consider ways in which we may harbor a Jonah-like lack of pity on those who have sinned against us.

A Spiritual Assessment

We should reflect on the errors revealed by Jonah's disgruntled attitude. We might start by realizing that resentment toward God's grace is a sure sign of spiritual decline. It is not surprising that such thoughts would be revealed even by the prophets in a time like Jonah's. The nineteenth-century expositor Hugh Martin describes them as

> "days of Israel's degeneracy, when faith gave place to formalism, and contrite gratitude to cold and supercilious ceremony; when self-righteous pride, singularly enough keeping pace with increasing iniquity and worthlessness, arrogantly claimed right to the privileges of the covenant in very proportion as all the spirit of the covenant was violated; when the close and narrow spirit of legalism, resting its claims on carnal distinctions, and saying, 'We have Abraham to be our Father,' superseded the true spirit of Israel."[4] A little reflection on Jonah's mentality will remind us of the spirit of the Pharisees in the time of Jesus. Martin comments that Jonah "enacts exactly the part of the Pharisee of the parable, while the publican may represent the waste of heathendom."[5]

How can we know if we also are approaching such an attitude? If our primary concern in worship is our consumer preferences rather than the God whose name we praise, if we gaze upon the wicked around us and see mainly a threat to our Christian lifestyles instead of perishing sinners in need of the gospel, and if we pray for forgiveness of our sins but justice for the agents of a wicked culture, then it cannot be doubted that the Pharisaical spirit of Jonah is in us.

Secondly, Jonah's resentment reveals a deep ignorance of God. He understood the Lord as his God and Israel's God, but not the God of Nineveh. Martin observes:

> Jehovah is the God of the spirits of all flesh, and ruleth over all the nations. Any other or more limited idea of His government, reduces Him, if not to the level, at least to the company, of the local, territorial, geographical gods of heathendom. And thus, by taking a wrong view of the relation of heathendom to the living and true God, the God of Israel, Israel virtually imbibed the very views of heathendom itself.[6]

4. Hugh Martin, *A Commentary on Jonah* (Edinburgh: Banner of Truth, 1870; repr. 1958), 6.
5. Ibid.
6. Ibid., 7.

The true God is God of all the earth and all peoples. If it glorifies him to extend saving grace to Israel and those who have taken the name of Christians, it glorifies him just as much to extend the grace of the gospel to every sinner in the world.

Jonah's resentment further reveals ignorance of himself as a sinner and of God's way of justification. Paul writes, "All have sinned and fall short of the glory of God, and are justified by his grace as a gift, through the redemption that is in Christ Jesus" (Rom. 3:23–24). The person who realizes this will never look on the gospel offer of forgiveness to everyone with anything other than wonder and joy. A spiritually vibrant Jonah would have gratefully received God's call to preach in Nineveh. He would have been reminded of the way he had been saved out of his sin and justified by free grace, received through faith alone, and would have run to Nineveh on refreshed legs. But it is always the case—as it was in his—that those who have come to stand before God with claims of their own merit, relying at least in part on their works or their heritage rather than wholly relying on God's free grace, will lose enthusiasm for the idea of saving grace for the wicked.

Grace for the Nations

The idea of the gospel call extending to the Ninevites was something new and appalling to the mind of Jonah. Up to this time, God's grace was restricted to Israel. Only Israel received the Passover. Only Israel possessed the temple of the Lord and the sacrifices for sin. But there had been signs of something more, scattered throughout the earlier prophets, especially in the ministries of Elijah and Elisha.

For instance, when Elijah announced a famine on Israel, he departed to live in Gentile regions. "Arise, go to Zarephath, which belongs to Sidon, and dwell there," God told him. "Behold, I have commanded a widow there to feed you" (1 Kings 17:9). Israel's prophet fed by the hand of a pagan, since Israel was famished! Notice the remarkable similarity of this with God's call to Jonah, "Arise, go to Nineveh." This suggests that God's call to Jonah was a warning to unbelieving Israel. If Israel hardened its heart, God would find believers elsewhere to receive his prophets.

Elisha also had dealings with the Gentiles. A Syrian general named Naaman suffered from leprosy and could find no cure. Then his Israelite slave girl told him of the prophet, so off went the Syrian to see Elisha. Naaman was healed and went home a worshiper of the true God. This declared that God's saving blessings are not restricted to one nation or tribe, but that all who come in faith will be saved.

These two episodes happen to be the very accounts Jesus cited when he addressed this same matter in the synagogue of Nazareth. Jesus had revealed himself as the promised Messiah, but his hometown would not receive him. So Jesus responded:

> I tell you, there were many widows in Israel in the days of Elijah, when the heavens were shut up three years and six months, and a great famine came over all the land, and Elijah was sent to none of them but only to Zarephath, in the land of Sidon, to a woman who was a widow. And there were many lepers in Israel in the time of the prophet Elisha, and none of them was cleansed, but only Naaman the Syrian. (Luke 4:25–27)

The Nazarenes thought in much the same way that Jonah did:

> When they heard these things, all in the synagogue were filled with wrath. And they rose up and drove him out of the town. (Luke 4:28)

This shows a clear trajectory between the experiences of Elijah and Elisha, the calling of Jonah to Nineveh, and Jesus' call of the gospel to the nations. God's call to Jonah was part of his grand program to bring salvation to the whole world. This had always been God's plan, just as he said to Israel's father, Abraham: "in you all the families of the earth shall be blessed" (Gen. 12:3).

Jonah had missed this truth. He believed in the grace of God, but resented it when God showed mercy to the wicked in Israel. And he certainly did not believe in the grace of God for all the world. In a sense, he wanted Israel to be glorified, or even just the righteous in Israel to be glorified. What he needed to know is that the purpose of God's grace is that God would be glorified and that his glory should be displayed in all the world.

Jonah feared that God's grace for Nineveh would come at Israel's expense. However, grace never works this way. Grace is not portioned out in servings—if for one, then not for the other. In God's plan, grace abounds through his gospel, so that God's blessing on Nineveh would result in blessing for Israel as well.

In fact, one of the best ways any person or nation can provide for their own need of the gospel is to spread it to others. An example is shown in the history of Christian missions. In the early medieval centuries, Christians on the continent of Europe took great pains to spread the gospel to the British Isles. Strongholds of Christian learning were established in those wild lands, especially the monasteries of Ireland and Scotland. Within a few centuries, however, barbarian invasions had darkened the continent, and in the turmoil the gospel was nearly lost. British Christians noticed this, and in the seventh and eighth centuries missionaries such as Columban from Ireland and Willibrord and Winfrid from Saxon England returned the light of the gospel to Europe. Only because earlier generations of Continental Christians had spread the gospel to Britain—by God's providential working—was the gospel preserved for their own descendants.

With this in mind, Jonah's devotion to Israel should have motivated him for the journey to Nineveh. But God had one additional purpose: by sending his grace into the heart of paganism and displaying there his power to save, God meant to provoke his own people to jealousy. This is what God had foretold in the time of Moses, should his people ever turn to idols: "They have made me jealous with what is no god; they have provoked me to anger with their idols. So I will make them jealous with those who are no people; I will provoke them to anger with a foolish nation" (Deut. 32:21). As Hugh Martin explains: God had "a design to rebuke Israel and provoke them to jealousy by sending His prophet to the capital of heathendom. He was giving them a preliminary warning of what their continued ingratitude would render inevitable—the removal of the vineyard from them, and the giving of it to a people who would bring forth the fruit thereof."[7]

It is difficult not to wonder whether something similar is taking place today in the once-Christian West with respect to the once-pagan lands of the developing world. In many places in Africa, South America, and Asia, the Christian church is expanding rapidly. Evangelists find ready hearers for their witness of the gospel, and missionary prayers seem answered practically as soon as they are uttered. Might God be seeking to provoke jealousy in Europe and America, where few seem interested in Christianity? Surely, this relative disparity in the success of the gospel urges us in the West to repent of our

7. Martin, *Jonah*, 23.

worldliness and seek the Lord for a renewed outpouring of his Holy Spirit on these lands that once shown brightly with the light of Christ.

It was out of mercy for Israel that God sent his grace to Nineveh, that his covenant people might renew their faith. It was the same mercy for the Jews that sent the gospel of Jesus Christ to the Gentiles (see Rom. 11:11), and it is surely in part out of his mercy for the now-decadent Western nations that God has displayed his saving grace to distant peoples throughout the world today.

LESSONS OF GRACE

These lessons are no less relevant today than in the time of the prophet. What are the lessons? First, God's grace must always be the chief delight of God's people; without a humble rejoicing in God's grace, no people, church, or nation can ever stand. Furthermore, the gospel gives a constant reminder to every believer that his or her own salvation is a sovereign, merciful, and unmerited gift from God, no different in kind from the grace received by the most notorious sinner imaginable. Grace humbles us before God, and grace lifts us up in saving faith. Lastly, to know God is to know his grace, and to feel God's grace is to run on winged feet to tell the world, even to tell the Ninevites of our own time.

Jonah's problem was no small one. It was a problem that unless remedied must bring him and Israel to ruin. Surely, this was why God chose Jonah for this mission; it was an act of grace for God to call him. Is God challenging you with his grace? Is God challenging your attitudes toward him, toward the church, toward people whom you resent and fear, and toward the whole world? If he is, it is not only because of his grace for them but also because of his grace for you.

2

BUT JONAH

Jonah 1:1–3

*Now the word of the LORD came to Jonah the son of Amittai, say-
ing, "Arise, go to Nineveh, that great city, and call out against it,
for their evil has come up before me." But Jonah rose to flee to
Tarshish from the presence of the LORD. (Jonah 1:1–3)*

The book of Jonah is not merely the story of the interesting
things that happened to this Old Testament figure. More than
that, Jonah was a representative of the people of Israel in their
disdain for God's grace to the nations. Ancient Israelites are not the only
ones who would profit from a study of Jonah, however. For if we look into
Jonah's mirror we will also see ourselves. Times change and situations vary.
But all of God's people find themselves in Jonah's position before God,
called by the Lord to serve his gospel in the world. And all too many find
their feet tracing Jonah's path of rebellion, in part because they misunderstand or even resent God's grace for all the world.

GOD'S SOVEREIGN CALL

God's call for Jonah to preach in Nineveh displays his grace for all the
world. But it also reveals God's sovereignty over his people. When we think of

God as sovereign, we usually think of his ultimate control over all the affairs of heaven and earth. Jesus said that not a single sparrow falls to the ground apart from the Father's will. But we also mean that God exercises sovereign rule over his kingdom. Sovereigns command. Kings and queens send forth their decrees, demanding obedience. God is no less sovereign. And just as God glorifies his grace by sending his gospel to the far corners of the world, he also glorifies his sovereignty by exercising his rule over his creatures.

Jonah begins, like many other Bible books, by affirming its message as God's Word. "The word of the LORD came to Jonah son of Ammitai" (Jonah 1:1). When we read statements like this we should be reminded of what we are handling when it comes to Holy Scripture. These are not the inspired thoughts of spiritual men, but the very Word of God revealed through human agents. The apostle Peter described the process of inspiration by saying, "Men spoke from God as they were carried along by the Holy Spirit" (2 Peter 1:21). But it is not just that in the Bible we have teaching from God himself, important an insight as that is. More than that, the Bible contains God's *sovereign* Word for his creatures. Just as the word of the Lord came to Jonah, the word of the Lord comes to us as we read the Bible. The right way to approach Holy Scripture is with humility, spiritually prostrate before our Sovereign, ready to learn and do all that he commands.

As the Bible records it, God's sovereign call to Jonah was brief, direct, and imperative. It did not come with an explanation. Many people today consent to obey God's Word only when it makes sense to them. But the sovereign God does not accept such an arrangement. God's call to Jonah was sudden, just as military commanders often receive sudden instructions based on concerns known only to their superiors. We, too, may have a sudden command from God's Word made known to us, and our duty to God is to obey immediately and submissively. As Isaiah replied when God first made his will known to him, we likewise should respond: "Here am I! Send me" (Isa. 6:8).

Not only was God's command to Jonah sovereign and sudden, it was also difficult. Nineveh was a great distance away, in the heart of a violent empire. Nineveh was among the largest cities in the ancient world, which is why God refers to it as "that great city Nineveh." Chapter 3 tells us "Nineveh was an exceedingly great city, three days' journey in breadth" (Jonah 3:3). It was also distant, about six hundred miles northeast of Israel, near present-day Mosul in Iraq. And God was sending Jonah alone, commanding him to pronounce a

message of doom: "Yet forty days, and Nineveh shall be overthrown!" (Jonah 3:4). Imagine receiving such a calling! Imagine the difficulties that would go through the mind, and the obstacles to any kind of success!

But God has and exercises the right to give the most difficult missions to his people. God called Abraham to leave his father's land and journey to a distant land. God told Moses to stand before Pharaoh and cry, "Let my people go" (Exod. 5:1). Moses replied the way that we often do: "Oh, my Lord, please send someone else" (Exod. 4:13). But God rejected this counsel; it was his will for Moses to be the one. God once directed the prophet Isaiah to walk naked and barefoot for three years as he preached judgment against Egypt and Cush (Isa. 20:2–3). God directed a teenage girl named Mary to have the Son of the Most High carried in her virgin womb, threatening her reputation and betrothal.

Why does God give such difficult commands? For his own sovereign purposes! But also for the purpose of his grace. When God gives the most difficult commands he typically intends the most marvelous acts of deliverance and salvation. Abraham was sent to Canaan to become the father of the people of faith (Gal. 3:7). Moses was sent to Egypt to lead the exodus. Mary as a virgin bore a child and delivered the Messiah to the world. Whenever we find that God has called us to a task that seems far more difficult than we think we can handle, our hope ought to be kindled that God intends to do something wonderful and great.

Of course, the most difficult of all commands was given by God the Father to God the Son. The Lord Jesus Christ submitted to the Father's will with joy, even when it meant a cruel death on a Roman cross. Jesus knew the prophecy that said of him, "It was the will of the LORD to crush him; he has put him to grief; when his soul makes an offering for sin" (Isa. 53:10). But Jesus replied, "Behold, I have come to do your will, O God, as it is written of me in the scroll of the book" (Heb. 10:7). Why did Jesus obey such a command as to die on the cross? He obeyed because he knew and trusted God the Father, just as we have every reason to do. He knew that God is faithful and that all his purposes are holy and good. Jesus loved the Father and delighted to do his will and display his glory. This, too, should be our attitude. Jesus also knew that God's purposes—however severe—are purposes of glory and grace. After Isaiah foretold the cross, he added, "He shall see his offspring; he shall prolong his days; the will of the LORD shall prosper in his hand" (Isa. 53:10).

So Jesus knew that beyond the cross there waited a resurrection crown of glory. Our crosses are similar in this respect: through obedience to difficult callings from God we can expect God's provision of power and God's reward of eternal glory.

Lastly, God's call to Jonah was righteous: "Arise, go to Nineveh, that great city, and call out against it, for their evil has come up before me" (Jonah 1:2). The incredible evil of Nineveh was known to the Lord. So it was right for him to send a representative and to declare his displeasure against the city. Jonah may not have liked the idea of going to Nineveh, but as a prophet of the Most High it was right for him to be sent there with this message of warning. Moreover, it was righteous of God to give that wicked city an opportunity to repent. They were his own creatures and, whether they knew it or not, God was their sovereign king as well. What could be more righteous than for the sovereign Lord to send his prophet to cry out against Nineveh?

The character of this command to Jonah—its sovereign, sudden, difficult, and righteous character—will be repeated in our own lives. Should we complain? Should we rebel? Should we drag our feet and kick back? Not if it is God who has given the command. He has the right and he has earned the trust to be taken at his bare word. Christians who know the Lord and understand his ways will therefore receive the word of the Lord in humble, submissive, and joyful obedience.

Jonah's Flight

That is not what Jonah did, however. God told Jonah to arise, and he arose all right. But he did not go to Nineveh. Instead, he went in precisely the opposite direction.

We can see this in two ways. First, "Jonah rose to flee to Tarshish from the presence of the Lord" (Jonah 1:3). There are debates regarding the location of Tarshish, but it seems to have been west in the Mediterranean Sea, through the Straight of Gibraltar, and somewhere on the western coast of modern-day Spain. The point is that it was in the opposite direction from Nineveh. We can imagine Jonah receiving God's command, getting up, but turning left instead of right and going as fast as he could away from the place he was ordered to go. His purpose was to flee "from the presence of the Lord." Tarshish seemed perfect for this, one of those far-off places where the name of the Lord was not heard. Tarshish was one of the places mentioned in Isaiah "that have not heard my fame or seen my glory" (Isa. 66:19). Douglas Stuart gives a good explanation: "Jonah, the ardent nationalist, therefore, attempted to flee to a place where no fellow believers would be found, hoping that this would help insure that God's word would not come to him again. If he stayed in Israel, he could expect to hear more from Yahweh, but if he left, he might hear nothing further."[1]

Secondly, Jonah sought a ship in the port of Joppa: "He went down to Joppa and found a ship going to Tarshish" (Jonah 1:3). Joppa was not an Israelite port, so there Jonah could be away from troublesome inquiries. Perhaps he could consort with unbelievers about his plans to flee from God without being troubled. In this respect, he is just like Christians who determine on a sinful course and avoid other Christians by not coming to church. They justify what they are doing and make excuses for their choices. If asked, they would deny the sinfulness of what they desire. But like Jonah, the fact that they avoid godly company demonstrates the true state of their hearts.

Jonah's flight from God was extremely sinful. To begin with, he was sinning against his confession of faith. Jonah was a professed Israelite, a worshiper of Yahweh, the One True and Most High God. He makes this statement while on the boat to Tarshish. "Where do you come from? What is your country? And of what people are you?" they asked him. Jonah replied, "I am a Hebrew, and I fear the LORD, the God of heaven, who made the sea and the dry land" (Jonah 1:8–9). His actions made a mockery of these words and compounded his sin.

The same is true of Christians who flagrantly disobey God's Word. It is one thing for professed atheists and other unbelievers to walk in sin. But when a Christian chooses sin it is far worse. Our profession of faith demands a life yielded to God. John Calvin comments, "All flee away from the presence of God, who do not willingly obey his commandments."[2]

One of the great problems today is that many people profess to be Christians—surveys show that almost a majority of Americans claim to be born again—but few follow up that profession with genuinely Christian lives. But it is practical godliness that validates a profession of faith. Had Jonah never repented, had he gone off to spend the rest of his days in Tarshish, we would

1. Douglas Stuart, *Hosea–Jonah*, Word Biblical Commentary 31 (Dallas: Word, 1987), 450.
2. John Calvin, *A Commentary on the Twelve Minor Prophets*, 5 vols. (1559; repr. Edinburgh: Banner of Truth, 1986), 3:31.

be justified in concluding that his profession of faith was false and that he did not believe in the Lord. The same is true for multitudes today who say the "sinner's prayer" or walk down the aisle at a revival but never show the fruit of a changed life.

Secondly, Jonah was sinning against his privileges. He was, after all, a prophet of the Lord. He benefited from a personal knowledge of God and direct revelation from heaven. In one sense, all Israelites lived in God's presence. They dwelt in the land of God and had access to God in his temple. But a prophet especially enjoyed this privilege. One might speak similarly of children raised in Christian homes and Christians provided with sound teaching of the Bible. The Word of God brings God's presence to us, and through our privilege of prayer we have access to the throne of grace. How great are our sins, especially the kind of open rebellion shown here by Jonah, in the light of these privileges. Privilege breeds obligation and compounds the sin of Christians who choose to disobey.

Thirdly, Jonah was sinning against reason. He thought he could "flee from the presence of the LORD." But his own profession of faith revealed how impossible this is. Unlike the pagans, Jonah knew that he did not serve a local or otherwise limited deity: "I fear the LORD, the God of heaven, who made the sea and the dry land," he said (Jonah 1:9). This being the case, there was no place where he could flee from God's presence. Psalm 139 serves as a commentary on his folly:

> Where shall I go from your Spirit?
>   Or where shall I flee from your presence?
> If I ascend to heaven, you are there!
>   If I make my bed in Sheol, you are there!
> If I take the wings of the morning
>   and dwell in the uttermost parts of the sea,
> even there your hand shall lead me,
>   and your right hand shall hold me.
> If I say, "Surely the darkness shall cover me,
>   and the light about me be night,"
> even the darkness is not dark to you. (Ps. 139:7–12)

I have known professing Christian men to leave their wives for other women, yet assure their friends: "This is for the best. God understands that

I need to feel more love. And things will work out fine for our children." But this is a great delusion. They are fleeing from God's clearly revealed will in the Bible. By gaining a new wife and a new circle of friends, and perhaps a more "tolerant" church where people won't judge, they will not be escaping God. There is no place where God is not found, and no path we can follow to escape either his presence or his hand of judgment.

The Bible's commentary on Jonah's actions is clear. God told Jonah to arise, but instead he went "down" to Joppa. It is always a movement downward when we rebel against God's commands. No doubt Jonah would have explained that he was avoiding narrow, legalistic Israelites, but in fact it was the presence of God that he was trying to escape. One of the major lessons of his story is that one can flee one's home, Christian fellowship, and church, but one can never flee from God. Jonah's flight was stalked by folly right from the start.

Let us learn the lesson from Jonah. Our profession of faith demands a life that is yielded to God in obedience. Our privileges carry a responsibility, so that our sin is compounded according to the measure of the grace and knowledge we have received. And our sin is always unreasonable. Sin always denies something about God. Sin either denies God as Provider, or Father, or Savior, or Judge. It denies God's attributes of goodness, power, holiness, and love. And sin always leads the direction that Jonah went: down. God told him to arise, but in the bitterness of his heart he descended "down to Joppa," "down into the inner part of the ship" (Jonah 1:3, 5), and finally down into the depths of the sea. Ultimately, sin will drag us down into the eternal depths of hell, away from the presence of God's mercy and grace—though not of his wrath—forever.

REASONS FOR JONAH'S FLIGHT

How do we explain Jonah's course of action? How can we account for this mad flight of folly by a prophet of the Lord?

Perhaps Jonah was afraid. After all, Nineveh was not only a great city, it was also a wicked and violent city. The Bible clearly represents it as such. Nahum prophesied against Nineveh: "Woe to the bloody city, all full of lies and plunder—no end to the prey! . . . Horsemen charging, flashing sword and glittering spear, hosts of slain, heaps of corpses, dead bodies without end—they stumble over the bodies!" (Nah. 3:1, 3). Frank Page writes:

19

Archaeology confirms the biblical witness to the wickedness of the Assyrians. They were well known in the ancient world for brutality and cruelty. Ashurbanipal, the grandson of Sennacherib, was accustomed to tearing off the lips and hands of his victims. Tiglath-Pileser flayed victims alive and made great piles of their skulls. Jonah's reluctance to travel to Nineveh may have been due to its infamous violence.[3]

Many of us sin out of fear. We fear to stand against the world. We fear persecution or worldly failure. We fear what other people will think or do. We sin as a way of protecting ourselves. But this probably does not explain Jonah's behavior, since there is not a word in the book to indicate that he fled from God because of fear for himself.

Perhaps, then, Jonah was alarmed at the difficulty of what God commanded. Did God really intend for Jonah to go alone into the heart of the most evil city in the world, and there to cry out a message of condemnation against it? It was not reasonable and it was not fair. Hugh Martin explains what must surely have occurred to Jonah: "To be despised and simply laughed at, as a fanatic and fool, must have appeared to him inevitable, if indeed his fate should not be worse."[4] The only course of action was to take matters into his own hands and out of God's hands. Christians sin this way frequently, refusing God's commands simply because they do not like them or do not think they will work out well. But going to Tarshish was not without difficulty either, so this does not seem to be Jonah's true reason.

Why, then, did Jonah rebel against God's command? The best explanation is that Jonah had developed such a deep hatred for Nineveh that he was not willing to obey God's command to go there and preach. He simply did not like God's command. Jonah believed in the power of God, and he acknowledged God's grace for sinners. This is precisely why he refused to preach God's message to these people. The Ninevites were the enemies of his people, so, as James Boice puts it, "Jonah would be damned (literally) before he would see God's blessing shed on these enemies." To understand Jonah's situation, Boice asks us to imagine "the word of the Lord coming to a Jew who lived in New York during World War II, telling him to go to Berlin to

---

3. Billy K. Smith and Frank S. Page, *Amos, Obadiah, Jonah*, New American Commentary 19B (Nashville: Broadman & Holman, 1995), 225.

4. Hugh Martin, *A Commentary on Jonah* (1870; repr. Edinburgh: Banner of Truth, 1958), 40.

preach to Nazi Germany." We should not be surprised if such a Jew went west to San Francisco instead, in order to board a boat headed to Hong Kong, just as Jonah fled for Tarshish.[5]

TENDING THE HEART

Solomon wrote words that address well Jonah's situation: "Keep your heart with all vigilance, for from it flow the springs of life" (Prov. 4:23). Jonah was likely a man of outstanding character and outward godliness, but he failed to tend to the affairs of his heart. There was bitterness there. There was anger. There was hatred and resentment. All of it was directed toward Nineveh, and with good reason. But none of it did Nineveh any harm—only Jonah. The same is true of Christians who refuse to forgive injuries done to them. They cultivate bitterness and resentment with careful attention, like a gardener tending a favored tree. But the only harm is done to themselves.

There are women whose husbands have betrayed and divorced them, and out of bitterness toward one man they render themselves incapable of love for any other man. There are children whose parents abused them, and out of devotion to their pain they refuse to trust anyone ever again, even God. But bitterness is an acid that destroys only its own container. The good news is that when Jesus set us free from sin, he included the sins of others against us. Forgiveness and grace are gifts of God, not only for us but to us. The words of the apostle Paul—"forgive as the Lord forgave you" (Col. 3:13 NIV)—are gospel, not law! Indeed, if we realize how much mercy we have received in being forgiven through the cross of Jesus Christ, we will offer our forgiveness to others as an offering of praise to the throne of God's grace.

Jonah sinned out of the bitterness of his heart. So let me conclude with advice on how we might tend our hearts and protect ourselves from foolish flights like Jonah's.

First, Jonah proves to us the value of Christian fellowship. Sin had deceived him, as often it will deceive us. His sin produced its own justification and rationalization, and Jonah was fully convinced. This is why the writer of Hebrews exhorts us: "Take care, brothers, lest there be in any of you an evil, unbelieving heart, leading you to fall away from the living God. But exhort

5. James Montgomery Boice, *The Minor Prophets*, 2 vols. (Grand Rapids: Baker, 1983), 1:266.

21

one another every day, as long as it is called 'today,' that none of you may be hardened by the deceitfulness of sin" (Heb. 3:12–13).

One of God's remedies against sin's deceit is Christian fellowship. Instead of going to Joppa, Jonah should have gone to the meeting place of the other prophets. He should have explained how he felt about God's command, and likely their help would have changed his mind.

This is one of the ways that regular attendance in public worship helps preserve us against sinful folly. The writer of Psalm 73 struggled with resentment for the happy wicked people he knew. "As for me," he writes, "my feet had almost stumbled, my steps had nearly slipped. For I was envious of the arrogant when I saw the prosperity of the wicked" (Ps. 73:2–3). What restored him? "I went into the sanctuary of God; then I discerned their end" (Ps. 73:17). The same is true for us. In the worship at church, our minds are reminded about the realities of heaven and hell, about the justice of God's economy, and about the grace for sinners like us who have been saved.

One last thing that would have greatly helped Jonah was prayer. Not once in his flight is he seen talking to God. Not once does he present his complaint directly to God, the way that Jeremiah did and was helped (see Jer. 12:1–17). Hugh Martin comments that when Jonah's feelings were starting to master him, "What would have been the remedy? Intercourse with God concerning them; a full statement in secret to his Father who is in secret, and who would in that case have rewarded him openly with a triumphant victory over the very evils of his own unbelieving heart."[6]

Do we realize the importance of tending our hearts? Then let Jonah warn us. If this prophet could flee from God's sovereign and righteous command, of what sins might we be capable? Let us make every use of the resources God has given us: his mighty Word, the blessing of Christian fellowship and counsel, regular attendance with God's people in worship, and the wonderful resource that is ours in prayer. Many a shipwrecked life would have been spared by such a course of action. Will this happen to you? It can. The book of Jonah was written not to condemn Jonah but to warn us. His folly need not be ours if we recognize the ease with which our hearts can fall into sin, and humbly attend upon God's precious means of grace.

---

6. Martin, *Jonah*, 42.

3

But the Lord

Jonah 1:3–4

But Jonah rose to flee to Tarshish from the presence of the LORD.
He went down to Joppa and found a ship going to Tarshish. So
he paid the fare and went on board, to go with them to Tarshish,
away from the presence of the LORD. But the LORD hurled a great
wind upon the sea, and there was a mighty tempest on the sea, so
that the ship threatened to break up. (Jonah 1:3–4)

A visit to the grocery store will usually offer tantalizing updates on the lives of the stars. We gain this information from the covers of the tabloids that are invariably posted along the checkout counters. I find these covers fascinating, with their tales of broken relationships, drug addictions, and ruined lives. I do not mean that I enjoy these magazines or that I find the covers entertaining. But the lives of the stars reveal a regular pattern to the life of sin from which we can learn. Time and again, an apparently innocent beauty is lured onto the path of stardom. Before long, her way of dressing changes to emphasize the sensual. Wealth and fame bring sinful attractions, including access to the nightclub scene and recreational drugs. Before too long, the tabloids reveal tidbits of sexual relationships, and, increasingly today, the stars rapidly fall in and out of marriage and even parenthood. The marriages do not last, the children become sources of conflict, and the pressures of sex, drugs, and public infatuation invariably lead to a breakdown. While still young, the starlets begin to look old and used, their lives wrecked and their souls scarred. Soon they are replaced by younger and fresher versions, bound for the same fate.

One lesson of the tabloids is that every train has a destination. Young men and women crave stardom, insisting that it will be different in their case. But once on the train, they find themselves stopping at all the regular stations, and soon they are dumped into the despair and destruction that is always the last stop.

The book of Jonah tells a similar story, though the prophet hardly counts as a star by today's definitions. In his case, Jonah boards a ship that has a fixed destination. The first verses of Jonah tell of his resolve to run from the Lord and from the Lord's calling. Jonah's flight leads somewhere, as sin always does. As he takes passage aboard a ship bound for Tarshish, he provides an important lesson in folly that can give us wisdom for serving the Lord.

JONAH'S FOLLY

In our last study, we considered the reasons for Jonah's flight from God, the primary one being his unwillingness to preach God's grace to the hated Ninevites. But we should also consider the flight itself, of which Jonah provides considerable detail.

The first thing we find is how easy the path of sin appeared, at least at first. God called Jonah to go north to Nineveh, but instead the prophet ran south to Joppa. Instead of going up to serve the Lord, he went down to serve his own rebellion. And what did he find upon his arrival in Joppa but "a ship going to Tarshish" (Jonah 1:3). We can only imagine how this encouraged Jonah in his rebellious course. He would have been mulling over his bitter reasons for fleeing God, and his conscience likely would have been wrestling with his decision. He may well have reasoned that if his course was wrong, then God would place obstacles in his path. But the opposite was the case in Joppa. There, waiting for Jonah's flight to the west, was a ship bound for a port as far from Nineveh as Jonah could have wished. The location of Tarshish is not precisely known, but scholars generally agree that it was on the west coast of modern-day Spain. "Ah," Jonah must have reflected, "providence has placed just the ship I need right in port as I have arrived."

Sin often works this way, though in his deceived state Jonah did not realize it. William Banks writes, "When a person decides to run from the Lord, Satan always provides complete transportation facilities."[1] Jonah's narrative shows how quickly our rebellious steps can lead us away from God. Verse three is terse in its progression of verbs, one leading simply to the other, without apparent space for reflection: Jonah rose, he went, he found, he paid the fare. How often sin works this way: once we have given ourselves permission to disobey God, the sinful world is likely to arrange for rapid progress. Jonah may have rationalized his disobedience by claiming God had "opened a door" for his flight to Tarshish. His folly reminds us that circumstances alone do not prove God's blessing; the confirmation we always need is the Word of God.

Jonah's situation reminds me of David's freefall into his grossest sin, the seduction of Bathsheba. Chapter after chapter of the Bible relates David's long progress in faith, but in three stunningly brief verses he falls. Second Samuel 11:2–4 tells us that David saw the beautiful woman, he sent a messenger, she came, and he lay with her. David was neglecting his duty, remaining in Jerusalem while his army was off to war. As soon as he took his eye off his duty, it rested on the bathing beauty. Before a second thought was given he had indulged in a sin that in certain respects he would never put behind him.

Jonah's flight was similar. All is action, with no deliberation or prayer. As David was in the grips of his lust, so Jonah was gripped by resentment. Having given over his heart, his legs worked just as quickly as David's hands entered into sin. More quickly than anyone could imagine, Jonah was aboard a ship to the ends of the world, hoping to put miles between himself and God. Once aboard, even if Jonah began to think about what he was doing, it was too late: the ship had set sail. Sin always takes us farther than we imagined we would go, faster than we ever intended.

There is an important lesson for us in this. If we have been toying with a sin and find that opportunity presents itself, we should not see the hand of good fortune but of Satan. It is not difficult, after all, for the devil to

---

1. William Banks, *Jonah: The Reluctant Prophet* (Chicago: Moody, 1966), 20.

arrange opportunities for sin. Perhaps you have allowed yourself to indulge in thoughts of a sexual affair; you should not then be surprised when an opportunity for adultery presents itself. This should raise your suspicions and lead you to repentance. Perhaps you have cheated on your taxes and not been caught, or indulged in pornography and no one has found out. This should alarm you as to what further sins you might be led to commit, and quickly bring you to your knees before the Lord.

Jonah also shows us that once we have resolved to sin against God, any of us can act in the most surprising ways. Jonah's foolish rebellion against the Lord involved him in the most irrational behavior. We remember that out of his hatred for the Gentiles, he sought to escape the presence of the Lord and even the presence of the Lord's people, lest he be forced to prophecy in Nineveh. But look at the company he ends up keeping: pagan, Gentile sailors whose ways were surely opposed to the Lord and his people. Moreover, he pays his own way, handing over what would surely have been a considerable amount of money, and commits himself to a large expenditure of time, since the voyage could take up to a year. Furthermore, he willingly accepts the very great dangers that sea travel involved in those days. Leslie Allen reminds us that the Hebrews were not a seagoing people. He writes, "That Jonah was prepared to entrust himself to an oceangoing boat rather than face up to God's call must have struck the hearers as proof positive of his mad determination."[2]

The same thing happens to Christians when they tread the path of sin. Sin is expensive and leads us into unwholesome company. It entails risks and dangers that a Christian ought not to desire, and often it simply makes us into fools. Sin is never good, but there is at least something reasonable about an unbelieving sinner engaging in the expense, time, risk, and company that sin involves. But a Christian? Christians may sin, but they seldom sin well, and their surprising behavior in sin is yet another warning of their need to repent.

The same can be said of the church. It is fine for worldly institutions to engage in cheap marketing or petty entertainments. But the church of Jesus Christ? Years ago, William Banks lamented, "Many of our churches have become obsessed with the physical and the temporal, and the mate-

2. Leslie C. Allen, *The Books of Joel, Obadiah, Jonah, and Micah,* New International Commentary on the Old Testament (Grand Rapids: Eerdmans, 1976), 205.

rialistic spirit has been nourished and fed at the expense of the cause of missions."[3] How much worse things are now! How surprising it always is to see the bride and body of Christ, his church, led into the ways of sin and worldliness.

Lastly, we observe the baleful effects of Jonah's foolish flight from God. Verse 3 says that he fled "from the presence of the LORD," and that he boarded the ship "to go with them to Tarshish, away from the presence of the LORD." We are tempted to think that Jonah foolishly believed that by putting physical distance between himself and Israel he was escaping God's actual presence. But given that Jonah was a prophet of the Lord, it is hard to believe that he knew so little about God as to think him limited by space. After all, he would have known the psalm that asks, "Where shall I go from your Spirit? Or where shall I flee from your presence?" (Ps. 139:7).

It is more likely that Jonah was seeking to separate himself from the Word of God and its appeal to his conscience. Douglas Stuart suggests, "Jonah hopes to avoid further revelatory contact with Israel's God by going some-place where there are no Israelites."[4] Moreover, there is evidence that the expression "away from the presence of the Lord" signifies someone who has refused the service that God has given. Gordon Keddie writes, "The person who chooses to flee from the presence of God, therefore, is refusing to serve God in the task he knows that the Lord has given him to do."[5] Perhaps Jonah believes that God will simply forget him, sending some other prophet on the undesired mission to Nineveh.

Both of these objectives—fleeing from God's people and from God's service—produce the most lamentable results. It is said that either God will keep us from sin, or sin will keep us from God. How many Christians have suffered for their sin-imposed absence from church and the preaching of God's Word, the very instrument that speaks God's grace for repentance and forgiveness! And how many Christians have made their lives unfruitful, turning their backs on useful ministry because of sin, and denying themselves "the blessing which is attached to happy obedience."[6]

3. Banks, *Jonah: The Reluctant Prophet*, 20–21.
4. Douglas Stuart, *Hosea–Jonah*, Word Biblical Commentary 31 (Waco, Tex.: Word, 1987), 452.
5. Gordon J. Keddie, *Preacher on the Run: The Message of Jonah* (Darlington, UK: Evangelical Press, 1986), 18.
6. Ibid.

SEVERE MERCY

The record of Jonah's flight involves two "buts" that structure the account. The first is "but Jonah," which tells of the prophet's unwillingness to heed God's sovereign call. God called Jonah to Nineveh, "but Jonah rose to flee" (Jonah 1:3). However, rebellious man never has the last word, so verse 4 gives another "but": "But the LORD." Jonah resigned his office as a prophet, but the Lord did not accept his resignation. Jonah fled from God's presence, taking a ship to far-off Tarshish, but the Lord did not let him go. Jonah went down into the ship's hold to sleep away his troubles (Jonah 1:5), "But the LORD hurled a great wind upon the sea, and there was a mighty tempest on the sea, so that the ship threatened to break up" (Jonah 1:4).

British poet Francis Thompson wrote a piece that describes well Jonah's situation, titled, "The Hound of Heaven."[7] This epic poem tells of God's undaunted pursuit of the man who flees him:

> I fled Him, down the nights and down the days;
> I fled Him, down the arches of the years;
> I fled Him, down the labyrinthine ways.

Those words might well have been penned by Jonah. Yet, as the poem recounts, it is not possible for those who belong to God to flee successfully from his mercy.

> Still with unhurrying chase,
> And unperturbed pace,
> Deliberate speed, majestic instancy,
> Came on the following Feet.

For Jonah, this must have been a rude awakening. We can imagine him in his sailing vessel, having pulled out from the harbor. He had made it! There would be no preaching to the hated Ninevites. But God had other plans; he was not going to let Jonah go so easily. For a tempest arose on the sea, as John Calvin explains: "not by chance, but by the certain purpose of God, so that being overtaken on the sea, [Jonah] acknowledged that he had been

---

7. *In Modern British Poetry*, ed. Louis Untermeyer (New York: Harcourt, Brace & Howe, 1950), 86–90.

deceived when he thought that he could flee away from God's presence by passing over the sea."[8] It is the Lord, writes Jeremiah, "who gives the sun for light by day and the fixed order of the moon and the stars for light by night, who stirs up the sea so that its waves roar" (Jer. 31:35).

The storm that Jonah experienced is a classic instance of divine chastisement. The Bible plainly states that God's wayward children can expect their Father's chastening hand. Hebrews 12:6 says: "For the Lord disciplines the one he loves, and chastises every son whom he receives." For this reason alone, Jonah could not expect to get away from God, any more than any child of God can expect to prosper in sin. "Jonah thought he could just walk away from a divine assignment. But the Lord was to make Jonah's voyage into a 'teachable moment.'"[9]

God's chastisement is a certainty for every one of those who belong to him, just as God's final judgment is certain for all those who do not. It does not always come immediately. Hugh Martin writes: "The Lord can afford to wait. You may trespass against Him, and pass on apparently unpunished, the Lord apparently uncognizant. But the path along which you pass has the punishment lining both sides of it, and looming dark at some fixed point further on."[10]

Jonah 1:4 makes it clear that the storm was a divine act of chastisement on Jonah: "the LORD hurled a great wind upon the sea." In other words, God targeted Jonah's ship with precision accuracy. We talk of "smart bombs" and guided missiles today, but they are nothing compared with God's chastisement! The word for "hurled" is used elsewhere of a javelin. O. Palmer Robertson explains, "He takes careful aim at the chosen target, and with all his strength he 'hurls' his chosen weapon."[11]

God has a chosen weapon to employ in the case of every rebellious Christian. As he showed in Jonah's case, he has the precise way of halting our sinful path. It may be a crushing job setback. It may be a deadly illness. It may be a sickening of the soul. It is common, for instance, for Christians to feel a plague in their conscience when rationalizing some plan to avoid doing God's will. A genuine Christian will never succeed in fleeing from God; at

8. John Calvin, *A Commentary on the Twelve Minor Prophets*, 5 vols. (1559; repr. Edinburgh: Banner of Truth, 1986), 3:33.

9. Billy K. Smith and Frank S. Page, *Amos, Obadiah, Jonah* New American Commentary 19B (Nashville: Broadman & Holman, 1995), 229.

10. Hugh Martin, *A Commentary on Jonah* (1870; repr. Edinburgh: Banner of Truth, 1958), 87–88.

11. O. Palmer Robertson, *Jonah: A Study in Compassion* (Edinburgh: Banner of Truth, 1990), 18.

a certain point of his own choosing, God is certain to step in, and when he does he will act with pinpoint accuracy. In Jonah's case, God sent a storm of such savagery that even the experienced sailors were driven to despair. God's clear purpose with this storm was to stop Jonah's westward journey dead in its tracks. The tempest was so mighty "that the ship threatened to break up" (Jonah 1:4). God will not be mocked, and even his own people will be chastened in their flight from his will.

God was not motivated by wrath toward Jonah, but instead by mercy. It was an instance of God's severe mercy, to save his own from sinful folly. Such chastisement inevitably displays God's fearful might, but it also reveals God's grace in halting a ruinous rebellion.

To be sure, God was sending a clear message to Jonah. The message was that his commands cannot be lightly rejected or successfully evaded. This is a message all of us should heed, lest we should refuse answering God's call to serve a struggling church, a difficult mercy ministry, or a relationship we would prefer to avoid. God does not intend for his sovereign plans to be disrupted, and he often displays his sovereign rule through chastening events like Jonah's storm.

God intended this storm as a teaching event for Jonah. Peter Williams summarizes, "He pursues us because he loves us and desires to draw us back to himself."[12] This shows that it is in the pursuing grace of God that every child of God finds true security. "God sometimes allows us to think that we can hide from him and evade his demands in order to teach us how much we need him, and how much he loves us. For he never gives up on us and will pursue us until we are drawn back to himself."[13] This was the message of the poem "The Hound of Heaven." The poem begins with the child of God's foolish words of flight. But they end with God's message of pursuing grace:

> All which I took from thee I did but take, not for thy harms,
> But just that thou might'st seek it in my arms.
> All which thy child's mistake
> Fancies as lost, I have stored for thee at home:
> Rise, clasp My hand, and come![14]

---

12. Peter Williams, *Jonah–Running from God: An Expositional Commentary*, Exploring the Bible (Epsom, Surrey, UK: Day One, 2003), 19.

13. Ibid.

14. *Modern British Poetry*, 90.

LINING UP WITH GOD'S WILL

The idea is widely held that Christians may lose the blessings that might have been theirs unless they remain constantly "in the center of God's will." That might be true, were it not for the pursuing grace of God. This is one way in which Christians are different from the media stars whose ruined lives keep tabloid sales going. The man or woman who has turned in faith to Jesus Christ has become a child of the God of grace. By his mercy, God stops our trains prior to their destination, just as he stopped Jonah's ship and redirected him on a path of blessing.

Jonah is not the story of a man who was blessed by remaining in God's will, but rather of a man who was mightily used of God despite his unbelief and sin, because of God's sovereign grace in his life. Jonah's message is not even that we must avoid all folly and rebellion, though we should, but rather that when we have strayed we should respond to the grace of God that calls us to repentance and new obedience.

The story is told of three fifty-foot posts lined up at the small port of the island of Inagua in the Bahamas. A visitor puzzled over the purpose of the posts, since they were placed on land. The answer was that the channel was too shallow for larger sailing boats. The posts were placed so that a ship's captain could align the posts so that from his perspective they were in a straight line, appearing as only one post. Lined up this way, the captain knew that he was in the narrow deep channel that would safely lead him to the dock.[15]

God's Word plays a similar role in our lives. The question facing each of us is whether we are willing to obey God's will as it is made known to us. Perhaps we have gone astray, but by God's intervening grace he has made known to us our need to repent and return to him. Are we willing to turn to God's Word for new direction? Are we willing to come to God, confessing our sins and seeking power for new obedience? Our unwillingness will never overrule God's sovereign plans, but by turning anew to the way of the Lord, responding either to gentle nudges in our hearts or to chastening storms in our circumstances, we can find anew the path—the way of the Lord—that is marked by his blessing.

15. Cited from Trent C. Butler, *Hosea, Joel, Amos, Obadiah, Jonah, Micah* Holman Old Testament Commentary (Nashville: Broadman & Holman, 2005), 277–78.

4

THE CHURCH IN THE WORLD

Jonah 1:5–6

*So the captain came and said to him, "What do you mean, you
sleeper? Arise, call out to your god! Perhaps the god will give a
thought to us, that we may not perish." (Jonah 1:6)*

In Alexander Dumas's novel *The Man in the Iron Mask*, Prince
Philip languishes in a prison while his twin brother, Louis XIV,
sits on the throne of France. Philip is forced by his captors to
wear an iron mask that hides his identity. The book of Jonah also tells of a
man who lost his identity, though for different reasons. Jonah the prophet
flees from the presence of the Lord to avoid God's command to preach in
hated Nineveh. Boarding a ship for distant Tarshish, Jonah hopes to hide
beneath the decks. But, whereas Dumas's Prince Philip is discovered and
restored to his throne by the Three Musketeers, it is the sovereign hand of
God that discloses Jonah's identity, challenging him to return to his high
calling as a prophet of the Lord.

THE MARINERS' PRAYER

Fleeing from the Lord, Jonah paid his fare for the journey to Tarshish. As
the boat pulled away from shore, his plan to run from God seemed to be a

success. But Jonah had not reckoned on the sovereign persistence of the Lord. Jonah 1:4 tells us, "But the LORD hurled a great wind upon the sea, and there was a mighty tempest on the sea, so that the ship threatened to break up."

It would be one thing for passengers to be frightened by a storm on the sea, but sailors are used to quite violent winds and waves. The mariners' alarm shows that this was a most terrific tempest, gravely threatening their ship and their lives: "The mariners were afraid, and each cried out to his god" (Jonah 1:5).

These sailors provide an instance of natural man's tendency to think of God only under extremity. There may be no atheists in foxholes, but once out of the foxhole most battlefield converts quickly revert to unbelief. This explains one of the reasons for the trials of this world: in his mercy, God seeks to gain man's attention. John Calvin observes: "Hardly any religion appears in the world, when God leaves us in an undisturbed condition. Fear constrains us, however unwilling, to come to God."[1] This tendency points to one of the ways that true believers differ from the rest of mankind. The Christian possesses an all-weather faith. The true spirit of prayer is not one that is summoned only in the midst of terror, but one that daily rises up from our loving relationship with the God we have come to know and trust.

The sailors did more than simply pray. We should always combine our prayers with the work given to us to do, and in this they are to be commended: "And they hurled the cargo that was in the ship into the sea to lighten it for them" (Jonah 1:5). It was likely a great deal of cargo that they threw overboard. The whole purpose of such ships was to convey goods from one place to another, so the mariners were throwing out not only their possessions but also their profit.

This reveals the relationship between our lives and our possessions, a difference that we are all too prone to forget. The cargo represented long labor and fond hopes of future wealth. But with their lives at risk, the sailors did not hesitate to jettison their possessions to gain only a slightly increased chance of safety. This is no less true for those with great possessions than for those with few. England's King Richard III cried out in the midst of his defeat in battle: "My kingdom for a horse!" Likewise, any of us would give up any amount of money or possessions to save our lives.

---

1. John Calvin, *A Commentary on the Twelve Minor Prophets*, 5 vols. (1559; repr. Edinburgh: Banner of Truth, 1986), 3:35.

More than that, possessions do not define even the quality of our lives. Jesus said, "One's life does not consist in the abundance of his possessions" (Luke 12:15). Countless people have reflected on this truth in the wake of tragedies. A friend told me of returning to his demolished home after it was struck by Hurricane Andrew. Looking at smashed furniture and scattered photographs, he realized that these were all just things; what mattered was his life. With what folly we accumulate material overabundance, seeking the fleeting pleasure of buying clothes, furniture, and toys—much of which is destined to be sold for a pittance at garage sales—while devoting so little effort to matters of the soul.

The actions of the frightened mariners show furthermore how superficially most people think about their problems. The root problem here was not the weight of the cargo, nor even the violence of the storm. Men think in such terms, focusing on circumstances and their proximate remedies. The problem with the ship bound for Tarshish was the sin residing under its decks. Likewise, mankind's problems arise from the guilt and misery incurred by sin. Like the mariners in the storm, natural man seeks God's help in removing danger but seldom gives any thought to removing sin. "We are casting overboard the ware and cargo, but the storm continues to rage because sin continues to rule in the hearts of those aboard the ship of life. Nothing weighs a man down as heavily as the burden of sin."[2]

A PRIMER ON NATURAL RELIGION

The example of the storm-tossed mariners provides a primer on natural religion. It shows that unregenerate men and women are aware of God. Nature displays God clearly, especially in the might of great phenomena such as hurricanes and other violent storms. The sailors, most of whom were probably Phoenicians, realized instinctively that a personal divine power stood behind the tempest. The reason that nature reveals the existence of God is that God created it for this purpose. Paul says, "What can be known about God is plain to them, because God has shown it to them" (Rom. 1:19). Moreover, the universality of prayer in the midst of storms shows that man knows God is able to help and that, properly solicited, he is also willing to help.

2. William Banks, *Jonah: The Reluctant Prophet* (Chicago: Moody, 1966), 27.

But there is a fatal limit to natural religion, as also shown by the sailors. While men know that God exists, they do not know God. "Each cried out to his god" (Jonah 1:5) is another way of saying that each sailor cried out to whatever god he thought might help him. They were like the Athenians of Paul's time who not only built idols to every god of their imaginations, but also tried to cover their bases with an idol "to the unknown god" (Acts 17:23). Their attitude is revealed in the ship captain's plea to Jonah: "Arise, call out to your god! Perhaps the god will give a thought to us, that we may not perish" (Jonah 1:6). He meant, in other words, "Maybe you know a god who can help. So give it a try!" This shows that the multitude of false gods worshiped and trusted in our world exist because of man's ignorance of the one true God. At the heart of all idolatry is the tragic problem that while man knows that God exists, man does not know who he is.

A second limitation is seen in their approach to prayer. Just as they do not know to whom they should pray, natural men and women also do not know on what terms their prayers may be answered. Calvin comments, "They know not whether they will obtain anything by their cries; they repeat their prayers; but they know not whether they pass off into air or really come to God."[3]

It is these two great problems of mankind that Christianity alone is able to address. Natural revelation, though displaying that there is a God, does not tell us who he is. This is why God gave us special revelation in the Bible. Moreover, God, having revealed himself through the prophets and apostles, has given an ultimate revelation of himself through his Son, Jesus Christ (see Heb. 1:2). To learn of Jesus in the Bible and have the Holy Spirit impress his truth upon your heart is to come to a personal knowledge of God. Jesus said, "Whoever has seen me has seen the Father" (John 14:9). Paul writes that Jesus "is the image of the invisible God" (Col. 1:15).

The believer in Christ therefore knows the God to whom he prays, for his salvation involves a personal relationship with the heavenly Father. Moreover, the Christian knows on what terms he hopes for his prayers to be heard. Since God's Son died for our sins, reconciling us to God the Father, the believer who prays in Jesus' name knows that his prayers are received by God as those of a beloved child. Praying in Christ's name, we say, "Our Father, who art in heaven" (Matt. 6:9, KJV).

3. Calvin, *Minor Prophets*, 3:42.

THE CHURCH ASLEEP

It was precisely to impart this knowledge to sinners that God commissioned Jonah to preach in the great and evil city of Nineveh. Now, on the ship bound for Tarshish, it was Jonah alone who could tell the mariners what they needed to know. The problem is that while the pagans were praying, Jonah was sleeping: "But Jonah had gone down into the inner part of the ship and had lain down and was fast asleep" (Jonah 1:5).

This is a remarkable situation, given the violence of the storm. It is hard to account for the fact that in this great tempest Jonah was soundly sleeping below. Some commentators have suggested that the strain and anxiety of his flight from God had utterly exhausted the prophet. Deep in the bowels of the ship, he had somehow managed to continue his sleep despite the violent storm.

However we account for it, Jonah's sleep is remarkable in what it says about his spiritual state. Thinking he had escaped God's presence, Jonah was unaware of approaching danger. His was "the sleep of one who has persuaded himself that he is safe, when in fact he is in grave danger."[4]

How many others are like him? They think themselves safe in their rebellion against or neglect of God. Life seems good; their affairs seem secure. Yet all the while a storm is fast approaching. Indeed, Christians can be the most presumptuous in this regard, because they have come to know the goodness of the Lord. Even though they are nurturing besetting sins or neglecting essential spiritual duties, they remain complacent. "God will forgive me," they think, "because that's what God is supposed to do."

It is true that the Bible reveals God as long-suffering and forgiving. But Jonah's experience reminds us that God's holiness demands an accounting for sin in the case of unbelievers and the repenting of sins in the case of his own people. The writer of Hebrews states, "The Lord disciplines the one he loves, and chastises every son whom he receives" (Heb. 12:6).

The mere fact that we may enjoy a spiritual state of peace says nothing about our actual situation with God. O. Palmer Robertson writes, "Jonah had plenty of peace. He was sleeping like a baby. At the very time when he was running from the will of God, he had great peace."[5] Yet at the time of

4. Gordon J. Keddie, *Preacher on the Run: The Message of Jonah* (Darlington, UK: Evangelical Press, 1986), 33.

5. O. Palmer Robertson, *Jonah: A Study in Compassion* (Edinburgh: Banner of Truth, 1990), 20.

God's choosing the terrible storm struck his ship. Like Jonah in his boat, many people today—Christians and non-Christians—think themselves safe from God's jurisdiction simply because they keep away from church. But God is able to strike in the world as well as in the church, at sea as well as on shore.

Jonah furthermore provides a picture of the relationship between the church and the world. Why were the mariners in such danger? It was not because of their sins, but because of the prophet's sin! In like manner, the condition of the world in any age may be traced to the condition of the church.

When the church is actively awake, exercising its duty of godliness, prayer, and gospel witness, things go well in the world. In this way, you may trace the world's advancement in the quality of life—whether through science, medicine, literature, or political science—to the influence of God's people. Just one example is the Great Awakening of the eighteenth century in both England and America in which large portions of society were converted to Christ. Many historians credit this revival with England's stability in an age of revolution, as well as with the civic virtue that made the American democracy possible. By God's common grace, some societies have flourished for a time apart from true religion (consider Egypt, China, or the Mayans). But wherever the footprints of Christian disciples have marked the earth, they lead to an increase of peace, prosperity, and well-being.

Conversely, the neglect of God and his Word, and especially the abandonment of fidelity to Christ, invariably foreshadows looming clouds of darkness and storm. One example is that of nineteenth- and twentieth-century Germany. In the nineteenth century, German scholarship assaulted the biblical foundations of the Christian faith. This led to a highly nationalistic church largely devoid of the gospel. In this spiritual vacuum, Adolf Hitler was able to raise the Nazi standard and engulf the world in war. Tragically, recent decades tell a similar state of decline in Europe and in America, the results of which are greatly to be dreaded.

In all of these cases, the situation can be largely traced to the failures of the Christian church. Like Jonah's flight, it begins with the rejection of God's Word. And like Jonah in the Tarshish-bound ship, doctrinely wayward Christians too often have sought refuge in the findings of science, the fashions of secular academia, and the waves of trendy culture, instead of standing fast on the solid rock of the Bible. The result is trouble not merely for the church but for the entire society.

This also happens on an individual level. O. Palmer Robertson comments that "you will invariably bring trouble to the life of others as well as to your own life if you are walking contrary to the will of God." He notes that those who minister in prisons have found the book of Jonah to resonate strongly with inmates. "They know they are running from God. They understand what it means to hurt other people, especially the ones they love, by going against God's will."[6]

Compare Jonah with the apostle Paul in a similar situation. Acts 27 records that Paul's ship was caught in a storm so violent that the crew tossed their cargo overboard (vv. 13–20). But whereas Jonah neglected his duty to arise, pray, and preach to the others, Paul busied himself in these very tasks. The apostle stood before the sailors and reported God's counsel. As a result, the mariners arrived safely on land despite the destruction of their vessel (Acts 27:21–44). In Jonah's case, as well as Paul's, it was the conduct of believers that determined the fate of the whole ship's crew.

This illuminates a tragedy in our own time, for like Jonah in the ship the church today is largely asleep in the world. We see this in the neglect of prayer, the lack of interest in theology in favor of lifestyle teaching, the casualness with which so many believers approach worship, and a lack of concern to witness the gospel to the surrounding world.

We may summarize the condition of sleep with four observations. First, the sleeping church is unaware of its condition. Sleepers gain consciousness only when they awake. Secondly, in their dreams sleepers often do things that would never happen in wakeful life. People say, "I had the wildest dream last night." Likewise, the sleeping church engages in behaviors wholly out of step with the godliness set forth in the Bible.

Thirdly, sleepers dislike an alarm. This is why those who seek to awaken the church are so often maligned and despised, just as the prophets were stoned in ancient Israel. No sleeper likes the sound of an alarm clock! Fourthly, as Jonah displays, a sleeper neither prays nor preaches the Word of God. A lack of prayer is especially a sign of a sleeping, backslidden church. Like Jonah in the ship, such Christians are embarrassed when others approach and ask for prayer.

6. Ibid., 18–19.

This is why it is such a mercy whenever God sends an awakening storm. It was grace that sent Jonah's storm! God could have let him sleep all the way to Tarshish, to a successful end of his rebellion, but in his grace God did not let him go. Likewise, the Bible reveals that famines, wars, economic depressions, and persecutions not only result from the sleeping state of the church in the world, but are often God's remedy to awaken his people. This is why, while the world is busy throwing cargo overboard or pursuing some other frantic attempt at survival, Christians should respond to God's storm by searching out their own sin. It is sin that disables our witness and work. It is sin that occasions God's chastening hand. Let us therefore be quick to repent and seek mercy from our gracious God. In that way alone can the church be a source not of danger to the world but of salvation.

THE WORLD'S CRY TO THE CHURCH

The book of Jonah is filled with ironies, and one of them is the sight of the pagan ship captain crying out to awaken the prophet. Jonah was there, after all, because he refused God's call to cry out to pagan Nineveh. Now, in his rebellion, it is an unbelieving voice that calls him awake: "The captain came and said to him, 'What do you mean, you sleeper? Arise, call out to your god! Perhaps the god will give a thought to us, that we may not perish'" (Jonah 1:6).

This was a *deserved* rebuke. To the captain's eyes, Jonah presented a remarkable instance of sacrilege, sleeping at a time when everyone should be calling on God! Jonah presented a shocking spectacle of irreligion, even though Jonah was in fact a holy prophet of the Lord. Yet, as Hugh Martin notes, "What can the world take you for, but what you appear to be?"[7] Christians tend to consider worldly rebukes to arise from malice, when often the world is rightly dismayed at the conduct of those who claim to know God.

Many Christians today deserve a similar rebuke from the world. Is our presence an instigation to peace and well-being? Are those who take the name of Christ living in a manner consistent with our creed? The world rightly expects us to do so. Martin asks, "Do not we often allow many a precious opportunity to pass without taking advantage of it? Are you

7. Hugh Martin, *A Commentary on Jonah* (1870; repr. Edinburgh: Banner of Truth, 1958), 101.

careful, believing brethren . . . in time of trial, adversity, poverty, anxiety, or bereavement, to show the world how the grace of God, how the faith of Jesus, how the fellowship of the Spirit, can suffice to keep your soul in perfect peace and perfect patience?"[8]

Secondly, it was a *needed* rebuke. In the midst of life's storms, the world has great need especially of the prayers of God's people. When a workforce is struck by layoffs, it is the Christians who should be active in the ministry of prayer for those whose jobs are lost. In times of war, Christians are the ones who must pray for peace. When tragedy strikes a family, Christian neighbors should arrive to help and pray. The world rightly expects and needs this. They do not know how to pray, but they know that we do! As a prophet, Jonah knew the way to gain God's help, so the captain rebuked him, "What do you mean, you sleeper? Arise, call out to your god!" The world either does or should give the same rebuke to Christians today.

The world is capable of achieving much on its own. The world can arrange for earthly riches and pleasurable lifestyles. By God's common grace, the world can solve economic problems and draft war plans. The world does not need the church for worldly things. But there are things for which the world urgently needs the proper witness of the church. The world does not know God. The world does not know the truth of God's ways. The world does not know how to find salvation from heaven. It is for these purposes that the church exists in the world. How great is the lament when the sleeping church becomes like the world! Let us take up this urgent calling, and, as Jonah was exhorted, let us arise before the world. Let us tell the world about God. Let us pray to God on the world's behalf and teach the world to pray. Let us preach the gospel of Christ, the one way by which the sinful world may find the blessing of heaven's God.

LORD OF THE STORM

In concluding this study of Jonah sleeping in the boat, we must remember another prophet—indeed, the Lord of the prophets—who also slept on a storm-tossed boat. The Gospels tell us of Jesus in the boat with his disciples, crossing the Sea of Galilee. The disciples woke him, crying, "Save us, Lord;

8. Ibid., 97–98.

we are perishing" (Matt. 8:25). Jesus slept not in rebellion against God but in the great peace of his sovereign might. So, unlike Jonah, who does not seem to have either risen or prayed, Jesus did arise. Mark 4:39 says, "He awoke and rebuked the wind and said to the sea, 'Peace! Be still!' And the wind ceased, and there was a great calm."

Jesus could do what no one else could, not even a prophet like Jonah. Jesus could still the storm because of his divine and sovereign might. Jesus can also still the storm of God's wrath on our sin. Jonah's sin had caused Jonah's storm, and likewise it is our sin that brings God's wrath. It was for this that Jesus died on the cross, paying the penalty our sins deserved and achieving for us an eternal peace with God.

Do you want to know what the mariners did not understand? Do you want to know how to pray so as to gain God's help and salvation? The answer is to pray in the name of Jesus, through faith in the shedding of his blood for our sins. God has made Jesus the way to salvation. John writes, "To all who did receive him, who believed in his name, he gave the right to become children of God" (John 1:12). As children of God through faith in Jesus, the Lord of the storms, we may know that our prayers are heard and that God is on our side.

If we realize this and have come to God through faith in Christ, then let us heed the world's and the Bible's cry to the church. Let us be active in worship, prayer, service, and witness. Paul exhorts: "Walk as children of light . . . and try to discern what is pleasing to the Lord. . . . 'Awake, O sleeper, and arise from the dead, and Christ will shine on you'" (Eph. 5:8, 10, 14).

5

FEARING THE LORD

Jonah 1:7—10

And he said to them, "I am a Hebrew, and I fear the LORD, the God of heaven, who made the sea and the dry land." (Jonah 1:9)

The book of Numbers records that as Moses led Israel toward the Promised Land, the tribes of Gad and Reuben asked to settle in the fertile lands east of the Jordan River. This troubled Moses, since Canaan, west of the Jordan, contained the Promised Land. He was willing to relent, however, on the condition that their armed men would fight with the others until the land had been secured for all twelve tribes. Gad and Reuben agreed, but Moses warned them: "If you will not do so, behold, you have sinned against the LORD, and be sure your sin will find you out" (Num. 32:23).

Moses' principle would be proved repeatedly throughout the Old Testament: "be sure your sin will find you out." It was learned by Achan, who stole forbidden treasure from the sacking of Jericho, so that God was angered and Israel was defeated in battle. It was discovered by King David, after he committed adultery with Bathsheba. David used all his royal power to tie the loose ends so that no one would learn of his sin. But, the Bible says, "the thing that David had done displeased the LORD"

(2 Sam. 11:27), and David's sin was found out and punished severely. So it was for Jonah: his sin found him out.

THE SINNER'S EVASION

Jonah had slept soundly in the hold of the ship bound for Tarshish. His flight from the Lord seemed to start well. But when a violent tempest struck the ship, Jonah's sin was brought under scrutiny. Not that everyone realized this at first: initially, the sailors simply woke Jonah and called him to pray (Jonah 1:6). When this failed to produce any positive results, the sailors struck upon another solution. "They said to one another, 'Come, let us cast lots, that we may know on whose account this evil has come upon us'" (Jonah 1:7).

The behavior of the mariners is telling. They seem to have been hard-working and competent men. But like dedicated public servants who seek to solve society's problems today, the difficulties were simply too great. Their confusion was not surprising, since the one man with the information to help them—the prophet Jonah—was sleeping in the hold. Whenever the world is desperate and confused, this is a sign that the church is asleep in the world. Unless the church gives light to the world, the world must persist in darkness. Hence the proliferation of psychic shops and astrology charts in the West: when the sleeping church ceases to speak God's truth to the world, the world becomes desperate.

The mariners' appeal to casting lots also typifies man's sense of sin. So terrific was the storm that they rightly concluded divine vengeance was its cause. They inferred that their ship contained someone who had offended the angered deity. Yet by casting lots, each of them deflected his own complicity. If God was angry, they believed, he must be angry with someone else, since none could think of anything he had done to incur such fierce wrath.

This perfectly depicts the natural man's attitude toward his own sin. People are willing to admit that they have not always done right and have sometimes done wrong. "But nothing that might deserve God's special wrath," they nonetheless conclude. People are willing to admit that they have faults, and even that they commit sins, but they will not admit that they justly come under the condemnation and wrath of God. This is why, when tragedy strikes, people are often angry with God rather than fearful of God. Jesus said, "Everyone who commits sin is a slave to sin" (John 8:34), and our master, sin, does not like to be exposed. But God is not deceived, and the terrible storm racking Jonah's ship exemplified God's wrath on all sin.

Had Jonah been occupied with his duty as a prophet, proclaiming both law and gospel to the world, the situation might have been different. As it was, instead of each sailor casting himself before God in repentance, the lots were brought forth to discern what great sinner was on board. The situation is the same today. So long as man's conscience remains dulled to his sin, he prefers other options to faith in Jesus Christ. Only when man has seen the justice of God's wrath toward his sin, for which purpose God has given his law, will man seek the Savior God has provided and yield his heart to Christ.

CASTING LOTS

The use of lots for divination was widespread in the ancient world. The Hebrew text's literal description of the sailors' procedure indicates that some kind of dice were likely used, just as the Roman soldiers did to divide Jesus' garments at the cross (Mark 15:24). God's people also used such means for divine guidance. The high priest's Urim and Thummim probably served this purpose (cf. Exod. 28:30). Saul was chosen as Israel's first king by the casting of lots (1 Sam. 10:21), and the law provided several circumstances in which God's people were to appeal to him for knowledge in this way (cf. Lev. 16:8; Num. 33:54).

The right use of lots was in seeking God's will and in acting so as to demonstrate impartiality. Casting lots was a way of saying, "Let it be God's will that decides." When appealed to in a right spirit, God spoke through the lots. But even when lots or other instruments of chance are used in an ungodly way, God's sovereignty is not overthrown. Proverbs 16:33 declares, "The lot is cast into the lap, but its every decision is from the Lord."

Are there godly uses of lots today? To answer, we must first realize how our situation is different from that of Old Testament believers. There are no examples in the post-Pentecost church of believers seeking information from God through instruments of chance. The last instance was the selection of Matthias to replace Judas as one of the twelve disciples (Acts 1:26). The uniqueness of this situation is obvious. But after the coming of the Holy Spirit to indwell God's people, lots were never used again. When the first deacons were selected, it was not by lots but by the Holy Spirit speaking through the will of the congregation (Acts 6:5). With the canon of Holy Scripture now complete, Christians are not to seek special means of divine revelation. Instead, James says, "If any of you lacks wisdom, let him ask God, who gives generously to all without reproach, and it will be given him" (James 1:5). William Banks writes: "The Holy Spirit, who now indwells all believers, teaches them and guides them into truth. The throne of God is accessible through the blood of Jesus Christ, and we have confidence that God hears and answers our prayers."[1]

But this does not mean there are no proper uses of lots today. There may be extraordinary occasions where a Christian rightly uses lots to cast himself upon God's providence. For instance, a general who cannot decide which unit to send into battle, and cannot bear the responsibility for the terrible outcome, might cast lots as an appeal to God's sovereign will. Another proper use of lots is to promote peace by avoiding partiality. Thus football games begin with a coin toss to determine which team will kick off first. My grandfather used this procedure in his will. Knowing that my father and uncle were not the best of friends, he directed that they take turns selecting from his personal items with a cut of the cards deciding who would go first. It was a wise and effective procedure that succeeded in avoiding ill feeling.

With these carefully limited categories noted, we should realize that in the vast majority of cases today the use of lots and other instruments of chance is ungodly. People love to rely on "luck" for easy riches or some other worldly gain. But there is no such thing as "luck." All things are determined by God's sovereign will. Jesus pointed out that not even a sparrow falls to the ground apart from God's will (Matt. 10:29). All the wealth we have comes from God, who generously answers the prayers of those who come to him with needs. Therefore, those who gamble in a spirit of pride and greed sacrilegiously mock God's sovereignty. Christians should lament the advanced state of civic depravity displayed by our state-run lotteries. Not only do these government lotteries undermine the virtues of hard work and prayer, while promoting the vices of sloth and greed, but they are proven to prey especially on the poor. A similar concern must be raised when raffles or lotteries are used to raise money for good causes, in which case greed may not be the motive.

1. William Banks, *Jonah: The Reluctant Prophet* (Chicago: Moody, 1966), 31.

Keddie rightly concludes: "Whether for the enrichment of a 'winner' or the benefit of 'a good cause,' [lotteries] are surely to be rejected as the circumvention of God's means for the provision of our needs—namely, work (2 Thess. 3:6–13) and genuine charity from individuals, the church and the state."[2]

SIN FOUND OUT

Whatever God thought of the sailors and their casting of lots, it was his own intention that Jonah should be exposed. Verse 7 thus reports, "So they cast lots, and the lot fell on Jonah."

The original readers of Jonah would immediately think of an earlier episode from Israel's history, in which another sinner was unmasked by lot. Joshua had led Israel across the Jordan River for their miraculous conquest of the fortress city of Jericho. God ordered that Jericho be completely devoted to destruction as an instance of divine judgment. He warned the people: "Keep yourselves from the things devoted to destruction, lest when you have devoted them you take any of the devoted things and make the camp of Israel a thing for destruction and bring trouble upon it" (Josh. 6:18). This was a stern and specific warning, but one Israelite fell into temptation. Achan took from Jericho a rich cloak, two hundred shekels of silver, and a large bar of gold. "I coveted them and took them," he later confessed, and he had buried them beneath his tent (Josh. 7:21).

What happened next shows how the sin of one person affects the entire church. After Jericho, the next city to be taken was Ai, which was so weakly held that an easy victory was expected. Instead, the Israelites were driven off with the loss of thirty-six dead. When Joshua complained to the Lord, God replied: "Israel has sinned . . . they have taken some of the devoted things; they have stolen and lied and put them among their own belongings. Therefore the people of Israel cannot stand before their enemies" (Josh. 7:11–12). The sin must be exposed and repented of, God insisted, before his favor returned to Israel's arms. Because one Israelite had sinned, Israel had sinned, and that sin needed to be dealt with.

God told Joshua what to do. All Israel was assembled the next morning and the lot was cast. The first lot revealed the tribe of Judah, so the whole

2. Gordon J. Keddie, *Preacher on the Run: The Message of Jonah* (Darlington, UK: Evangelical Press, 1986), 40.

tribe was brought forth. The next lot showed the clan of Zerah. The next lot fell on the house of Zabdi. Imagine the tension as the house of Zabdi stood before Joshua and the Lord. The lot was cast again, and it fell on Achan. Joshua approached him and said, "My son, give glory to the Lord God of Israel and give praise to him. And tell me now what you have done; do not hide it from me" (Josh. 7:19). Achan confessed, "Truly I have sinned against the Lord God of Israel" (Josh. 7:20). Achan's stolen goods were revealed, and then not only Achan but also his sons and daughters, his oxen and donkeys and sheep, his tent and all that he had, as well as the silver and the cloak and the bar of gold he had stolen, were taken to the Valley of Achor. There Achan and his family were stoned to death and the whole was put to fire. Finally, a great heap of stones was erected atop Achan's household as a memorial to future generations.[3]

With this in mind, imagine the look on Jonah's face when it was announced that lots would be cast. See him cringe as every footstep thumped on the planks down into the hold as the captain came to bring the news. "Jonah," he may have begun, and Jonah would have already started to nod his head, "the lot has fallen on you."

How would you respond if you were Jonah? Would you contest the falling of the lots? Would you rack your mind for some desperate denial? Would you play it cool and shrug it off? Jonah did none of these, for he saw in the lots the finger of God. So he replied, "I am a Hebrew, and I fear the Lord, the God of heaven, who made the sea and the dry land" (Jonah 1:9). Then he told them all about his flight from the presence of the Lord (Jonah 1:10).

One wonders whether Jonah remembered Joshua's words to Achan: "My son, give glory to the Lord God of Israel," as well as Achan's reply, "Truly I have sinned against the Lord God of Israel." This is what God calls each of us to do: to own our sin before him and glorify him in his righteous judgment. This is the plea that comes to us in the cross of Jesus Christ. Just as the captain brought Jonah the message that his sin was found out, the cross tells us all that God has seen our sins. Even when the holy Son of God was

---

3. The judgment of Achan's family along with him reflects the Bible's idea of covenantal solidarity. As the head of his household, Achan acted on behalf of his whole family so that God judged the entire household for Achan's sin. The harshness of God's judgment is typical for his response to great sins at key turning points in redemptive history, and the placing of memorial stones tells us that the Lord intended this unusually severe judgment to serve as a special warning to Israel against unfaithfulness in the land the Lord was giving to them.

bearing our sins, God did not relent from pouring out his just wrath on Jesus. The cross tells the world that God has seen our sin and that the wages of sin is death (Rom. 6:23).

Yet those who know God also know that he is a God of grace. Jonah should have known this. His prior labor as a prophet involved preaching God's grace in Israel, and it was out of resentment for God's offer of grace to wicked Nineveh that he boarded this ship for Tarshish. Jonah shows our great need not merely to understand the doctrines of grace but to feel our personal need for the grace of the doctrines. God proclaims this grace at the same cross that displays his uncompromising justice against our sin. In the cross of his only beloved Son, God offers us a way of salvation, through faith in the blood of the Lamb of God, who bore our sins in his body on the tree. Though we suffer temporal effects from our sin, as Achan did and Jonah would, God offers salvation for our eternal souls. Jonah does not seem to have been ready to seek God's grace, but at least he confessed his sins. John Calvin comments: "If then we wish God to approve of our repentance, let us not seek evasions, as for the most part is the case; nor let us extenuate our sins, but by a free confession testify before the whole world what we have deserved."[4]

FEARING THE LORD

This pivotal episode in Jonah's life provides a number of useful observations. The first is its clear statement of the church's true occupation. The sailors asked Jonah: "Tell us on whose account this evil has come upon us. What is your occupation?" (Jonah 1:8). Having awakened from sleep, Jonah gave the proper answer: "I am a Hebrew, and I fear the LORD" (Jonah 1:9). The New International Version renders this, "and I worship the LORD." The connection is a good one, because to worship God is to fear him. William Banks explains, "The fear of the Lord is not a servile, cringing type of fear but involves the idea of worship. It means reverential awe, trust, and respect."[5] This is what Christians are called by God to do in this world; worshipful fear of God is the proper occupation of the church.

4. John Calvin, *A Commentary on the Twelve Minor Prophets*, 5 vols. (1559; repr. Edinburgh: Banner of Truth, 1986), 3:52.
5. Banks, *Jonah*, 35.

The fear of the Lord contrasts with fear of the world. Christians are to do God's work in God's way for God's purposes. When we seek the world's work or the world's ways or the world's purposes we lose our relevance and our usefulness to the world, just as Jonah did to the ship and its crew. R. T. Kendall writes, "The solution to making the message of the church 'relevant' to the world is not to be found by concealing our identity. . . . We have been told what we need to do is mix with the world. . . . The idea is that we must adjust our message so that the man in the street will now accept it. We have been doing it for years, bringing the message down, step by step; yet 'modern man' is unimpressed."[6]

So it was with Jonah: the mariners did not even know who he was. They did not know his occupation or who was his God. The church, like Jonah, is called to fear the Lord, and the result of a God-fearing church is that the world knows what it stands for, and which God it serves. It is the sleeping church that fears the world and looks for relevance in worldliness. But when the church is truly awakened, the first sign is that it fears the Lord. However incomplete Jonah's repentance was to this point, he still gave the very definition of a true, awakened Christian: "I fear the Lord."

Secondly, note the relationship between Jonah's fear and the sailors' fear. Jonah declared himself a fearer of the one true God, "the God of heaven, who made the sea and the dry land" (Jonah 1:9). What was the result? "Then the men were exceedingly afraid" (Jonah 1:10). The storm had made them "afraid" (Jonah 1:5), but learning of the God who not only sent the storm but created the sea and dry land made them "exceedingly afraid." Literally, the text says, "They feared a great fear." They were shocked that Jonah had sinned against this God, showing an awe for the God they did not know that exceeded Jonah's fear for the God he did know.

The mariners likely would have heard about the Hebrews and their frightening God. He was the God who broke Pharaoh's power in order to set his people free, and who parted the waters of the Red Sea for the Hebrews to pass through, but then drowned the pursuing Egyptians. This was the stern God who took his people into the wilderness for forty years to teach them to fear him, but then led them into Canaan with such frightening power. Therefore, they realized, fearing a great fear, that "this was a great God, this

---

6. R. T. Kendall, *Jonah: An Exposition* (Atlanta: Authentic, 2006), 38.

God of the Hebrews; and it was this God, not a weak god, who was pursuing them for the sake of Jonah."[7]

The mariners' reaction to Jonah's answer shows that when the church is awake, God uses the church to awaken the world. Christians wonder why there is no fear of God in the society around us. The reason is that there is so little fear of God in the church. History reveals that great revivals always begin in the church: Christians regain their vision of the great and holy God they serve; they fear him; they revere him; they grasp with awe the saving message of grace in Jesus Christ. From such a church, the fear of God spreads out to the world, so that many seek the salvation God has provided in the gospel of his Son. But until the church regains its own identity and awakens to the fear of its God, there is no way for the world around to fear the Lord either.

Realizing this leads to a third point that Jonah shows us: those who fear the Lord will show the world who the Lord is. Pagans like these mariners tended to think in terms of territorial gods. There were the gods of Babylon, the gods of Philistia, the gods of Egypt, the god of Israel, and so on. They had learned that Jonah was fleeing from his God "because he had told them" (Jonah 1:10; the tense of this verb indicates that Jonah had told this some time earlier). But they likely thought the matter resolved, since Jonah's God was the god of Israel and, after all, they were on their way to Tarshish. Yet now, with the terrifying storm raging about them, the prophet reveals, "I am a Hebrew, and I fear the LORD, the God of heaven, who made the sea and the dry land" (Jonah 1:9). Where our English Bibles read "the LORD" (in small capital letters), the Hebrew text uses God's covenant name, Yahweh. "I fear Yahweh," Jonah states, and he is "the God of heaven, who made the sea and the dry land." This may have made little impact on the mariners back when Jonah boarded the ship in Joppa, and much less as their ship pulled farther away from Israel, where they understood this particular god Yahweh to operate. But now, with the divine storm raging and ripping their boat, they realized the truth of Jonah's words: Yahweh is the true God, not merely of this place or that, but everyplace and everywhere.

In like manner, God's dealings in the lives of his people are designed to show the world the truth about him. When he answers our prayers, when

---

7. James M. Boice, *The Minor Prophets*, 2 vols. (Grand Rapids: Baker, 1983), 1:276.

he chastens us with trials, and when he blesses us with power, God shows himself to the world through his dealings with his people. It is especially the awakened church that serves this end, by speaking and preaching the truth of God to the world. The awakened, God-fearing church preaches God's Word boldly to the world, and finds anew that God's Word is a mighty, sharply edged sword, before which even the boldest of men tremble before God. Amid the howling winds of divine wrath, Jonah's answer to the mariners' question caused them to fear the Lord, with a newly awakened understanding of who and what God really is.

It is from this vantage point that we see what a blessing it is when God sends a storm to bring his people to repentance. It was a hand of divine grace that tore the mask from Jonah and uncovered his sin. God's purpose was to restore the prophet's godly fear. This is why God did not shut down the storm as soon as Jonah confessed. The storm still raged as Jonah and the mariners trembled; the temporal consequences of sin must still be felt. Hugh Martin writes:

> Therefore, to deepen your repentance and confirm it; to inspire you with a holy terror of like iniquity in time to come; to grave painfully and burningly into your heart and memory experiences and recollections that shall rise swiftly to the aid of your integrity and virtue, if tempted to like offence again; God may see meet to prolong the storm that He has awakened, even after it may have been blessed to bring you to repentance.[8]

So let us learn our lesson early and well. Let us bless the hand of chastisement, seeing the grace that directs it. Let us embrace God's call to repentance for our sin and slumber, and let us long to fear the Lord. Are you willing to do this? Are you ready and eager for the state of your soul to be searched? Are you confident that your ship contains no Jonah—that there is no Achan in your camp? If there is, will you give glory to God when it is revealed? Be assured, Christian, that God has found out your sin and will bring it to light. Be assured that the Lord of the storm intends for you to fear him as you ought.

But rest assured as well, that there is no greater good that God might perform in your life and no better way for him to give meaning to your

---

8. Hugh Martin, *A Commentary on Jonah* (Edinburgh: Banner of Truth, 1870; repr. 1958), 169.

time in this world. For when God's discipline has brought you back to his cross—the place where sin is confessed and cleansed—you may stand before heaven and earth and exult with unmasked heart: "I am a Christian, and I fear the Lord, the God of heaven, who made the sea and dry land, and sent his own Son with boundless love to redeem me through his blood, that I may declare his glory forever." Then God will use you to bring his message of fear and grace to the world.

6

JONAH THE SCAPEGOAT

Jonah 1:11—16

*He said to them, "Pick me up and hurl me into the sea; then the
sea will quiet down for you, for I know it is because of me that this
great tempest has come upon you." (Jonah 1:12)*

In the early hours of October 16, 1946, Lutheran minister
Henry Gerecke paid a visit to members of his small congregation in Nuremberg, Germany. This was no ordinary congregation, since the men he was visiting were about to be executed for
committing the vilest crimes imaginable. One by one, Gerecke walked
with his congregants to the gallows. When the noose was placed over the
first man's head and he was asked for his last words, he gave testimony to
his faith in Jesus Christ: "I place all my confidence in the Lamb who made
atonement for my sins. May God have mercy on my soul." His name was
Joachim von Ribbentrop, and until the previous year he had been the
foreign minister of Adolf Hitler's Nazi Germany. When first visited by
Gerecke in the Nuremberg prison where the war crimes trial was taking
place, Ribbentrop had listed a long string of objections to the Christian
faith. But under the faithful preaching of the gospel in the prison chapel,
he had been thoroughly converted and saved.

Not all of Gerecke's parishioners were converted. One of them was Hermann Goering, chief of the German Luftwaffe and Hitler's closest colleague. Goering also attended chapel, but when Gerecke visited him on that last evening, Goering mocked Christianity. Within minutes after the pastor left him, Goering committed suicide.

Others were more like Ribbentrop. When Gerecke first visited the cell of Field Marshal Wilhelm Keitel, chief of the German armed forces, he found Keitel reading his Bible and professing Christ. Two others, Fritz Sauckel, the Nazi head of labor supply, described as the cruelest slave master since Pharaoh, and Wilhelm Frick, who as minister of the interior oversaw a reign of terror that had targeted many Christians, went to the scaffold confessing their sins and asking forgiveness from God through faith in Christ. Eight of the Nazi war criminals were accepted at the Lord's Table by Chaplain Gerecke on the basis of a credible profession of faith in Christ.[1]

THE MARINERS' MERCY

Not everyone is prepared to accept the idea of the grossest sinners finding salvation in Christ. This explains why Gerecke received so many abusive letters when he returned to America for ministering to the Nazis. Had the prophet Jonah been living, he might have sent one of these letters. God had ordered Jonah to preach for the salvation of the savage murderers in Nineveh, but Jonah decided to abandon God rather than accept the job. Jonah's experience has shown the futility of running from God. But as the story unfolds and Jonah falls under judgment, the irony of his rebellion is revealed through the actions of the pagan mariners on board Jonah's ship.

Terrified by the great storm God had hurled at their ship because of Jonah, the sailors first prayed to their own false gods. Then they cast lots to identify the sinner responsible for the divine wrath. When the lot fell on Jonah, they began quizzing him. Jonah confessed, "I am a Hebrew, and I fear the LORD, the God of heaven, who made the sea and dry land" (Jonah 1:9).

The sailors were "exceedingly afraid" when they realized that Jonah was rebelling against such a great God. So they appealed to Jonah, who was still a prophet of the Lord in spite of himself: "What shall we do to

---

1. Cited from Don Stephens, *War and Grace: Short Biographies from the World Wars* (Darlington, UK: Evangelical Press, 2005), 253–71.

you, that the sea may quiet down for us?" (Jonah 1:11). Jonah answered, "Pick me up and hurl me into the sea; then the sea will quiet down for you, for I know it is because of me that this great tempest has come upon you" (Jonah 1:12).

What then happened was remarkable because of the nobility of the mariners' conduct. Hugh Martin writes, "A perfect stranger he was to them. No ties of friendship, or acquaintance, or kin, or country could he plead; and the subject of a strange but strong God, bringing down his God's wrath on them—verily, they had little to thank him for."[2] The only thing Jonah had ever done for them was bring them into trouble. So one could excuse them if they simply tossed him overboard, especially since these were pagan idolaters and since Jonah himself had suggested this solution.

Instead, the sailors were motivated by the sanctity of Jonah's life, and perhaps by fear of the divine consequences of needlessly shedding blood. So instead of tossing Jonah overboard, "the men rowed hard to get back to dry land, but they could not, for the sea grew more and more tempestuous against them" (Jonah 1:13). The Hebrew text indicates that the sailors "dug into" the waves, so hard did they row in their attempt to win Jonah's safety ashore. They realized that their safety required his removal, but they exerted themselves to the utmost to spare his life. Whether their respect arose from his special status as a prophet or merely from his general standing as a human being, the fear of the Lord is manifested in their conduct. These men show us that just as a disregard for God always shows forth in cruelty toward man, the fear of the Lord invariably produces both justice and mercy.

What a reproach this was to Jonah! After all, the reason he was on the ship was his hardness of heart toward Gentiles. O. Palmer Robertson comments: "He, the believer, closes his heart toward the massive metropolis of Nineveh. Although his people had experienced the grace of God for generations, he closes his heart to another people. But in dramatic contrast these coarse sailors do everything they can to spare the life of Jonah, even after he has caused the loss of all their cargo, and now may cause their loss of life."[3]

Apparently, God did not cooperate with the merciful mariners. However hard they rowed, they could not overcome the increasingly raging seas. It was

2. Hugh Martin, *A Commentary on Jonah* (1870; repr. Edinburgh: Banner of Truth, 1958), 174.
3. O. Palmer Robertson, *Jonah: A Study in Compassion*, 24–25.

God's will for Jonah's chastisement to continue, so nothing the sailors could do succeeded in sparing his life. "Therefore they called out to the LORD, 'O LORD, let us not perish for this man's life, and lay not on us innocent blood, for you, O LORD, have done as it pleased you.' So they picked up Jonah and hurled him into the sea, and the sea ceased from its raging" (Jonah 1:14–15).

Here, too, we see the impact of Jonah's unwitting witness on the sailors. Faced with no alternative but to accept Jonah's counsel, they first prayed to Yahweh asking him not to hold them responsible, since it was obviously his sovereign will that controlled their situation.

How do we account for the nobility of these men who did not know the Lord? The answer is found in God's common grace. Common grace observes that God is at work in the world even apart from the realm of salvation. God instills virtue in heathen kings and inspires a reverence for life among even the pagans. God provides this common grace for the sake of the gospel, so that the world might continue and his church be preserved in the midst of a wicked world, and also to preserve the world for the sake of those who yet will be saved.

The mariners also display an awareness of what is called natural law. It is doubtful that they had ever read the Ten Commandments, with God's mandate that "You shall not murder" (Ex. 20:13). Yet they still knew it is wrong to take human life needlessly. John Calvin comments: "There is by nature implanted in all an abhorrence of cruelty. . . . Though these men had never known the doctrine of the law, they were yet so taught by nature that they knew that the blood of man is dear and precious in the sight of God."[4]

Both common grace and natural law are still in evidence today. Sometimes the virtue of pagans embarrasses the people of God who possess saving grace and know the written law of God. We think, for instance, of the heroism by which the New York City firefighters cast away their lives trying to save others in the World Trade Center on September 11, 2001. Many of them were probably not true believers in Christ, yet their valor exceeds that of many Christians. Whenever God's people witness such virtue in unbelievers, we should feel challenged to respond to God's saving grace by becoming the men and women the Lord desires us to be.

---

4. John Calvin, *A Commentary on the Twelve Minor Prophets*, 5 vols. (1559; repr. Edinburgh: Banner of Truth, 1986), 3:60.

THE MARINERS CONVERTED?

A question arises at this point for which there is little scholarly consensus. The question is whether or not the account in Jonah reveals a true conversion of the mariners. Were they operating strictly out of common grace, or at some point did they come to a true and saving knowledge of the Lord?

An impressive array of voices concludes that there is not sufficient reason to see this as a true conversion, including John Calvin, George Hutchinson, Douglas Stuart, John Mackay, William Banks, and Peter Williams. Calvin states that they "were not suddenly so changed as to devote themselves to the true God . . . it was not such a real and thorough conversion of the soul as changed them into new men."[5] Douglas Stuart supposes that instead of embracing true Old Testament faith, the sailors merely "added Yahweh to the god(s) they already believed in."[6] William Banks assesses: "The fear they showed could have been only temporary, lacking true piety."[7] As a pastor, I understand this skepticism. I have found that those who profess faith in Christ with an ulterior motive are often found to have done so insincerely. A man wants to marry a Christian woman, so he professes faith to her father. Or soldiers in battle promise religion in order to get out alive. Such professions of faith should be viewed skeptically until true faith is evidenced in a changed life.

Nonetheless, I think there is ample evidence to believe that these mariners were truly converted through their experience with Jonah's God. This is the view held by James Boice, R. T. Kendall, Thomas McComiskey, Hugh Martin, O. Palmer Robertson, Jacques Ellul, and Gordon Keddie. What is the evidence for this positive view?

First, I am influenced by the way such a conversion fits in the overall narrative of Jonah. The prophet had feared that his preaching in Nineveh would lead pagans to find mercy in God's grace. It follows that God should teach him a lesson in the conversion of the pagan sailors. Moreover, the mariners' conversion should be considered no more implausible than that of Pastor Gerecke's Nazi war criminals—or, for that matter, anyone else's conversion. It took no more grace for them to be saved than it takes for any Christian to be saved.

5. Ibid., 3:64.
6. Douglas Stuart, *Hosea–Jonah* Word Biblical Commentary 31 (Waco, Tex.: Word, 1987), 464.
7. William Banks, *Jonah: The Reluctant Prophet* (Chicago: Moody, 1966), 42.

In addition, the language of the mariners' prayer suggests more than that they simply added Jonah's God to their list of false gods. Calvin, who writes so strongly on this point that we almost should list him as being both against and for the idea of the mariners' conversion, says, "The sailors and the passengers were not only touched with the fear of God, but that they also had the impression that the God of Israel was the supreme King of heaven and earth." Realizing this, they also saw that "they were previously deluded, and that whatever the world had invented was mere delusion, and that the gods devised by the fancies of men were nothing but mere idols."[8] Bryan Estelle points out that the phrase "you, O LORD, have done as it pleased you" corresponds to three other Old Testament texts that make a similar statement (Pss. 115:3; 135:6; Isa. 46:10). In each of the other cases the context features the rejection of false gods, so it is reasonable to take it with this meaning here as well.[9]

Furthermore, we read that the sailors "offered a sacrifice to the LORD and made vows" (Jonah 1:16). They called on God's covenant name, Yahweh, and while they did not know the proper procedures for the Levitical sacrifices in Jerusalem, they seem to have understood their need for some offering of atonement for sin. The taking of vows is probably to be understood as a confession of covenant fidelity. Calvin writes: "When, therefore, the sailors vowed a vow to God, they renounced their own idols. . . . Now then they made their vows to the only true God; for they knew that their lives were in his hand."[10]

The sailors had experienced an unforgettable, once-in-a-lifetime divine encounter. In this way, God had sent the storm not only to awaken his wayward prophet, but also to provide the pagans a display of his saving power. Who knows but that these Tarshish-bound mariners were the seeds for the later and wider knowledge of God in Spain. We remember the apostle Paul's fervent desire to preach the gospel in Spain; perhaps God was preparing the ground through these sailors (see Rom. 15:24). Joyce Baldwin summarizes their experience: "The sailors have made a life-changing discovery because they have come into contact with the living God. They make such offerings

---

8. Calvin, *Minor Prophets*, 3:64.

9. Bryan Estelle, *Salvation through Judgment and Mercy: The Gospel According to Jonah* (Phillipsburg, NJ: P&R Publishing, 2005), 53–54.

10. Calvin, *Minor Prophets*, 3:69.

as they can then and there, but plan to do more, formulating their intentions into vows to be carried out later."[11]

What lessons should we learn from this conversion? One lesson is not to be intimidated by the world's unbelief, so that we lower our message to its level. The same God "who made the sea and the dry land" (Jonah 1:9) and converted the pagan sailors is able to win converts through our witness to anyone. We should also learn that God will save whomever he desires, whether we are faithful and obedient or not. Jonah's willingness to witness to the Gentiles did not determine God's will for their salvation; all it determined was whether or not Jonah would be blessed by it. As it was, Jonah went beneath the waves without witnessing the mariners' sacrifice or hearing their vows. James Boice writes:

> What God is going to do, he will do. . . . But notice, God can do this through the obedience of his children, as he does later with Nineveh through Jonah, in which case they share in the blessing. Or he can do it through his children's disobedience, as here, in which case they miss the blessing. . . . Which will it be in your case? Will you resist him? Will you refuse his Great Commission? Or will you obey him in this and in all matters?[12]

JONAH THE SCAPEGOAT

When we turn our consideration toward Jonah, we also have a question on which there is disagreement. When Jonah asked to be thrown into the sea, did this express his sincere repentance over his sin, or rather his hardened resolve to suffer even death rather than to give in to God's will? Those who argue for Jonah's repentance say that his acknowledgement of guilt made him willing to suffer death in order to spare the pagan sailors. But there is one main reason why I do not believe Jonah had yet relented in his rebellion to God: there is no suggestion of him resolving to return and carry out the commission God had given him. Jonah does not repent until chapter 2, and when he does repent he goes to Nineveh and preaches as God commanded. William Banks comments, "If the tempest served to harden Jonah's will, it meant that

11. Joyce Baldwin, *Jonah*, in Thomas McComiskey, *An Exegetical & Expository Commentary on the Minor Prophets*, ed. Thomas E. McComiskey, 3 vols. (Grand Rapids: Baker, 1993), 2:563.
12. James M. Boice, *The Minor Prophets*, 2 vols. (Grand Rapids: Baker, 1983), 1:280.

Jonah was willing to perish rather than to preach. Bigotry can become so ingrained in the human personality that not even the threat of physical harm or punishment will eradicate it, nor will arguments and appeals to reason."[13] With this bitter spirit, Jonah faced the waters of his doom. He would rather die than preach for the salvation of hated Nineveh. Whereas the sailors were willing to submit to the revealed will of God, Jonah, who knew better what the will of God is, would rather be consigned to the waves.

Anyone who has witnessed or read about burials at sea knows how solemn they are. How much more so when the victim is still alive and is cast over to drown in the deep! The sailors all expected Jonah's sacrifice to calm the storm, just as they acknowledged it to be a just punishment for Jonah's sin. But if anything proves that a believer can become so hardened by sin as to destroy his or her life in this world, the experience of Jonah proves it. No wonder the writer of Hebrews tells us, "Exhort one another every day, as long as it is called 'today,' that none of you may be hardened by the deceitfulness of sin" (Heb. 3:13).

But more important than Jonah's subjective state of mind is the objective role he plays in God's redemptive history. In the Bible's teaching of redemption, Jonah's "death" beneath the waves looks both backward and forward. Looking backward, Jonah plays the same role as the scapegoat on Israel's Day of Atonement. On the one day each year when the sin of Israel was dealt with, God ordained that the high priest would come to the tabernacle with two live goats. One of the goats, chosen by lot, would be sacrificed for sin; the other goat—the scapegoat—was sent away into the wilderness (Lev. 16:7–10). This was the role Jonah played for the salvation of the mariners. Just as Aaron laid his hands on the scapegoat, placing Israel's sins on its head, and sent it away into the distant wilderness (Lev. 16:21–22), so also Jonah removed God's wrath by taking his sin into the wilderness of the deep. Even the use of lots to identify Jonah suggests an intentional connection. His sacrifice removed God's wrath from the ship so that peace was restored between man and God.

Jonah's "death" in the deep also looks forward in redemptive history, finding its ultimate meaning in the death of Jesus Christ. It was Jesus who compared his own death to that of Jonah: "For just as Jonah was three days

---

13. Banks, *Jonah*, 37.

and three nights in the belly of the great fish, so will the Son of Man be three days and three nights in the heart of the earth" (Matt. 12:40). There are major differences between Jonah and Jesus, of course. Jonah is guilty of his own sin, having refused God's will. Jesus bore only the sins of others, in obedience to the will of the Father. Yet Jonah is a type of Christ; he is an Old Testament figure who represents at least one aspect of Jesus and his saving work. Jacques Ellul explains the connection: "If it is true that the sacrifice of a man who takes his condemnation can save others around him, then this is far more true when the one sacrificed is the Son of God."[14]

Jonah's "death" in the waves, bringing the storm to an end, shows that God's way of salvation involves the placing of sins upon one who will die. And just as salvation for Nineveh comes from Jonah's resurrection-like salvation after three days in the cold tomb of the great fish, so also the resurrection of Jesus Christ brings salvation to the world. In Jonah, Robertson explains, "God pursues one man to the death that he might bless the many." Likewise, "God pursued his own Son even to the death that many from every nation under heaven might be saved."[15]

BUT JONAH, BUT THE LORD

God used the sleeping witness of his rebellious prophet to reveal himself to the sailors. The "but Jonah" that led to his rebellion was overcome by the "but the LORD" that sent the storm. How often this has been the case with God's people: "The fact that the church is not what she ought to be at the present moment does not mean that God cannot use us. For God can use a crooked stick to draw a straight line and that is precisely what happened in the case of Jonah."[16] But how much better it would have been for Jonah had he softened his heart to God's gracious will! In that case, he could have been on the deck instead of descending through the cold sea as the converted sailors began worshiping on the ship. How much better for us, too, to accept God's sovereign call on our lives, serving the cause of the gospel wherever God sends us and marveling at the grace by which we and others are saved.

14. Jacques Ellul, *The Judgment of Jonah* (Grand Rapids: Eerdmans, 1971), 37.
15. Robertson, *Jonah: A Study in Compassion*, 26–27.
16. R. T. Kendall, *Jonah: An Exposition* (Atlanta: Authentic, 2006), 57.

Jonah's experience holds a message for those who have not yet believed, too. Learn from the grace that God extended to the sailors. James Boice offers God's generous invitation: "You have not yet perished in your godless state because God, who made the sea around you and the dry land on which you walk, preserves you. Do not remain indifferent to him. Turn to him. Approach him on the basis of the perfect sacrifice for sin made once by his own Son, Jesus Christ, and follow him throughout your days."[17]

17. Boice, *The Minor Prophets*, 1:280.

7

JONAH'S GREAT FISH

Jonah 1:17

And the LORD appointed a great fish to swallow up Jonah. And Jonah was in the belly of the fish three days and three nights. (Jonah 1:17)

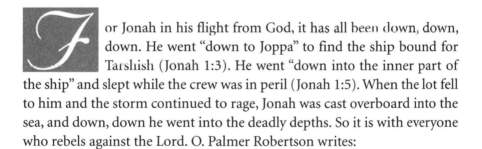 or Jonah in his flight from God, it has all been down, down, down. He went "down to Joppa" to find the ship bound for Tarshish (Jonah 1:3). He went "down into the inner part of the ship" and slept while the crew was in peril (Jonah 1:5). When the lot fell to him and the storm continued to rage, Jonah was cast overboard into the sea, and down, down he went into the deadly depths. So it is with everyone who rebels against the Lord. O. Palmer Robertson writes:

> The sinner goes down. He begins the descent by his own acts of folly. He tries to run from the will of God, and he trips on his own dangling shoelaces. It is just a fact: nothing can be in its right order when you are living in rebellion against the will of God. . . . The circumstances of life will bring you down. Your own inner spirit will bring you down. The hand of the Lord will bring you down.[1]

1. O. Palmer Robertson, *Jonah: A Study in Compassion* (Edinburgh: Banner of Truth, 1990), 28.

The bad news for Jonah is that for every action he takes, God acts in return. Yet what seems like bad news is actually good news when it comes to God's people, since even God's hand of chastisement is ultimately meant for blessing. Believers will sometimes go down into the pit even when they have trusted God. Joseph discovered this when he was placed in prison for obeying the Lord. But he found that God was with him in the pit. The greatest instance of this principle was the descent of Jesus into the darkness of death. Robertson writes, "From the cross he descended into the tomb. But from there he rose in glory to reign at the right hand of the Father."[2] Jonah may not seem to fit in that company, since his descent stemmed from his sin. But even he discovered the grace of God in the deep. He too, as a child of God, discovered the power of the resurrection, so that in the abyss he found the saving grace of God.

MIRACLE OR MYTH?

Jonah 1:17 introduces the most famous feature in this book, since it tells of the great fish that rescued Jonah from the deep. It states that "the LORD appointed a great fish to swallow up Jonah." It is unfortunate that questions concerning the whale or great fish have preoccupied most readers, since this distracts us from the real meaning of the book. Thomas Carlisle wrote of making this mistake: "I was so obsessed with what was going on inside the whale that I missed seeing the drama inside Jonah."[3] As Lloyd Ogilvie has pointed out, "The subject of the . . . sentence is not the great fish, but the Lord,"[4] so our attention should be on what God did and not on the fish.

One reason for the excessive attention on the great fish—the Hebrew word is a generic word for fish, not necessarily a whale—is that liberal scholarship has brought its guns to bear on this verse. By showing that the Bible is clearly in error about Jonah's whale, they hope to undermine the overall authority of Holy Scripture. Liberals argue that Jonah tells a fable, since it is impossible to believe that a man was swallowed by a fish and lived inside for three days before being vomited onto the shore. At the heart of the liberal objection, of course, is the unwillingness to admit the possibility of the miraculous.

2. Ibid., 28.
3. Cited in James M. Boice, *The Minor Prophets*, 2 vols. (Grand Rapids: Baker, 1983), 1:282.
4. Lloyd Ogilvie, *Hosea, Joel, Amos, Obadiah, Jonah* (Dallas: Word, 1990), 410.

Only by first ruling out the supernatural are the liberals able to rule out the possibility of Jonah's fish.

A couple of specific objections should be considered, however. One states that since the larger whales eat plankton, none of them have throats large enough to swallow a man whole. In the early twentieth century, it was argued that even a sperm whale would have difficulty swallowing an orange, much less a man. Since then, however, botanists have identified subspecies of sperm whales with throats large enough to swallow a small house.[5] The second issue deals with whether or not a man could breathe enough air inside such a creature to survive a three-day submarine voyage. The answer is that it is possible, although it would be a very uncomfortable journey.

The most famous answer to the liberal objections is the episode of the whaling ship Star of the East, which spotted a large sperm whale in February 1891. Harpoon boats were launched, one of which capsized with two men overboard. In time the whale was killed and drawn to the ship where it was secured and its blubber removed. The next day its stomach was hoisted onto the deck, and inside was sailor James Bartley, who was unconscious but alive. After being revived, he resumed his duties aboard the ship.[6]

DEATH IN THE DEEP

It is important for us to defend the validity of the text. But for those who can accept that God performs miracles in our world, the more important point is the text's meaning. The first theme we should consider is the relationship between Jonah's descent into the deep and the atoning death of Jesus Christ. As the ancient church father Tertullian wrote, "What he endured was a type of the Lord's suffering, by which pagan penitents also would be redeemed."[7]

In this respect, we should note the symbolism of death embedded in Jonah's language about the deep sea. When we think about Noah's flood, Moses in the Red Sea, and Joshua crossing the Jordan, we realize that the sea symbolizes the power of death to swallow and destroy. Jacques Ellul

5. Cited from Boice, *Minor Prophets*, 1:283.
6. Ibid., 2:284.
7. Tertullian, in Alberto Ferreiro, ed., *The Twelve Prophets*, Ancient Christian Commentary on Scripture, Old Testament XIV (Downers Grove, Ill.: InterVarsity, 2003), 135.

comments: "The waters are the power of death and drowning. He who is plunged into them is plunged into death; he who traverses them traverses death."[8] Likewise, the devouring fish symbolizes the powers of chaos and death that engulf the impenitent. Isaiah, for instance, symbolizes God's final judgment with imagery of the slaying of a great sea creature: "In that day the *Lord* with his hard and great and strong sword will punish Leviathan the fleeing serpent . . . and he will slay the dragon that is in the sea" (Isa. 27:1). Moreover, the statement that "Jonah was in the belly of the fish three days and three nights" (Jonah 1:17) speaks of death, since that was the length of time traditionally understood to confirm a death.[9] For instance, Jesus waited until his friend Lazarus had been four days in the grave before he arrived to raise him (John 11:39), so that none would doubt that Lazarus truly had died. Of course, Jesus himself lay dead in the tomb for three days, in part to confirm to all that he had not merely swooned but truly had suffered death.

Indeed, our interpretation of Jonah's descent into the great fish must be shaped by the teaching of the Lord Jesus. Some Pharisees had demanded that Jesus prove himself by performing miracles, to which Jesus replied: "An evil and adulterous generation seeks for a sign, but no sign will be given to it except the sign of the prophet Jonah. For just as Jonah was three days and three nights in the belly of the great fish, so will the Son of Man be three days and three nights in the heart of the earth" (Matt. 12:39–40). This indicates that Jonah's "death" in the belly of the fish prefigured the days of death that Jesus Christ would experience in the grave, after his crucifixion for our sins.

Jonah's experience in the watery grave teaches us at least three things about the death and resurrection of Jesus Christ. The first is that the end of God's judgment is death. When Jonah was swallowed by the great fish, this was the climax of his judgment from God. So far as he was concerned, his entombment was a final judgment beyond remedy. Jacques Ellul writes, "It is damnation. The fish is in fact hell. Jonah has thus traversed the agony and death and come to this hell prepared by God to enforce the total separation of man and God."[10]

---

8. Jacques Ellul, *The Judgment of Jonah* (Grand Rapids: Eerdmans, 1971), 41.

9. See D. A. Carson, *The Gospel According to John*, Pillar New Testament Commentary (Grand Rapids: Eerdmans, 1991), 411, where Carson makes this observation regarding Lazarus having been dead for four days prior to Jesus' arrival in Bethany.

10. Ellul, *The Judgment of Jonah*, 44.

This reminds us that hell is the end of every desire to flee from God. Jonah was looking for a place where he could escape the presence of the Lord, and the belly of the great fish in the deep was the achievement of his rebellious desire.

All this and more is what Jesus endured in our place through his death on the cross. The Lord of glory and life suffered damnation in that final judgment of death. "My God, my God, why have you forsaken me?" Jesus cried (Matt. 27:46). His experience on the cross was not less dreadful than its corollary of Jonah in the belly of the fish; if anything, it was more dreadful. Jesus voluntarily took to himself the death that we deserved by our sins. As Cyril of Jerusalem preached long ago:

> Jonah was cast into the belly of a great fish, but Christ of his own will descended to the abode of the invisible fish of death. He went down of his own will to make death disgorge those it had swallowed up, according to Scripture: "I shall deliver them from the power of the nether world, and I shall redeem them from death."[11]

Like Jonah, every sinner has embraced a path of sin that can only lead to the damnation of death; but in his grace, Jesus has endured this death in our place on the cross. Just as Jonah's death in the deep removed the storm from the sailors above, so Jesus' cross removes the wrath of God from our sins. Gordon Keddie writes:

> By it, Jesus paid the penalty of sin (expiation), placated the displeasure of God against the sinner (propitiation) and restored believers to the favour and fellowship of God (reconciliation). Jesus' death procures a new heart (regeneration), a new record (forgiveness) and a new future (eternal life) for all who will trust in him as their Savior and Lord. Jesus went through the hell of the earth for the sake of people like us. . . . Jonah's three days in the fish emphasized that the wages of sin is death and that, if anyone was ever to be forgiven the consequences of his sin, then there had to be an atonement sufficient to cover the need. In this sense, Jesus' death and burial was the "sign of Jonah" for his own generation.[12]

11. Cyril of Jerusalem, in Alberto Ferreiro, ed., *The Twelve Prophets*, Ancient Christian Commentary on Scripture, Old Testament XIV (Downers Grove, Ill.: InterVarsity, 2003), 135.

12. Gordon J. Keddie, *Preacher on the Run: The Message of Jonah* (Darlington, UK: Evangelical Press, 1986), 71–72.

Secondly, to all appearances, the descent into the deep was the end of Jonah, just as Jesus' death on the cross seemed to be his end. When Jonah went beneath the waves, the mariners may have stood reverently for some time, but then they would have moved on, never to see the prophet again. So it must have seemed to the Jews and the Roman soldiers when Jesus breathed his last on the cross. Yet it was not the end, because through the death of his servant, God intended to bring life not just to him but to the world. Peter Williams comments: "Just as Jonah was delivered from his watery grave to continue the work of preaching repentance and salvation to the Ninevites, so Christ through his resurrection continued—through the gift of the Holy Spirit to the church—to preach the gospel of salvation to the whole world."[13]

The history of God's people has shown this pattern at work time and again. Williams writes:

> Witness what happened in the old Soviet Union under communism when the church was persecuted, believers imprisoned, and the Bible outlawed. God's power was at work and it came to life again. The same happened in China when Christian missionaries were expelled and the church closed down. Many then thought that that was the end of the great vision of Hudson Taylor, but God was at work, and today there are more believers in China than ever before. The last word is never with men, but with God's power.[14]

SALVATION BY SOVEREIGN GRACE

The third point made by Jonah's descent into the great fish deserves extended treatment. For the sea creature was not only a sign of God's judgment, but a sign of God's sovereign grace through that judgment. We can consider this by asking: "Where did the great fish come from?" The answer is obvious: it was God who arranged for the sea creature to be at just the right spot at just the right time, with just the right amount of hunger so as to want to swallow a foolish prophet who had just been cast overboard.

The key word here is "appointed": "The LORD appointed a great fish to swallow up Jonah" (Jonah 1:17). Some versions translate this as saying God

13. Peter Williams, *Jonah—Running from God: An Expositional Commentary*, Exploring the Bible (Epsom, Surrey, UK: Day One, 2003), 42.
14. Ibid., 43.

"prepared" the great fish that would swallow Jonah. Together the two words render the idea perfectly. God had long since been preparing his plans for the appointed fulfillment of his saving will for and through the prophet. This is a theme that recurs throughout this book, with its strong emphasis on the sovereign grace of God. Later God appoints and prepares a plant to shade Jonah, then he appoints a worm to destroy the plant, and finally God prepares an east wind to blow on the prophet in order to achieve his will. Williams writes: "Each of these instances was a deliberate act by God to provide for the outworking of his purpose. As the omnipotent God he not only ordains the end, but also provides the means to that end."[15]

This theme of God's sovereignty in salvation is not new to the Bible with Jonah. All through God's Word we read of God providing and preparing that which would advance his redemptive plan. God had Noah prepare the ark for saving him and his family through the great flood (Gen. 6:14). When Abraham obeyed God by taking his son Isaac up Mount Moriah as an offering, God provided him with a ram appointed to be sacrificed in Isaac's place (Gen. 22:13–14). Likewise, when Elijah was hiding at the brook, God appointed ravens to bring him his daily bread (1 Kings 17:5–6). When the Ethiopian eunuch was reading the prophet Isaiah, God prepared and appointed that Philip the deacon be on hand to explain the meaning of the gospel (Acts 8:26–40). Williams comments: "In all these instances we are meant to see how God prepares the way, and provides the means for the outworking of his eternal purposes."[16] We might continue all through the New Testament, in which the sovereign God prepared and appointed the means of his saving purpose at every step, whether it was Peter's need to meet Cornelius in order to take the gospel to the Gentiles or Paul's need for the earthquake to deliver him and Silas from the Philippian jail.

When we turn back to the cross of Christ, we see that the same is true. God prepared for the Messiah to come through the prophecies of the Old Testament and the ministry of John the Baptist. God appointed that his Son would be betrayed by Judas and delivered by the Jews into the hands of the Gentiles, and that together representatives of the whole world would nail Jesus Christ to the cross. The sham trial and murder of Jesus took place, Peter said, "according to the definite plan and foreknowledge of God" (Acts

15. Ibid., 40.
16. Ibid., 41.

2:23). And God appointed that Jesus would rise from the dead on the third day, arriving back in the world in resurrection power, just as Jonah would in time come to Nineveh as proof of God's sovereign, forgiving, and life-giving grace for all who will repent and believe.

From this perspective, we can see that all along God's purpose had been working even in Jonah's flight of rebellion. God purposed to bring wicked Nineveh to repentance. He did this out of mercy for them and also for the display of his own glory. However, it was not God's plan for Jonah simply to embark from Israel to arrive in the enemy capital with a message from Israel's God. Instead, God appointed and prepared that Jonah would first join them in rebellion, that Jonah would experience the kind of death about which he would warn them, and Jonah would serve as an emblem of the resurrection life that comes as the gift of a gracious God. In this way, the Jonah that God intended to use for the salvation of Nineveh was himself a trophy of saving grace. It was a bedraggled, humbled, and God-reliant prophet who emerged onto the shore from the belly of the fish, ready and now equipped to serve God's purpose in the world.

God intends for our lives to bear this same message to our world. The Christian witness is not that of good and faithful people who have merited God's favor by our own actions, and whose lives display the power of virtue and success. That is the way the religions of the world seek to achieve their aims. But the Christian witness is that of rebellious sinners who have been delivered from a just condemnation by the sovereign grace of God through the atoning death of his Son.

After he had experienced his own deliverance, Jonah found mercy in his heart to preach to wicked Nineveh. Every Christian should look on the world with the same realization. It was as a prophet of God's mercy that Jonah was fit to speak grace to the wicked, and so it is with each of us. Like Jonah, every redeemed sinner who has experienced the death of conviction of sin and the spiritual resurrection of the new birth is sent forth by God to serve his gospel. We are to preach salvation as those who have been redeemed and bear a new life within our souls. Realizing that in our need for forgiveness from sin and deliverance from the abyss we find the great unity of all mankind, we are to break through every barrier that might separate us from others in the world.

Lastly, Jonah's experience speaks to those who have yet to believe. Jonah typifies the inevitable end of your own rebellion against God. "The wages of sin is death," says the Bible (Rom. 6:23). But through faith in Jesus Christ, who died to conquer sin and death, the sea monster of judgment is tamed so as to deliver us onto the shores of a new life. Can you see your need of such a deliverance? Will you look to the God of sovereign grace for your own redemption and deliverance into resurrection life?

If you will not, then Jesus will not be the only one to condemn you for unbelief. Having spoken of his own death as the sign of Jonah for his generation, Jesus added that the Ninevites would also have a testimony to give: "The men of Nineveh will rise up at the judgment with this generation and condemn it, for they repented at the preaching of Jonah, and behold, something greater than Jonah is here" (Matt. 12:41). If wicked Nineveh repented at the sight of resurrected Jonah, how much more ought we to repent of unbelief and sin, having witnessed the risen Christ in the Word of God. And seeing such grace for sinners, how eagerly we ought to embrace the gospel offer of the Son of God, who died for our sins and rose to give us eternal life.

8

PRAYER FROM THE DEEP

Jonah 2:1–7

Then I said, "I am driven away from your sight; Yet I shall again
look upon your holy temple." (Jonah 2:4)

*T*here are things about the realm of grace that those outside
it simply cannot understand. This is demonstrated by much
criticism of the second chapter of Jonah. Among liberal scholars, this chapter is almost universally regarded as a later editorial addition,
for the simple reason that its message seems unbelievable. They argue that
a later editor sought to explain the story that Jonah was swallowed and
then vomited forth by a whale with a psalm that seemed to make sense.
Jacques Ellul comments: "The great argument against the validity of this
psalm, however, is that it is not a psalm of appeal and petition, but an act of
thanksgiving and praise."[1]

PRAYER IN THE DEEP

Jonah chapter 2 records one of the Bible's great prayers. This is especially remarkable in that up to this point Jonah has not been found praying.

1. Jacques Ellul, *The Judgment of Jonah* (Grand Rapids: Eerdmans, 1971), 47.

When God summoned him for a mission to Nineveh, Jonah did not pray to consider the right response. When fleeing to Joppa, Jonah did not pray for guidance. When purchasing passage aboard the ship bound for Tarshish, he did not pray. Nor did Jonah pray when the captain besought him during the great storm. This is not coincidental, for this path of prayerlessness charted Jonah's descent into folly, rebellion, and ruin. Jonah did not pray because he did not want to talk with God, much less to hear from God. The whole objective of Jonah's flight was to escape "away from the presence of the LORD" (Jonah 1:3), and prayer would hardly have served that end. We will find the same to be true in our lives. Disobedience leads to prayerlessness, prayerlessness leads to folly and sin, and folly and sin lead to disaster.

What has changed in Jonah's life to make him a man of prayer? Back on the ship, he refused to pray even when the captain implored him. But things are different inside the great fish. What has happened? The answer is that God in his grace has brought Jonah low. Now brought to the ultimate destination of his foolish flight, Jonah is faced with the real consequences. He is separated from God, from the fellowship of God's people, and from the witness of God's Word. For many of us, the journey that Jonah took will involve the whole of our lives—a slow but steady descent into darkness. However, God in his grace gave Jonah a sudden experience of the abyss into which his life was heading. You might call it a sneak preview of coming attractions. Cast overboard, Jonah was encased in the living grave that is the belly of the fish, deep beneath the surface of the waves. Because of God's gracious deliverance, which precedes Jonah's prayer, he finally was enabled to pray.

In his best-selling book *Disappointment with God*, Philip Yancey explores the experience of an increasing number of people who express their dissatisfaction over God's care. One young mother's joyful faith turned to bitterness after her daughter was born with spina bifida. She wrote of ruinous medical bills and a marriage that broke under the strain of the child's disease. Unlike Jonah, whose situation was caused by his own sin, her life had descended into the abyss simply as a result of this childbirth. Having trusted God, she now wrote of anger and doubt. In another case, a homosexual wrote Yancey to tell of the hell of his life. For a decade and more he had sought a "cure" for his sexual orientation, involving every manner of treatment including electrical shock. But nothing seemed to work, and finally the man abandoned himself to perverse promiscuity and rejected Christianity. Yet another woman wrote of her ongoing depression. She really had no reason for her despair, but most days she could not think of a single reason to go on living. She wrote to say that she had pretty much given up on God and doubted that he even cared.[2]

These are all examples—common enough in our day—of people who found their lives descending into the deep and who responded with resentment toward God. Their one theme was that God has disappointed them by not delivering them from their severe trials. We can imagine Jonah doing the same thing. He might have complained that God was wrong to ask him to go preach to the Ninevites, and that his flight on the Tarshish-bound ship was only a reasonable response. But that is not what Jonah did. Instead, Jonah acknowledged that it was God who had cast him into the deep, and only God could rescue him. His key insight is found in verse 3, where Jonah says, "For you cast me into the deep, into the heart of the seas, and the flood surrounded me; all your waves and your billows passed over me." Jonah realized that while it was the sailors who physically tossed him over the rails, and while this was all his own idea, it was God's sovereign hand that had cast him into the deep. It was "your waves" and "your billows" that passed over him.

Jonah acknowledged that everything that had happened to him was caused by God, while at the same time realizing that it was all his own fault. There is no accusation against God's justice. As he explained to the sailors, "I know it is because of me that this great tempest has come upon you" (Jonah 1:12). Now, he might have added, "And I know it is because of my sin that I am dying in this great fish." Instead of turning against God, Jonah was willing to turn on himself, on his sin.

Yet the reality did not break through to Jonah until he began descending into the deep. While still on the boat, his doctrine was right but his heart was wrong. That is why he refused to pray. But it was only when final darkness gathered around him, when all the options had closed down, leaving only his just condemnation, that Jonah's heart responded to his formal confession of sin. Now only God could help him, so Jonah turned in prayer to God: "I called out to the LORD, out of my distress," he reports (Jonah 2:1). Jacques Ellul writes:

> Obviously, when man has somewhere to turn he does not pray to God and God does not come to him. As long as man can invent hopes and methods, he

2. Philip Yancey, *Disappointment with God* (Grand Rapids: Zondervan, 1988), 21–22.

naturally suffers from the pretension that he can solve his own problem. . . . When the sailors tried to save the ship by their nautical skill, Jonah slept. All these aids had to be shattered, all solutions blocked, and man's possibilities hopelessly outclassed by the power of the challenge, to cause Jonah to return to God.[3]

The contrast between the call of the ship captain and the response of God is revealing. The captain cried, "Arise, call out to your god!" (Jonah 1:6). But God sent Jonah down, not up, to pray. It is as if God was saying, "Go down before me and then you will be able to pray, Jonah." Sometimes the very best thing that can happen to us is the very thing we most dread, for the simple reason that it strips away our self-reliance, humbles our pride, and removes from us every other hope save that of God. Sometimes this is what it takes for us really to pray.

The Bible does not specify any particular posture for prayer. We see people standing or sitting in prayer, and either is appropriate. Yet in the Bible, as in life, when men or women pray out of the anguish of desperation and terrible need, they fall to their knees before the Lord. In order for Jonah to look away from his own willful plans and turn to God in hope, he first had to be brought to his knees. We read in the Bible, "Humble yourselves, therefore, under the mighty hand of God so that at the proper time he may exalt you" (1 Peter 5:6). Yet we do not readily humble ourselves before God, so God in his grace will do it for us, all out of his wonderful purpose of salvation.

How does this fit the case of those who find themselves in despair with no obvious blame to themselves? What about the woman who despaired of God because of her daughter with the birth defect? The answer is but a variation on Jonah's theme. In order truly to turn to God we must accept that God is sovereign. Not only that, but God is holy, just, and good. We must acknowledge that God is the sovereign, saving Lord. Just as Jonah had to bow to God's sovereign call in his ministry, we must bow to God's sovereign purpose in our circumstances. In some cases, God is calling us to repent of some open sin. In other cases, God is fitting us for a calling or trial. In either case, God is humbling us into a right sense of worship and reliance on his grace. He demands, "I am God and there is no other" (Isa. 45:22; 46:9). Therefore, our answer is found, first, by acknowledging

3. Ellul, *The Judgment of Jonah*, 57.

God's holy, right, and good sovereignty in all our callings, and, secondly, by turning to him as the only One who is able to save us.

In the end, it is not merely out of his knowledge of God's sovereignty or God's holiness that Jonah repents and prays. Rather, it is his remembrance of God's grace that turns his heart to the Lord. "Then I said, 'I am driven away from your sight,'" Jonah recalls. This is the prophet's admission of God's sovereign justice in his life. But he adds, "Yet I shall again look upon your holy temple" (Jonah 2:4). This is Jonah's remembrance of God's merciful grace, and it is by renewed reliance on God's grace that Jonah is moved once more to pray.

When we come to such a point of surrender to the one true and living God, the result will always be the same: we will pray. We will seek his mercy and power for our salvation. Later, we will be able to say, "I called out to the LORD, out of my distress, and he answered me; out of the belly of Sheol I cried, and you heard my voice" (Jonah 2:2).

JONAH'S PSALM

This raises an important question, however: how did Jonah remember God's sovereign grace? We have considered when Jonah remembered God's grace so that he returned in prayer: it was at his final extremity within the great fish in the deep. But how did Jonah remember God's grace?

To answer this, imagine plucking Jonah's prayer out of this book and reading it. What book of the Bible would you think you were hearing? There is one answer that everyone who is familiar at all with the Bible will give: it is the book of Psalms. We might find ourselves saying, "Now which psalm is this? I should know this psalm!" In fact, Jonah is not quoting any particular psalm, but rehearsing the themes of the psalms in general. A study of Jonah's prayer will show allusions or references to Psalms 3, 5, 16, 18, 31, 42, 50, 65, 88, and 120.

The whole perspective of the psalms—on God and man, life and death, despair and hope, fear and faith—is flowing out through Jonah's heart and mouth. So how is it happening that Jonah suddenly becomes an oracle of psalmody while in the belly of this great fish? The only answer can be that he had been raised and nurtured in the psalms. He had recited and sung the psalms all his life. The psalms were inside him because of his life among the people of God. So now, brought to this terrible extremity beneath the waves and inside the great fish, when Jonah is moved to pray, the vocabulary and faith of the psalms find expression in his prayer.

This is as strong an advertisement as can be arranged for the value of the book of Psalms. In the psalms of the Bible, through the miracle of inspiration, God places on the lips of his worshipers the words of faith, worship, and life. In the psalms, we encounter man in every circumstance—frequently in need and distress—looking up to God in search of faith. In the psalms we read the very complaints we have uttered in our own hearts, along with the remedy to those complaints through a renewed grasp of God's glory and grace. The psalms wrestle with every human emotion, every human experience, every high and low, all in such a way that the believer finds himself restored to faith in God. In this way, the psalms present the doctrines of salvation in lived experience and struggle. The psalms present the saving truths of God's Word as light fighting through the foggy mist of human struggle to restore the believer's vision of heaven. The psalms may be the Bible's best answer to the remarkable prayer once offered to Jesus, "I believe; help my unbelief!" (Mark 9:24).

For these reasons, Jonah's long experience with the psalms results in the greatest of all helps in his darkest hour of need: his mind is returned to the Lord and his heart is refreshed in God's grace. Christians who make it their practice to stroll frequently through the garden of the psalms, who make a practice of singing the psalms and committing them to memory, will be well repaid in their hours of darkness, doubt, and despair with words fitted just for their troubled situation, words designed to take their faltering faith by the hand and lead it once again to the Lord.

We might well speak similarly of the whole Bible, of course. Here again, Jonah provides us with a lesson. His book starts with a disturbing call from God. Jonah's faith is staggered by the call to preach in Nineveh. The sin inhabiting his hatred of the Ninevites rears its willful head and sends him on his flight away from the Lord. Instead of praying, Jonah stops his ears and flees from the influence of God's Word. He finds the solution to his distress in the ship bound for Tarshish. And how many versions of the Tarshish-bound ship there are, to which Christians make appeal in their struggle with God's commands! How many churches today recoil against the difficult calling of faithfulness by boarding ships to Tarshish—worldly substitutes for the ministry of God's Word conveniently at our disposal and fiendishly made available by our enemy the devil. Yet all along, the true answer to our need and distress is found in the Bible.

It is only when the influence of God's Word is felt again that Jonah-like believers are restored to God in repentance. It is the influence of God's Word that turns our hearts back to God in prayer instead of away from God on ships bound for Tarshish. Therefore, both in the individual believer's experience and in the life of the church, it is always true that "faith comes from hearing, and hearing through the word of Christ" (Rom. 10:17).

The way to experience God's grace is to turn to God's Word. Peter spoke this way of a sinner's conversion to saving faith: "You have been born again . . . through the living and abiding Word of God" (1 Peter 1:23). Jesus spoke this way of God's grace for the growth and restoration of those already saved: "Sanctify them in the truth," he prayed. "Your word is truth" (John 17:17). So whether we are being humbled before God for the first time, or we have come for a return visit to the convicting darkness of the fish's belly, the grace of God that we need is found and experienced through the Word of God.

Jonah's Prayer of Deliverance

Exactly what, then, was Jonah trusting when he turned anew to God in prayer? We have considered the *when* of Jonah's prayer: he prayed when God had cast him down into the darkness. We have studied the *how* of Jonah's prayer: he prayed as he remembered the Lord as God's grace was recalled to him through the psalms. Now we should consider the *what* of Jonah's prayer. What did he pray for? What did he seek in his prayer from the deep?

Jonah's prayer is focused on a single theme, introduced at the beginning, God's merciful answer to him in need: "I called out to the Lord, out of my distress, and he answered me; out of the belly of Sheol I cried, and you heard my voice" (Jonah 2:2). He came to this realization, first, by recognizing his true situation; second, by remembering his relationship with the Lord; and third, by appealing to God's provision of grace for sinners like himself.

First, Jonah describes his dire straits in the tomb of the great fish. He was in "distress" (Jonah 2:2). He was in "the belly of Sheol," so that he considered himself to be in a hellish grave. "The flood surrounded me," he writes, reminding us of psalms that speak of troubles rising up like a flood, though in Jonah's case it was true more than metaphorically. There, Jonah realized that he was dying: "My life was fainting away" (Jonah 2:7). Moreover, his plight was truly miserable: "weeds were wrapped about my head at the roots of the mountains. I went down to the land whose bars closed upon me forever" (Jonah 2:5–6). Jonah saw his delivering fish as a kind of prison, fast shut with the tightest of bars.

This is a dramatic version of the kind of situation into which sin and folly cast us. None of us are likely to have Jonah's precise plight, but we may feel the same emotions for other reasons. For some, it is a career path that has led them to dismay. For others it is an ungodly relationship that has sown destruction in their lives. Some people experience this through financial folly; the burden of their debt seems like a prison.

But worst of all was Jonah's awareness that he was separated from God: "Then I said, 'I am driven away from your sight'" (Jonah 2:4). This was the whole point of Jonah's flight from the Lord. But now that he had tasted the ultimate fruit of his rebellion against God, the full bitterness of his hopeless situation choked his soul. Encased in the fish, Jonah had reached the bitter end.

This realization of his true situation was the turning point of Jonah's life. It will often work out in our experience as well, that it is only when we understand the depths to which we have sunk that we are ready to seek God's way of deliverance. Jonah realized the folly of his sin. He realized his need of the Lord. How then could he be restored?

The answer is seen throughout the rest of this prayer. We read that "Jonah prayed to the LORD his God" (Jonah 2:1). Having first recognized his true plight, Jonah, second, remembered his relationship with God. All along, he had been a man in covenant with God. He was a believer and Yahweh was his God. This makes his rebellion all the more foolish, but it also marks the beginning of his hope.

We can trace the path of Jonah's thought. He knew he was separated from God in his unbelief and in his circumstances. The Lord had driven him away from his sight (Jonah 2:4). But what he knew about the Lord reminded him that there was a way of hope. God's promise of grace remained despite Jonah's folly in sin. He had deserted God, but the very fact that he had not yet drowned proved that God had not deserted him.

In times of despair, every believer should remember God's promise never to desert his people. God has said, "I will never leave you nor forsake you" (Heb. 13:5). Paul celebrated this truth in rhetorical prose:

> Who shall separate us from the love of Christ? Shall tribulation, or distress, or persecution, or famine, or nakedness, or danger, or sword? . . . No, in all these things we are more than conquerors through him who loved us. For I am sure that neither death nor life, nor angels nor rulers, nor things present nor things to come, nor powers, nor height nor depth, nor anything else in all creation, will be able to separate us from the love of God in Christ Jesus our Lord. (Rom. 8:35, 37–39)

Behind this conviction is the Bible's teaching of God's unbreakable love for his own. "I have loved you with an everlasting love," God tells his people (Jer. 31:3). "I will make with them an everlasting covenant," he says, "that I will not turn away from doing good to them" (Jer. 32:40). Therefore, in every trial we may look to the mercy of God as a man in the night looks for the sure coming of dawn.

Remembering God's faithfulness in mercy, received through simple faith alone, transformed Jonah's petitions into praise. This is what the liberal critics of Jonah cannot understand. He now is confident of God's salvation. This is remarkable because at no point do we read of Jonah asking God to deliver him from the fish. Yet now he exults, "I called out to the Lord, out of my distress, and he answered me; out of the belly of Sheol I cried, and you heard my voice" (Jonah 2:2). This is the sign that we are restored to faith: that so long as we know the Lord's favor, we no longer need to be delivered from our trials.

How did Jonah know that God had heard and answered him? The answer is that he recognized the kindling of his own repentance and faith. Simply to remember the Lord is proof that the Lord has answered your cry. Simply to be able to acknowledge humbly your unworthiness and sin and to praise God for his faithful love is proof that God is with you to save.

Jonah sees an analogy between his physical situation and the spiritual situation in which he had languished: "I went down to the land whose bars closed upon me forever; yet you brought up my life from the pit, O Lord my God" (Jonah 2:6). His real prison was the unbelief and resentment toward God in which he suffered in darkness; the stomach of the great fish was merely the analogy. God had delivered him by restoring him to faith, and this was all that Jonah needed in order to know that he would be restored fully, either in this life or the next: "When my life was fainting away, I remembered the LORD, and my prayer came to you, into your holy temple" (Jonah 2:7). His remembrance of God as Savior was enough to assure him of the certainty of his salvation. Do you realize that the bare fact of your faith in Christ testifies to God's saving work in your life? Do you know that if you are restored to God, you are safe and secure even in the midst of the darkest trial?

The third feature of Jonah's prayer is his appeal to God's grace for sinners. Jonah not only regained a general confidence in God's mercy, but specifically remembered the provision God had made for the salvation of people like him. This focus is discernible in his prayer: "I am driven away from your sight; yet I shall again look upon your holy temple" (Jonah 2:4).

Why did Jonah think of God's temple? He may have thought of the temple as the place where God dwells, and thus where his prayers were directed. This way of thinking is indicated in verse 7: "My prayer came to you, into your holy temple." But this does not account for the pivotal statement of verse 4: "I shall again look upon your holy temple." Hugh Martin takes up the question:

> Jonah thought of "the temple;" and why? Because God had placed His name there. Because there He gave the symbol of His presence as a God of love, and especially a God of propitiated favour; a God dwelling between the cherubim, God on the blood-sprinkled seat of mercy, on the throne of grace.[4]

In short, Jonah remembered that God had ordered sacrifices as a way of restoring sinners to himself. It was for the sake of these sacrifices that the temple existed, as the blood of lambs was shed for the forgiveness of sin. And it was by the mercy granted by God through sacrificial blood that Jonah had a hope for salvation.

Jonah's prayer is a model for our own prayer of salvation. For what Jonah looked to in faith received its fulfillment in Jesus Christ. Each of us, no matter how fallen, may look to the altar on which the Lamb was slain for reconciliation with God. Each of us, no matter how dark the circumstances of life, may look to the cross of Christ as the proof of God's unrelenting love. The apostle

---

4. Hugh Martin, *A Commentary on Jonah* (1870; repr. Edinburgh: Banner of Truth, 1958), 200.

John wrote, "If anyone does sin, we have an advocate with the Father, Jesus Christ the righteous. He is the propitiation for our sins" (1 John 2:1–2). Paul added, "If God is for us, who can be against us? He who did not spare his own Son but gave him up for us all, how will he not also with him graciously give us all things?" (Rom 8:31–32). This means that whatever trials and suffering we experience in this life—because of our own sin or not—Christians may see in the cross all the proof they need of God's conquering love, God's holy love, God's providing love, and God's unfailing love. With the cross firmly in mind, the writer of Hebrews urges, "Let us then with confidence draw near to the throne of grace, that we may receive mercy and find grace to help in time of need" (Heb. 4:16).

THE SALVATION OF THE LORD

Realizing the danger into which he had fallen by sin, then remembering God's covenant faithfulness, and finally appealing to God's saving grace through Christ's blood, Jonah concluded his prayer with a great exclamation that has encouraged multitudes of God's people: "Salvation belongs to the LORD!" (Jonah 2:9). Jonah may have meant, "Only God can save me," and surely that is something he had learned. Or he could have meant, "Salvation is what God delights to do." That would have been equally true. But speaking personally—and Jonah's was the most personal of prayers—there is little doubt that Jonah had come to a stunning conclusion that changed his attitude toward everything in his life. Jonah now realized that God sent him into the deep darkness, into the great fish, not to destroy him but to save him. Do you recognize God's saving purpose as you ponder his providence in your life? God is not destroying you in your trials. The Lord is saving you. He is restoring you from sinful rebellion, from foolish self-reliance, from ignorant pride, and from unbelieving stubbornness—to which all of us are natively prone in our fallen condition—so that you learn to turn to him for grace. Jonah's prayer is one that every believer is invited to learn, so that we rejoice together with the ancient prophet: "I called out to the LORD, out of my distress, and he answered me .... Salvation belongs to the LORD!" (Jonah 2:2, 9).

9

SALVATION OF THE LORD

Jonah 2:8–10

"But I with the voice of thanksgiving will sacrifice to you; what I have vowed I will pay. Salvation belongs to the LORD!" (Jonah 2:9)

During most of the centuries of the church, Christians have debated the sovereignty of God in salvation. In some periods those who emphasized God's sovereign grace have been called Calvinists, and in other periods Augustinians; all have derived their doctrine from the sacred writings of apostles such as Paul and prophets such as Isaiah, and especially the teachings of Jesus Christ. At the same time, there have been others who objected to the idea of divine election in salvation. Some, including the Arminians, have contended for a rational doctrine of free will. Others, such as the heretical monk Pelagius, have rejected the biblical doctrine of sin and denied the need for grace altogether.

The story of the prophet Jonah sheds considerable light on the question of God's sovereignty in salvation. As Charles Spurgeon saw it, the characters in Jonah 2:9–10 represent both sides of the debate. Jonah's "Calvinism" can be seen in his great exclamation: "Salvation belongs to the LORD!" The Arminian position is represented by the great fish that had swallowed him. Spurgeon is reputed to have jested, "We know that the great fish was an Arminian.

Because no sooner did Jonah pray, 'Salvation is of the Lord!' than the great fish spat him out of its mouth!"

In God's dealings with Jonah and in the prophet's penitent prayer, we may see not only the general truth that salvation is of the Lord, but more specifically that salvation is of the Lord in its initiation, its power, and its successful conclusion.

Salvation's Source

The question of salvation's source is an important one both for individuals and for the ministry of the church. Does salvation occur because of what we do for God or because of what God does for us? Do sinners come to God for salvation or does God come to sinners in order to save? The Bible's answer is found in Jonah's prayer: "Salvation belongs to the Lord!" or, as some translations render it, "Salvation is of the Lord!" (Jonah 2:9).

We can see that God is the source of salvation, first, in his *plan* of salvation. Spurgeon writes: "No human intellect and no created intelligence assisted God in the planning of salvation; he contrived the way, even as he himself carried it out."[1] This is the emphasis of the Bible. The apostle Paul tells us that we are saved, "having been predestined according to the purpose of him who works all things according to the counsel of his will" (Eph. 1:11). The plan of salvation originated in the counsel of God's will, according to his own purpose and by his predestination. The plan of salvation is of the Lord.

When we reflect on the gospel message, we see how this must be so. For who but God could devise a way by which guilty and corrupted sinners could be approved by his relentless justice and accepted into his holy presence? Donald Grey Barnhouse exults: "He alone could have found the way to declare ungodly men godly and justified. He alone could have taken fallen children of Adam and made it possible for them to sit upon the throne of the universe with Himself. He alone could have taken those who were joined to the harlotry of sin and turned them into the pure bride of Christ."[2] For

---

1. Charles Haddon Spurgeon, *Spurgeon's Sermons*, 10 vols. (Grand Rapids: Baker, 1883, reprint n.d.), 3:195.
2. Donald Grey Barnhouse, *Exposition of Bible Doctrines, Taking the Epistle to the Romans as a Point of Departure*, 10 vols. (Grand Rapids: Eerdmans, 1954), 3:212.

this reason, our salvation serves to display the glory of God's wisdom, and especially of his grace. Nothing outside God led him to devise the plan of our salvation, and no influence outside his own glorious being led God to save us. Thus Paul writes that God's sovereign and eternal plan of our salvation is "to the praise of his glorious grace" (Eph. 1:6).

This continues to be true when we consider God's *accomplishment* of salvation. All the work performed for our salvation is of the Lord. The Christian gospel does not consist in instructions for what we might do to achieve our own salvation. Rather it is the proclamation of what God has done for us. We see this from the start of Jesus' life on earth. When the angels heralded the birth of the child to a virgin, they were not calling on mankind to gather together for a great initiative. Instead, they proclaimed good news of what God had done: "For unto you is born this day in the city of David a Savior, who is Christ the Lord" (Luke 2:11). God sent his Son to be born under the law and so to fulfill the law for us. God then directed his Son to the cross, there to offer his life as a sacrifice and shed his own blood for our sins. God then raised up our Lord Jesus from the grave that he might conquer not only sin but even death for us. So it had to be if we were ever to be saved, for man could do nothing of his own to remedy the problem of sin. Man cannot offer his own sacrifice for sin, since every human being has his or her own sins to pay for and thus cannot pay for another's. Man cannot offer good works, for all our works are corrupted by the sin that pollutes our very being. But what we could never do, God has done for us. Salvation is all "of the LORD" in its initiation and achievement.

Jonah provides a choice example of God as the source of salvation. As we look on the prophet turning his heart back to God and praying in renewed faith, we ask, "What has Jonah done to save himself?" "What has Jonah contributed to this story?" The answer is that Jonah contributed only his unbelief, rebellion, folly, and sin. When Jonah was thrown into the waves, there was nothing he could do for his own salvation. But God had willed that Jonah would be saved and therefore God "appointed a great fish to swallow up Jonah" (Jonah 1:17). When Jonah arrives in Nineveh to preach God's message of warning, it will be because he was saved by God's sovereign grace. Realizing this sovereign initiative in his deliverance, Jonah thus prays from the belly of the fish, "Salvation belongs to the LORD!"

SALVATION'S POWER

Some astute observers may reply: "Yes, Jonah was saved because God sent the great fish. But Jonah still had to turn to the Lord in faith. After all, this chapter begins with Jonah telling us, 'I called out to the LORD.'" Here, we consider the *application* of salvation to the individual sinner. We have seen that the plan of salvation and the accomplishment of salvation are initiated by God. But what about the application of salvation to the individual? Arminians will argue this point especially. "Yes, God has offered salvation by his own initiative. But we must take the initiative in receiving this salvation in order to be saved." "Isn't it true," they will argue, "that when God gave Jonah one last chance by sending the great fish, Jonah responded to this grace by changing his heart to turn back to the Lord?" What would Jonah say to this? We know what Jonah said, and it applies not only to the offer of salvation but also to the power to receive it: "Salvation belongs to the LORD!"

Indeed, we could not say that salvation is wholly of the Lord if salvation required that we take the lead in exercising our wills to believe the gospel. Instead, we would have to say, "Salvation is of the Lord in its offer, but in terms of its receipt, salvation is of the sinner's own will." But that is not what Jonah says. Speaking of his whole deliverance, he insists, "Salvation is of the LORD."

When we understand the Bible's teaching about man's condition in sin, we see why this must be the case. Jesus said, "Everyone who commits sin is a slave to sin" (John 8:34). This being true, our wills are not free to turn to God; our nature is bound in the chains of sinful corruption. The apostle Paul made this clear when he wrote: "The natural person does not accept the things of the Spirit of God, for they are folly to him, and he is not able to understand them because they are spiritually discerned" (1 Cor. 2:14). The apostle stresses not only that the unregenerate sinner *does not* accept God's Word but also that he *cannot*. In Ephesians chapter two, where Paul outlines the doctrine of salvation, he begins by describing the unsaved as "dead in . . . trespasses and sins" (Eph. 2:1). So if salvation requires the sinner to bend his own will to receive the gospel, and man's will is enslaved to sin and man's spirit is dead to God, then it is impossible for man to be saved. This is why the biblical gospel is such good news, for as Jesus said to Peter, "What is impossible with men is possible with God" (Luke 18:27). Therefore, even in receiving the gospel, the power to believe is "of the Lord."

Charles Spurgeon reflected on our need for God's regenerating power during a visit to Carisbrooke Castle on the Isle of Wight. This is where King Charles I was held prior to his execution after the English Civil War. On one occasion an escape attempt was arranged. Everything was provided for Charles's escape: his followers were waiting outside the wall and boats were ready to take him to safety. All the fallen king had to do was get out the window of his room. But Charles could not get the window open and all the efforts on his behalf came to nothing. Spurgeon writes:

> So with the sinner. If God had provided every means of escape, and only required him to get out of his dungeon, he would have remained there to all eternity. Why, is not the sinner by nature dead in sin? . . . And if God does require of the sinner—dead in sin—that he should take the first step, then he requireth just that which renders salvation as impossible under the gospel as ever it was under the law, seeing man is as unable to believe as he is obey, and is just as much without power to come to Christ as he is without power to go to heaven without Christ. The power must be given to him of the Spirit.[3]

This was a major point of debate in the Protestant Reformation. The Roman Catholic apologists argued against salvation by grace alone by arguing the point of free will. The great answer was given by Martin Luther: "Free will, after the fall, exists in name only. . . . For the will is captive and subject to sin. Not that it is nothing, but that it is not free except to do evil." Luther showed that this was not a new debate, but quoted Augustine in his earlier struggles with Pelagius and other heretics: "Free will without grace has the power to do nothing but sin. . . . You call the will free, but in fact it is an enslaved will."[4] Instead of by free will, we are saved by the power of God at work in the soul through the effectual call of the gospel. Jesus called, "Lazarus, come out!" and the dead man rose and came (John 11:43–44). Jesus approached Levi the tax collector and called, "Follow me"; the tax collector came forth as Matthew the disciple (Matt. 9:9). Likewise, Christ calls to sinners today in sovereign power through his gospel, and as the Holy Spirit gives new birth to the soul, the sinner believes and is saved. This is why the apostle Paul described even

3. Spurgeon, *Spurgeon's Sermons* (Grand Rapids: Baker, 1883, reprint, n.d.), 3:197.
4. Martin Luther, *Basic Writings of Martin Luther* (Minneapolis: Fortress, 1989), 39–40.

faith as "the gift of God" (Eph. 2:8), and why Jonah cried in the deep, "Salvation belongs to the LORD!"

If there was ever a picture of man dead in sin, then Jonah within the great fish is such a picture. This is true not only of his external situation, but especially of the inward state of his soul. Jonah had hardened his heart to God's command, fleeing "from the presence of the LORD" (Jonah 1:3). So bound was his will in cords of sin that when God's wrathful storm was crushing his ship, even then he did not repent and turn his heart to God. "Pick me up and hurl me into the sea" (Jonah 1:12) was the only counsel his bitter spirit could offer. When Jonah finally reckons with God in the darkness of his deep tomb-like experience, and he is able to say, "When my life was fainting away, I remembered the LORD," how does he explain the change in his heart? "Salvation is of the LORD!" he exclaims.

When we remember that Jesus labeled his own death with "the sign of the prophet Jonah" (Matt. 12:39), we see how important this statement is to the Christian gospel as a whole. For the power animating both Jonah's deliverance and Jesus' death and resurrection is "of the LORD." Jonah's words at the moment when he was typifying Christ are a motto for the whole of Christ's saving work: "Salvation is of the LORD!" It is not the power of man that accounts for salvation at any point, but only the power of God. And just as it was God's power that turned Jonah's heart in the darkness of the fish's belly, it is God's power that turns sinners' hearts to faith today in the shadow of the cross. The cross of Christ, like Jonah's great fish, is a sign to the world of the sovereign grace of God. "Salvation is of the LORD!"

SALVATION'S COMPLETION

From the moment when Jonah turned to the Lord in repentance and faith, he was saved. We see this in that Jonah never asks God to rescue him from inside the great fish, but instead thanks God for the deliverance he has already gained: a deliverance from his folly and sin. Yet Jonah's salvation would not have been complete had he remained inside the fish's belly. Likewise, our salvation will not be complete until we are delivered out of this dark and evil age to arrive safely on the shores of heaven.

The last question to ask, then, is who will ensure that our salvation is successfully completed? Having been saved by sovereign grace, do we remain saved by our own efforts or by that same sovereign grace of God? Jonah, again, provides a model, for his resurrection from the grave of the fish's belly was not the result of his own labors. Rather, in its successful conclusion, as in its initiation and its application, he rejoices, "Salvation is of the LORD!" Jonah's thankful confidence in God was well rewarded, for "the LORD spoke to the fish, and it vomited Jonah out upon the dry land" (Jonah 2:10).

This does not mean that Christians are inactive in their faith. Having first been saved by a faith that receives—we might refer to it as a passive faith—we advance in salvation by a faith that works—that is, by an active faith. Moreover, it is absolutely necessary that Christians persevere in faith. Those who think that they may rest upon a fleeting spiritual experience of belief in Christ, apart from a life-long walk of faith in the Lord, are tragically mistaken. Paul states this plainly: "He has now reconciled [you] . . . , if indeed you continue in the faith, stable and steadfast, not shifting from the hope of the gospel that you heard" (Col. 1:21–23). For this reason, the only solid ground of assurance of salvation is a present, active faith in Jesus Christ.

Yet even this is "of the LORD." God's people do not persevere in their own power, but in the preserving grace of the Lord. The Bible teaches that our perseverance is the result of God's ongoing grace in our lives. Our salvation will be successfully concluded because God the Father refuses to forsake his dear children. Paul writes, "He who began a good work in you will bring it to completion at the day of Jesus Christ" (Phil. 1:6). Peter adds that "by God's power [we] are being guarded through faith for a salvation ready to be revealed in the last time" (1 Peter 1:5). Our salvation is also secured by our faithful Shepherd, Jesus Christ. Jesus said, "My sheep hear my voice, and I know them, and they follow me. I give them eternal life, and they will never perish, and no one will snatch them out of my hand" (John 10:27–28). Finally, our perseverance in faith is guaranteed by the Holy Spirit's presence in our lives. Paul comments, "When you heard the word of truth, the gospel of your salvation, and believed in him, [you] were sealed with the promised Holy Spirit, who is the guarantee of our inheritance until we acquire possession of it, to the praise of his glory" (Eph. 1:13–14).

Jonah's prayer from within the great fish was modeled on the psalms, so it is no surprise to learn that his statement, "salvation belongs to the LORD," is a quote from Psalm 3. This is one of David's affliction psalms, attributed to the time of the rebellion led by his son Absalom. "O LORD, how many are my foes," David begins (Ps. 3:1). David, not unlike Jonah, finds himself in a desperate situation, beyond the hope of human salvation. So he lifts up his heart to God: "You, O LORD, are a shield about me, my glory, and the lifter of my head" (Ps. 3:3). David's enemy has overwhelmed him, and while he can find no hope in himself or any other man, he knows that God is able to deliver him from his troubles. David concludes: "For you strike all my enemies on the cheek; you break the teeth of the wicked. Salvation belongs to the LORD; your blessing be on your people!" (Ps. 3:7–8).

Just as David sought his only hope for the future in God, and just as Jonah looked up from the deep with hope in the Lord, so also we should rest our hopes of deliverance into the blessed realm of glory in the sovereign grace of God. Martin Luther comments: "It is the Lord alone that saves and blesses: and even though the whole mass of all evils should be gathered together in one against a man, still, it is the Lord who saves: salvation and blessing are in his hands. What then shall I fear?"[5] "Salvation belongs to the LORD!"

THE BELIEVER'S RESPONSE TO SOVEREIGN GRACE

Having considered the doctrine expressed in Jonah's prayer, we should conclude by reflecting on our response to the sovereign grace of God. Verses 8 and 9 serve as a postscript to Jonah's prayer, capturing the lessons he learned in what Spurgeon referred to as the "strange college" of "the whale's belly."[6]

When Jonah turns to God in his despair, he realizes afresh the vanity of the idols of the world. He says, "Those who pay regard to vain idols forsake their hope of steadfast love" (Jonah 2:8). In the presence of the true and sovereign God, the idols are unmasked and Jonah looks upon them with repulsion.

This is a lesson that today's Christians need to learn as we reflect on the sovereignty of the one true God. Peter Williams comments:

> The essence of idolatry . . . is anything that commands the central place in our lives, and to which we give the loyalty and devotion, which rightly belongs to God alone. . . . For some people money is their god, and the pursuit of materialistic goals dominates their lives. . . . But we can make an idol of anything,

---

5. Martin Luther, cited in Charles Spurgeon, *A Treasury of David*, 3 vols. (Peabody, Mass.: Hendrickson, n.d.) 1:32.

6. Charles Spurgeon, *New Park Street Pulpit*, 6 vols. (1857; repr. Pasadena, Tex.: Pilgrim, 1975), 3:193.

sport, sex, drugs, politics, career, even home and family. Anything that nudges God out to the perimeter of our lives can become idolatrous.[7]

What is the result of worshiping idols? Williams says,

They become worthless "lying vanities," and will always let man down, because—however much he tries to manipulate them for his own happiness—they will always fail to deliver in the long run on what they promise.[8]

Jonah had refused to allow the Lord to be God over his life, instead seizing the reins of his life in a rebellious flight away from Nineveh, the place of God's calling. How had that worked out for Jonah? In contrast, those who turn to the Lord as God receive a "steadfast love" that will save them in the end.

Secondly, note the change in Jonah's attitude toward the lost world (2:8). The whole point of Jonah's rebellion against God's command was his loathing of the idea of preaching to the pagan Gentiles. But now he laments over them, knowing that in their idolatry they "forsake their hope of steadfast love."

What will cause us to look on the world with new and merciful eyes? Jonah's example suggests that it is a glorious vision of God's grace. We realize that our own salvation is "of the LORD"—we were saved by sovereign mercy, which pitied us in our darkened state of sin. Paul reminds us that "God shows his love for us in that while we were still sinners, Christ died for us" (Rom. 5:8). From that point of view, the vilest, most offensively unbelieving sinners—even those who pose the most danger to ourselves—can only be regarded as those in dire need of the same mercy by which we were saved. We will pray for the lost, preach the Word, and witness the gospel, realizing that by their unbelief sinners "forsake their hope of steadfast love."

Lastly, Jonah expresses the response of a heart that is newly yielded to God: "But I with the voice of thanksgiving will sacrifice to you; what I have vowed I will pay" (Jonah 2:9). This was the end to which God in his grace was working. Jonah's salvation bears the good fruit of a willingness to follow God's call in his life. His intestinal education could end now that Jonah combined mercy for the lost with a will that was obedient to God's Word.

7. Peter Williams, *Jonah—Running from God: An Expositional Commentary*, Exploring the Bible (Epsom, Surrey, UK: Day One, 2003), 63.
8. Ibid.

So the Lord responded by directing the fish to disgorge the prophet back into the world.

Jonah could not know that his words were practically identical to the ones spoken by the converted mariners after they had cast him into the deep. Jonah 1:16 says "they offered a sacrifice to the LORD and made vows." That both the Gentile sailors and the Jewish prophet responded to God's grace in the same way shows that this must be the universal response of all who are saved. Likewise, Christians are saved by relying on the atoning blood of Christ, and by our baptism we are pledged to bear the name of God in obedience to his Word.

Have you responded like this to God's grace? Do you realize that the sovereign God of the universe has planned and achieved a single way of salvation in the sin-atoning blood of his only Son? No other offering can remove the debt of your sin and no other salvation has entered the councils of the wisdom of God. In response, we offer a living sacrifice of thankful praise for the gift of his Son to be our Savior. Do you realize further that when God saves you by his sovereign grace, he remains sovereign over your life? Jonah confessed, "What I have vowed I will pay" (Jonah 2:9). What must you vow as a believer? The answer is that you must enter into a covenant of faith with the Lord, surrendering the rule of your life into his sovereign control.

Jonah shows that the sovereignty of God is more than a doctrine to affirm; it is also a commitment to be kept. Perhaps some of us, like Jonah, will need to renew our commitment to the Lord. Such a commitment will find expression not merely in our hearts or with our mouths, but also with our hands: "In the end, there is only one evidence of a personal, saving relationship to the Lord—and that is the keeping of his commandments."[9] For if "salvation belongs to the LORD," then those who are saved belong to him, too.

9. Gordon J. Keddie, *Preacher on the Run: The Message of Jonah* (Darlington, UK: Evangelical Press, 1986), 62–63.

10

THE GRACE OF THE LORD

Jonah 3:1–5

Then the word of the LORD came to Jonah the second time, saying, "Arise, go to Nineveh, that great city, and call out against it the message that I tell you." (Jonah 3:1–2)

he book of Jonah records the education a prophet received in the school of God's grace. Those who study this topic will often speak of God's plan of grace. Having permitted mankind to fall into sin, God worked out his gracious plan in human history, centered on the coming of his Son, Jesus Christ. The God who planned his grace in the great sweep of history does the same in individual lives. The third chapter of Jonah shows how God's gracious purposes always succeed, although they often follow a path that is surprising to the human observer. Jonah's experience proves the words written so much later by the apostle Paul: "The foolishness of God is wiser than man's wisdom, and the weakness of God is stronger than man's strength" (1 Cor. 1:25, NIV).

THE GRACE OF THE LORD

God's grace is first revealed in this chapter by the second chance that God provides to Jonah: "Then the word of the LORD came to Jonah the second time, saying, 'Arise, go to Nineveh, that great city, and call out against it the message that I tell you'" (Jonah 3:1–2).

We remember that this book opened with very similar words, a calling to preach to the Ninevites, which Jonah rejected. Unwilling to obey, he fled for Joppa, and from there he boarded a ship bound for the most distant port possible. But God intervened with a great storm that threatened to destroy Jonah's ship. To save the ship, the crew cast Jonah overboard. But instead of drowning, he was swallowed by a great fish or a whale that God had sent. In the belly of the fish, Jonah recognized his utter need for the very grace he had been withholding from Nineveh. The prophet repented and called out to God, and the Lord answered his prayer by delivering him safely to dry ground.

Now Jonah is called a second time to God's task. This tells us a good deal about God's grace. O. Palmer Robertson comments: "God forgets, and never holds the thing against you. Think of how wonderful are the implications of that one fact for your life. God simply does not hold grudges against people who humble themselves and ask his forgiveness through Jesus Christ."[1]

Jonah was given a second chance by God, just as God's people often receive second, third, and seventy-seventh chances when they repent and call upon the Lord. Abraham received a second chance when he had stopped short of the promised land, but God called him again to go forth. Moses received a second chance after he had murdered an Egyptian slave driver and was forced to flee across the desert. Perhaps most poignantly, Peter was given another chance after he had denied his Lord three times on the night of Jesus' arrest. What an encouragement it is to know the second chances of God as you face your disobedience and sin, repent, and seek the grace of the Lord again.

God's second chance also meant that the Lord intended to get his way with his servant. Jonah's deliverance through the belly of the great fish was not a way out of God's calling on his life. God still called Jonah to preach in Nineveh, so Jonah's restoration to God's presence included the restoration of his calling to serve.

Consider what marvelous grace it was that not only forgave Jonah and restored him to God's favor, but also restored him to his office before the Lord. Hugh Martin writes:

---

1. O. Palmer Robertson, *Jonah: A Study in Compassion* (Edinburgh: Banner of Truth, 1990), 42.

It would have been a very conspicuous instance of gracious condescension and forgiving love, had the Lord simply forgiven the penitent prophet his great sin in disobeying the heavenly command and fleeing from the presence of the Lord. . . . In bringing His erring servant to repentance, and reinstating him in favour, He reinstates him in office also; sealing to him the assurance of his own personal forgiveness by the restoration of his holy calling.[2]

It is to the glory of God's grace that our salvation progresses beyond forgiveness to full restoration. Mankind fell from his status as God's image-bearing son by Adam's sin in the garden. But our salvation in Christ restores us both to our lost calling and to our lost status. Christians are children of God and lights in the world, declaring God's praises through our witness and works. Every Christian who has turned to the Lord for forgiveness from sin also finds the great purpose and meaning of his life that had been lost in the paths of sin.

THE GRACE OF JONAH

When Jonah receives God's calling again to preach in Nineveh, he goes forth as a living testimony to the grace of the Lord. In this way we realize that Jonah's rebellion had actually served the purposes of God. God is never to blame for our sin, yet in his sovereign plan of grace he uses even our folly, sin, and rebellion as occasions for achieving the designs of his grace. So when Jonah received his second call to Nineveh, he answered it as a man who had been changed by grace.

Another way to say this is to observe that God's hand of chastisement in the lives of his children is guided by his purpose for our lives. John Calvin notes that through Jonah "we . . . learn how well God provides for us and for our salvation, when he corrects our perverseness; though sharp may be our chastisements . . . we know that nothing is better for us than to be humbled under God's hand."[3] Having been changed by God's disciplining grace, Jonah is now ready to serve as an instrument fit for God's design in preaching the gospel.

2. Hugh Martin, *A Commentary on Jonah* (1870; repr. Edinburgh: Banner of Truth, 1958), 226–27.

3. John Calvin, *A Commentary on the Twelve Minor Prophets*, 5 vols. (1559; repr. Edinburgh: Banner of Truth, 1986), 3:94.

We can mark the change in Jonah's life by first realizing that he now knew himself to be *a sinner who had been forgiven*. Earlier, Jonah had refused to preach to Nineveh because he did not think that such great sinners deserved to receive God's grace. But what an education he had received while at sea! Hugh Martin comments: "As a sinful man, whose sin had been forgiven, [Jonah] could not fail to accept at the hand of the Lord, the mission now assigned him in a spirit of reverence and dutifulness—of gratitude, submission, and obedience . . . Jonah would not only be prepared, but desirous to be engaged again in his Master's service."[4]

Why was Jonah more fit for God's mission now that he knew himself as a sinner forgiven? The answer can be seen in a small detail in the Hebrew text. In Jonah's first calling, God had directed him to rise and go to Nineveh and call out "against" it. But in this second calling, there is a slight but significant change. Now Jonah is called to arise and go to Nineveh and preach God's message "to" it. In both cases, Jonah would go to the same place and do the same thing. But God would have him go with a different attitude: an attitude of grace. Jonah was to seek earnestly the repentance and forgiveness of Nineveh, and for this he needed to know himself as a penitent and forgiven man. Now Jonah could arrive in Nineveh and declare: "Look at me! Forgiveness and restoration are possible even for those who disobey and run away from God."[5]

Jonah's lesson is one that God wants all his servants to learn. This is one reason why the Lord permits us to slide back into sin. When he has called us to repentance, we are ready to serve him again in the joy of his amazing grace. "Amazing grace, how sweet the sound that saved a wretch like me. / I once was lost but now am found, was blind but now I see." Those whose hearts readily sing these words are most useful for the gospel in this world.

The change in Jonah's life is reflected immediately in his response to God's renewed call. The first time God called Jonah to preach against wicked Nineveh, the prophet fled from the Lord's presence. But this time, "Jonah arose and went to Nineveh, according to the word of the Lord" (Jonah 3:3). His gratitude for God's grace showed forth in new obedience. Martin comments: "Thus a true reception of the true forgiveness fills the soul, in the very instant, with reverential submission, quickening and calling forth a

4. Martin, *Jonah*, 230.
5. Robertson, *Jonah*, 44.

promise and pledge—yea, a longing desire and a loyal endeavour—to obey."[6] Forgiveness fuels the zeal of God's people to serve him. It was, for instance, after Isaiah had realized the depths of his sin, and felt the angel press to his lips a coal from the atoning altar, that he answered God's call to service by exclaiming, "Here am I! Send me" (Isa. 6:8). We will experience the same passion for the spread of the gospel as we likewise see the truth of our sin and receive the forgiving grace of the Lord for ourselves.

Jonah had been changed in a second way that also shaped his response to God's renewed call. Now he was *a man who had prayed and been heard by God*. Having been in the belly of the whale, Jonah knew what it was like to be in total need and utter dependence on God's answer to prayer, only to find how faithful the Lord is to all who call on him in faith.

It is easy for us to underestimate what it meant for Jonah to obey the Lord's calling to Nineveh. He was about to make a long and perilous journey into the heart of the most violent empire of that day. God described Nineveh as "that great city." Jonah was then to call out against it, God said, "for their evil has come up before me" (Jonah 1:2).

> Jonah was about to enter, unprotected, a city, whose inhabitants were pre-eminently wicked and violent; and he was to threaten them in the name of the Almighty with speedy and complete destruction. It was as going into the lions den. Nothing but an implicit reliance on the presence, the faithfulness, the power, and the protection of God could possible bear him through, in the calmness and courage befitting an ambassador of God.[7]

It was by grace that Jonah obeyed the Lord, a grace that he learned in desperate prayer while in the belly of the great fish. This is always how it is with God's mightiest servants. Gordon Keddie writes, "The experience of prayer, together with the answers to that prayer, constitute the most profound encouragements to a deepening commitment to the Lord."[8]

A notable example of learning godliness through prayer is Hudson Taylor, founder of China Inland Mission. Early in his Christian life, Taylor undertook to make a trial of God's faithfulness in prayer. He prayed for

6. Martin, *Jonah*, 232.
7. Ibid., 238–39.
8. Gordon J. Keddie, *Preacher on the Run: The Message of Jonah* (Darlington, UK: Evangelical Press, 1986), 84.

everything, often ignoring even prudent means for seeing to his needs. When his employer forgot to pay him, Taylor said nothing but only prayed. Then the employer remembered his mistake and made good on his debt to the young believer. Taylor later admitted that he had been immature in much of his approach, yet the lesson he learned as a man who knew that his prayers were heard would shape the rest of his ministry.

Believing that God had called him to take the gospel to the inner regions of China, Taylor faced tremendous opposition. One minister asked him how he expected to get to so distant a place with no money. Taylor replied that he did not know. "It seemed to be probable," he writes, "that I should need to do as the Twelve and seventy had done in Judea, go without purse or scrip, relying on Him who had sent me to supply all my need." Unable to find a suitable missionary society to support him, Taylor concluded, "So God and God alone is my hope, and I need no other."[9]

History records that Hudson Taylor did go to China and founded the China Inland Mission, a great missionary society that ultimately succeeded in reaching millions of people with the gospel of Christ. Taylor was a man of vision, courage, and love. But above all he was a man who had experienced God's faithfulness in answering prayer. Howard Taylor said of his missionary father that for forty years the sun never rose over China without God finding Hudson Taylor on his knees.

One feature of Jonah's obedience to the Lord should be especially noted by everyone called to teach and preach God's Word. Jonah 3:3 tells us that "Jonah arose and went to Nineveh, according to the word of the LORD." In other words, his obedience was defined by his faithfulness to the command of God's Word. The message Jonah spoke in Nineveh was the very message God had given him to speak. So it must be with all who proclaim God's message. The preacher is not invited to invent his own sermon, much less to tailor his preaching to tickling the fancies of his hearers. Peter Williams writes: "It is the preacher's task and privilege to declare, as clearly and as powerfully as God will enable him, the truth revealed in the Bible."[10] The faithful servant of God, writes J. I. Packer, must "take care to make clear that what he offers is not his own ideas, but God's message from God's book . . . to let the text talk

9. Cited from Marshall Broomhall, *The Man Who Believed God* (Chicago: Moody Press, 1929), 41–52.

10. Peter Williams, *Jonah—Running from God: An Expositional Commentary* Exploring th Bible (Epsom, Surrey, UK: Day One, 2003), 74.

through him."[11] As the apostle John noted: "He whom God has sent utters the words of God" (John 3:34).

There is a third aspect we should note regarding how God's grace had changed Jonah. Through the trials brought on by his own sin, he was *a man who had known affliction and found the blessing of God*. We should never glamorize God's chastisement, and we can be sure that Jonah's afflictions in the fish's belly were very great indeed. Yet it was through these afflictions that he was blessed. Hugh Martin comments:

> Before he was afflicted, he went astray; but now he will keep God's word. Chastened and subdued, of a meek and quiet spirit, overwhelmingly convinced that no device of man can prosper against the strong hand of the Most High, he would return with a readiness to render implicit and unquestioning obedience to whatever the Divine oracle should enjoin. . . . Not any less than the royal Psalmist could he say, "I believed, therefore have I spoken; I was greatly afflicted."[12]

The effect of Jonah's experience and the change worked in him by the grace of God went beyond mere obedience. It conveyed to him a holy boldness about God's work. We can scarcely imagine traveling through all the neighborhoods of one of our great cities today—through the business district, the ghettos, the markets, and the parks—crying out a message like Jonah's: "Yet forty days, and Nineveh shall be overthrown!" (Jonah 3:4). We could hardly expect anything short of rejection, abject failure, ridicule, and possibly official abuse. How much more boldness did Jonah require to preach in this way as he crossed for three days the "exceedingly great city" of Nineveh! But he had learned the reality of God's power and the tenacity of God's purposes. He had been afflicted greatly at the hands of God, and he had experienced the great blessing of God's grace. Therefore, writes John Calvin, "He is not now moved in any degree by the greatness of the city, but resolutely follows where the Lord leads. We hence see that faith, when once it gains the ascendancy in our hearts, surmounts all obstacles, and despises all the greatness of the world."[13]

11. J. I. Packer, in Samuel T. Logan Jr., ed., *The Preacher and Preaching: Reviving the Art in the Twentieth Century* (Phillipsburg, NJ: Presbyterian and Reformed, 1986), 8.

12. Martin, *Jonah*, 240. The citation is from Psalm 116:10 (KJV).

13. Calvin, *The Minor Prophets*, 3:93.

To our surprise, we now realize that Jonah's flight had been in a straight line toward God's objective all along. God draws straight lines with crooked sticks. The detours of trial and even sin are shaped by God for his precise purposes in our lives, fitting us through an increased awareness of our own forgiveness, an intense experience of answered prayer, and deep afflictions that end in blessing from the Lord, for the sake of his gospel of grace in the world.

THE GRACE OF NINEVEH

In our next study we will consider the remarkable revival that took place in the world's greatest and most evil city in Jonah's day. But while still reflecting on the grace of God for Jonah, we should observe the grace of God through Jonah's preaching in Nineveh.

Jonah finally arrived in the great city and began preaching: "Yet forty days, and Nineveh shall be overthrown!" (Jonah 3:4). This was a warning of God's judgment, apparently according to instructions that God had given. This may not seem to be a very gracious message, until we realize what a blessing such a warning is. William Banks writes: "The warnings of judgment are evidence of God's mercy, for He is not willing that any should perish."[14] While we must properly distinguish between the law and the gospel—that is, between God's just requirements and his promise of salvation—we also should realize that "the message of God's judgment is itself evangelistic. It is an evidence of God's mercy and grace, a warning to men and women of what awaits them if they do not repent."[15]

This is where the grace of the gospel properly begins, with warnings of God's certain judgment on sin. There is always a great danger that Christians would be so concerned to "win over" their hearers that they would withhold the unpleasant reality of judgment for which the gospel is the answer. Martyn Lloyd-Jones writes:

> The essence of evangelism is to start by preaching the law; and it is because the law has not been preached that we have had so much superficial evangelism. . . . So evangelism must start with the holiness of God, the sinfulness of man,

14. William Banks, *Jonah: The Reluctant Prophet* (Chicago: Moody, 1966), 80.
15. Williams, *Jonah—Running from God*, 77.

the demands of the law, the punishment meted out by the law and the eternal consequences of evil and wrong-doing. It is only the man who is brought to see his guilt in this way who flies to Christ for deliverance and redemption.[16]

If God's grace in Nineveh began with the law, then where was the gospel? The answer is that Jonah himself presented the gospel; he was a living sermon on the grace of God that brings life to the dead and delivers sinners from just condemnation.

Many of us do not expect to see mighty works of God, looking at things as we often do from a strictly human perspective. So we do not expect to see our witness blessed with the salvation of a neighbor or friend, and we little imagine that God can use our church to reach great masses of people. Such a limited view of God's grace would not expect much from Jonah's mission to Nineveh. But how wrong it would be. For God sent Jonah to Nineveh, and God's purposes are attended by God's power. Therefore, we read of the beginning of one of the greatest revivals in the history of the world: "And the people of Nineveh believed God" (Jonah 3:5).

Practically as soon as Jonah began preaching, people started to believe and repent. We are told that they not only believed Jonah, but they "believed God." O. Palmer Robertson remarks:

> It was not the force of the argument presented by the prophet that moved the people. It was the power of God's truth that pierced to the heart. Never rely on your own persuasive powers as the way to save sinners. Never wait until you have confidence in yourself to speak up for Christ. It is God and his truth that people believe. You must remain only the instrument.[17]

When God sends his message of grace, he sends it to save. We must therefore pray for God's mercy upon those to whom he would have us witness and preach, believing that nothing is too great or difficult for the almighty power of God working through his gospel.

Furthermore, we note that God gave the Ninevites grace to act on Jonah's message: "They called for a fast and put on sackcloth, from the greatest of them to the least of them" (Jonah 3:5). This was the proper response to

16. D. Martyn Lloyd-Jones, *Expositions on the Sermon on the Mount* (Grand Rapids: Eerdmans, 1959), 1:235–36.
17. Robertson, *Jonah*, 49.

Jonah's message, just as confession of sin and mourning for our guilt is always the sign that God's gospel has been believed. Repentance, like faith, is the gift of God (Eph. 2:9), and even the most hardened sinner will humble himself before the Lord when the law and the gospel go forth in the power of God's grace. Peter said that Jesus was exalted "to give repentance" (Acts 5:31), and the book of Acts adds that, through the gospel, God "has granted repentance that leads to life" (Acts 11:18).

THE GRACE OF JESUS TODAY

Lastly, we should observe the similarity between Jonah's ministry to Nineveh and Jesus' ministry to the world. Like Jonah, Jesus was sent from the Father with a message of warning and salvation to the world. Jesus said of himself: "Whoever believes in him is not condemned, but whoever does not believe is condemned already, because he has not believed in the name of the only Son of God" (John 3:18). Like Jonah eventually did, Jesus obeyed God's command and faithfully delivered the message from heaven. And like the earlier prophet, Jesus went forth in the power of God so that the most unlikely and hardened sinners responded in repentance, by God's grace believing God as he spoke through the witnessed gospel.

The situation in our world is little different from that of Nineveh. The call of warning and invitation is still going out today. Jonah gave Nineveh a warning with a specific time period for response: "Yet forty days, and Nineveh shall be overthrown!" (Jonah 3:4). The number forty is often used in Scripture for times of preparation or warning. The rain of Noah's flood fell for forty days, and Israel was tried for forty days while Moses met with God on the mountain. Perhaps most notable is that Jesus was tempted by the devil in the desert for forty days. Forty days therefore speaks of a definite time established by God before his coming either in judgment or in grace.

So it is today. The Word of the Lord has come to the wicked corner of the world in which we live. The time is established by God, with a definite opportunity for grace, after which comes judgment. The day of judgment may or may not be tomorrow, but it will certainly come at the definite time of God's appointment. Jesus has come in the power of his death and resurrection, and if you will believe, the amazing grace of God will come to restore you, to change you, and then to use you to carry the message of this grace to others in the world.

11

THE GRACE OF REPENTANCE

Jonah 3:5–10

When God saw what they did, how they turned from their evil
way, God relented of the disaster that he had said he would do to
them, and he did not do it. (Jonah 3:10)

f all the great revivals in the history of this world, few can compare with the mass repentance of ancient Nineveh. Hugh Martin comments on the magnitude of this event:

> A great and proud city suddenly smitten into the most profound humiliation, from the greatest of its inhabitants unto the least of them—from the king on the throne to the meanest citizen—is a spectacle to which, I suppose, history affords no parallel. Cities, and countries, and communities have oftentimes, with not a little unanimity, given themselves to humiliation and fasting. But there is no event on record that can at all be compared with the fast and the repentance of Nineveh.[1]

This great revival occurred through the preaching of one man, the prophet Jonah. As always with revivals, it began with the awakening of

1. Hugh Martin, *A Commentary on Jonah* (1870; repr. Edinburgh: Banner of Truth, 1958), 260.

the messenger. Revivals begin in the repentance and renewed faith of the church, just as the repentance of Nineveh began with Jonah's contrition and spiritual renewal. Seeing the genesis of this work in Jonah's own experience, we realize that the revival of Nineveh was a mighty act of God in his mercy. According to the Lord Jesus Christ, this event stands through all history "as a sign and witness against both the poverty of our obedience to the Lord and our low expectations for the success of the gospel in our own time" (see Luke 11:30–32).[2]

NINEVEH'S REPENTANCE

Jonah had obeyed God's call to preach in Nineveh, crying throughout the city: "Yet forty days, and Nineveh shall be overthrown!" (Jonah 3:4). To the astonishment of history, the wicked Ninevites did not respond with violence against the prophet, or even with mocking indifference to his call. Instead, they presented one of the classic instances of corporate repentance, as an entire society turned from sin and called upon the Lord.

A biblical definition of repentance will include at least three vital elements, each of which is present in the case of Nineveh. The first is a *sorrowful mourning over sin*. We see this in that the Ninevites "called for a fast and put on sackcloth, from the greatest of them to the least of them" (Jonah 3:5). False repentance grieves only over the consequences of sin; people are not sorry that they sinned but that they got caught. True repentance grieves over the sin itself. But the Ninevites tore their hearts in conviction for their sin and the offense they had given to Jonah's God.

We see the Ninevites' sorrow for sin in three ways. The first is that they "called for a fast." Fasting has several biblical purposes, one of which is a public expression of penitence. It is interesting that in this case, even the animals of Nineveh were required to fast. The king decreed: "Let neither man nor beast, herd nor flock, taste anything. Let them not feed or drink water" (Jonah 3:7). The intent may have been to display to God the total repentance of their society. Moreover, the lack of food and water would cause the beasts to moan and cry, increasing the intensity and seriousness of the city's repentance.

2. Gordon J. Keddie, *Preacher on the Run: The Message of Jonah* (Darlington, UK: Evangelical Press, 1986), 87.

Secondly, the Ninevites' sorrow was acted out by the wearing of sackcloth, "from the greatest of them to the least of them" (Jonah 3:5). Sackcloth was coarse and rough cloth used for making sacks, which normally only the poorest of people wore. Like fasting, sackcloth expressed lament, grief, and humiliation.

Thirdly, the king of Nineveh set an example for his subjects by sitting in ashes. When he heard Jonah's preaching, "he arose from his throne, removed his robe, covered himself with sackcloth, and sat in ashes" (Jonah 3:6). Taking off his rich and costly robes, donning sackcloth, and then squatting in ashes was the ultimate public display of self-humiliation.

Inevitably, people wonder whether such public expressions as fasting and the wearing of sackcloth and ashes are appropriate today. The answer depends on the sincerity of the actions; where there is a genuine conviction before the Lord, as seems to be the case here (there being no apparent ulterior motive behind his public remorse), public, civic expressions of repentance may be quite appropriate. If a nation loses a great battle in war, for instance, expressions of public lament may be a legitimate way of expressing their inward groaning for divine favor and mercy. But we are warned by Jesus against hypocritical public displays. He said, "Beware of practicing your righteousness before other people in order to be seen by them" (Matt. 6:1). Fasting, especially, may be a useful way of stimulating prayer or chastening the soul, but only when accompanied by the corresponding inward reality. Calvin urges: "We must bear in mind that these things are set before us as the outward signs of repentance, which, when not genuine, do nothing else but provoke the wrath of God."[3]

All these actions by the Ninevites expressed repentance in terms of sorrow for sin. But repentance also requires an actual *turning from sin*. J. I. Packer writes, "Repentance is a change of mind issuing in a change of life."[4] We see this in the king's proclamation: "Let everyone turn from his evil way and from the violence that is in his hands" (Jonah 3:8). Nineveh was notorious for violence, so here its king acknowledges the evil of their ways and calls the people to repudiate their chief and characteristic sin.

3. John Calvin, *A Commentary on the Twelve Minor Prophets*, 5 vols. (1559; repr. Edinburgh: Banner of Truth, 1986), 3:104.
4. J. I. Packer: *A Passion for Faithfulness: Wisdom from the Book of Nehemiah* (Wheaton, Ill.: Crossway, 1995), 58

Thirdly, repentance culminates in *a turning to God in renewed faith*. Thus the king of Nineveh decreed, "And let them call out mightily to God" (Jonah 3:8). He was summoning the people to pray to the God of Jonah for mercy. Throughout the Bible we find sinners who repent turning to God in prayer and discovering his grace in reply. Solomon's prayer at the dedication of his temple establishes the principle for us all:

> If they sin against you—for there is no one who does not sin—and you are angry with them . . . if they turn their heart . . . and repent and plead with you . . . , then hear in heaven your dwelling place their prayer and their plea, and maintain their cause and forgive your people who have sinned against you (1 Kings 8:46–47, 49–50).

Presumably, the Ninevites had never heard of Solomon's prayer; nor could they plead with God as his own covenant people. But they understood enough to repent, having heard Jonah's warning of judgment. How much more should Christians, knowing more than the Ninevites and even more than Jonah—looking back as we do on the grace of God in the blood of Christ—freely and eagerly turn in repentance to God for his mercy. The apostle John has given us a great assurance of success, writing: "If we confess our sins, he is faithful and just to forgive us our sins and to cleanse us from all unrighteousness" (1 John 1:9).

THE GRACE OF REPENTANCE

The repentance of Nineveh was a truly extraordinary event and, from a human perspective, totally surprising. How can we account for this unprecedented repentance?

The first answer is found in the initial words of Jonah 3:5: "And the people of Nineveh believed God." This shows us that repentance is always a firstfruit of belief in the Word of God. They repented because they believed the message Jonah preached. We may assume that Jonah's preaching involved a fuller exposition of the warning that in forty days the city would be overthrown. Doubtless, he proclaimed the reasons for their coming judgment and the holiness of the God who threatened them. Believing Jonah's message, their faith was the catalyst for the repentance that followed.

Nor was it merely that they repented because they believed the word of judgment against them. They must also have believed that God might have mercy if they turned from their sin. So their king mused: "Who knows? God may turn and relent and turn from his fierce anger, so that we may not perish" (Jonah 3:9). This hope of mercy was essential to their change of heart; true repentance is always grounded not merely in the law of God but also in the hope of the gospel. True repentance is evangelical repentance; it is actuated not merely by fear of wrath but also by hope of grace. Paul says, "The grace of God has appeared . . ., training us to renounce ungodliness and worldly passions" (Titus 2:11). It was the hope of salvation that spurred Nineveh's repentance. Calvin comments: "No one can willingly submit to God, except he has previously known his goodness, and entertained a hope of salvation; for he who is touched only with fear avoids God's presence; and then despair prevails, and perverseness follows."[5]

But where would the Ninevites have gotten any idea of God's mercy? Two sources are apparent. The first is the offer of mercy implied by Jonah's warning. When the electric company warns that your power will be turned off unless you pay your bill, that warning implies that if you pay the bill the threat will not be carried out. Likewise, the Ninevites saw hope of mercy in the fact that God had offered them a warning. Compare their situation with that of Sodom. No messenger from God wended through Sodom's streets alerting them of the fire from heaven that would destroy them. So why was Nineveh given the warning that Sodom was denied? The evident reason was God's purpose to spare them through faith in his message.

We should view the threats of judgment in the Bible from this perspective. Why, after all, does God warn that "the wages of sin is death" (Rom. 6:23a)? The obvious reason is to draw us to "the free gift of God is eternal life in Christ Jesus our Lord" (Rom. 6:23b). Peter warned, "The day of the Lord will come like a thief, and then the heavens will pass away with a roar, and the heavenly bodies will be burned up and dissolved" (2 Peter 3:10). What was his point? "Since all these things are thus to be dissolved, what sort of people ought you to be in lives of holiness and godliness?" (2 Peter 3:11).

In addition to the mercy implied in Jonah's warning, the Ninevites' faith must also have latched onto Jonah himself. Here we remember Jesus'

5. Calvin, *Minor Prophets*, 3:110.

teaching that Jonah "became a sign to the people of Nineveh" (Luke 11:30). This would seem to indicate that the Ninevites had learned of Jonah's amazing history. They knew that he had disobeyed God and that his flight from God's presence led to his apparent death in the sea. They also would have learned that Jonah was nonetheless spared by God's mercy, receiving a sort of resurrection through the belly of the great fish. The very sight of such a redeemed sinner as Jonah must have encouraged the king that God might have mercy for his people as well.

If Jonah's reemergence from the great fish spurred the Ninevites to a hopeful repentance, how much more ought we to be persuaded by the resurrection of Jesus Christ. As Jesus argued, "[Nineveh] repented at the preaching of Jonah, and behold, something greater than Jonah is here" (Matt. 12:41). Jesus went into the grave not for his own sins but for ours. Therefore, his resurrection offers a hope of new life sufficient to persuade us to trust in him and repent. The sight of Jesus risen from the grave and exalted in glory proclaims to us God's acceptance of his atoning death on our behalf, and assures us of God's mercy for sinners who humbly seek forgiveness.

So Nineveh's repentance was grounded in their belief in God and the message of his servant. This leads to a second source behind their repentance, namely, the grace of God.

The mass repentance of the most wicked metropolis of the ancient world was clearly the result of God's supernatural working. There is no other sufficient explanation for this remarkable event. Who could expect that the arrival of one bedraggled prophet into the heart of violent, arrogant paganism would be received the way Jonah was received? Yet this one man brought low the capital of a bloodthirsty empire simply by the message that he preached! How did this happen? It happened by the secret working of God's Spirit in and through the Word of God that was preached.

Our repentance must also be empowered by the grace of the Lord. It is not easy for any man or woman to repent. We must pray when seeking a radical change in the life of someone we love. When it comes to our own repentance, we should bow our hearts before the God of grace and plead for him to do the work that so often our own hearts cannot perform. "Create in me a clean heart, O God, and renew a right spirit within me," King David prayed (Ps. 51:10). God will answer such a prayer offered up in trusting faith. Repentance, like salvation, is by grace and through faith, in the power of God's Holy Spirit bearing witness to God's Word.

What a blessing it is to repent! Too often, believers and nonbelievers alike think repentance an unpleasant topic, however necessary the Bible says that it is. Yet it is through repentance that many of God's choicest graces enter our experience. If each of us took stock of our habitual sins and earnestly pleaded with God in persistent prayer, relying on the power of his grace, then the freedom we would gain from breaking just one sinful habit would revolutionize our lives. If we studied passages such as Paul's list of the fruit of the Spirit (Gal. 5:22–23), finding there the most obvious defect in our character, and then earnestly sought God's grace for repentance, the change in our manner of living would bring scarcely imagined blessing into our homes, marriages, and other relationships.

Realizing this, we see why this king of Nineveh is so worthy of praise. Those who exercise authority in society, the church, or the home have no higher duty than to lead their people in sincere repentance. Likewise, there are few more baleful curses upon any people than to be ruled by those who make light of sin, spurn the warnings of God's Word, and harden not only their own hearts but the hearts of the people against God. By setting an example of humble contrition—rising from his throne, removing his royal robes, covering himself with sackcloth, and sitting in ashes—the king of Nineveh offered the best possible service for the well-being of his people. May we seek such leaders for ourselves, and beg God's mercy in providing them.

GOD'S REPENTANCE

The chapter closes with the strongest encouragement for us to repent, for it tells of God's response to the humbling of Nineveh. The wicked people having repented of sin, God repented of his plans for their destruction: "When God saw what they did, how they turned from their evil way, God relented of the disaster that he had said he would do to them, and he did not do it" (Jonah 3:10).

First, notice what it is that God desires to see: "how they turned from their evil way." It was not outward ceremonies that God desired to see. God relented not because he observed that they abstained from food and water for a time, or briefly wore cheap material in the place of their normally luxurious dress. It was not because sacrifices of animals or money were made in an effort to purchase God's favor. It was because they repented: their hearts turned from their evil ways.

God desires the same from us. We may go to church and worship him. We may recite liturgies of repentance. We may offer fervent songs of praise. We may bring large amounts of money to the coffers of the church. We may become experts of theological learning. But what God desires to see is a sincere turning from our sins, because we have believed the message of both his law and gospel, that is, because we have truly grieved for the wickedness of our sins and have cast ourselves upon God's mercy in Jesus Christ. So it was that Jesus began his preaching ministry with this call: "Repent, for the kingdom of heaven is at hand" (Matt. 4:17).

When Nineveh repented, a city whose wickedness was so great and whose guilt was piled as high as the pyramids of skulls its conquering rulers delighted to construct, God relented of his judgment. This shows us that God can and will forgive anybody who believes and repents. Calvin writes: "We hence learn for what purposes God daily urges us to repentance, and that is, because he desires to be reconciled to us, and that we should be reconciled to him."[6]

Some translations of Jonah 3:10 state that God "repented" of his judgment. This has led some to question the omniscience of God, as if he had previously judged them in error; or the immutability of God, that is, his changelessness, since he appears to have changed his mind. There are several answers to these suppositions. One is that God accommodates his Word to our mode of understanding. Just as the Bible ascribes human physicality to God, speaking of "the hand of the Lord" or "the ears of the Lord," so also does Scripture ascribe human reasoning to God when it speaks of him "repenting." John Mackay writes: "When God is said to change his mind, matters are viewed from our human perspective. It appears to us that there has been a change in God, but what has in fact changed is our human conduct."[7] The point is that in "repenting" of his threatened judgment, God was exposing not his changeableness but rather his unfailing consistency and faithfulness. Hugh Martin explains this well:

6. Calvin, *Minor Prophets*, 3:113.
7. John L. Mackay, *Jonah, Micah, Nahum, Habakkuk and Zephaniah: God's Just Demands*, Focus on the Bible (Ross–shire, UK: Christian Focus, 1998), 47.

It was wicked, violent, unrighteous, atheistical, proud, and luxurious Nineveh which God had threatened to destroy. A city sitting in sack-cloth and ashes, humbled in the depths of self-abasement, and appealing as lowly suppliants to his commiseration—a Nineveh like that—*that* Nineveh, he had never threatened. *That* Nineveh he visited not with ruin. He had never said he would.[8]

It is precisely because God is unchanging that we are encouraged to repent. God is unfailing in both his wrath against sin and his mercy toward faithful repentance. There is no variation in his opposition to wickedness; thus, we are always called to repent of our sin. There is no variation in his delight in receiving sinners who call on the name of the Lord and lay hold of his mercy through faith in his Word.

Yet we may still wonder, "How could God forgive a city as wicked as this? How could God look past their many and gross sins, relenting to avenge the blood of their thousands of victims?" But the same question could be asked of each of us: "How could God really forgive the things that I have done? How could he just look past the blasphemies that have dishonored him from my tongue, the injuries I have caused other people, and the pain I have inflicted?"

The answer is found in the Hebrew word used to describe the repentance of God. The word *shubh* describes the repentance of Nineveh: it signifies the turning from evil to good. But a different word is used of the repentance of God, since God has no evil from which to turn. Here it is the word *nucham*, which denotes an inward suffering. It is perhaps best rendered as saying that God was "moved to pity."[9] The answer to how God can forgive sin is found at the cross of Jesus Christ. God literally suffers in repenting from judging our sins; he suffered at the cross of Jesus Christ. Jacques Ellul states: "He takes upon himself the evil which was the wages of man's sin. He suffers the very suffering which in his justice he should have laid on man. God causes the judgment to fall on himself; this is the meaning of his repenting."[10] God placed the evil of all those who turn to him on the cross of Christ, so that he might justly repent of his holy obligation to condemn us, all because of the merciful grace that calls us to believe and repent.

8. Martin, *Jonah*, 290.

9. Joyce Baldwin, *Jonah*, in Thomas E. McComiskey, ed., *The Minor Prophets: An Exegetical & Expository Commentary* (Grand Rapids: Baker, 1993), 560.

10. Jacques Ellul, *The Judgment of Jonah* (Grand Rapids: Eerdmans, 1971), 99–100.

The Witness of Nineveh

The great need of our world today is a legion of Jonahs, fresh with the awareness of God's grace in their own lives, who call out to the world with the same message of grace. God will and must judge the wickedness of our world. God will and must visit your sins with the fire of his wrath. Yet he has sent his own Son into this world to bear the sins of those who believe. This is the message that Christian pulpits must preach and the witness that Christian lives must present. In this respect, the ministry of Jonah stands as a perpetual encouragement to preaching the gospel of Christ.

But the response of the Ninevites also stands as a perpetual witness. Their repentance and God's relenting of judgment stands as a testimony to the grace of God for all who will humble themselves in faith. Jesus said, "As Jonah became a sign to the people of Nineveh, so will the Son of Man be to this generation" (Luke 11:30). Jesus offers forgiveness to all who believe, repent, and seek his saving grace. But for all who refuse God's offer of mercy, who harden their proud hearts to the gospel of salvation, it will not only be Jesus who bears witness against them on the day of judgment. For, he adds, "the men of Nineveh will rise up at the judgment with this generation and condemn it, for they repented at the preaching of Jonah, and behold, something greater than Jonah is here" (Luke 11:32).

12

GROWING IN GRACE

Jonah 4:1–5

But it displeased Jonah exceedingly, and he was angry. And he
prayed to the LORD and said, "O LORD, is not this what I said when
I was yet in my country?" (Jonah 4:1–2)

onah chapter 4 completes the Bible's record of this fascinating prophet as he reacts to the great public repentance of evil
Nineveh. As we prepare to bid farewell to our study of Jonah, it
would be good to recall his progression in the Lord's school of grace.

Jonah previously had been employed by the Lord to deliver a message
to King Jeroboam II, informing the wicked monarch about the undeserved
mercy he had been shown by God (2 Kings 14:25–27). The book of Jonah
starts with God giving Jonah another mission that would stretch his appreciation for grace even further, summoning him to preach in the wicked
Assyrian capital of Nineveh. At this, the prophet snapped. Giving himself
over to resentment, he fled "from the presence of the LORD" (Jonah 1:3),
boarding a ship bound for the distant port of Tarshish. In response, "the
LORD hurled a great wind upon the sea, and there was a mighty tempest" that
threatened the ship (Jonah 1:4). In a bitter spirit, Jonah advised the pagan
sailors to throw him overboard. Chapter 1 might have ended as a classic tale

of sin and judgment. But Jonah learned that just as he could not flee from God's presence, he could not flee from God's grace: "The LORD appointed a great fish to swallow up Jonah" (Jonah 1:17).

In the fish's belly, Jonah found grace to repent. His repentance and renewed faith expressed themselves in the classic words, "Salvation belongs to the LORD!" (Jonah 2:9). Repentance and faith also inspired renewed faithfulness, as chapter 3 records Jonah's obedience to God's commission to preach in wicked Nineveh. In an astonishing display of divine power, Jonah's preaching provoked one of the greatest mass expressions of repentance: "They called for a fast and put on sackcloth, from the greatest of them to the least of them" (Jonah 3:5).

Against this background, we might expect Jonah's story to conclude in triumph. But chapter 4 tells us otherwise. Jonah's story reminds us that few believers follow an unbroken ascent from unbelief upward into gloriously victorious faith. Instead, we tend to progress with steps and halts, advances and slips. R. T. Kendall speaks for many when he writes, "Jonah had such a marvelous revelation of God's mercy and grace to him that, humanly speaking, we might expect he would never have a serious problem again. For, after once seeing God in this extraordinary way in his own life, that should set him up for life."[1] Instead, Jonah shows us that when it comes to growing in God's grace, none of us is set up for life; we all have need for continual and perpetual growth in the grace of God. So it is that Jonah's final chapter begins with a most distressing report: "But it displeased Jonah exceedingly, and he was angry" (Jonah 4:1).

JONAH'S ANGER

It seemed that Jonah had come so far in his spiritual journey, but here is Jonah right back where he was at the beginning. God had saved Jonah and God had used Jonah for the sake of his grace. But far from being exultant over God's decision to relent from the judgment of Nineveh, Jonah instead burned with great anger.

The basis for Jonah's new complaint is provided in Jonah 4:2: "O LORD, is not this what I said when I was yet in my country? That is why I made haste

---

1. R. T. Kendall, *Jonah: An Exposition* (Atlanta: Authentic, 2006), 204.

to flee to Tarshish; for I knew that you are a gracious God and merciful, slow to anger and abounding in steadfast love, and relenting from disaster." This shows that Jonah's previous repentance had not been so thorough as it seemed: he justifies his prior conduct on the basis of God's unreasonable grace. Instead of thinking he was wrong for disobeying God, he now reveals that he thinks he was right all along: "I knew you were going to forgive those wicked Ninevites!" Unlike most people, who sin in ignorance of what God is really like, Jonah's heart rebels precisely because he knows the truth about God, and because the truth conflicts with his own heart's desires.

We can assess Jonah's anger from three perspectives. The first and most obvious is *his resentment over God's mercy for sinners.* Jonah was committed to the judgment of the wicked; this is what seemed right in his eyes. When God's anger toward Nineveh ends, Jonah's anger is still burning strong. Jonah is upset because he thinks God is soft on sin. "The Lord might be rejoicing 'in the presence of the angels' over sinners come to repentance, but Jonah was seething with discontent and bitter revulsion."[2]

It is tempting to think Jonah has forgotten that he is himself a sinner. But a more complex answer seems to be required. More likely, Jonah simply thought that there were sinners, and then there were *sinners.* He was in the former category—a basically good and religious person with some issues to work out—while the Ninevites were in the latter category of wicked miscreants worthy only of destruction. Many people think this way. While they admit to some sin issues in their lives, they do not think they deserve to be sent to hell. When you bring up a really big sinner—someone like Adolf Hitler or Osama bin Laden—they are quick to agree that *that sinner* deserves the wrath of God. Once again, Jonah shows us that the only way to glory in the grace of God for everyone is to realize our own dire need of God's grace for the forgiveness of our own transgressions of his holy law.

Perhaps the best commentary on Jonah's attitude was given by Jesus in one of his most famous parables, the parable of the prodigal son. While this story is beloved by many people, its point is lost on most. Jesus told of a son who demanded his portion of the inheritance in advance. When he received it, he journeyed far away, squandering his money in reckless sin. As a result he became destitute, falling so low as to covet even the slop that was fed to

2. Gordon J. Keddie, *Preacher on the Run: The Message of Jonah* (Darlington, UK: Evangelical Press, 1986), 105.

115

pigs. In that defiled condition, the son came to his senses and resolved to return home. He would no longer be a son but would be content just to be a servant. Yet as he approached, his father spied him. Racing to meet his son along the road, the father "embraced him and kissed him" (Luke 15:20). Calling to his servants, he had a rich robe draped over the son's shoulders, a ring put on his hand, and shoes placed on his feet. Then the whole community held a joyful feast to celebrate the prodigal son's return. The loving father exclaimed, "For this my son was dead, and is alive again; he was lost and is found" (Luke 15:24).

Most people delight in this parable as a picture of God's merciful love for lost sinners who come home. So it is. But this was not the primary point of Jesus' parable. To get this, we have to keep reading, for we learn of the older brother who resents the mercy shown to his sibling. He had never run off with his father's money. He had never disgraced his father's name. "Yet," he complained, "you never gave me a young goat, that I might celebrate with my friends. But when this son of yours came, who has devoured your property with prostitutes, you killed the fattened calf for him!" (Luke 15:29–30). Do you see Jonah's attitude in the older brother's words? Jonah wants to die because God has shown mercy to the heinous Ninevites and the Lord has used bitter Jonah to do it!

Jesus concluded his parable by making his point: "I tell you, there will be more joy in heaven over one sinner who repents than over ninety-nine righteous persons who need no repentance" (Luke 15:7). The joy of salvation! The marvel of God's grace! If we want to understand the heart of God, we have to grasp this rejoicing for redemption. There is no glory in heaven or on earth to compare with the glory of the forgiveness of sins. But like the older brother in Jesus' parable, Jonah thought it best for the Ninevites' gross sin to be condemned and judged. It never dawned on him that it was more glorious for God to provide for their forgiveness through repentance and faith.

A second perspective on Jonah's anger arises from *his hostility toward the salvation of the Gentiles.* We see this in his emphasis on "my country" (Jonah 4:2). Jonah could embrace the grace of God for his countrymen, but not for alien pagans like the Ninevites. He knew, he says, that God was gracious and merciful, slow to anger and abounding in steadfast love. It was wrong, he believed, for these blessings to be shown to the Gentiles—especially Gentiles who had shown such violence to the covenant people of God, the nation of Israel.

Jonah's confession of God's gracious attributes seems consciously to recall God's call to Israel in Joel 2:13: "Return to the LORD, your God, for he is gracious and merciful, slow to anger, and abounding in steadfast love; and he relents over disaster." It also echoes an important episode in Israel's history, namely, God's self-revelation to Moses in Exodus 34:6, "The LORD, the LORD, a God merciful and gracious, slow to anger, and abounding in steadfast love and faithfulness." In Jonah's mind, this knowledge of God was the exclusive property of Israel, who received it through Moses in the exodus. Jonah reasoned, Why should the Gentiles enjoy the covenant blessings that belong to Israel alone?

We may critique this view with another of Jesus' parables—the parable of the laborers in the vineyard. Some men had been working all day in the vineyard, each receiving a denarius in payment. But then they learned that other workers who had come only during the last hour had also received a denarius in pay. So they grumbled, "These last worked only one hour, and you have made them equal to us who have borne the burden of the day and the scorching heat" (Matt. 20:12). But the master replied, "Friend, I am doing you no wrong. Did you not agree with me for a denarius? Take what belongs to you and go. I choose to give to this last worker as I give to you. Am I not allowed to do what I choose with what belongs to me? Or do you begrudge my generosity?" (Matt. 20:13–15). Jonah *did* begrudge God's generosity to Nineveh, wrongly thinking that God thereby cheated his ancient people Israel.

This leads to the last perspective on Jonah's anger: *his disgust over God's sovereign will*. The Lord challenged him, "Do you do well to be angry?" (Jonah 4:4). By his actions, Jonah answered, "Yes, I do!" Jonah saw God's saving purpose as lacking in justice. This seems to be the cause of Jonah's tantrum: "Therefore now, O LORD, please take my life from me, for it is better for me to die than to live" (Jonah 4:3). If only Jonah was God, how different things would be! So offensive is God's plan of grace that Jonah no longer wants to live: "'Over my dead body' is his vehement reaction to God's grace."[3]

Jonah's objection reveals great pride. How else could Jonah presume to think better of things than God does? Yet many object to the Bible's doctrines of grace in just this way. When Paul wrote of God's sovereign grace

3. Leslie C. Allen, *The Books of Joel, Obadiah, Jonah, and Micah*, New International Commentary on the Old Testament (Grand Rapids: Eerdmans, 1976), 229.

in Romans 9, he rehearsed two objections. The first demanded, "Is there injustice on God's part?" (Rom. 9:14). People frequently object this way to the doctrine of election: the Bible says that God sovereignly chose his people from all eternity (Eph. 1:4; Rom. 8:30), but people object, "Isn't that unfair?" Paul rejoined, "By no means! For he says to Moses, 'I will have mercy on whom I have mercy'" (Rom. 9:14–15). Paul reminds us that when we are talking about the salvation of any sinners, the proper category is God's mercy, not God's justice (or fairness). To claim injustice when it comes to grace is simply to confuse categories: no one deserves to be saved; if anyone is saved at all, it is only because of God's mercy. The second objection to sovereign grace is equally wrong: "You will say to me then, 'Why does he still find fault? For who can resist his will?'" (Rom. 9:19). This is a common objection to sovereign election: if God decides everything, how can we be blamed? But notice Paul's answer: "Who are you, O man, to answer back to God?" (Rom. 9:20).

Paul's reply is the right answer to Jonah's narrow-minded complaint. Jonah is lashing out at God from the folly of his self-absorbed, sin-bound perspective. Notice that God does not even dignify the prophet with an answer. Jonah wants to die because of God's sovereign, saving grace; the prophet's idea of justice has collided with the reality of sovereign mercy. But how much better for Jonah, and for us, simply to let God tell us about salvation. A better example for us to follow is that of Job, who had voiced complaints about God's ways until he came before the Lord face-to-face. Then he changed his mind and his whole approach to God's truth: "Behold, I am of small account; what shall I answer you? I lay my hand on my mouth" (Job 40:4). Job sets us a good example of sitting humbly under God's revealed Word: being taught by God rather than thrusting our ideas onto him. In contrast, Jonah's request to die warns us about the suicidal folly of placing human wisdom against the mind and heart of God.

JONAH'S FALL FROM GRACE

In his scathing epistle to the Galatians, the apostle Paul denounces his opponents, saying, "You have fallen away from grace." Paul's point was not that true believers had lost their salvation, as is sometimes taught. Rather, he argues that his opponents had fallen away from the doctrine of grace: "You who would be justified by the law; you have fallen away from grace" (Gal. 5:4).

The same argument might be made against Jonah. He agreed with God's grace for Israel; he just rejected the grace of God for anybody else! This raises a question about Jonah's prior repentance, since he effectively renounces it here. But Jonah's true repentance should not be doubted. After all, he had not only turned to the Lord for salvation, but had followed up by submitting to the Lord's call. So how do we explain Jonah's change of heart?

First, we can observe a vital error in Jonah's thinking about salvation. He does not reject the salvation by grace he had celebrated within the fish's belly. But he does misunderstand the *extent* of that grace. Behind this is his spiritual pride, which imagines that only Israel deserves to be saved by grace. He is angry with God because God is not doing what Jonah wants him to do. What Jonah wants God to do is to reward only Israel with compassion and grace.

How widely spread is the Jonah syndrome! Some Christians think this way in terms of race. If God is for us, then he must be against them. It is right for God to show mercy to our race—whether we are white, black, or brown—but not to those of another race. We can also think this way nationally, especially in times of war. If God is to bless our country, then he must judge our enemies. But are we prepared for God to show mercy to those who hate us? We can even think this way with respect to divisions in the church. We look around and see churches that do not seem to be following God's Word. "They don't deserve to experience God's grace," we say. If a refreshing of God's Spirit should occur in such churches we may be disappointed or even angry with God. But Jesus asks, "Do you begrudge my generosity?" (Matt. 20:15). Gordon Keddie comments: "If Paul could rejoice when Christ was preached, 'whether from false motives or true,' then so can we when we see Christ preached today and lives changed by his grace!"[4]

Even more significant than the problem of Jonah's thinking is the problem of his heart. Jonah reveals a deep-seated bitterness against the Ninevites, no doubt nurtured in response to Nineveh's sins against Israel. His was an advanced case of the kind of resentment that spoils so many hearts. A woman is betrayed by her husband, so she nurtures bitterness toward men. A man

4. Keddie, *Preacher on the Run*, 109.

119

is taken advantage of by lawyers, so he seethes whenever he meets a legal professional. Such bitterness may involve hatred toward other nations or other regions of the nation. It may include churches and denominations. It may involve different races or specific people and families.

Notice what this heartsickness has done to Jonah's spiritual life, for a failure to love other people will always poison our relationship with God. "I knew you would forgive Nineveh!" Jonah objects. So because of his hatred for Nineveh, he fled from the presence of the Lord, nearly ruining his eternal soul. Now, having witnessed in Nineveh a striking display of the glory of God's grace, Jonah seethes with anger. "If the Assyrians were in on the love of God," writes James Limburg, "then Jonah wanted out."[5] If God was going to show love to Nineveh, then Jonah did not want God's love. He would rather die.

Against this background, we see why the New Testament makes such a point about the spirit of forgiveness. Our hearts cannot be right with God unless they are right toward other men. Jesus said, "If you are offering your gift at the altar and there remember that your brother has something against you, leave your gift there before the altar and go. First be reconciled to your brother, and then come and offer your gift" (Matt. 5:23–24). Paul states that if we have a complaint against another, we must "[forgive] each other; as the Lord has forgiven you, so you also must forgive" (Col. 3:13). Notice that Paul does not say that we forgive others when they have deserved it, or even when they have sufficiently repented. We forgive out of gratitude for God having forgiven us. We forgive others because we are aware that we have received a far greater, far more costly forgiveness through the blood of Jesus.

So essential is our forgiving to our salvation that Jesus said, "If you forgive others their trespasses, your heavenly Father will also forgive you, but if you do not forgive others their trespasses, neither will your Father forgive your trespasses" (Matt. 6:14–15). His point was not that we earn forgiveness by forgiving others, but that an unforgiving spirit is so alien to God's grace that it is fundamentally inconsistent for one to be forgiven by God and yet to hold grudges against others.

In our assessment of Jonah's spiritual state, we have taken counsel from the parables of Jesus, and here another parable will help us to see the impor-

5. James Limburg, *Hosea–Micah*, Interpretation (Atlanta: John Knox, 1988), 155–56.

tance of a merciful attitude toward other sinners. A certain servant owed his king a vast sum of money. The man could not pay, so his family was to be sold into slavery. But the man came to the king and begged for his mercy. "Out of pity for him, the master of that servant released him and forgave him the debt" (Matt. 18:27). Shortly afterward, the man found a fellow servant who owed him a much smaller amount of money. But when the man begged his forgiveness, he refused and had the man put into prison. News of this action reached the king, who called him back and rebuked him for his own lack of mercy, throwing him into prison. Jesus concluded, "So also my heavenly Father will do to every one of you, if you do not forgive your brother from your heart" (Matt. 18:35).

JONAH'S GROWTH IN GRACE

This parable shows us on what shaky ground Jonah has placed himself. In fact, where he placed himself informs us precisely of his spiritual attitude: "Jonah went out of the city and sat to the east of the city and made a booth for himself there. He sat under it in the shade, till he should see what would become of the city" (Jonah 4:5). Nurturing his malice toward Nineveh, Jonah separates himself from the city, and watches. No doubt he is nursing his wrath and hoping their repentance will not last.

As we conclude our assessment of Jonah, for all the discouraging signs we see in his attitude toward Nineveh's repentance, there is yet evidence of his growth in grace. We should notice one striking difference between Jonah in chapter four and in chapter one. When he first was called to preach in Nineveh, Jonah responded by fleeing from the presence of the Lord. But now, for all his bitterness over Nineveh's repentance, Jonah responds by turning to the Lord: "He prayed to the LORD" (Jonah 4:2).

The significance of this cannot be overstated. Hugh Martin observes: "Agitated and alarmed, he fled *from* the Lord. Agitated and alarmed now again, he flees *to* the Lord. . . . He does not seek a refuge from God. He makes God his refuge."[6] In this respect, Jonah recalls the experience of Asaph in Psalm 73. Asaph confesses that he envied "the prosperity of the wicked" (Ps. 73:3). As a result, he says, "My feet had almost stumbled, my steps had nearly slipped"

6. Hugh Martin, *A Commentary on Jonah* (1870; repr. Edinburgh: Banner of Truth, 1958), 350.

(Ps. 73:2); "my soul was embittered" (Ps. 73:21). So how did he avoid falling altogether? "When I thought how to understand this, it seemed to me a wearisome task, until I went into the sanctuary of God" (Ps. 73:16–17). Asaph turned to God. And in the house of God he remembered the grave peril of the wicked. "You make them fall to ruin," he realized. "How they are destroyed in a moment, swept away utterly by terrors!" (Ps. 73:18–19). Instead of resenting God's forebearance in judgment, Asaph became thankful for God's mercy in his own salvation: "For me," he concludes, "it is good to be near God; I have made the Lord GOD my refuge" (Ps. 73:28). It would overstate Jonah's case to imply that he rejoiced over God's mercy as Asaph did, but by turning to the Lord he was taking the steps that Psalm 73 depicts as leading to spiritual recovery.

This is the kind of growth that most of us need as well. We need to realize that the grace of God is not an offense to our sense of justice, but rather the only hope of our own salvation. At all times we will celebrate mercy and grace, since by them we gained our own forgiveness. Instead of drawing back from God in perplexity, we should learn to draw near to God for refuge. Jonah had learned this, and because of it he was moving in the right direction.

So how does Jonah turn out in the end? As his book concludes, we gain no definitive answer. But I think we have good reason for hope. Jonah is in the hands of the gracious God, and the chapter concludes with God patiently leading Jonah forward into grace. The fact that Jonah himself must be the source of this material suggests that he wants us to profit from his experience and grow in grace with him.

Indeed, this is the proper approach to considering Jonah's tale. How do we feel about God's mercy for those who have wronged us? Do we resent God's grace for others? Or do we rejoice in every display of divine favor and mercy, remembering the kindness God has shown to us? How do we respond when we are perplexed at God's actions in the world? What do we do when God doesn't seem to be answering our prayers the way we think he should? Do we pull away from God in anger? Or do we draw near to God, even in our consternation? Jonah's example would suggest that God is never the problem, but always the answer. He especially teaches us that God's grace should ever be the chief of all our glories and delights. If we begin to grasp these mighty truths, then we are indeed growing in grace.

13

FOR PITY'S SAKE

Jonah 4:5–11

Should not I pity Nineveh, that great city, in which there are more
than 120,000 persons who do not know their right hand from
their left, and also much cattle? (Jonah 4:11)

hy does God ask questions? Some theologians argue that God's
questions in the Bible indicate a deficiency in his knowledge;
God simply doesn't know. But this view is at odds with the
Bible's teaching about God. Job, for instance, tells us that God "looks to
the ends of the earth and sees everything under the heavens" (Job 28:24).
Moreover, this approach makes poor sense of the passages in which God
asks questions. When God asked newly fallen Adam, "Where are you? . . .
Have you eaten of the tree of which I commanded you not to eat?" (Gen.
3:9, 11), it was not because God did not know where Adam was or what
he had done. The purpose was to drive home to Adam the enormity of
his sin. Likewise, when God asked Cain, "Where is Abel your brother?"
(Gen. 4:9), it was not because God did not know about the human race's
first murder. Rather, it was to demand an account of Cain's actions in his
own words. God's questions, writes Peter Williams, "are meant to teach
us something, or to expose to us our inner selves when we are guilty of

sin or disobedience. . . . So whenever we read the Bible and come across God asking a question, we ought to ask ourselves, 'Is God addressing that question to me, and if so what am I meant to learn from it?'"[1]

JONAH'S PITIFUL ATTITUDE

This is a good approach to take with the three questions that God asks Jonah in the conclusion of this book. Jonah was exceedingly angry that God had spared wicked Nineveh, so angry that he wanted to die. So God asked him, "Do you do well to be angry?" (Jonah 4:4). Jonah thought that he did, so he set up a booth to the east of the city, sitting out in the hot sun to watch what would happen. God responded to Jonah's situation by appointing a plant to come up over Jonah and shade his head. Then, at dawn the next day, God appointed a worm to attack and kill the plant. Again, Jonah was so unhappy that he said, "It is better for me to die than to live" (Jonah 4:8). So God asked a second question, "Do you do well to be angry for the plant?" Jonah replied bitterly, "Yes, I do well to be angry, angry enough to die" (Jonah 4:9).

God's purpose in these questions was first of all to expose Jonah's self-centered attitude. We see this, first, in what makes Jonah happy. Amid all the complaints from Jonah that fill his book, there is only one time when he is glad. Jonah was not happy when God blessed his preaching with the mass repentance of Nineveh. Instead, he was comically miserable, since they did not meet his ethnic and moral requirements for salvation. Undoubtedly, most of their practices were out of accord with Scripture and their grasp of doctrine was outrageously deficient. Jonah responded as a most determined fundamentalist: he would not associate with the newly saved Ninevites; he would not mingle in their city; he would not share in their worship or participate in ministry with them. Despite the clear evidence that God had accepted Nineveh's repentance, Jonah did not accept them. Instead, he set up his booth outside Nineveh's east gate, willingly accepting isolation and needless hardship, all of which he embraced as a sign of his exceptional holiness. Jonah would do his own thing, and his own thing was to watch miserably for signs of their failure and demise.

1. Peter Williams, *Jonah—Running from God: An Expositinal Commentary*, Exploring the Bible (Epsom, Surrey, UK: Day One, 2003), 95.

If Nineveh's salvation did not make Jonah happy, then what did? The answer is given in verse 6: "Now the LORD God appointed a plant and made it come up over Jonah, that it might be a shade over his head, to save him from his discomfort. So Jonah was exceedingly glad because of the plant." Perhaps the most amazing instance of grace in the book of Jonah is God's provision of this plant to cover Jonah from the burning Mesopotamian sun. Whatever materials Jonah found to make his little booth, it could not have offered much protection from the searing elements. So God appointed a supernaturally growing plant—scholars believe that it was a gourd or a castor-oil plant, which grows quickly and produces broad leaves—to give Jonah shade. At this, the prophet was "exceedingly glad." More literally, the prophet who "was angry with a great anger" over Nineveh's salvation (Jonah 4:1) now "rejoiced with a great joy" over his castor-oil plant. How wonderful things now were for Jonah! In the comfort of the shade provided by God's wonderful grace toward him, he could watch and wait for God's terrible wrath to annihilate the city of Nineveh.

In doing this, God was exposing Jonah's self-centered attitude toward God's grace, with the miserable spirit it inevitably produced. This spirit is all too common among God's people. What amazed Jonah about grace was only what it meant to him personally—whether in the form of a great fish or a little plant—along with the narrow circle of people he cared about. What the gospel might mean for others concerned him little, except that he had personal reasons not to want grace for the Ninevites. So there he sat in misery, seething outside the city, while the wind and the sun blasted his body and mind.

Not only did Jonah's self-centered attitude toward God's grace make him miserable, but it also rendered him useless. God can judge others without our help! What he calls his people to do is enter into his work of salvation. Jonah should have been mingling among the Ninevites, encouraging their newborn faith, gently correcting their manifold errors, and lovingly teaching them the gospel. James Boice comments: "[Jonah] was not called to be a spectator, any more than Christians are called to be spectators of the world's ills and misfortunes today. He was called to identify with those people and help them as best he could by the grace of God."[2]

2. James M. Boice, *The Minor Prophets*, 2 vols. (Grand Rapids: Baker, 1983), 1:308.

Like the other questions in the Bible, God's questions to Jonah call for us to consider ourselves. Do we look upon the gospel as a consumer product for our personal benefit? Have we set up our little booths outside the culture, content to enjoy God's mercy for us while savoring the misfortunes of a God-alienated world? To put it in Jonah's terms: what makes us glad? Are we grateful for God's grace to us and delighted about signs of grace in others? Or do we delight in being right, and that others are wrong?

GOD'S GRACIOUS DEALINGS WITH JONAH

God was gracious in providing Jonah with his plant, but his true purpose is revealed in his sovereign, patient, and wise dealings with the miserable prophet. God had a plan for Jonah's plant, starting with a worm that he appointed to arrive the following morning: "When dawn came up the next day, God appointed a worm that attacked the plant, so that it withered" (Jonah 4:7). And God wasn't done: "When the sun rose, God appointed a scorching east wind, and the sun beat down on the head of Jonah so that he was faint. And he asked that he might die and said, 'It is better for me to die than to live'" (Jonah 4:8). This led to God's second question: "God said to Jonah, 'Do you do well to be angry for the plant?' And he said, 'Yes, I do well to be angry, angry enough to die'" (Jonah 4:9).

This whole episode shows God's *sovereignty* in dealing with his people. The expression "God appointed" appears over and over in Jonah. In chapter 1, God sovereignly "hurled a great wind" at Jonah's ship (Jonah 1:4), and then "the LORD appointed a great fish to swallow up Jonah" when he was cast into the sea (Jonah 1:17). Now in chapter 4, God "appointed a plant" to shade Jonah (Jonah 4:6), then "appointed a worm that attacked the plant" (Jonah 4:7), and "appointed a scorching east wind" (Jonah 4:8). The outward circumstances of Jonah's experience were sovereignly appointed by God. So it is in our circumstances: it is God who appoints the great fish that delivers us, the shade that gives us comfort, and the worm and east winds that try our souls. The lesson is that it is always God with whom we have to do, as he sovereignly appoints even the little details of our lives.

This episode also shows God's gracious *patience* in dealing with his servants. How much the Lord had put up with in Jonah! But he was still patiently prodding, patiently challenging Jonah's thinking, patiently correcting the attitude of Jonah's heart. It is in this patient grace of God that any of us finds hope to persevere in faith, since we are so much like Jonah in our indwelling sin. How many times God might well have given up on us! But he does not. In amazing condescension—more patient than the most loving mother of toddlers or the most enduring father of teenage children—God bears with our weakness and sin and never gives up on our salvation. He sees the end from the beginning and knows the glory he will win for himself through his patiently persevering grace.

On one occasion, Jesus expressed a sanctified frustration in his wayward disciples, exclaiming: "O faithless and twisted generation, how long am I to be with you and bear with you?" (Luke 9:41). The answer is best seen in Jesus' ensuing ministry. How long would he endure his disciples' failings with loving patience? All the way to the cross, where he died for their sins, and then to the open tomb, by which he secured the ministry of the Holy Spirit to sanctify our souls.

God's dealings with Jonah also show the *wisdom* of God's dealings with his people. In granting and then destroying Jonah's dearly beloved plant, God had a two-point program for his growth in grace. The first point was to show Jonah that he needed to get out of himself. Jonah was consumed with his own petty affairs; his view of life was dominated by his narrow opinions and his personal comfort.

Indeed, Jonah shows that a self-centered person will grow increasingly petty and ridiculous. At the start of the chapter, he wanted to die because God did not conform to his narrow view of salvation; now Jonah is angry enough to die because his precious plant had withered. He shows us that if we are consumed by our own problems and outlook, our spiritual life shrivels. Jonah's spirit had been reduced to the level of the plant, easily withering under the slightest assault. He was consumed by a little nothing of a gourd. Many Christians are this way: what concerns them most are all the little nothings of church life—the color of the carpet, their standing in the church pecking order, minor details of the musical performance—while giving no concern to the greater matters of the gospel. Even the greatest of believers—like the prophet Jonah—can reduce themselves to spiritual pigmies unless they elevate their perspective above the small concerns of self.

Experience shows that self-centered people are the most unhappy people: they constantly complain, are never satisfied, take no joy out of life, and give little joy to others and precious little glory to God. Unless our hearts become consumed with causes and glories far greater than those of self, we waste our gifts and calling and sit miserably under the beating sun of the world's trials, wishing we could die. Beneath it all was Jonah's bitterness for the Ninevites. Jonah's path to the loathing of life began with his loathing of Nineveh. He began, "How can I live when the Ninevites are saved?" *This* was the worm eating at his soul: God's grace for his enemies. So Jonah now complains, "How can I live in a world that allows my precious little plant to die?" Leslie Allen writes, "A Jonah lurks in every Christian heart, whimpering his insidious message of smug prejudice, empty traditionalism, and exclusive solidarity."[3] How, then, do we get out of ourselves?

FOR PITY'S SAKE

This is the point of God's third question, and the second point of God's message to Jonah: "You pity the plant, for which you did not labor, nor did you make it grow, which came into being in a night and perished in a night. And should not I pity Nineveh, that great city, in which there are more than 120,000 persons who do not know their right hand from their left, and also much cattle?" (Jonah 4:10–11).

God's point is that the way out of our self-consumed misery is to lift up our hearts to glory in the great scope of God's salvation, entering into his compassionate concern for the lost. The most joyful and most useful Christians are those with a passion for the gospel. They are also the ones who are growing in grace, their souls expanding as they are filled with excitement for God's mercy in the world.

God reasons this carefully with Jonah, arguing from the lesser to the greater. Jonah had loved his little plant, for which he exerted no effort, and which arose over him in a single night. It was a tiny, perishing little nothing. Yet there before him was a great city, filled with soul-bearing people. "Should I not pity Nineveh, that great city, in which there are more than 120,000 persons?" (Jonah 4:11). Even the cattle and other possessions were of far greater significance than Jonah's plant. Should not the temporal and the eternal well-being of thousands be of interest to Jonah, as it is to God?

3. Leslie C. Allen, *The Books of Joel, Obadiah, Jonah, and Micah*, New International Commentary on the Old Testament (Grand Rapids: Eerdmans, 1976), 235.

Not only should Jonah note the sheer value of so many people and so great a city, but he should also have compassion on their plight. God describes Nineveh as a city "in which there are more than 120,000 persons who do not know their right hand from their left" (Jonah 4:11). Some commentators argue that "persons who do not know their right hand from their left" refers only to the children in Nineveh. They argue from this the moral innocence of those who have not come of age, and sometimes even for the certainty of salvation for all children. But the Bible teaches neither, and this is not a likely explanation here. Archaeological studies indicate that the whole population of ancient Nineveh could not have been much greater than 120,000 people.[4] Moreover, God is not arguing for the rightness of his mercy for some of the people in Nineveh, but for the entire great city. Therefore, "the expression refers to the spiritual and moral ignorance of the whole population of Nineveh."[5]

The point is that God has mercy on sinful mankind, trapped in ignorance and corruption. Man's spiritual bondage is man's own fault, but God still has compassion on sinners. Is it not glorious that he does? Jonah thought it right to have pity on a worthless little plant, just as we are often consumed by our petty affairs. But can we not see the glory of God's saving pity for a world lost in sin? Do we not see the glory in the words of Jesus Christ, suffering at the hands of cruel men: "Father, forgive them, for they know not what they do" (Luke 23:34)? The sinful human race, like ancient Nineveh, is wicked and evil, guilty on account of its own sins and corrupted as the result of its self-centered choices. Yet God has mercy on the world! Should we not enter into his saving pity, opening our hearts to those bound fast in ignorance and darkness? If we do, we will tear down our little booths, enter into the world with holy love, and spread the grace of our saving God, making his cause of grace our own cause and in the process expanding our own souls.

God's final question to Jonah reveals not only the glorious motive for God's saving grace, but also its scope. God has mercy not only for the in-group but also for the out-group. God looks with saving pity on even the most wretched and wicked. And God's salvation concerns not only the spiritual aspect but also the physical and moral well-being of life, as he pities not only the Ninevites but also their cattle. David sang, "Man and beast you

4. Ibid., 234.
5. Williams, *Jonah*, 101.

save, O Lord" (Ps. 36:6). What greater cause is there to fill our hearts? But are our hearts lifted up to God's saving grace for the world? Do we marvel at the pity of God for the lost? And do we glory in the vast scope of God's salvation—redeeming sinners of all kinds and transforming not only their eternal destinies but also their temporal lives?

It is surely significant that the book of Jonah ends with God's last question. Indeed, the most important verse in the book of Jonah may be the verse that isn't there: Jonah 4:12. We read nothing of Jonah's response. More important is how we respond to God's call of merciful grace, not only for us but also for the world. The best and only fitting reply is to offer all that we have to the cause of his gospel:

> When I survey the wondrous cross on which the Prince of glory died
> My richest gain I count but loss and pour contempt on all my pride . . .
> Were the whole realm of nature mine that were a present far too small
> Love so amazing, so divine demands my soul, my life, my all.[6]

THE GOD OF THE BOOK OF JONAH

With this in mind, the best way to conclude our study of the book of Jonah is to recall its display of God and his glorious attributes.

First, Jonah displays the Lord in all his *sovereign* majesty. God's commands were sovereignly given to his prophet, and sovereignly supervised by the chastening and empowering hand of God. Jonah could refuse God's call to preach in Nineveh, but he could not avoid God's ordained purpose through him. Jonah could flee to Tarshish but he could not avert the chastising storm sent by the Lord. But just when God's sovereignty might have seemed bad news to Jonah, he learned that it is exactly what he needs, for God sovereignly sent the great fish to swallow and deliver the prophet. Even in the small matters of Jonah's life, it was God who sovereignly helped him and disciplined him to grow in grace. And it was by God's sovereign grace that an entire wicked city repented at the word of God's prophet. God said through Isaiah: "My counsel shall stand, and I will accomplish all my purpose . . . I have spoken, and I will bring it to pass; I have purposed, and I will do it" (Isa. 46:10–11). If there is any story in the Bible that proves the

---

6. Isaac Watts, *When I Survey the Wondrous Cross*, 1707, 1709.

truth of God's unremitting sovereignty, that story must be Jonah's. And if we realize the sovereign hand of God in all things, then we will receive the commands of his Word as sovereign calls to humbly obey.

The book of Jonah also reveals the Lord as a *holy* God. It was God's holy anger at Nineveh's sins that started Jonah on his way: "Arise, go to Nineveh, that great city, and call out against it, for their evil has come up before me" (Jonah 1:2). It was because of that same divine holiness that God did not accept Jonah's rebellion. The great tempest that God hurled at Jonah's ship is but a picture of the greater judgment awaiting all who turn from his ways. The message God commissioned Jonah to preach in Nineveh is a warning to all the world: "Yet forty days, and Nineveh shall be overthrown!" (Jonah 3:4). Because God is a holy God, the wicked will not continue forever, and their liberty to sin has a divinely appointed end in fearful judgment. Because God is holy, those who are spared judgment by his mercy are then called to a life that is like God's: "You shall be holy," God says to us, "for I am holy" (1 Peter 1:16).

Thirdly, Jonah reveals the Lord as a *mighty* God, indeed, an omnipotent deity. Not only did Jonah fail to escape God's reach, but he also could not escape God's power. "I fear the LORD, the God of heaven, who made the sea and the dry land," Jonah witnessed to the pagan mariners (Jonah 1:9), and God's demonstrated power over the created realm was proof of his words. Moreover, God has power to change the hearts of beasts and men. He called the great fish and it answered his summons; God caused his word to be preached to the most wicked of kings, and the ruler of Nineveh "arose from his throne, removed his robe, covered himself with sackcloth, and sat in ashes" (Jonah 3:6), calling all the city to repentance. If God is so mighty as this, and if God is for us in our salvation, then surely we must live without fear before the world. Especially in our witness to an evil generation, God's revealed power calls us to enter into the Ninevehs around us, proclaiming his justice and mercy with holy boldness.

But above all, Jonah presents to us the sovereign, holy, and omnipotent Lord as a God who is *merciful* and *gracious*. Why else would God's plea of pity for the ignorant sinners of Nineveh be given the final word? One of our hymns declares, "There's a wideness in God's mercy, like the wideness of the sea."[7]

7. Frederick William Faber, "There's a Wideness in God's Mercy," 1862.

Jonah learned that God's mercy was wider than the boundaries of his native Israel, wide enough to include people from all lands and tongues, wide enough to bring in the most vile of sinners, including a vicious tyrant like the king of Nineveh and a self-absorbed prophet like Jonah.

How wide is God's mercy? Its true measure is the length of the outstretched arms of Jesus Christ, God's only Son, on the cross of Calvary to die for our sins. If anyone will come to the Savior at his cross, pleading the mercy of God, that sinner will find God's mercy wide enough to enter into eternal life. At that same cross, God calls us to lift up our eyes above our petty little selves and see the glory of his grace as he looks in pity on the world. Looking at the eyes of God's Son gazing out from the cross, how can we not look on the lost with a similar pity? Let us, for pity's sake, love the world in his name, offering to any and all sinners the mercy and grace that God has shown to us.

Micah

AFTER DARKNESS, LIGHT

14

A Tale of Two Cities

Micah 1:1

The word of the LORD that came to Micah of Moresheth in the days of Jotham, Ahaz, and Hezekiah, kings of Judah, which he saw concerning Samaria and Jerusalem. (Mic. 1:1)

*I*t was the best of times, it was the worst of times, it was the age of wisdom, it was the age of foolishness, it was the epoch of belief, it was the epoch of incredulity, it was the season of Light, it was the season of Darkness, it was the spring of hope, it was the winter of despair, we had everything before us, we had nothing before us, we were all going direct to Heaven, we were all going direct the other way."[1]

So begins Charles Dickens' *A Tale of Two Cities*, considered by some to be the finest novel ever written in English. Dickens sought to chronicle the spirit of the French Revolution in the late eighteenth century A.D., but he could just as well have been writing of another time long before: the late eighth century B.C. in Israel and Judea. For what Dickens wrote about the cities of London and Paris is similar to what the prophet Micah had to say to Samaria and Jerusalem. The themes of Micah are precisely

---

1. Charles Dickens, *A Tale of Two Cities* (New York: Nelson Doubleday, n.d.), 9.

those cited by Dickens: wisdom and folly, belief and unbelief, light and darkness, hope and despair, heaven and hell.

Micah of Moresheth

Who was the prophet Micah? While the name is fairly common in the Old Testament (fourteen men are named Micah), there are only two biblical references to this Micah who prophesied in Jerusalem during the late eighth and early seventh centuries B.C. One of these is in the opening verse of Micah's book: "The word of the LORD that came to Micah of Moresheth" (Mic. 1:1). The other reference is in the book of Jeremiah, written a hundred years later. Jeremiah identifies Micah as the prophet whose warnings of judgment persuaded King Hezekiah to repent and seek the Lord (Jer. 26:18–19).

Reflection on these two passages will provide at least some clues about the identity and personality of this prophet. First, we should note that his name has theological significance. "Micah" means "who is like the LORD?" Bruce Waltke comments, "It reveals the essence of his parents' faith, who wished above all to praise [Yahweh], and it portends our prophet's message."[2] Micah employs his own name at the book's end, praising the Lord with the words, "Who is a God like you, pardoning iniquity and passing over transgression for the remnant of his inheritance?" (Mic. 7:18). This indicates that Micah identified with his name, and it shows that for all his oracles of judgment, at the heart of his faith was joy for the saving grace of God.

In addition to his name, we are told Micah's town of origin. He is known as "Micah of Moresheth." This was an agricultural town in the lower lands to the west of Jerusalem, about halfway to the sea. It was the kind of place whose traditional values were being undermined by the decadent rich from the capital city, and therefore an ideal place to produce a reforming prophet like Micah. David Prior writes: "His instinctive empathies were with the farmers, shepherds and small holders of the [agricultural region]. . . . He was not lured away by the glittering façade of the new culture—fine houses, advanced fashions, get-rich-quickly businesses—but kept a firm grip on the moral realities that make for true national greatness."[3]

2. Bruce Waltke, *A Commentary on Micah* (Grand Rapids: Eerdmans, 2007), 38.
3. David Prior, *The Message of Joel, Micah & Habakkuk, The Bible Speaks Today* (Downers Grove, Ill.: InterVarsity, 1998), 107.

A Season of Darkness and Light

Just as important as Micah's identity is the question of when he lived and served. He says that he prophesied "in the days of Jotham, Ahaz, and Hezekiah, kings of Judah" (Mic. 1:1). This follows the Old Testament convention of keeping time by means of the kings. Micah preached during the reigns of Jotham, Ahaz, and Hezekiah, which places his ministry between 740 and 687 B.C., a period of 53 years. Micah therefore followed the prophetic ministries of Hosea and Amos, and served in Jerusalem alongside the better-known prophet Isaiah.

Two great concerns dominate this period of Israel's history, one external and one internal. The external concern was the spreading power of the Assyrian empire: the same Assyria whose capital had been brought to repentance by the preaching of Jonah about a generation earlier. By now Assyria had returned to its rapacious ways. As the superpower of its time, and under new and vigorous leadership, Assyria cast its shadow far and wide. Assyria's policy was to recruit a vast standing mercenary army that was practically invincible in battle. To pay for these forces, they intimidated their surrounding kingdoms to extract crushingly high tributes. "In other words," writes Waltke, "the conquered nations supported the international army that raped them."[4] The political history of this era consisted mainly of rebellions small and large against this policy, to which Assyria would respond with overwhelming and savage force. Conquered peoples would be relocated en masse into the vast Assyrian domains, and conquered lands were organized as permanent Assyrian provinces.

This was the backdrop for the great crises that dominated the reigns of Jotham, Ahaz, and Hezekiah. Through our studies of Micah, we will learn much about the power and depredations of such Assyrian conquerors as Tiglath-Pileser III, Shalmaneser V, Sargon, and Sennacherib. We will also learn about the weakness of Judah's king Jotham, the perfidy of Ahaz, and the triumphant faith of Hezekiah.

As the prophets saw it, the political and military problems were mere symptoms of a greater and deeper problem: the moral and spiritual condition of Jerusalem. Just as Western civilization has abandoned its Christian foundations in our time, Judah had abandoned its religious heritage.

---

4. Waltke, *A Commentary on Micah*, 5.

Despite an outward embrace of biblical religion, Jerusalem had turned its heart away from the Lord, and the fruit of its unbelief was rampant corruption and vice.

The Old Testament prophets as a group were greatly concerned with societal standards of justice and mercy. But Micah is particularly pronounced in his concern for civic godliness. In his day the rich got richer and the poor got poorer, often by the most violent and ungodly means. Micah is sometimes considered a defender of the poor, but really he particularly defended what we today call the middle class. Their land was unlawfully seized (Mic. 2:2); deceitful business practices were rife (6:10–12); community and family life had broken down (7:5–6). Above all, Micah denounced the corrupt leaders and false prophets. Leslie Allen writes: "Even religious leaders—priests and prophets—did little more than echo the spirit of the period, buttressing the society that gave them their livelihood."[5]

In both of these respects—our attitude toward outside threats and the reality of our inward spiritual state—the prophet Micah speaks powerfully to our time. For just as Judah's kings had to respond to danger, we too live in a threatening world, and Micah calls us to a calm reliance on our faithful God. And just as Jerusalem's true religion was revealed by its outward conduct, our profession of faith is likewise tested by our obedience to God's Word.

THE WORD OF THE LORD

Perhaps the most important words in this opening verse are the very first: "The word of the LORD that came to Micah." This makes the essential statement, common to all the biblical writers, that what Micah wrote did not originate with himself. John Mackay writes: "The message that follows is not to be attributed to the insight of human genius. It is rather a word *that came*. This message was revealed by divine initiative. Micah does not ask for any credit for having thought it up. What he claims is that it is the *vision he saw*."[6] Notice that the prophet is passive in this action: Micah is the recipient, the action of revelation having been taken by the Lord (Yahweh,

---

5. Leslie C. Allen, *The Books of Joel, Obadiah, Jonah, and Micah*, New International Commentary on the Old Testament (Grand Rapids: Eerdmans, 1976), 240.

6. John L. Mackay, *Jonah, Micah, Nahum, Habakkuk and Zephaniah: God's Just Demands*, Focus on the Bible (Ross–shire, UK: Christian Focus, 1998), 59.

the covenant name of Israel's God, which appears in most English Bibles as LORD, with small capital letters).

The divine authorship of this book of Scripture, as with the rest of the Bible, carries several key implications. One of them is that it is *inerrant*. Certainly the prophet himself was subject to error, as well as bias and sin. But because the all-knowing God of truth is the ultimate author, we may be assured that everything contained in this book—its history, its ethics, and its message of salvation—is true and without error, and thus is completely trustworthy. Secondly, because of its divine authorship, we may interpret Micah in light of the entire Bible. Divine authorship is the basis of the *unity* of the Bible and all its books. What Bruce Waltke says of Micah may be said of the Bible as a whole: "In this book the invisible God becomes audible."[7]

Most importantly, since Micah's message came "from the Lord," it carries the very *authority* of God, and is to be believed and obeyed today. John Calvin comments: "We owe to the Scripture the same reverence which we owe to God, because it has proceeded from Him alone."[8] For the same reason, the message of the prophet Micah is completely *relevant* to us, since God and his ways never change. This is why when New Testament authors cited the Old Testament, they typically described it speaking in the present tense: "As the Holy Spirit says" (Heb. 3:7); "for the Scripture says," writes Paul (1 Tim. 5:18).

To be sure, we must interpret Micah's book in light of his own historical context. But we must not stop there. We must ultimately interpret it in light of the completed revelation of the whole canon of Scripture, with its focus on the saving work of Jesus Christ. Micah's ministry played a role in the unfolding drama of Christ and his gospel, and its most important message is in anticipating, revealing, and, in some of Micah's prophecies, foretelling the coming of Jesus.

Lastly, because of the divine authorship of Scripture, it must be *precious* to all God's people. An example is seen in the coronation service of a king or queen of the United Kingdom. The moderator of the Church of Scotland presents the new monarch with a Bible and utters these words: "The most precious thing this world affords, the most precious thing that

---

7. Waltke, *A Commentary on Micah*, 37.

8. John Calvin, cited from John Piper, *The Legacy of Sovereign Joy: God's Triumphant Grace in the Loves of Augustine, Luther, and Calvin* (Wheaton, Ill.: Crossway, 2000), 137.

this world knows, God's living Word."⁹ So it is, in all its parts, including the Word of the Lord that came to Micah.

THE PROPHETIC MESSAGE OF JUDGMENT

The final statement of verse 1 tells us that, like Dickens' novel, the message of Micah is a tale of two cities: "The word of the LORD that came to Micah of Moresheth . . . which he saw concerning Samaria and Jerusalem." Samaria was the capital of the northern kingdom of Israel, which broke off from Jerusalem during the days of Solomon's son Rehoboam, with ten of Israel's twelve tribes. The history of this kingdom is an unbroken record of evil, idolatry, and apostasy. During Micah's lifetime, the Assyrians would utterly destroy Samaria and deport the ten tribes into historical oblivion. Micah's concern is primarily over Jerusalem, the capital of the southern kingdom: he sees the judgment of Samaria as a dire warning that Jerusalem must heed to avoid divine wrath. Samaria's wound, he says, "is incurable, and it has come to Judah, it has reached to the gate of my people, to Jerusalem" (Mic. 1:9).

With this in mind, Micah is rightly identified as a prophet of doom. His message of divine wrath on sin is in keeping with that of the prophets as a whole; one of the prophets' chief functions was to deliver God's warning of judgment against his faithless people.

This is why the prophetic message of judgment is one of the Bible's most important themes. We can summarize it by asking four key questions. The first is, Does God have expectations and demands of people? This is an important question because many people assume that God really doesn't care how we conduct our individual lives, to say nothing of our corporate behavior in society.

Does God demand anything of us? The answer of the prophets, including Micah, is a resounding "Yes!" Micah's very first message says: "Hear, you peoples, all of you; pay attention, O earth, and all that is in it, and let the Lord GOD be a witness" (Mic. 1:2). Micah's later summary of God's demands declares: "He has told you, O man, what is good; and what does the LORD require of you but to do justice, and to love kindness, and to walk humbly with your God?" (Mic. 6:8). God demands reverent holiness, and Micah preached that

---

9. James M. Boice, *Genesis: An Expositional Commentary*, 3 vols. (Grand Rapids: Baker, 1998), 2:740.

God would come to Jerusalem in judgment for sin: "For behold, the LORD is coming out of his place, and will come down and tread upon the high places of the earth. . . . All this is for the transgression of Jacob and for the sins of the house of Israel" (Mic. 1:3, 5).

One of the dangers of reading these oracles of ancient judgment is to assume that God is talking about someone other than you. James Boice rightly warns:

> When we read of judgment on others we almost sigh in relief, assuming wrongly that if judgment is spoken against them, it is therefore not spoken against us. But this is wrong. God is no respecter of persons. Consequently, if we are going our way and not God's way, as the people of Jerusalem were doing, then we must do as they eventually did and turn back to God. It is the way we ourselves will escape God's judgment.[10]

A second question to ask of Micah's prophecy is, Should sin be rebuked? This is a sensitive topic, because our society generally believes that everyone should mind his own business. But Micah clearly shows that sin is to be exposed and rebuked. There is something deeply wrong with a society that stands by while the innocent are injured and the weak are oppressed. There is something wrong with leaders who make excuses for violence, greed, and hatred. And there is something wrong with individuals who stand by doing and saying nothing while evil is openly worked around them. Micah set a good example for all of us, especially for preachers, when he denounced on God's behalf the sinful ways of the people: "Woe to those who devise wickedness and work evil on their beds!" (2:1). God's judgment on sin has been declared in the Bible, and the only loving thing for Christians to do is to speak out against sin and warn people against God's coming judgment. "Save yourselves from this crooked generation," cried Peter on the day of Pentecost (Acts 2:40). Christians today must likewise sound the warning of Micah and Peter.

Thirdly, we should ask, What are the effects of sin? This, too, is an important question for our times, because it is popularly believed that a happy life is an uninhibited life. But is this true? Not according to Micah, who carefully chronicles not only the sin of Jerusalem but also its misery: "You shall eat,

10. James M. Boice, *The Minor Prophets*, 2 vols. (Grand Rapids: Baker, 1986), 2:316.

but not be satisfied, and there shall be hunger within you; you shall put away, but not preserve, and what you preserve I will give to the sword. You shall sow, but not reap; you shall tread olives, but not anoint yourselves with oil; you shall tread grapes, but not drink wine" (Mic. 6:14–15). These warnings do not pertain to ancient Jerusalem alone: they simply declare that the sinful life is unsatisfying, unsafe, and unsavory. And it is God who makes the sinful life that way. Mark Dever applies this directly to our times:

> We humans have mastered the art of caring about ourselves more than we care about others as well as about God. Yet learning to cultivate our selfish desires by getting drunk, lying, sleeping with someone who is not our spouse, stealing, or murdering both embitters life and belittles our experience of it.[11]

Sin not only brings misery, it also leads to a final judgment from God that is furious, deadly, and eternal. God's judgment meant death for Samaria, as the people simply disappeared into slavery and the nation vanished from history. This would happen to Jerusalem too, unless the city repented, and the same is true for us all. Paul writes of those who are judged in the end: "They will suffer the punishment of eternal destruction, away from the presence of the Lord and from the glory of his might" (2 Thess. 1:9). Jesus speaks even more fearfully, rehearsing the words that multitudes will hear at the end: "Depart from me, you cursed, into the eternal fire prepared for the devil and his angels" (Matt. 25:41). This warning of divine wrath is the message Micah delivered to Jerusalem. He warned of death for the nation and its people, delivering God's uncompromising threat, "I will strike you with a grievous blow, making you desolate because of your sins" (Mic. 6:13).

THE PROPHETIC MESSAGE OF SALVATION

This leaves a fourth and all-important question, Does God offer a way for sinners to escape this judgment? The good news of the prophet Micah—Micah's gospel, we might say—is that the answer is "Yes!" In fact, Micah stands out among the prophets in the sheer beauty and intensity of his message of salvation hope.

11. Mark Dever, *The Message of the Old Testament: Promises Made* (Wheaton, Ill.: Crossway, 2007), 795.

Micah's message of salvation contains three main points. The first is a call to repentance. Here is Micah's good news: Jerusalem can be saved by turning from her evil ways and calling on the Lord. Micah's first section concludes with a promise that God will lead his people to repentance: "I will surely assemble all of you, O Jacob; I will gather the remnant of Israel; I will set them together like sheep in a fold, like a flock in its pasture, a noisy multitude of men" (Mic. 2:12). Micah would live to see this happen when King Hezekiah repented and prayed to God so that the city was delivered. But so deeply ingrained were the habits of sin that a hundred years later Jerusalem was destroyed at God's hand for its persistent sin of idolatry.

Micah's second encouraging message of salvation pertains to the gracious character of God. It turns out that God does not desire to destroy his people, but delights in showing mercy. This is how Micah's third and final section ends, with a celebration of God's marvelous grace: "Who is a God like you, pardoning iniquity and passing over transgression . . . ? He does not retain his anger forever, because he delights in steadfast love. He will again have compassion on us; he will tread our iniquities under foot" (Mic. 7:18–19).

This offers a compelling reason for us to seek salvation from God today. His character has not changed and his promises cannot be broken. If we come to him seeking forgiveness, we will find him ready to offer us mercy and love.

But how can a holy God forgive sinners? The answer is the central point of Micah's salvation message: God will send a Savior to deliver us from his own judgment on our sin. This message forms the heart of the book, at the end of his second section. Here we find Micah's most famous prophecy, announcing the birth of the Savior Jesus Christ:

> But you, O Bethlehem Ephrathah, who are too little to be among the clans of Judah, from you shall come forth for me one who is to be ruler in Israel, whose origin is from of old, from ancient days. . . . And he shall stand and shepherd his flock in the strength of the LORD, in the majesty of the name of the LORD his God. And they shall dwell secure, for now he shall be great to the ends of the earth. And he shall be their peace (Mic. 5:2, 4–5).

Micah foresaw that Jerusalem would eventually be judged for its sins; God's people would suffer death as a nation, trudging off into Babylonian captivity. So how could those consigned to death end up with life? Micah's answer was the coming of a Savior, the Lord Jesus Christ, the Good Shepherd who would lay down his life for his sheep (John 10:15). Israel would receive a Messiah, who alone deserved to live and yet would die for the sins of his people. He would then rise from the grave, and through union with him in faith, the people of God would receive everlasting life. The words Micah spoke to his foes might be more fittingly said by the promised Savior: "Rejoice not over me, O my enemy; when I fall, I shall rise; when I sit in darkness, the LORD will be a light to me" (Mic. 7:8).

Does God offer sinners a way of salvation? Micah's answer is "Yes," and God's answer through him is his promised Son, Jesus Christ. In Christ's fall into death on the cross and then his rise to resurrection life, God's people are delivered from the death we deserve and enter into the eternal life God desires to give. If you believe in Jesus the Savior, his blood will cleanse you of your sins and he will lead you to walk humbly and righteously with your God forever.

15

HEAR, YOU PEOPLES!

Micah 1:2–7

Hear, you peoples, all of you; pay attention, O earth, and all that is in it, and let the Lord GOD be a witness against you, the Lord from his holy temple. (Mic. 1:2)

icah is a book of prophecy. A prophet both forthtold— speaking from God about the present, and foretold— speaking from God about the future. Typically, a prophet preached in the form of an oracle, that is, a divine utterance. There are oracles of judgment, condemning sin and foretelling divine wrath, and there are oracles of salvation, which promise redemption for God's people. The book of Micah is composed of these two kinds of oracles, summing up the prophet's preaching in Jerusalem in the late eighth and early seventh centuries B.C. Each of the oracles may be seen as a sermon outline. David Prior describes the book of Micah as "a distillation of what must have been a costly, demanding and . . . extremely unpopular ministry."[1]

Micah presents his oracles of judgment and salvation in three cycles, each of which begins with a call to hear the Word of God (1:2; 3:1; 6:1). The first

---

1. David Prior, *The Message of Joel, Micah & Habakkuk*, The Bible Speaks Today (Downers Grove, Ill.: InterVarsity, 1998), 103.

cycle begins with the oracle of judgment in 1:2–7, probably preached in the early days of Micah's ministry, during the reign of Jotham. Judah had enjoyed peace and prosperity during the fifty-two years of Uzziah's kingship (792–740 B.C.). Overall, affairs were not perfect, but the times were not too bad. To the north, Samaria, the capital of Israel, had grown rich and decadent, and troubling noises were heard from a resurgent Assyria. If trouble was coming, it seemed far off. If there was a need for reformation, there seemed to be plenty of time, with no immediate worries. Into this scene, the prophet Micah began his ministry by calling the people to listen to the accusations of God.

A CALL TO HEAR

Micah's first oracle thus began with a call for all people to listen to God: "Hear, you peoples, all of you; pay attention, O earth, and all that is in it, and let the Lord GOD be a witness against you, the Lord from his holy temple" (Mic. 1:2).

The great need of every generation is to pay attention to God. Yet the recurrent theme of history is that people tend to forget God, especially when times are good. But we forget God at our peril, as we are easily lulled into a false security. Grave danger may be right around the corner, but we don't know it. The causes of danger are in our midst, but we don't recognize them. "Hear, you peoples," then, is the message we always need. God speaks to us today in the Bible, and if we are too fixed in our ways to listen to God we will pay a steep price for our folly.

Micah's first oracle is deliberately universal: he calls not merely Jerusalem but all the earth to attend to God's Word. This asserts the sovereignty of God over all, as stated in Micah's expression, "the Lord GOD," which translates literally as "sovereign Yahweh" (Mic. 1:2). Micah is about to describe the great political and military affairs of his time as acts of divine sovereignty; he insists that the explanation for all history is theological.

Even though God is going to deal with Israel, he summons the nations to teach them a vital lesson. For God's dealings with his people always have a universal importance, speaking to everyone at all times. The great events of the time resulted from God's anger over his people's sins, and the Lord's

146

punishment of Samaria and Jerusalem, announced by Micah, served as a model for his future judgment of all the earth.

FIRE ON THE MOUNTAINS

False security was the hallmark of God's people during the reign of Jotham. They wrongly expected Assyria to remain quiet, but even more wrongly expected the Lord to tolerate their sins. Were they not, after all, the people of God? Was not Jerusalem the place where God dwelt in his temple? How could God judge his own beloved city? This was the presumption with which Jerusalem justified its decadence and idolatry. But Micah reminded them that the temple was home to a holy God: "Behold, the LORD is coming out of his place, and will come down and tread upon the high places of the earth" (Mic. 1:3).

The religious leaders serving in Jerusalem's temple might speak lightly about sin, but the Lord who dwells in the heavenly temple will come to "tread upon the high places of the earth." High places were strategic military positions, and mountain peaks symbolized unassailable might. Micah probably refers to Samaria and Jerusalem, both of which were built on mountains— Jerusalem especially resting in seeming security on its high terrain. Moreover, this expression may refer to the ruling classes, those who are high and mighty among God's people. Jerusalem on high was the source of Judah's mounting sinfulness, and its leaders promoted this new decadence. Lastly, "high places" is biblical terminology for the mounts on which pagan worship was offered to false gods such as Baal and Asherah. God would come from his holy temple and tread upon such high places.

More threatening still is the effect of God's coming: "And the mountains will melt under him, and the valleys will split open, like wax before the fire, like waters poured down a steep place" (Mic. 1:4). This is classic prophetic language, describing the coming of God in terms of natural cataclysm. The point of this description of mountains melting and valleys split is not just to show God's power over nature, but to emphasize his terrifying might against rebellious mankind. The ancient church scholar Jerome said: "As wax cannot endure the nearness of the fire, and as the waters are carried headlong, so all of the ungodly, when the Lord comes, shall be dissolved and disappear."[2] John

2. Jerome, in Alberto Ferreiro, ed., The Twelve Prophets, Ancient Christian Commentary on Scripture, Old Testament XIV (Downers Grove, Ill.: InterVarsity, 2003), 152.

Calvin writes: "Such figures of speech symbolize how defenseless we are, how totally unable to resist God. For if God should suddenly appear, who could withstand his furor?"[3] Ultimately, the scene of creation melting at God's approach belongs to the last day, but that final judgment "is anticipated in every prior intervention of God in judgment in the affairs of men."[4]

With this prophetic language, Micah foretold the coming of Assyria's armies to invade and conquer Samaria, and to threaten Jerusalem. Bruce Waltke explains: "The blind eyes of unbelievers saw only the immediate cause of Samaria's fall, the inexorable march of Assyria's crack international army under the leadership of its brilliant kings. But Micah's open eyes saw behind the juggernaut the invincible march of God."[5]

The same situation exists today, as secular humanists look upon the increasingly tenuous state of Western civilization, yet never dream that God might be acting to judge our sins. In that ancient world God sent forth his prophets to denounce false worship, and the sins that it engendered: societal injustice, sexual defilement, and decadent materialism. In our world God calls for his church to honor him with true worship and speak out against these same evils. Unless the people repent, Micah says, "The Lord is coming out of his place, and will . . . tread upon the high places of the earth" (Mic. 1:3).

Judgment on the House of God

One common feature of prophetic literature is irony. It fell to the prophets to declare what the people never imagined possible. This is probably the case in Micah's first oracle. Until this time in the Bible, the vision of God coming from heaven was a welcome one, signaling the overthrow of Israel's enemies. Recall the exodus from Egypt: it was through cataclysmic judgments on Pharaoh that the people of God were set free. The same was true during the days of Joshua, when God caused the sun to stand still to allow the Israelites to complete their victory over the Canaanites (Josh. 10:12–14).

So up to this point in his sermon, Micah may have been praised by his listeners. God was coming to judge the wicked, which surely meant nations

3. John Calvin, *Sermons on the Book of Micah* (Phillipsburg, NJ: P&R Publishing, 2003), 25.

4. John L. Mackay, *Jonah, Micah, Nahum, Habakkuk and Zephaniah: God's Just Demands*, Focus on the Bible (Ross–shire, UK: Christian Focus, 1998), 64.

5. Bruce Waltke, *A Commentary on Micah* (Grand Rapids: Eerdmans, 2007), 58.

like Assyria. But Micah gets more specific: "All this is for the transgression of Jacob and for the sins of the house of Israel. What is the transgression of Jacob? Is it not Samaria?" (Mic. 1:5).

In speaking of Jacob and the house of Israel, Micah refers to the northern kingdom, whose capital was Samaria. It is their judgment that God comes to bring. This, too, would have won approval in Jerusalem. Had not the ten northern tribes rebelled against the Davidic throne? Had they not set up false rivals to the true temple in Jerusalem? Was not Samaria a veritable snake pit of sensuality, greed, and idolatry? How appropriate for God to judge Samaria!

It is true that Micah's oracle directly concerns the destruction of Samaria, which God engineered at the hands of the Assyrian kings Shalmaneser V and his son Sargon. Yet the target of this oracle is really the people of Jerusalem. Therefore, Micah continues: "And what is the high place of Judah? Is it not Jerusalem?" (Mic. 1:5).

This stunning declaration is the turning point in Micah's sermon. Up to this point, the people would have been relieved. God will destroy Samaria: how fitting! But then the knife comes home. Has not Jerusalem become like Samaria? Are not the sins of Samaria the very sins currently cherished in Jerusalem? God is coming to trample the high places: but look around and notice that Judah's capital itself is one such high place in its arrogance and idolatry.

What a shock this must have been to Micah's hearers. They were the heirs of Abraham, Moses, and David, the people who possessed the Bible and worshiped at God's true temple. Yet corruption had set in. False worship was tolerated. Sexual promiscuity had become common. Greed dominated civic government, injustice grew rife, and the ruling class oppressed those beneath them. God had warned Jerusalem through the prophet Amos, but few had listened. Now, under the weak leadership of King Jotham, God was setting up Jerusalem for fire and destruction. God would come to judge, for, as the apostle Peter later wrote, "It is time for judgment to begin at the household of God" (1 Peter 4:17).

Do we see how similar this situation is to that of the Christian church in the West today? We are the heirs of faithful generations, but presuming on God's kindness, the Christian church has tolerated man-centered worship, false doctrine, and unholy living. Like Jerusalem of old, Christians in the

West look out and see a culture awash in moral depravity. In comparison, we think we are doing pretty well. But the Lord says, "No, I am coming to cleanse *you*, my people. The problem is not how the world is living, but how the church is living. Your loose sexuality, your lack of interest in my Word, your self-absorbed approach to worship, your lack of mercy for the needy and poor, your low motivation for evangelism—for these and many other sins I am causing your labors to fail, permitting your children to stray, and allowing the wicked to achieve their aims." This is how Micah's message relates to the church today. We see what is happening in the world and affirm God's judgment on it. But God applies his Word directly to us, saying, "The church has become like the world, worshiping the world's false gods, and so will fall under my judgment."

In this way, the judgment promised for Samaria was also being threatened upon Jerusalem. Micah's oracle says that God would come to judge two things: transgression and sin. "All this is for the transgression of Jacob and for the sins of the house of Israel" (Mic. 1:5). Transgression (Hebrew, *peshah*) means rebellion against God's commands. It encompasses both the actions that violate God's Word and the rebellious heart that wills those actions. The word for sin (Hebrew, *hattat*) means to be wayward and to fall short. Put together, transgression and sin spelled Israel's comprehensive breaking of God's covenant, especially in Samaria's rampant idolatry.

The story of Samaria's fall is recorded in 2 Kings 17, which tells of Shalmaneser's siege and the city's fall. But the explanation is theological and covenantal:

> This occurred because the people of Israel had sinned against the LORD their God . . . and had feared other gods and walked in the customs of the nations whom the LORD drove out before the people of Israel . . . . They built for themselves high places in all their towns, from watchtower to fortified city. They set up for themselves pillars and Asherim on every high hill and under every green tree, and there they made offerings on all the high places, as the nations did whom the LORD carried away before them. . . . of which the LORD had said to them, "You shall not do this." Yet the LORD warned Israel and Judah by every prophet and every seer, saying, "Turn from your evil ways and keep my commandments and my statutes . . . ." But they would not listen, but were stubborn, as their fathers had been, who did not believe in the LORD their God. They despised his statutes

and his covenant that he made with their fathers and the warnings that he gave them (2 Kings 17:7–15).

The passage goes on to cite the city's most abominable sins, including the burning of their children in idol worship. For these transgressions and sins, "the LORD was very angry with Israel and removed them out of his sight. None was left but the tribe of Judah only" (2 Kings 17:18). But the writer of Kings adds this note, which was Micah's particular point: "Judah also did not keep the commandments of the LORD their God, but walked in the customs that Israel had introduced" (2 Kings 17:19). Therefore Jerusalem, along with all the world, including the Bible's readers today, should take heed of God's judgment on the transgressions and sins of Samaria. "Keep watch on yourself, lest you too be tempted," warns the apostle Paul. "God is not mocked, for whatever one sows, that will he also reap" (Gal. 6:1, 7).

JUDGMENT EXPERIENCED

Micah's first oracle concludes with a two-pointed description of Samaria's experience of God's judgment. First, all that Israel had built in rebellion to God would be cast down: "Therefore I will make Samaria a heap in the open country, a place for planting vineyards, and I will pour down her stones into the valley and uncover her foundations" (Mic. 1:6).

The city of Samaria was founded by Israel's King Omri and completed by his son, Ahab. These ruthless kings were brilliant and wicked statesmen and empire builders, with Samaria as their crown jewel. The city was constructed of "exquisitely dressed stone—a style of masonry dressing which was not equaled in Palestine, or indeed anywhere else in the Near East."[6] Ahab added a gorgeous palace, built in the highest luxury. Instead of being a light in the darkness, Samaria became a den of sensual indulgence and idolatry. The prophet Amos rebuked Samaria for its decadent affluence: "Woe to those who lie on beds of ivory and stretch themselves out on their couches" (Amos 6:4).

But God would cast it all down: "[The Lord] used the battering rams of the Assyrian army under Shalmaneser V to carry out his sentence against . . .

6. K. M. Kenyon, cited in Waltke, *A Commentary on Micah*, 58.

the proud stones of her retaining walls and royal residence."[7] The haughty city would become "a heap in the open country," like a pile of stones a farmer tosses up beside his fields. It would become "a place for planting vineyards." This meant a complete undoing of all that Israel had built, since Samaria previously had been a land of vines. "And I will pour down her stones into the valley and uncover her foundations" (Mic. 1:6). The whole site would be leveled in shame. In fact, the Assyrians did not demolish Samaria in quite this way; Shalmaneser's successor, Sargon, rebuilt the city for his own use. But the words did come true in due time, when Judah's John Hyrcanus completed Samaria's demolition in 107 B.C.

God not only tore down all that the idolaters had built, but he also smashed and disgraced the idols they served: "All her carved images shall be beaten to pieces, all her wages shall be burned with fire, and all her idols I will lay waste, for from the fee of a prostitute she gathered them, and to the fee of a prostitute they shall return" (Mic. 1:7).

We should note well the link between sexual sin and idolatry, because pagan worship typically involved a sex-offering to the gods. The luxurious artifacts that fill today's museums were paid for by offerings to the cultic prostitutes at the high places, in the belief that through ritual sex "the forces of life in nature . . . were revived . . . ensuring fertility of the crops and of the wombs."[8] David Prior warns that this union of magic and sexual promiscuity is replicated in the New Age practices of our time. One need only read Dan Brown's mega-best-selling novel *The Da Vinci Code* to see the worship of Samaria being revived today. Whether under the guise of mother-earth Gaia, sophisticated talk of ying and yang, or explicit references to ancient idols such as Isis and Osiris, "they all turn out to be another recycling of pagan beliefs which place no moral obligations or boundaries on their adherents, pander to our naturally self-centered desires, and constitute a direct rejection of our creator God."[9]

God's judgment typically involves the handing over of idolaters into total bondage to the idols they worshiped (see Rom. 1:24). Such was the case for Israel as the northern kingdom was marched off in chains to inner Assyria. There, the spoils of their city would be offered in payment to other cultic

7. Waltke, *A Commentary on Micah*, 52.
8. Prior, *The Message of Joel, Micah & Habakkuk*, 116.
9. Ibid.

prostitutes and used to adorn pagan temples. Micah explains: "for from the fee of a prostitute she gathered them, and to the fee of a prostitute they shall return" (Mic. 1:7).

All of this prefigures a greater judgment that will occur at the end of history in the return of Jesus Christ. Then, God will act not merely through surrogate armies like that of Assyria, but the Lord Jesus himself will come with wrath and divine war. In the book of Revelation, the apostle John records seeing heaven open and the Lord appearing on a white horse: "In righteousness he judges and makes war. . . . From his mouth comes a sharp sword with which to strike down the nations, and he will rule them with a rod of iron. He will tread the winepress of the fury of the wrath of God the Almighty" (Rev. 19:11, 15). Christ will then establish his own eternal city. The angel said to John: "Blessed are those who wash their robes, so that they may have the right to the tree of life and that they may enter the city by the gates. Outside are the dogs and sorcerers and the sexually immoral and murderers and idolaters, and everyone who loves and practices falsehood" (Rev. 22:14–15).

This prospect raises questions. What are you building in this life? Are you living for the glory of God and the advance of his kingdom? Or are you piling up the luxuries of the world so as to enjoy the lifestyle of idolatry? The Bible says, "Each one's work will become manifest, for the Day will disclose it, because it will be revealed by fire, and the fire will test what sort of work each one has done" (1 Cor. 3:13). All that is built for the praise of man and the service of sin will be destroyed in God's coming judgment. Then there is an even more important question: What god do you worship and serve? In what do you trust for your life and lifestyle? The only true God is the God of the Bible, and the only true Savior is the Lord Jesus Christ, who gained our forgiveness with his own blood on the cross. When he returns, all false gods and those who trust them will be put to the sword of divine wrath, but those who trust in Jesus Christ will be saved.

A SIMPLE WAY TO ESCAPE JUDGMENT

Micah presents us with a fearful message of divine wrath. But he also offers us a simple way to escape God's judgment. It comes in the very first word of Micah's first oracle: "Hear." It was a failure to hear that ultimately caused Samaria's demise and threatened Jerusalem with the same. God sent his prophets, but his wicked people would not listen. Micah's prophecy still speaks to our world today. God's Word speaks to you. If you will hear and listen, then you will fear the Lord and turn from your transgressions and sins.

Fortunately, God did not stop speaking to the world with the prophets. In time, he sent the Great Prophet, his own Son, Jesus Christ. Jesus called out to the world with a message of mercy and grace, a call of forgiveness and new life through faith in him. Jesus will deliver you from God's judgment on your sins. "Truly, truly, I say to you," Jesus declares, "whoever hears my word and believes him who sent me has eternal life. He does not come into judgment, but has passed from death to life" (John 5:24). Hear, listen, and believe on Jesus Christ, and you will be saved.

Finally, Jesus calls on his people in the church to hear his Word and obey his commands. "I am the light of the world. Whoever follows me will not walk in darkness, but will have the light of life" (John 8:12). Are you walking in the light of Christ, or are you dabbling in the darkness of sin and worldliness? If you are not following Jesus in a holy life, then remember God's threat to chastise Jerusalem. Yes, God will destroy Samaria—but what of Jerusalem and its very same sins? Do not walk in darkness. Follow Jesus, and you will have the light of his life.

16

A Death in the Family

Micah 1:8–16

For this I will lament and wail; I will go stripped and naked;
I will make lamentation like the jackals, and mourning like
the ostriches. (Mic. 1:8)

One of the most endearing moments of King David's life was his response to news of his rival King Saul's death. Given the way Saul had persecuted him, we might expect David to spew out bitter venom: "It's only what Saul deserved!" But instead, David wept in lament for King Saul: "Your glory, O Israel, is slain on your high places! How the mighty have fallen! . . . You daughters of Israel, weep over Saul" (2 Sam. 1:19, 24). Despite all his failings in life, it is no wonder that God called David "a man after his own heart" (1 Sam. 13:14). While David suffered under Saul's sins, he always looked on him as what God had made him: the anointed king of the holy nation, a man of valor and might, with heroic potential—even if that potential was never achieved.

Lamentation for Samaria

A parallel to David's song of lament for King Saul is found in the prophet Micah's lament for fallen Samaria. His first oracle pronounced God's judgment on the northern kingdom of Israel and the demolition of its capital, Samaria. Since Judah and Israel were estranged, we might expect him to gloat over this development, but instead Micah takes up a funeral lament of great intensity: "For this I will lament and wail; I will go stripped and naked; I will make lamentation like the jackals, and mourning like the ostriches" (Mic. 1:8). Jews are known for their intense and vocal mourning, and Micah enters into such grieving for the loss of Samaria. Walter Kaiser comments: "As a sign of his grief, he goes about naked (v. 8). His wail is like the banshee cries of jackals and the gruesome screech of the ostrich (v. 8). The jackals and ostriches embody wildness and desolation."[1] In this way, Micah vents the frustration and pain of his heart over "a nation that could have been saved if she had listened to the repeated warnings from God's prophets."[2]

Micah lists two reasons for this intense public lament. First, he will lament and wail "for this"—for the promised destruction of Samaria. Micah never forgot who the Samarians were, no matter how wayward they became or how hostile to God's Word: Samaria was the capital of Israel, and Israel was the holy nation of God. John Calvin observes, "they were yet a part of the holy race, they were the children of Abraham, whom God had received into favour. . . . The Prophet . . . shows the fraternal love which he entertained for the children of Israel, as they were his kindred, and a part of the chosen people."[3]

Micah's lament understands the conquest of Samaria and the exile of the ten northern tribes as a death in the family. Family members may have their differences, but when a brother or sister dies it is time to mourn and lament. Israel had lost forever that portion of the Promised Land assigned to them by God. They lost their identity, their culture, and all ties to their God. The conquest and exile of Israel, completed by the Assyrians in 722 B.C., was the death of a people who were God's covenant children, however wayward.

And it was God who put them to death. They had given their land over to idol worship, so after decades of patient warnings, God took their land away. They had debased their culture with immorality and saturated their religion with false worship and teaching, so God gave them over completely to the pagan idolatry they had come to love. The ten tribes disappeared from

---

1. Walter C. Kaiser Jr., *Micah–Malachi*, The Communicator's Commentary (Dallas: Word, 1992), 34.
2. Ibid.
3. John Calvin, *A Commentary on the Twelve Minor Prophets*, 5 vols. (1559; repr. Edinburgh: Banner of Truth, 1986), 3:171.

history and will never be found, for God executed his penalty of death on their transgressions and sins. The judgment of Samaria was a foretaste of the final judgment of all the world for its sins. Yet for all his disgust with the sins of Israel, Micah rightly lamented and wailed.

It is apparent that Micah's funeral mourning took place before Samaria's fall, for he says "her wound is incurable" (Mic. 1:9). He knew that God's decision to judge Samaria was final and that her hardness of heart made Israel beyond repentance. But he also laments for a second reason: "For . . . it has come to Judah; it has reached to the gate of my people, to Jerusalem" (Mic. 1:9). The kingdom of Judah, with the tribes of Judah and Benjamin, had been infected with Israel's disease of idolatry, and the prophet foretells that the disaster that befell Samaria will come to the very gates of Jerusalem. It is for the benefit of Jerusalem that he laments: clad only in a loincloth, the prophet sounded the calls of jackals and ostriches in the streets of God's holy city, arousing Jerusalem to recognize this plague that threatened the whole family.

The reader of the New Testament cannot fail to compare Micah's actions with those of the Lord Jesus Christ during his final and fatal visit to Jerusalem. Jesus presented himself as the last and greatest of the prophets, crying out to arouse the Jews from their unbelief and lamenting the destruction they would experience as a result. Looking upon Jerusalem just days before his crucifixion, Jesus mournfully cried: "O Jerusalem, Jerusalem, the city that kills the prophets and stones those who are sent to it! How often would I have gathered your children together as a hen gathers her brood under her wings, and you would not! See, your house is left to you desolate" (Matt. 23:37–38).

Christians should look on a godless world through these same eyes of Christ. Do we weep over the lost state of the world? Are our hearts burdened over the judgment that family and friends are securing by their stubborn unbelief? Like Jesus and the prophets, we are to tell people the truth about the death that awaits them in hell unless they repent of their sins. But notice the attitude with which we should announce God's judgment. People are offended by the Bible's prophetic message, but what if they saw tears in our eyes and a heart that is broken for them? How heartless it is when Christians denounce the sins of the culture, but make little effort to point out the way to God's mercy through faith in the blood of Christ.

157

Tell It Not in Gath

Micah seems deliberately to associate his prophetic grief with the earlier grief of David over fallen King Saul. From verse 10 to verse 15, his oracle speaks of disaster befalling the cities of Judah. He puts bookends on this section with two references to David's darkest hours. First, he says, "Tell it not in Gath" (Mic. 1:10). Gath was the hometown of the giant Goliath, to which David foolishly fled from King Saul and ended up disgracing himself before the Philistines. The last reference, in verse 15, is to Adullam. It was in the caves of Adullam that David found refuge from Saul's violent attempts on his life. This suggests that God's judgment on Samaria and Jerusalem meant the undoing of David's kingdom and a return to the time when David and his band were holed up in caves.

"Tell it not in Gath," is also a direct quote from David's funeral dirge over Saul. The full citation reads: "Tell it not in Gath, publish it not in the streets of Ashkelon, lest the daughters of the Philistines rejoice, lest the daughters of the uncircumcised exult" (2 Sam. 1:20). David's point, picked up by Micah, is that the Jews should avoid exulting over Samaria's deserved judgment, because this would give the unbelieving world a cause to rejoice in Israel's downfall.

Nothing so delights the unbelieving world as to see God's people falling under divine chastisement. Therefore, "Micah did not want the pagan people of Gath to have the pleasure of gloating over the downfall of God's people."[4] David prayed that God would not allow his enemies to jeer on his account (Pss. 30:1; 89:49–51), and it should be our desire to live in obedience to God so the world will not have reason to scoff. Micah was not only concerned for God's glory, but he also realized that the Gaths of the world had no hope of salvation so long as they disparaged God's holy name. Salvation came only through faith in Israel's God. We, too, should be motivated evangelistically in the example we set before the world.

It was too late for this when it came to the downfall of Samaria and God's judgment on Jerusalem. Even though Micah urges the people, "weep not at all" (Mic. 1:10), what follows shows that the coming calamity was so great that weeping would be inevitable. The prophet thus reminds us that believers

---

4. Kenneth L. Barker and Waylon Bailey, *Micah, Nahum, Habbakuk, Zephaniah*, The New American Commentary (Nashville: Broadman & Holman, 1999), 57.

in crisis should conduct themselves with an aim to the glory of God and the witness of his gospel in the world.

Disaster at the Gates

After the Assyrian king Shalmaneser V captured Samaria in 722 B.C., his successor Sargon moved south to invade Philistia, along the seacoast directly to the west of Judah. Then, in 701 B.C., his successor Sennacherib turned toward Jerusalem. While the city was spared by the divine intervention recorded by the prophet Isaiah, the outlying region known as the Shephelah was overrun. These were the agricultural communities in the valleys and foothills between Jerusalem and the sea, as well as the military fortresses that guarded the approaches to the capital. Both the Bible and secular history record that Sennacherib captured this entire region; according to his royal records, the Assyrian took into exile two hundred thousand Jewish slaves. While Jerusalem itself was spared, so great was the calamity that disaster came to the very gates of the city.

Micah foretells this by making puns from the names of ten cities in the Shephelah. For instance, the name Beth-le-aphrah meant "house of dust," so Micah says, "Beth-le-aphrah, roll yourselves in the dust" (Mic. 1:10). There is no mere wordplay in this. Rather, the prophet takes the place-names as omens of doom in God's judgment for their sin. For an English-language equivalent, imagine a Scottish preacher declaring, "Crieff will know grief. Forfar will forfeit. Craill will be frail. Wick will be burned. Stornaway will be blown away. Edinburgh will be no Eden. For Tain, there will only be pain."[5]

The first town Micah mentioned is Beth-le-aphrah, named "dust-town." He says, "In Beth-le-aphrah roll yourselves in the dust" (Mic. 1:10). This was the most intense mourning, by which the people would throw themselves on the ground and roll in the dust to express their grief.

The second city is Shaphir, which means "beauty." To them he cries, "Pass on your way, inhabitants of Shaphir, in nakedness and shame" (Mic. 1:11). Depending on her attire, a beautiful woman may be either a delight or a disgrace. Micah foretells that Shaphir's sin would produce the latter. Third is

---

5. Cited from Peter C. Craigie, *Twelve Prophets*, Daily Study Bible series 2 vols. (Louisville: Westminster John Knox, 1985), 2:14.

Zaanan, meaning "going out": "the inhabitants of Zaanan do not come out" (Mic. 1:11). Just as the beautiful city will be disgraced, the people of "going-out town" will be shut up behind their walls until their city falls.

Next is Beth-ezel, which probably means "standing place." So Micah writes, "The lamentation of Beth-ezel shall take away from you its standing place" (Mic. 1:11). Just as the people of Zaanan "did not come forth to help the inhabitants of Shaphir, Beth-le-ezel offers no defense either because its mourning inhabitants have been deported."[6] Similarly, Micah predicts, "The inhabitants of Maroth wait anxiously for good, because disaster has come down from the LORD to the gate of Jerusalem" (Mic. 1:12). Maroth comes from the word for "bitter," and though the people there seek the sweetness of peace and prosperity, their fate as slaves will be bitter indeed.

When Micah turns to his sixth city, Lachish, he makes an important note: "Harness the steeds to the chariots, inhabitants of Lachish; it was the beginning of sin to the daughter of Zion, for in you were found the transgressions of Israel" (Mic. 1:13). Lachish was one of King Solomon's chariot cities and an important fortress. First Kings 10:26 states that Solomon recruited 1,400 chariots and 12,000 horsemen, which he stationed in the chariot cities. But this violated God's commands, since Israel was to rely not on military technology but on God's might alone. Psalm 20:7 says, "Some trust in chariots and some in horses, but we trust in the name of the LORD our God." By recruiting his cutting-edge force of chariots, Solomon was hedging his reliance on God by appealing to worldly sources of security.

According to Micah, this is how a sinful lifestyle starts: by adopting secular priorities and resorting to worldly strategies for security and prosperity. "It was the beginning of sin to the daughter of Zion," Micah says of Lachish. Secularism always fails, so the people of Lachish will "harness the steeds to the chariots." The word for *steeds* (Hebrew, *rekesh*) is that for racehorses, not warhorses. When the Assyrians came, the chariots of Lachish would be used not for attack but for a hasty flight to safety. Sennacherib's capture of this fortress was so significant that relief sculptures from his palace in Nineveh cite the capture of Lachish as one of his greatest triumphs.

This reminds us of the important principle that nothing of this world is a true source of safety. America has the words "In God We Trust" on our

6. Bruce Waltke, *A Commentary on Micah* (Grand Rapids: Eerdmans, 2007), 77.

coins, but the reality is that it is the coin itself that we really trust, along with the hardware it enables us to buy. Chariots were cutting-edge technology in Solomon's day. But Bruce Waltke warns us: "People like those at Lachish, who trust the latest technology instead of God, will fall into all kinds of sins that spring from man's autonomous, rebellious spirit. Their technology will prove worthless in the time of God's judgment against sin."[7]

What Judah's kings should have done was to purge from their midst the leaven of secularism in places like Lachish, for, Micah says, "in you were found the transgressions of Israel" (Mic. 1:13). We, too, will either purge the seedbeds of worldliness from our lives or be corrupted by them into sin and judgment. For example, many Christians are practically addicted to television shows that advocate sexual promiscuity, crass speech, and a general self-centeredness. This secular influence leads them into these same sins. This also happens on a national level. Waltke comments, "Modern cities like Hollywood promote adultery, and like Reno or Las Vegas give impetus to easy divorce and gambling, and like San Francisco give status to homosexuals."[8] The influence of such places must inevitably spread, ultimately causing God to come in judgment for sin.

If Lachish was the source of Judah's sin, the final four cities mentioned by Micah illustrate the wages of sin. The first is Micah's own hometown of Moresheth: "Therefore you shall give parting gifts to Moresheth-gath" (Mic. 1:14). Moresheth sounds like the Hebrew word for "bride," and Moresheth will be offered as a bridal gift to the king of Assyria.

Achzib means "deceitful," and it "shall be a deceitful thing to the kings of Israel" (Mic. 1:14). Any trust placed in this city by Jerusalem's king will be betrayed when invasion comes. Likewise, Micah cries, "I will again bring a conqueror to you, inhabitants of Mareshah" (Mic. 1:15). This name sounds like the word for "possessions gained by conquest," but instead Mareshah will be forfeited by conquest. As a result, Micah prophesies, "The glory of Israel shall come to Adullam" (Mic. 1:15). Adullam was the cave region seven miles northeast of Mareshah, where David gathered an army from those dispossessed by King Saul. But now it will be "the glory of Israel" that is penned in and gathered for captivity; since David's lament for King Saul referred to him as "your glory, O Israel." This probably refers to the aristocratic families and

7. Ibid., 90.
8. Ibid.

their children. It is often said that "the children are our future," and Judah's future would be deported for slavery to the inner regions of Assyria.

Micah's inventory of these calamities prompts some reflections. The first is that everything good we have is granted to us by God. Just as God has given us all things, God is able to take them away. If we fail to be thankful to God or if we put our trust in the gifts rather than in the divine Giver, we can expect God to take his blessings away. Are we trusting in retirement accounts or real estate holdings? God is perfectly able to cause the markets to crash and real estate values to plummet. Are we trusting in armed might? God is able to bring our armies to defeat. So it is with every worldly blessing: God's people are to receive them thankfully and in stewardship to God. But the only things worthy of our faith are the grace of God for those who trust in him and the promises of his Word.

Secondly, we should realize that sin often appeals to us as something that will give us pleasure, success, and security. But sin never works out this way. Walter Kaiser responds to Micah's catalogue of judgment by asking, "In retrospect, I wonder if the sins of Israel and Judah were worth all the trouble that resulted?"[9] The obvious answer is that they were not. Neither are the sins we cherish. John Calvin comments: "If ever there was a city that God wanted to spare, it was Jerusalem. Nevertheless, Micah proclaims that its downfall is coming. Hence, his purpose is to show that, wherever iniquity reigns, God's judgment will come to pass. No place of sanctity or position of privilege will protect anyone, for our Lord judges with complete impartiality."[10]

CHILDREN INTO EXILE

Micah began his message with his own intense lamenting over the fall of Samaria, which he saw as a death in God's family, and he concludes by calling the people of Jerusalem to lament for deaths that would take place in their own families. He writes: "Make yourselves bald and cut off your hair, for the children of your delight; make yourselves as bald as the eagle, for they shall go from you into exile" (Mic. 1:16). The prophet refers the people to the practice of cutting the hair as an expression of grief. Micah cites the

9. Kaiser, *Micah–Malachi*, 37.
10. John Calvin, *Sermons on the Book of Micah* (Phillipsburg, NJ: P&R Publishing, 2003), 55.

bald-appearing head of an eagle or vulture and urges that the people shave their heads to create a similar effect.

The calamity Micah predicts for the towns of the Shephelah was the greatest kind of disaster known to the ancient world. Armies of the wicked would overrun the country, despoiling and destroying. Communities where children played in the street and neighbors gathered in friendship would be consumed in fire and blood. Worst of all, "the children of your delight . . . shall go from you into exile" (Mic. 1:16). Imagine being a parent who escaped behind the walls of Jerusalem, only to realize that your children have been captured and even now are bound in chains to be enslaved in a far land from which they will never return. Could anything be more grievous? Wake up from your sinful slumber, Micah cries! Realize what is coming and lament intensely for what your sins are bringing upon you!

The same cry needs to be sounded in our generation. In the towns and cities where we live, babies are slaughtered inside their mothers' wombs, promising lives are destroyed in the insanity of drug abuse, and innocents are abused by men whose hearts are twisted by pornography. God will judge all these things. But if we can go about our comfortable lives, knowing all this but saying nothing, doing nothing, and feeling nothing, then something is just as wrong with us as it was with Micah's original audience. Even more pointedly, if we are participating in the sins that are consuming our society—including sins of materialism, racism, sexual impurity, and sensually hedonistic entertainment—our hearts should be mortified by the realization of what is being reaped from what we are sowing. Realizing also that one consequence of our worldliness may be the loss of our own children to the bondage of sin—and ultimately, perhaps, to hell—we should wake up and lament before it is too late.

A Call for Godly Grief

It has been said that those who forget the lessons of history are doomed to repeat them. Unless the ways of God have changed since the time of the Bible—and they have not—then our society is poised on the brink of a judgment every bit as fierce as that which befell Judah. If God did not spare the towns listed by Micah, filled with his own covenant people, and if God ultimately did not spare the holy city of Jerusalem the judgment for its sins, he will most certainly not spare America or the other nations of the decadent West.

Micah called the people to bitterly lament the loss they would suffer for their sins. But his ultimate purpose was to seek a greater and deeper repentance. True repentance is not merely a grieving over sin's loss, but a grieving over sin itself and for the offense it has caused to our loving and holy God. The apostle Paul differentiated between worldly and godly grief. "Worldly grief produces death," he wrote, meaning that sorrowing over the consequences of sin provides no remedy. But godly grief is different, he said: "For godly grief produces a repentance that leads to salvation without regret" (2 Cor. 7:10).

Godly grief is that which mourns over the sin itself and the alienation from God that results. Godly grief does not merely sorrow but repents: that is, it turns from sin and turns to God for mercy and grace. This is the good news of the gospel of Jesus Christ, that the same holy God who must punish all sin is also a loving God who delights in showing mercy to those who repent and believe. This is the message to which Micah is leading his readers. He says at the end of his prophecy: "Who is a God like you, pardoning iniquity and passing over transgression for the remnant of his inheritance? He does not retain his anger forever, because he delights in steadfast love. He will again have compassion on us; he will tread our iniquities under foot. You will cast all our sins into the depths of the sea" (Mic. 7:18–19).

Salvation could still be had by Jerusalem if it turned in faith to the God of all grace, the God whose temple stood in their city and whose Word had been entrusted to them. And salvation can be had by us today, no matter how great our sins, because that same God fulfilled his promises of old and sent his Son to bear our sins on the cross. With this in mind, let me conclude with words from the end of John Calvin's sermon on this text:

> Now, let us observe that what Micah was saying to his time applies also to ours. What must we do, then? Since our Lord graciously wishes to govern us, let us be subject to him in everything. Let us learn to place ourselves again in his hand; and, since God declares that he cares for us [see 1 Peter 5:7], let us put our trust in his promise.[11]

11. Ibid., 59.

17

A Rebuke to the Greedy Rich

Micah 2:1–5

Woe to those who devise wickedness and work evil on their beds!
When the morning dawns, they perform it, because it is in the
power of their hand. (Mic. 2:1)

There is a scene in the film version of J. R. R. Tolkien's *The Two Towers* in which the prophet Micah would fit very well. King Theoden has been released from the evil enchantment that had tormented his mind. His face regains its natural light and his sword arm recovers its strength. Now his eyes begin to dart around the throne room, flashing with menace. He spies his chamberlain, Grima Wormtongue, the evil agent used to take Theoden captive. Theoden rages, and soon Wormtongue is violently tossed out the palace doors, his body bounding down the hard steps that lead below.

A similar scene unfolds in the second chapter of Micah. The first chapter presented two oracles of judgment, Micah prophesying the destruction of Samaria and threatening Jerusalem with the same. Now, in his third oracle, Micah's eyes dart around in the same manner as King Theoden's: he is searching for those most responsible for this calamitous situation. Setting his gaze upon the wealthy elite of Jerusalem, he cries out in fury: "Woe to those who devise wickedness and work evil on their beds!" (Mic. 2:1).

WICKEDNESS DEVISED

Having spoken generally about Jerusalem's sins, Micah's accusation now becomes specific. He lifts back the veil on the practices of Jerusalem's land barons, those who insatiably added to their already excessive wealth by oppressing the small landowners. In chapter 1 Micah spoke of the "transgression" and "sins" of Israel and Jerusalem (1:5), referring to their iniquity before God. But those who violate God's law always end up harming people, too; accordingly, Micah now cites their "wickedness" and "evil" against their fellow man.

By the inspiration of the Spirit, the prophet is so well informed about the wealthy elite that he knows what they are doing even in the secrecy of their bedrooms. He thus reminds us that everything we do is laid bare before the eyes of God (Heb. 4:13). When God looked upon the greedy rich of Jerusalem in their bedchambers, he found them busy scheming: they "devise wickedness and work evil on their beds" (Mic. 2:1). Leslie Allen describes this as "a scathing word-sketch of dedicated and unscrupulous villains."[1] These are not sinners who fell under sudden temptation and gave into weakness, but determined oppressors.

Rest is one of God's greatest blessings. The psalmist says, "he gives to his beloved sleep" (Ps. 127:2). Nighttime is when God's people normally should be enjoying God's rest or thanking him in prayer. But these greedy rich people were gripped by an insatiable desire for more and more wealth, racking their brains with plans for wickedly defrauding those with lesser means. So it is today! When we read accounts of the excessively wealthy, we often learn of their plans to acquire even greater wealth by buying up unsuspecting companies or exploiting vulnerable markets. One might wonder why someone with more money than he could ever spend would lie awake at night scheming after more money!

The answer is given in the opening words of verse 2: "they covet." To covet is to be gripped with desire for what you do not have, especially when

1. Leslie C. Allen, *The Books of Joel, Obadiah, Jonah, and Micah*, New International Commentary on the Old Testament (Grand Rapids: Eerdmans, 1976), 287.

someone else has it. Covetousness breeds discontentment with what God has given. The Tenth Commandment expressly forbids this: "You shall not covet your neighbor's house; you shall not covet your neighbor's wife, or his male servant, or his female servant, or his ox, or his donkey, or anything that is your neighbor's" (Exod. 20:17).

Covetousness is a sin we all commit. The apostle Paul stated that even in his previously self-righteous state, he had to admit that he was convicted by the Tenth Commandment (see Rom. 7:7–8). So universal is this sin that whole economies are based on it: the advertising industry utterly relies on the insatiable coveting of consumers, the commercials seeking to incite boundless desire in order to bolster corporate profits.

Micah reminds us that we must strive against a covetous spirit. Those who covet are enslaved by their possessions and dominated by a spirit of greed. This is why Paul wrote, "There is great gain in godliness with contentment" (1 Tim. 6:6), and why he warned, "The love of money is a root of all kinds of evils" (1 Tim. 6:10). The land barons of Jerusalem provide a prime example. Instead of being blessed by their wealth, they were dominated by a scheming desire for more, even lying awake at night devising evil.

Unfortunately, their wickedness was not confined to the dark hours, for, Micah continues, "When the morning dawns, they perform it, because it is in the power of their hand" (Mic. 2:1). The word for "morning" signifies the first breaking of morning twilight; having schemed all night, the greedy rich were up at the crack of dawn to put their plans into effect.

Micah leaves no doubt as to these plans: "They covet fields and seize them, and houses, and take them away; they oppress a man and his house, a man and his inheritance" (Mic. 2:2). Wealthy oppressors were scooping up land and houses from simple freeholders to add to their already massive estates. Much as the small shopkeeper and farmer are squeezed out of business by large corporations today, family-size agricultural plots were being bought out in Micah's day. Peter Craigie explains the result:

> The small landowner, who could provide for himself and his family was suddenly destitute. Where once he was self-sufficient, he now became dependent on others, his livelihood lost to the unscrupulous dealers in real estate. And the small landowner lost not only his own livelihood, but also his "inheritance" (verse 2), that which he might have bequeathed to

his children for their future support and survival. . . . The greed of the wealthy created a category of "new poor." A section of society that once fended for itself now could no longer do so; the nation's socio-economic foundation was crumbling.[2]

Micah's outrage was directed not merely at the end result, but also at the means employed. Consider the verbs in verse 2: "covet . . . seize . . . take . . . oppress." The land barons were not achieving their fortunes through fair enterprise but through deceit, guile, and manipulation. Since Micah speaks of them acting at morning's first light, he may hint that they are using their control of the courts, since Jewish courts met at the break of day. Craigie writes, "They are hungry for land, fields and houses, because land represents both power and wealth. And only one thing stands in the way of further acquisitions: the owner of the land! But owners can be bullied, cheated, and oppressed, until at last they are willing to turn over their land for a song."[3] One common tactic was to make ill-advised loans, only to foreclose at the slightest provocation. Hailing from small-town Moresheth, Micah probably knew families who had lost their property through such means, and the anger must have stuck in his craw.

It is important to note that neither Micah nor the Bible condemns honestly acquired wealth. Those who create wealth can be a blessing to society, opening up jobs and increasing the overall standard of living. Those who become wealthy by providing useful products or offering valuable services should be admired, not resented or envied.

But Micah was not describing such people. Likewise, many people gain gross wealth today by means that the Bible labels as wicked and evil. Consider some insurance companies who gain customers by making lavish promises of care in need, but who then make every effort to pay out as little as possible when need arrives, often by means of legal technicalities written in fine print. Such actions are simply wicked. Or consider the Enron scandal of 2000, in which fabulously wealthy executives falsified the books to disguise losses. When their financial house of cards collapsed, they had arranged vast payoffs for themselves while thousands of their employees lost almost everything they had saved for retirement.

2. Peter C. Craigie, *Twelve Prophets*, Daily Study Bible Series, 2 vols. (Louisville: Westminster John Knox, 1985), 2:18.
3. Ibid.

Less personal but equally efficient in defrauding their fellow man are those who make their living manipulating stock markets, or exploiting market inefficiencies to skim off vast amounts of wealth that they did nothing to create. All such covetous activity is deemed evil by God, and should be shunned by Christians and opposed by just government. The sins of Jerusalem's land barons expose the dark side of Western capitalism today and warn many against God's vengeful judgment.

What made this situation even more woeful in Jerusalem was the economic structure established by God in the old covenant. When Israel entered the Promised Land, parcels of land were distributed by lot to the households of the nation (see Joshua chapters 14–21). The idea was that the land belonged to God, and families were to work and benefit from their apportioned land perpetually. Maintaining the family inheritance was their duty and privilege before the Lord. J. L. Mays writes, "In Israel's societal order a man's identity and status in the community rested on his household or family dwelling place and land. . . . Lose it, and he lost all the rights which were based on its possession, he had no 'place' in the community."[4] This is why, when King Ahab sought to purchase the vineyard from his neighbor Naboth, Naboth refused to accept even a fair price offered by the king. "The LORD forbid that I should give you the inheritance of my fathers" (1 Kings 21:13), Naboth replied. When Ahab's evil wife Jezebel arranged Naboth's murder to get his land, the prophet Elijah promised God's vengeance against her.

So it would be with the land barons of Micah's day. Woe to them! the prophet cries (Mic. 2:1). Proverbs 6:18 declares that God hates "a heart that devises wicked plans, feet that make haste to run to evil." Ralph Smith explains that the prophetic woe designates "persons guilty of covenant-breaking who are in imminent danger of experiencing judgment from God."[5] God would not stand for such wickedness, so the prophet pronounces God's warning of woe against the greedy rich.

JUDGMENT DEVISED

Micah points out that Jerusalem's oppressive land barons were making one crucial mistake. They assumed that while they were up scheming,

4. Cited from Gary V. Smith, *Hosea, Amos, Micah* NIV Application Commentary (Grand Rapids: Zondervan, 2001), 464.

5. Ralph L. Smith, *Micah–Malachi*, Word Biblical Commentary 32 (Waco, Tex.: Word, 1984), 24.

everyone else was asleep. But everyone else was not asleep, for God was fully awake and watching. Micah informs them: "Therefore thus says the LORD: behold, against this family I am devising disaster, from which you cannot remove your necks, and you shall not walk haughtily, for it will be a time of disaster" (Mic. 2:3).

There are a couple of parallels between the scheming of the land barons and the Lord's devising of judgment. One is that just as they were methodical and cunning in working out their schemes, so also the Lord works out his judgments with deliberate care. He bides his time, issuing warnings and developing his plans. When the judgment finally comes, it will be the result not merely of worldly forces, though it may seem that way to some, but God's deliberate response to their sin. John Calvin summarizes God's message: "While you are thus busying yourselves on your beds, while you are revolving many designs, . . . you think me to be asleep, you think that I am all the while meditating nothing; nay, I have my thoughts too, and those different from yours; for while you are awake to devise wickedness, I am awake to contrive judgment."[6]

There is a second parallel in that God's judgments always fit the crime. The Lord charged the land barons with evil, and the same word is used of God's threatened response. "I am devising disaster," he says, but the literal reading is, "I am devising evil." They plotted evil against the disempowered people, so God plotted evil against the oppressors.

Micah is taking advantage of the fact that the same word that means "evil" also is used for "disaster." God is never evil, of course. But just as God thought that what the greedy rich were doing was evil, they would look upon his judgment as a great evil upon themselves. David Prior comments: "The point is that rebellious humanity and God have entirely different definitions of what is evil and offensive. We deem evil anything which impairs our convenience and comforts. God deems evil anything which ignores his commandments and character."[7]

The disaster God brings will be unavoidable—a disaster "from which you cannot remove your necks" (Mic. 2:3). An animal in a yoke may thrash and heave, but it is not able to free itself. Likewise, Jerusalem will not escape its

6. John Calvin, *A Commentary on the Twelve Minor Prophets*, 5 vols. (1559; repr. Edinburgh: Banner of Truth, 1559, reprint 1986), 3:188.

7. David Prior, *The Message of Joel, Micah & Habakkuk*, The Bible Speaks Today (Downers Grove, Ill.: InterVarsity, 1998), 128.

coming judgment. Since their lifestyle was characterized by haughty pride toward God and their neighbors, the Lord's judgment has the effect of humbling the city in shame. When God's warnings are ignored, the judgment he threatened will come with unfailing certainty, righting wrongs and breaking the haughty will.

Note, too, that God is personally involved in his judgments. Sin is not judged by some arbitrary machinery. Sin is judged by God *personally*. The reason is that he is personally offended. Our sins against others are an affront to the holiness of our Creator. Sins against God's own precious people especially spur personal indignation from the Lord. God says to his own, "he who touches you touches the apple of [my] eye" (Zech. 2:8). What a comfort this is to afflicted believers. Not only may you hope for justice eventually to set things right: you may look for God himself to intervene on your behalf, either in this life or in the final judgment. High-handed sinners like Jerusalem's violent oppressors should tremble at the knowledge of the personal enmity of almighty God. While they are working their misdeeds, God is devising their overthrow and humiliation.

God's Portion Removed

Micah's woe oracle concludes with a fearful description of God's judgment when it finally falls on Jerusalem's corrupt elite. First, he speaks of their public humiliation: "In that day they shall take up a taunt song against you" (Mic. 2:4). Those who once walked so proudly among men will be vilified as the source of calamity for the nation. The King James Version renders "taunt song" as a "parable": the oppressive landlords will be offered as "an example to be shunned, a lesson to others not to travel the path that leads to this disastrous end."[8] History shows numerous similar examples. Bully Dawson was a swaggering gambler in seventeenth-century London. His first name became a byword for a brutal coward. When Benedict Arnold betrayed West Point to the British during the American Revolution, he secured infamy as the very definition of treasonous betrayal. Likewise, the land barons of Jerusalem would be vilified as those whose wickedness ruined the nation.

8. Allen, *The Books of Joel, Obadiah, Jonah, and Micah*, 290.

Micah had made it clear that the judgment of which he speaks will come in the form of invasion from the mighty Assyrians. That judgment came during the prophet's lifetime, when Sennacherib's army advanced to the gates of Jerusalem. All the real estate so wickedly plundered by Jerusalem's wealthy elite was then turned over to new management! Micah warns that when the day came, the landlords would lament: "We are utterly ruined; he changes the portion of my people; how he removes it from me! To an apostate he allots our fields" (Mic. 2:4).

This is the second aspect of God's judgment: the portion he had granted to his people—the allotted land for Judah's families—will be reallocated by the invaders. Having broken God's covenant with respect to the land, the real estate prospectors learn that it really was not theirs to take; it belonged to God, who can give and remove his portion from his people. Their attitude was like that of stockbrokers who hurled themselves from high-rise buildings during the crashes of 1929 and 2008. Having lived for money, they could not live without it. "We are utterly ruined," the land-grabbers cried. Having once made others landless by their scheming, they are now landless themselves. "How could God do such a thing—take away my land?" they cry.[9]

The meaning of the word "apostate" is not entirely certain. The Hebrew word means "those who have turned away," and refers to those who are outside the covenant. In this case, it probably means the Assyrians, although it could also refer to the common people, on whom the elites looked down with contempt. When the Assyrians took ownership, they probably turned the land over to the poor, having carried the upper classes off into exile. We know this happened when Jerusalem was destroyed a century later. The prophet Jeremiah records that Nebuchadnezzar "left in the land of Judah some of the poor people who owned nothing, and gave them vineyards and fields at the same time" (Jer. 39:10). In this way, God restored the land to his poor people from whom it had been stolen.

This reminds us all that God's gifts in this life are provisional. He gave the land to the Jews, but when they broke covenant with him, he took it away. This, by the way, makes an important point with respect to current claims by Jewish people to have a divine right to Palestine. According to the Bible, in light of their breaking of the old covenant, and especially their rejection

9. Ibid.

of God's new covenant in Christ, that right has been forfeited. But the same can also be true of Christians and churches. The exalted Christ threatened the seven churches of Asia Minor: "I will come to you and remove your lampstand from its place, unless you repent" (Rev. 2:5). The ruins of those churches in Turkey, a land almost devoid of Christianity for centuries, bears eloquent testimony to the seriousness of Christ's warning. The same is true for churches that cease to teach God's Word faithfully. American cities are filled with large, majestic churches, once filled but now empty. Some of them are being put to use as restaurants, museums, and even mosques. It is blessedly true that those who are truly saved can never lose their salvation (see John 6:37–40). But God nonetheless visits temporal judgments upon his unruly people. Nations, churches, and families that squander their spiritual inheritance through worldliness and sin should expect to have their gracious allotment taken away.

Worst of all is the final threat of judgment: "Therefore you will have none to cast the line by lot in the assembly of the LORD" (Mic. 2:5). The land barons lamented their utter ruin when they lost their real estate. But that was not their true ruin. Micah refers to the assignment of land by lot described in Joshua 18:8–10. There is an implicit promise here that after the fall of Jerusalem there would be another allotment of land to God's people. But these land-grabbers, their entire families destroyed or carried off into exile, will have no one to represent them in that lottery, so they are cut off from the land forever. The recent experience of the northern kingdom of Israel provided a sobering warning: the ten lost tribes of Israel were removed from history forever. Micah now threatens the greedy rich with a similar judgment. David Prior writes: "In effect, this punishment was a sentence to exclusion from the life of the people of God. They would be banned from the land, and thus from the life of God, for ever."[10]

When we turn to the prophecy of Jeremiah, the prophet called to witness Jerusalem's fall, we realize that the future restoration implied in verse 5 takes place in the new covenant that God would bring through his Son, Jesus Christ. Amid the ashes of the holy city, Jeremiah foretold: "Behold, the days are coming, declares the LORD, when I will make a new covenant with the house of Israel and the house of Judah" (Jer. 31:31). Jesus made it plain

10. Prior, *Joel, Micah, & Habakkuk*, 130.

that this was the new covenant in his own blood (Luke 22:20). Likewise, Jeremiah foretold the building of a new city of God, one that "shall not be uprooted or overthrown anymore forever" (Jer. 31:40). This is the eternal city witnessed by the apostle John, "the holy city, new Jerusalem, coming down out of heaven from God" (Rev. 21:2), the eternal home where God will dwell with his people forever.

To be excluded from this salvation is to be utterly ruined. The covetous rich lost not just their real estate but their place in "the assembly of the Lord" (Mic. 2:5). Their exile would be an eternal one, not just from the land of their fathers but from the blessed presence of God. With this heavy blow for the land-grabbers but with an implied promise for the faithful poor, Micah concludes his oracle of woe. Bruce Waltke summarizes, "The hard-fisted land barons are consigned to eternal death; the righteous remnant have a future hope."[11]

On That Day

The day of the Lord's coming is always a day of woe for the ungodly, but a day of hope for God's afflicted righteous people. It was a day the land-grabbers never saw coming, despite all the warnings from God's messengers. In their final ruin, they are a picture of all covetous people who fail to heed God's warnings of wrath. The book of Revelation depicts such people in the final judgment crying out in woe to the mountains and rocks: "Fall on us and hide us from the face of him who is seated on the throne, and from the wrath of the Lamb, for the great day of their wrath has come, and who can stand?" (Rev. 6:16–17).

The day of the Lord is coming. It will arrive either with the return of the Lord Jesus Christ or with the hour of our death, when we will stand before God. Jesus once told a parable about a covetous rich man who was not prepared for that day. Like the greedy rich of Jerusalem, the rich fool of Jesus' parable lay awake thinking about where to store all his riches for his own enjoyment. But the day finally came for the rich fool, as it must for us all. "God said to him, 'Fool! This night your soul is required of you, and the things you have prepared, whose will they be?'" (Luke 12:20). Jesus added,

11. Bruce Waltke, *A Commentary on Micah* (Grand Rapids: Ecrdmans, 2007), 104.

"So is the one who lays up treasure for himself and is not rich toward God" (Luke 12:21).

This raises a question, What do you think about as you lie down at the end of the day? Is your mind racing with new schemes to get ahead and get rich, to succeed in the world, perhaps even at the expense of your fellow man? Realize that the day is coming for you. Jesus warned, "Be on your guard against all covetousness, for one's life does not consist in the abundance of his possessions" (Luke 12:15).

We should consider, instead, how to be rich toward God. We are rich toward God when we receive the matchless grace poured out in the blood of Christ's cross and in God's gift of eternal life through his Son. We are rich toward God when we offer prayers of thanksgiving from our beds, and when we devise ways of honoring God with our lives and doing good to those in need. We are rich toward God when we spend our energies not in attaining excessive wealth and worldly prestige but in the kingdom work of Christ, and when we use the wealth we have for the advance of Christ's gospel of salvation.

If we are rich toward God, then our names will be spoken with praise and affection on the lips of God's beloved people, not reviled in taunt songs on the judgment day. If we are rich toward God we will have nothing to fear with the coming of the Lord; indeed, that will be the day of our hope fulfilled, the day of our greatest blessing, the day of the allotment of our eternal real estate and our entry into that assembly of the Lord that will rejoice to sing his praises forever.

18

A Display of False Prophets

Micah 2:6–11

"Do not preach"—thus they preach—"one should not preach of such things; disgrace will not overtake us." (Mic. 2:6)

I t is sometimes cynically said that no good deed ever goes unpunished. That may be practically true in a world like ours. But it is definitely true that no faithful ministry of God's Word ever goes unopposed. The devil opposes the gospel by both attacking its messengers and blinding the hearts of its hearers. On a human level, the preaching of God's Word is opposed in two main ways. The first way is to reject or even attack the faithful preachers. The second is to pay your own preachers to give sermons more to your liking.

It was the second kind of opposition that especially galled the prophet Micah. Having been threatened with divine judgment, the greedy land barons got their own prophets to preach that nothing of the sort would ever happen. Micah's contemporary, Isaiah, regarded this situation as proof of Jerusalem's apostasy: "For they are a rebellious people, lying children, children unwilling to hear the instruction of the Lord" (Isa. 30:9).

Stop Preaching!

It was not that Jerusalem's greedy rich were intolerant of preaching, only that they refused preaching that made them uncomfortable. People with great wealth usually do not have difficulty finding a preacher to suit their tastes, and such well-financed mouthpieces are eager to take on annoying prophets. This was the situation in Micah's Jerusalem. As Peter Craigie puts it, "The best way to deal with a preacher is to set other preachers upon him."[1] Micah begins his fourth oracle complaining about these false prophets: "'Do not preach'—thus they preach—'one should not preach of such things; disgrace will not overtake us'" (Mic. 2:6).

The word for "preach" in this verse is not the usual term for prophesying. Its root meaning is that of "dripping," which suggests a pejorative slant on preaching: "Stop preaching at me!" The New King James Version translates it as "prattle." But Micah turns this back on his enemies, using the same word in saying, "thus they preach." We might translate the verse to read, "'Stop your incessant preaching,' they incessantly preach."

What bothered the false prophets so much was that Micah and his colleagues declared God's condemnation and judgment on the ruling classes of Jerusalem. As a result of their counter-message, Micah not only had the difficulty of standing up to the wealthy exploiters of the poor, but "he must also cope with the army of preachers whose public proclamations supported their patrons."[2]

False prophecy is a common and baleful phenomenon in the history of God's people. All through the Bible, God's true messengers are set upon by false prophets. This happened during the exodus, when the false prophet Korah led the people to rebel against Moses' leadership. Korah became so obnoxious that God finally opened the ground to swallow him (Num. 16:32–33). But the people paid a fearful price for listening to the false prophet, including defeat in battle, the loss of thousands in a plague sent by God, and ultimately God's refusal to allow them to enter the Promised Land, so that almost the entire generation died in the wilderness (see Num. 14, 16).

After Israel settled in Canaan, they continued to be plagued with false prophets. Each of their unbelieving kings had his stable of false prophets,

1. Peter C. Craigie, *Twelve Prophets*, Daily Study Bible Series, 2 vols. (Louisville: Westminster John Knox, 1985), 2:22.
2. Ibid.

who declared the Lord's approval and received the king's favor in response. In one famous example, Judah's righteous king Jehoshaphat was asked to assist Ahab in a foolish military expedition. Jehoshaphat was suspicious when Ahab's gaggle of false prophets assured them of victory, so he asked, "Is there not here another prophet of the LORD of whom we may inquire?" (1 Kings 22:7). He meant that he desired a prophet who was not paid off by the king. Ahab's answer was revealing: "There is yet one man by whom we may inquire of the LORD, Micaiah the son of Imlah, but I hate him, for he never prophesies good concerning me, but evil" (1 Kings 22:8). Despite Micaiah's warning of disaster, Ahab listened to his false prophets, losing the battle and his life as a result.

Indeed, all the true prophets were opposed by false counterparts. Amos was accused of treason by the false prophet Amaziah for prophesying judgment on Samaria, so Amos responded with a woe of doom on Amaziah (Amos 7:17). When Jeremiah warned Jerusalem of coming destruction a hundred years after Micah, the false prophet Hananiah assured the people that all would be well (Jer. 28:1–4). As a result, Jeremiah was cast into a cistern, and the unbelieving city fell to the Babylonian sword. Of course, the most notable instance is the opposition of the Pharisees and scribes to the preaching of Jesus. Speaking for all the prophets before him, including Micah, Jesus warned, "Woe to you, scribes and Pharisees, hypocrites! For you shut the kingdom of heaven in people's faces. For you neither enter yourselves nor allow those who would enter to go in" (Matt. 23:13).

False prophecy remains the bane of God's people. Whether Bible-believing Christians confront evolution, abortion, the sexual debaucheries of pornography and homosexuality, racism, or supercharged materialism, at the forefront of our opposition are false prophets who assuage sinful consciences and lull people into a deeper and deeper moral slumber.

Micah records the substance of the false preaching directed against him and his faithful colleagues: "one should not preach of such things; disgrace will not overtake us" (Mic. 2:6). Micah's opponents were complaining about his prophecy of coming judgment on Judah's idolatry and sin. This is the hallmark of all false prophecy: a denial of God's judgment of sin. False prophets today loathe above all else the Bible's teaching on sin and judgment, and therefore its teaching on the atoning blood of Christ. Increasing numbers of supposedly evangelical scholars now scorn the teaching that Jesus died in the place of sinners, receiving the wrath of God their sins deserved.[3] In place of the Bible's teaching on sin and the cross, false preaching today emphasizes human goodness, moralistic works, health, wealth, and prosperity, and life-style training that mimics self-help psychology. It was by false prophecy that Satan coerced Adam and Eve into the fall of our race, saying to Eve, "Did God really say . . . ?" (Gen. 3:1, NIV). False prophecy remains one of Satan's most potent weapons.

In the Old Testament, the typical result of false prophecy was to give the people a false sense of security. When the people fell into sin and idolatry, God sent the prophets to warn them, but the false prophets assured them that God would never judge them. "'Peace, peace,' they say, when there is no peace," Jeremiah complained (Jer. 6:14, NIV). This same message persists today, as lying pulpits assure the sexually immoral, greedy, and unbelieving that all is well with God, even though the Bible insists, "The wages of sin is death" (Rom. 6:23).

SMOOTH THEOLOGY

The Bible's critique of false prophecy indicates that the most vital insti-tution of any nation or people is the church pulpit. True preaching awakens the mind and heart to the truth of God, but false preaching deadens the heart to sin and darkens the mind with eloquent lies. Yet how common it is, in ways small and large, for the pulpit to become captive to moneyed interests! It happens when the pastor declines to preach messages deemed unpopular by large givers in the church. It happens when Christian orga-nizations expand their donor base by broadening their message, or enter into political alliances that limit the range of their preaching. It happens when consultants convince churches that a more "relevant" message than that of the Bible will increase the size of the church. The worst form of this pulpit perversion occurs when corrupt rulers enter into an adulterous mar-riage with false prophets, so that the most unfaithful preachers become the society's most influential. When this occurs, the people's departure from the ways of God is dramatically hastened.

3. For a detailed discussion of this problem, see Richard D. Phillips, *Precious Blood: The Atoning Work of Christ* (Wheaton, Ill.: Crossway, 2009), 205–25.

How do false prophets support their perverted doctrines? The answer is illustrated by Micah's description of the smooth theology of the false prophets he faced. They argued: "Should this be said, O house of Jacob? Has the Lord grown impatient? Are these his deeds?" (Mic. 2:7).

First, we see a false theology based on only one facet of God's character, without painting the whole portrait: "Has the Lord grown impatient?" they asked. The false teachers were reminding the people of a glorious truth: God's long-suffering grace. After all, God had revealed himself to Moses: "The Lord, the Lord, a God merciful and gracious, slow to anger, and abounding in steadfast love and faithfulness, keeping steadfast love for thousands, forgiving iniquity and transgression and sin" (Exod. 34:6–7). "Isn't this the character of our God?" the false prophets insisted. So how could Micah go about threatening God's people with judgment, when God had promised mercy, grace, and infinite patience? The problem is not with the truth the false prophets taught, but with the other truths they so carefully left out. In this case, they stopped reading before God was done declaring who he is. If they read all the way to the end of the sentence they would have included this teaching: "but who will by no means clear the guilty" (Exod. 34:7). The God of grace is also a holy God of justice who punishes sin. This was the inconvenient truth that the false prophets smoothed out. Their attitude was that of an atheistic philosopher who quipped that if it turned out there is a God he was not afraid, because as Voltaire is often quoted as saying: "God will forgive; that's what he's there for."

The false prophets' second argument had to do with what God had done in the past: "Are these his deeds?" They were pointing to God's great acts in their history, especially God's deliverance of Israel from the bondage of Egypt. "God has always blessed and protected us," they argued, "and so he always will!"

This shows why such people are called false *prophets* or false *preachers*: because they manipulate and pervert what God and the Bible have said. They present a smooth theology: everything difficult taken out, and their message of convenient half-truths sanded down and polished by the most studied eloquence and the most profound oratorical pauses, to appeal to the senses of carnal men and women. Leslie Allen comments, "Such was the case of the optimistic prophets, so plausible in its half-truths, so convincing to those who longed to believe it. Who could be so foolish as to want to demolish such comfortable doctrine?"[4]

I once counseled a young man who had been raised in a liberal church. He had decided to divorce his wife on the grounds that he realized he didn't love her after all. When I pressed upon him God's condemnation of his proposed action, he glibly replied, "I don't believe in the God you talk about. My God is a God of love." I replied to him that this was precisely his problem. It is because God is a God of love that he hates divorce. It is because God is a God of love that he could be counted on to take up the cause of his injured wife. It is because of God's holy and true love that he will judge those who violate his loving commandments. But so ensnared was the young man by the false but convenient preaching of his upbringing that my warning had no apparent effect. On the one occasion when I spoke to him afterward, he informed me that his hometown pastor had convinced him against my "narrow-minded" and "legalistic" counsel.

False prophecy not only deadens the conscience of hearers against the moral demands of God, but it also cheapens God's grace. God's true grace produces a harvest of holiness and peace, but cheap grace winks at sin and evil. Dietrich Bonhoeffer, who coined the term, explained: "Cheap grace is the preaching of forgiveness without requiring repentance, baptism without church discipline, Communion without confession, absolution without personal confession. Cheap grace is grace without discipleship, grace without the cross, grace without Jesus Christ, living and incarnate."[5]

In reality, cheap grace is no grace at all. Cheap grace incites a false presumption that will prove perilous when God's judgment falls on sinners who have trusted it. But cheap grace is alive and well in the pulpits of our time. Comparing our situation to that of Micah's Jerusalem, Bruce Waltke warns: "Just as dangerous today are false teachers who apply the doctrine of the believer's security to those who disown their Lord in their lifestyles and who do not bring forth the fruit of repentance from sin."[6] There is a true security in salvation, but it belongs only to those with a living, trusting faith in Jesus Christ and in God's Word.

---

4. Leslie C. Allen, *The Books of Joel, Obadiah, Jonah, and Micah*, New International Commentary on the Old Testament(Grand Rapids: Eerdmans, 1976), 295.

5. Dietrich Bonhoeffer, *The Cost of Discipleship* (New York: Touchstone, 1995), 43–45.

6. Bruce Waltke, *A Commentary on Micah* (Grand Rapids: Eerdmans, 2007), 127.

Along these same lines, Micah's message was one of blessing and hope for those who receive God's Word in faith. So he breaks in with a question to the smooth theology of the false prophets: "Do not my words do good to him who walks uprightly?" (Mic. 2:7).

This question is an appeal to receive and obey God's true Word. It is true that God is full of grace and mercy. Therefore, we ought to receive his entire Word as a source of blessing, including its warnings. When God teaches us to live a certain way, it is for our good in living upright lives. Not only is it a sin to oppose or pervert God's Word, but there is no good reason why we should do so. David reasons to this effect in Psalm 19: "The law of the LORD is perfect, reviving the soul; the testimony of the LORD is sure, making wise the simple; the precepts of the LORD are right, rejoicing the heart; the commandment of the LORD is pure, enlightening the eyes" (Ps. 19:7–8). If this is true of God's Word generally, it is especially true of those teachings we find hard at first but which through faith become most precious to our souls.

SOFT PREACHING, HARD HEARTS

A smooth theology of cheap grace is to be loathed because it does violence to God's Word and brings discredit on the true God of holiness and grace. But Micah's rebuke focuses on the terrible reality that false teachers produce enemies of God. Jesus insisted that a tree is revealed by the fruit it grows, and in this vein Micah condemns the false prophets for the kind of followers they raise up: "But lately my people have risen up as an enemy" (Mic. 2:8). The soft preaching of the false prophets had made hard hearts, just as it does today.

Because the blame for false prophecy lies equally with those who pay and applaud them, Micah addresses the evil landlords who stood behind the false teaching: "You strip the rich robe from those who pass by trustingly with no thought of war. The women of my people you drive out from their delightful houses; from their young children you take away my splendor forever" (Mic. 2:8–9).

Such was the callous malice of the smug adherents of cheap grace that they were like bandits who ripped the robes off unsuspecting passersby. This may suggest that the rich land barons hired gangs of thugs to take even the clothes off the backs of those who owed debts from their usurious loans.

They went so far as to evict women and children from their homes, casting them out with nothing. This violated God's loving provision to his people in the Promised Land. The common homes may not have stacked up against the regal estates of the rich, but Micah calls them "their delightful houses." He refers to the land God had given for the bounty of his people as "my splendor." In order to add increments to their already vast wealth, the greedy land barons drove out "forever" the women and children of Israel—so precious to God—from their God-glorifying inheritance.

Verse 8 uses an expression that is rendered differently in various translations. The English Standard Version reads that the hard-hearted rulers strip the robe from those who pass by "with no thought of war." This suggests their victims were unsuspecting, with no idea that an attack was near. Probably a better translation is given by the New King James Version, which says the bandits conduct themselves "like men returned from war." Those returning from war are sometimes calloused in their spirits and at ease with violence. Especially in the ancient world, they would often come home with ravenous appetites. This is what the smooth preaching of the false prophets engendered: hard-hearted, greedy, and violent abusers of power; in short, enemies of God.

Not that the targets of Micah's rebuke did any of this with their own hands. They would have remained high up in the capital city, issuing callous directives from their estates before hustling off to present their elegant persons at the temple, there to receive a polished sermon of half-truths from God's Word. No wonder God said through Amos, "I hate, I despise your feasts, and I take no delight in your solemn assemblies. . . . But let justice roll down like waters, and righteousness like an ever-flowing stream" (Amos 5:21, 24).

The business practices of Jerusalem's greedy rich are replicated in our society. The effect of the modern corporate structure is that those who make the business decisions are carefully distanced from the human results of their actions. The result of this removal of human factors from decision making is that a company's stock value wholly defines its success. When I attended a graduate school of business, I remember hearing that it was the duty of executive decision makers to place the stock value above all other considerations, even if one's decisions resulted in pollution to the environment, ruin to low-level employees, or corruption in the government—and this was in a business ethics class! Considered this way, the company exists solely to make money for its stockholders. If small businesses operated by families for generations are wiped out, if widows are evicted from their homes, if layoffs reduce loyal workers to penury, these things are simply "the cost of doing business." The only sacrifices that cannot be made are in the stock price and the ever-soaring executive compensation packages. All the while, the board members and CEOs live in a fairy-tale land far removed from the common people about whom they neither know nor care—a world of rich estates, private jets, skyscraper views, and—all too often—richly appointed churches with smooth and elegant preachers whose wagging tongues assure them of God's favor.

The assumption that only short-term profits matter is simply irrational, creating a bubble of poor decisions that must ultimately burst. Moreover, this way of thinking is evil, and it is only a matter of time before the God of holiness and love strikes back with vengeance upon the greedy rich who work violence against the common people.

It is with such a word of judgment that Micah concludes his message to the land barons who bought their false preaching with their ill-gotten money: "Arise and go, for this is no place to rest, because of uncleanness that destroys with a grievous destruction" (Mic. 2:10). Having evicted God's people from the homes and land God had lovingly provided, now the wealthy elite are evicted from the land. The invading Assyrians will drag them off into an exile of slavery in a pagan wasteland. Peter Craigie explains, "Those who by their actions had made others leave their homes would be required to 'arise and go.' The greed of the land-grabbers did not only destroy others, widows and children, but would eventually return in the divine scheme of things to destroy themselves."[7]

This reminds us that God's blessings are to be used for God's purposes. Position, power, and wealth are not to be employed with violence or neglect for others, or for personal gain alone. The land God gave to Israel was to be a land of pleasant rest in which holy people enjoyed God's loving bounty. Micah describes the land barons' policy as an abomination to the land: "uncleanness that destroys with grievous destruction" (Mic. 2:10). Just as the abominable nations who occupied Canaan before the Israelites were driven out and destroyed, so it would be with the apostate people of Jerusalem.

7. Peter C. Craigie, *Twelve Prophets*, 2:24.

Allen observes: "Their dirty conduct in ill-treating their needy neighbors has rendered them unfit to tread Canaan's soil any longer. So they are doomed to suffer agonizing ruin, involving loss of land, livelihood, and liberty."[8]

Do we realize that a similar loss of God's blessing is taking place today in the midst of our fevered Western affluence? Our land of liberty is increasingly a land of bondage to the most vile and destructive sins, including spiraling domestic abuse, sexual perversion, and the slaughter of unborn children. Our version of peace and prosperity is increasingly nothing of the sort. Rich only in money, we are more and more becoming poor by every other standard. In many respects, the decadent rich are their own chief victims. Slaves to pride and avarice, they are unable to enjoy the most basic and most important blessings of life: covenant faithfulness in marriage, joyful harmony in the home, godly contentedness, wholesome purpose and satisfaction, the ability to enjoy life and the courage to face death. This is why the rates of depression and suicide seem to be so high in the most affluent sectors of society: those who live for money, pride, and greed increasingly find it impossible to live at all.

WHAT KIND OF PREACHING?

Micah suggests that the most telling indicator of our spiritual condition is revealed by our answer to this question: what kind of preaching does your heart crave: soft and false, or hard and true? Micah's most pointed condemnation of the people of his day reviles them for the choice they would make: "If a man should go about and utter wind and lies, saying, 'I will preach to you of wine and strong drink,' he would be the preacher for this people!" (Mic. 2:11).

This is the kind of preaching that the hell-bound world delights to hear. First, Micah derides it as "wind and lies." It is just so much empty noise, for all the smiling charm and smooth eloquence with which it is delivered. Worse than empty, it is "lies." Smooth preaching falsifies God's Word even as it quotes selected Bible verses for its message of cheap grace. Micah mocks such preaching as saying, "I will preach to you of wine and strong drink." Probably the best way to render this today is "wine and beer preaching." His

8. Allen, *Joel, Obadiah, Jonah, and Micah*, 298.

point is not that it promotes alcoholism, but that it promotes a good time in general. "Eat, drink, and be merry!" it extols. "All is well, and no matter what evil we work in God's sight, we will still have a good time! Do not fear God's judgment: God is a God of love."

Is this the kind of preaching you prefer? The apostle Paul wrote of another kind of preaching, to which you would do better to listen. Summarizing his ministry in Ephesus, he said, "I did not shrink from declaring to you the whole counsel of God" (Acts 20:27). By this he meant the teaching that God is love and that God is light, permitting no evil at all. He meant the teaching of God's judgment on sin, as well as God's mercy for sinners through the precious blood of his Son. Paul meant the truth that "the unrighteous will not inherit the kingdom of God," including the sexually immoral, idolatrous, adulterers, homosexuals, thieves, the greedy, drunkards, revilers and swindlers, along with the truth that "such were some of you. But you were washed, you were sanctified, you were justified in the name of the Lord Jesus Christ and by the Spirit of our God" (1 Cor. 6:9–11).

We hear it said, "You are what you eat." Far more profound is the truth that you are what you hear. Soft preaching makes hard hearts, and hearts hardened by sin will perish under God's wrath. But hard preaching that teaches what we need to hear, whole teaching that presents both deliverance and judgment, mercy and wrath, forgiveness and repentance, leads to soft hearts that receive salvation from the God of truth and love.

19

A Shepherd for God's Remnant

Micah 2:12–13

*I will surely assemble all of you, O Jacob; I will gather the
remnant of Israel; I will set them together like sheep in a fold,
like a flock in its pasture, a noisy multitude of men.*
(Mic. 2:12)

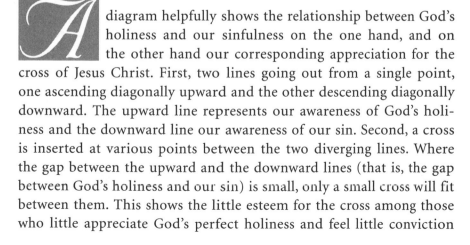

diagram helpfully shows the relationship between God's
holiness and our sinfulness on the one hand, and on
the other hand our corresponding appreciation for the
cross of Jesus Christ. First, two lines going out from a single point,
one ascending diagonally upward and the other descending diagonally
downward. The upward line represents our awareness of God's holiness and the downward line our awareness of our sin. Second, a cross
is inserted at various points between the two diverging lines. Where
the gap between the upward and the downward lines (that is, the gap
between God's holiness and our sin) is small, only a small cross will fit
between them. This shows the little esteem for the cross among those
who little appreciate God's perfect holiness and feel little conviction

over their own sin. But as the gap gets larger—as the line depicting God's holiness gets higher and the line depicting our sin gets lower—the cross gets bigger. The point is that those who best comprehend the greatness of God's surpassing holiness and the depths of our own abominable sinfulness are those who most glorify and trust the grace of God in the cross of Christ.

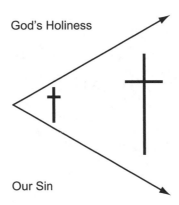

Micah presents a vastly holy God who burns with indignation against sin and threatens terrible judgment on the wicked of Jerusalem. But for this very reason, Micah preaches a gospel of wondrously amazing grace, raising high the hopes of God's people, having first driven them to their knees in conviction over sin.

So sharp is Micah's transition from condemnation to salvation that some commentators suspect these verses recount more vain assurances from the false prophets. But the text is clear that Micah himself concludes his oracles of woe with a clarion call of hope for the faithful and righteous poor of Jerusalem. James Boice explains:

> The city will fall and they will go into exile. This is just. But what, we may ask, of the poor whom [the rich] have exploited? If the city falls and the wicked are punished, will not the poor be punished too? Will the innocent not suffer with the guilty? Micah seems to say that they will. But he has good news for them too: for the remnant of the upright, there will be a restoration.[1]

1. James M. Boice, *The Minor Prophets*, 2 vols. (Grand Rapids: Baker, 1986), 2:329.

THE HOLY REMNANT SHELTERED

Micah continues to prophesy against the backdrop of a coming invasion from the mighty northern empire of Assyria. His first cycle of oracles, comprising chapters 1 and 2, sees this violent intrusion as God's response to the idolatry and sin of Israel and Jerusalem. The first oracle (Mic. 1:2–7) foresaw the northern capital of Samaria destroyed by Assyria. The second oracle (Mic. 1:8–16) pointed out that Jerusalem had fallen in with Samaria's ways; therefore, the disaster of enemy conquest would come to Jerusalem's very gates. The third and fourth oracles (Mic. 2:1–5 and 2:6–11) lay the blame on the oppressive land barons and the false prophets who supported them. Now, as Micah offers a ray of hope to the faithful who are left, he sees a godly remnant holed up behind the walls of Jerusalem, relying on God's saving might for their defense. To this end, Micah writes, "I will surely assemble all of you, O Jacob; I will gather the remnant of Israel" (Mic. 2:12).

The theme of a holy remnant is important to all the preexilic prophets. They predicted that only a small number of Israelites would be left after God's judgments. Amos said, "The city that went out a thousand shall have a hundred left, and that which went out a hundred shall have ten left to the house of Israel" (Amos 5:3). This drastic reduction would be a penalty for sin and unbelief. This was precisely the situation when Sennacherib's conquering army arrived at Jerusalem's gate in 701 B.C. The northern kingdom was entirely in exile, and all the region around Jerusalem was lost. All that was left of the once-great nation of Israel were those thousands huddled behind the stone ramparts of God's city. Though only a remnant of the nation was left, God promised, "I will surely assemble all of you, O Jacob." This indicates that this faithful remnant is the true people of God, the true covenant children of Jacob, and the true Israel of faith.

In addition to being small, three characteristics define God's faithful remnant. First, they are weak and poor, having forfeited their worldly goods and might. Second, they are holy: that is, they are those who have retained their faith in God and have not abandoned his ways in the midst of widespread unbelief and depravity. Third, they are therefore strong in the Lord, who shows forth his glory by saving his holy remnant. Weak in the flesh, holy to the Lord, and strong in his might: these are the characteristics of the remnant of God's people.

This pattern is repeated throughout the Bible. The holy remnant was delivered in Micah's time, but Isaiah foretold another, greater judgment in which Jerusalem would fall. The entire nation would go into exile in Babylon. Yet, Isaiah promised, "A remnant will return, the remnant of Jacob, to the mighty God" (Isa. 10:21). Centuries later, after Jerusalem had rejected and crucified her promised Messiah, Jesus Christ, the city again fell to the sword in one of the most devastating conquests ever: the fall of Jerusalem in A.D. 70. Over a million Jews were slaughtered by the invading Romans.[2] Only a small number of believers, the followers of Jesus Christ, escaped. This holy remnant remembered Jesus' prophecy, "When you see Jerusalem surrounded by armies, then know that its desolation has come near" (Luke 21:20), and following Jesus' command they fled to the mountains and were spared.

The Bible's theme of the holy remnant assumes a lamentable situation: out of all the vast peoples of the earth, and sometimes even the church, only a minority are true followers of the Lord. Just as the great majority of the people in Micah's time fell to the sword of God's judgment, and in later judgments it could rightly be said that the entire nation was destroyed, so today it is true that "the whole world lies in the power of the evil one" (1 John 5:19). But there is good news as well. There always remain those who do not bow to the world's idols, and who for all their sin and folly remain true in their faith. At one point in history, the prophet Elijah thought he was the only believer left. But God reminded him of the remnant he preserved, "seven thousand in Israel, all the knees that have not bowed to Baal" (1 Kings 19:18), through which God would continue the march of redemptive history. This holy remnant in every generation can expect to suffer as part of God's general judgment on the world, but it may also look for the Lord to display his glory by saving his weak but holy people.

It was this salvation that Micah held before Jerusalem: "I will surely assemble all of you, O Jacob; I will gather the remnant of Israel" (Mic. 2:12). As the Bible records, Sennacherib king of Assyria came up and captured the fortified cities of Judah, and then came before Jerusalem with his great army. His representative, the Rabshekah, came forward and taunted the Jews. He pointed out that all their worldly stratagems and alliances had failed and that Israel's God had obviously given them over to judgment

2. Josephus, *The Jewish Wars*, VI.9.3.

(2 Kings 18:19–25). Moreover, since none of the gods of other lands had been able to stop the Assyrian might, the Jews should not trust their God to do any better (2 Kings 18:33–35). But Hezekiah was fortified by the prophetic message of Micah and the personal counsel of Isaiah. Isaiah informed him that God had promised Assyria's fall: "Do not be afraid because of the words that you have heard, with which the young men of the king of Assyria have reviled me. . . . I will make him fall by the sword in his own hand" (Isa. 37:6–7). God answered when Hezekiah prayed in faith for deliverance, and by the Lord's intervention the remnant that had fled to Jerusalem was gathered safely not just behind its high walls but in the mighty hands of God.

This example offers a clear message to us today as we tremble in weakness with the trials of this world. Sennacherib believed that God had gathered his remnant to hand them over to their enemies. That was why they were so weak and afflicted, he reasoned. But the Christian can know that when the storms of life drive us to our knees, with only God to help us, sometimes even by God's own chastening hand, God's purpose is not to destroy us or to humiliate us in judgment. God gathers his people near to himself, depriving us of every other solace and hope, in order to save us. He gathers us so that we would remember his goodness and love, so that we would realize the folly of our love for the world, and so that he might display his glory through a salvation that is by his sovereign might alone.

For this reason, the biblical image of God as a fortress and refuge has always been precious to afflicted believers. Psalm 46 declares, "God is our refuge and strength, a very present help in trouble. Therefore we will not fear though the earth gives way, though the mountains be moved into the heart of the sea, though its waters roar and foam, though the mountains tremble at its swelling. . . . The LORD of hosts is with us; the God of Jacob is our fortress" (Ps. 46:1–3, 7). With this refuge in mind, Hezekiah called the remnant of God's people to gather into Jerusalem to escape Sennacherib: "With him is an arm of flesh," he told them, "but with us is the LORD our God, to help us and to fight our battles" (2 Chron. 32:8). This is why the worst thing to do in times of darkness or doubt is to flee from the Lord. Since God is our refuge and strength, weak and broken believers should flee *to* the Lord, who delights to "gather the remnant of Israel" and "set them together like sheep in a fold" (Mic. 2:12).

THE HOLY REMNANT SHEPHERDED

In addition to the great Bible theme of the holy remnant finding refuge in God, Micah adds that God is the good shepherd who cares for his sheep. He writes, "I will set them together like sheep in a fold, like a flock in its pasture, a noisy multitude of men" (Mic. 2:12).

This heartwarming message brings with it a sobering assessment of our need. In all the many passages that depict believers as sheep, the underlying truth is that we greatly need God's shepherding care. Sheep are unable to defend themselves, having no weapons of any use in a fight. They are easily panicked and debilitated. In fact, sheep need to be protected from themselves—they are notorious for wandering away from good pastures and sources of water, for destroying what good grass is available, and for placing themselves in irretrievable situations. This is the Bible's depiction of our spiritual state, and it seems to account for Micah's description of the flock as "a noisy multitude of men." Charles Spurgeon wrote: "[Sheep] are prone to wander, and ready for all sorts of mischief, but they never assist the shepherd in the slightest degree. In this respect, we are all just like the silly sheep, yet our good Shepherd supplies all the needs, pities all the infirmities, and pardons all the wanderings of his poor wayward flock."[3]

There is one positive thing to say about God's sheep: they always have a shepherd. This was the only hope of Micah's generation, as it is our only hope. By their own sins against God, the Jews had brought God's judgment. By their own foolish political and economic policy, they found themselves besieged behind the city gates. But they still had one great resource: the Lord, God of heaven, was their shepherd. Their Lord would be faithful to his covenants and so would not abandon the holy remnant. The Lord looks with love and pity on his afflicted people, and so he helps them. Psalm 34:17–18 says, "When the righteous cry for help, the LORD hears and delivers them out of all their troubles. The LORD is near to the brokenhearted and saves the crushed in spirit." For this reason, Micah consoles the weak but holy remnant, "I will set them together like sheep in a fold, like a flock in its pasture" (Mic. 2:12).

The image of the Lord as our shepherd is one of the Bible's primary pictures of a believer's relationship with God. It tells us that, first, what matters

---

3. Charles H. Spurgeon, *Metropolitan Tabernacle Pulpit*, 63 vols. (Carlisle, Pa.: Banner of Truth, 1971), 52:600–1.

most in life is that we come under the care of the right shepherd. How often in the Bible were the people led by false shepherds who cared nothing for the sheep! The prophet Zechariah had complained, "their own shepherds have no pity on them," so they are "doomed to be slaughtered" (Zech. 11:5, 7). Jesus pointed out that false shepherds, like robbers only interested in selfish gain, abandon the sheep when danger draws near (John 10:12).

This lack of a true shepherd remains the great problem of most people today. The great mass of people have either committed themselves to false ideologies and leaders, or allow no one at all to serve as their protector and guide. Many brazenly sing, "I did it my way," all the way to destruction. Jesus looks on this state of the world with pity, seeing the masses "harassed and helpless, like sheep without a shepherd" (Matt. 9:36). The godly of Micah's day turned to the Lord for their salvation. Jesus came to the whole world as the great Savior God has sent to us, and he presents himself as the true and good shepherd, who guides our souls safely into the pastures of God.

PROTECTED AND PROVISIONED

Having trusted Jesus to be our good shepherd, we also need to know what to expect of him. The Bible is honest in assuring us of many troubles. But there are two great blessings for everyone who enters the flock of Christ. The first is that our souls are personally protected by the Lord. This is what Micah promised the holy remnant of Jerusalem: they would be "like sheep in a fold" (Mic. 2:12). A shepherd protected his sheep by bringing them into a fold, a walled shelter with only one entryway. The shepherd then lay down across that entry, guarding the sheep with his own life.

This is what Jesus meant when he said, "I am the door of the sheep" (John 10:7). Nothing can reach his precious sheep without passing through him. Christ's sheep are protected from everything that might truly harm us, beginning with the righteous judgment of God on our sins. "I am the good shepherd," said Jesus. "The good shepherd lays down his life for the sheep" (John 10:11). Jesus died for the sins of his sheep; and having risen from the grave, he lives today to keep every last one of us secure. "I give them eternal life," he declares, "and they will never perish, and no one will snatch them out of my hand" (John 10:28).

The second blessing secured by the good shepherd is provision for all our needs. Micah wrote that the remnant of Jerusalem would be "like a flock in its pasture" (Mic. 2:12). A shepherd prepares green pastures and leads his flock to them. Psalm 23:2–3 says, "He makes me lie down in green pastures. He leads me beside still waters. He restores my soul. He leads me in paths of righteousness for his name's sake." In just this way, God arranged for supplies of food and water in Jerusalem so that the remnant that fled there would find provision during Sennacherib's siege. Hezekiah, Judah's godly king, had not only purged Jerusalem of idolatry and restored worship in the temple so as to point the people to the Lord, but also gathered stores and constructed a remarkable tunnel that would provide the besieged city with water (see 2 Kings 20:20; 2 Chron. 32:2–3; 27–30).

Likewise, if we will only enter the flock of Jesus Christ by faith in him, and then follow him through obedience to his Word, we will find both the supply for all our needs and the satisfaction of soul that only he can give. Jesus said, "If anyone enters by me, he will be saved and will go in and out and find pasture. . . . I came that they may have life and have it abundantly" (John 10:9–10).

In sum, the Bible states that those who turn to God to be their refuge will find him to be our good and faithful shepherd. God's protection of the holy remnant in Jerusalem was just one example. Our trials are designed by the Lord to draw us to him, and he will keep us safe. He will guard us and provide for our needs. And he will lead us out of this world, even passing with us through the valley of the shadow of death, so that we arrive safely in the green fields of everlasting life.

Have you recognized your own need for such a Savior? Do you still think you can make it through life in your own strength? Or are you following ideologies and false saviors who lead you astray and seek only to use you for their own selfish designs? The key to life is recognizing Jesus Christ as the only true Savior, believing his Word and trusting in him, and then following him by listening to the voice of his Word. For those who have Jesus as their shepherd, and those alone, the concluding words of Psalm 23 are precious and true: "Surely goodness and mercy shall follow me all the days of my life, and I shall dwell in the house of the LORD forever" (Ps. 23:6).

THE REMNANT LED OUT IN VICTORY

One of the indications that Micah is referring to Sennacherib's invasion is the language of verse 13: "He who opens the breach goes up before them;

they break through and pass the gate, going out by it." This precisely fits the situation that unfolded in Jerusalem's salvation.

Sennacherib had Hezekiah and his people penned into the city. A record on one of the reliefs in his palace, which archaeologists have unearthed, boasts that Sennacherib had "shut up Hezekiah inside Jerusalem his royal city like a bird in a cage."[4] There were the two kings, the stronger gloating over the weaker. But Micah reminds us that there is another king, the almighty King of heaven, and he would come to break the siege around his people. The people who fled for refuge would come out to safety, for "their king passes on before them, the Lord at their head" (Mic. 2:13).

As Micah envisions it, the Lord opens the breach. The Hebrew term means to break open a wall, though more broadly it may speak of someone opening a way by striking out with great might. John Mackay writes that this "is a presentation of the Lord as a warrior overthrowing his enemies."[5] This same description is given of the Lord Jesus Christ, who in the New Testament is called the "captain" or "forerunner" of our salvation (Heb. 2:10; 6:20), having overthrown our enemies through the blood of his crucifixion. Behind the Lord, Micah says, the people "break through and pass the gate, going out by it" (Mic. 2:13), led by their king, with the Lord at their head. We are thus reminded that God's people are saved not by bow or sword or warhorse, but rather God says, "I will save them by the Lord their God" (Hos. 1:7).

Isaiah tells us how Jerusalem's deliverance transpired. After Sennacherib's emissary mocked Hezekiah and his faith, he sent a letter to the king. Hezekiah took this letter into the temple and spread it out before the Lord. There, he offered up a model of God-centered prayer. Hezekiah began: "O Lord of hosts, God of Israel who is enthroned above the cherubim, you are the God, you alone, of all the kingdoms of the earth; you have made heaven and earth" (Isa. 37:16). He continued, "Incline your ear, O Lord, and hear; open your eyes, O Lord, and see; and hear all the words of Sennacherib, which he has sent to mock the living God" (Isa. 37:17). Hezekiah then admitted the overwhelming supremacy of the Assyrian might, but concluded, "So now, O Lord our God, save us from his hand, that all the

4. Cited from Leslie C. Allen, *The Books of Joel, Obadiah, Jonah, and Micah*, New International Commentary on the Old Testament (Grand Rapids: Eerdmans, 1976), 302.

5. John L. Mackay, *Jonah, Micah, Nahum, Habakkuk and Zephaniah: God's Just Demands*, Focus on the Bible (Ross–shire, UK: Christian Focus, 1998), 83.

kingdoms of the earth may know that you alone are the LORD" (Isa. 37:20). God replied by sending an answer through Isaiah: "Out of Jerusalem shall go a remnant, and out of Mount Zion a band of survivors. The zeal of the LORD of hosts will do this. . . . For I will defend this city to save it, for my own sake and for the sake of my servant David" (Isa. 37:32, 35).

This reminds us that God hears and answers prayer. It shows that when God enters into covenant with us through faith, he considers his name bound to our defense. So it was that God struck Sennacherib that very night: "And the angel of the LORD went out and struck down a hundred and eighty-five thousand in the camp of the Assyrians. And when people arose early in the morning, behold, these were all dead bodies. Then Sennacherib king of Assyria departed and returned home and lived at Nineveh" (Isa. 37:36–37). So spectacular was this supernatural deliverance that a version of it is recorded in the secular history of the Greek chronicler Herodotus.[6]

God's deliverance of the Jewish remnant in Micah's time is not an isolated incident, but God's manner of saving all his people from a condemned and violent world. One of our hymns captures the spirit of this salvation, with a vision of the countless host of God, that remnant from the world, rising up to follow the Lord, triumphant in all the battles of this life against sin. God allows us to be weak in this world, beset by mighty enemies, yet always he is our refuge and strength:

> Thou wast their Rock, their Fortress and their Might;
> Thou, Lord, their captain in the well-fought fight;
> Thou, in the darkness drear, their one true light. Allelluia! Allelluia!

That is what the remnant of Jerusalem discovered as God led them into his shelter, a Rock and Fortress for those who trust in him. The hymn rejoices that when the darkness is past, everyone who hopes in the Lord Jesus Christ may look forward to a glorious rising, a resurrection even from the grave. The Lord himself leads us out into the everlasting pastures of heaven:

> But lo! There breaks a yet more glorious day;
> The saints triumphant rise in bright array;
> The King of Glory passes on His way. Allelluia! Allelluia!

6. Herodotus, *The Histories*, 2:141.

196

This is why God's people rejoice in a salvation by his sovereign grace and might, and why we will lift up our hearts in praise to him for all the long years of eternity:

> From earth's wide bounds, from ocean's farthest coast;
> Thro' gates of pearl stream in the countless host,
> Singing to Father, Son, and Holy Ghost. Allelluia! Allelluia![7]

The words of this hymn are a fitting conclusion to the first cycle of Micah's prophecy. Micah proclaims an unyielding message of divine holiness, for God is certain to judge any wicked and idolatrous people. The prophet admits that God's faithful remnant is afflicted in this world at the hands of the greedy and false, and suffers with them through God's acts of judgment on the world. The gap between God's righteous standards and man's sinful performance is so wide that divine judgment is inevitable. But into that gap Micah inserts a towering promise of the hope of God's grace. God speaks with the most definite resolve: "I will surely," he promises (Mic. 2:12), guaranteeing that his remnant will be sheltered, shepherded, and led in triumph. Likewise, the Lord Jesus Christ speaks in equally definite terms, having won on the cross our victory over sin, evil, and death: "Truly, truly, I say to you, whoever hears my word and believes him who sent me has eternal life. He does not come into judgment, but has passed from death to life" (John 5:24).

7. William Walsham How, "For All the Saints," 1864.

197

20

WOLVES IN SHEPHERDS' CLOTHING

Micah 3:1–4

Then they will cry to the LORD, but he will not answer them; he will hide his face from them at that time, because they have made their deeds evil. (Mic. 3:4)

eople often picture religious zealots as wild-eyed fanatics, holding up signs declaring, "God's Judgment Is at Hand!" We see this image in cartoons and religious lampoons. It is, in fact, a fairly accurate portrait of the prophet Micah, perhaps more so than any other Old Testament figure. In chapter 1, Micah records going around Jerusalem practically naked, loudly lamenting God's coming judgment with sounds like that of jackals and ostriches (Mic.1:8). As we begin chapter 3, which opens his second cycle of sermons, Micah returns to form, warning the false prophets and especially targeting the governing magistrates: "Hear, you heads of Jacob and rulers of the house of Israel!" (Mic. 3:1).

The middle section of Micah's prophecy, consisting of the oracles or sermons in chapters three to five, continues his pattern of preaching judgment followed by grace. Chapter 3 delivers severe denunciations on sin, and chapters 4 and 5 present soaring promises of salvation. Through these messages, Micah sought to spark the people's consciences so they would repent and turn back to the Lord.

The question might be raised, "Does such preaching make any difference? Is there any point to warning people against the perils of sin and reminding them of God's grace?" According to the prophet Jeremiah, such preaching can have a powerful, redeeming effect. Writing a hundred years later, Jeremiah reminded his hearers of Micah's preaching. Hezekiah, Judah's king during this period of Micah's ministry, responded by repenting, turning to the Lord, and leading the people in a national reformation, with the result that disaster was averted (see Jer. 26:18–19). This encourages us that by preaching the Bible's warnings against sin and heralding the gospel promises of God's grace, we may hope for reformation and revival in our own time.

To the Heads and Rulers

Micah addresses himself to the "heads of Jacob and rulers of the house of Israel" (Mic. 3:1). Originally, each tribe and clan was overseen by its elder men and by those of proven ability (see Exod. 18:25). Under the kingship, Jehoshaphat had appointed his own officials to judge over the affairs of the cities and towns. It is probably these royal officials to whom Micah refers. The word "rulers" literally means "deciders," so these were the magistrates who ruled the local and national courts in the name of the king.

Micah has a question for these heads and rulers: "Is it not for you to know justice?" (Mic. 3:1). Above all others in Israel, the ruling officials should know what constitutes justice, he argues. His point is not merely that they should know the laws, but that they should operate with the law in their hearts. Bernard Renaud comments that Micah's idea of knowing justice "implies a power of discerning and of making judgment, even a sympathy for the outcasts of fortune. . . . In short, 'to know the law' is to let reign inside the community a climate of justice and brotherhood."[1] Isaiah made a similar plea to the leaders of Jerusalem, urging them to "learn to do good" and "seek

1. Cited from Bruce Waltke, *A Commentary on Micah* (Grand Rapids: Eerdmans, 2007), 155.

justice." Isaiah also gives the Bible's definition of justice: "correct oppression; bring justice to the fatherless, plead the widow's cause" (Isa. 1:17).

According to the Bible, this mandate for justice pertains not merely to Old Testament officials, but to all civil leaders even today. The apostle Paul made this clear when he taught Christians to submit to civil authority: "For there is no authority except from God, and those that exist have been instituted by God" (Rom. 13:1). All authority is derived from God, and every ruler has been put in place by God's providence. Therefore God holds all rulers to account for the exercise of moral and social justice. Paul says, "He is the servant of God, an avenger who carries out God's wrath on the wrongdoer" (Rom. 13:4). This is in keeping with Jehoshaphat's instructions to the officials of his kingdom: "Consider what you do, for you judge not for man but for the LORD. . . . Now then, let the fear of the Lord be upon you. Be careful what you do, for there is no injustice with the LORD our God, or partiality or taking bribes" (2 Chron. 19:6–7).

In most Western nations, where rulers are elected, these instructions are helpful to those entrusted with casting votes. If God calls all rulers to enforce sound morals and equitable justice, then the first qualification for any candidate must always be that of personal character and discernment. When Moses sought rulers, these were his priorities: "Look for able men from all the people, men who fear God, who are trustworthy and hate a bribe" (Exod. 18:21).

We are constantly told today that character doesn't matter, only competence. But the Bible condemns such thinking as sheer folly. For one thing, a candidate for high office can seldom predict the challenges he or she will face once elected, so wisdom and moral courage are at a premium. Moreover, given the great power invested in civil officials, especially at the national level, the first prerequisite should always be a demonstrated trustworthiness to wield such authority. Therefore, Moses' priorities for leadership included proven ability, reverence before God and his Word, and high personal integrity. We should select our leaders by these same priorities, in society and especially in the church.

Micah's point in asking his question, "Is it not for you to know justice?" was to show that they did not know justice. The ancient preacher Theodoret of Cyr paraphrases: "Was it not you who had responsibility for judging, for punishing the guilty and letting the innocent go free without blame? How did you, then, who were entrusted with administering the law, turn from the practice of good works and ardently support evil?"[2]

Such was the crisis of leadership in Micah's day that he could honestly describe the Jewish officials as "you who hate the good and love the evil" (Mic. 3:2). This is not the kind of thing the judges would readily have admitted. But their actions and rulings proved Micah's accusation. As Jesus said, "the tree is known by its fruit" (Matt. 12:33), and the character of one who wields authority is revealed by the decisions he makes. Micah's language is colorful: these rulers found the good to be repulsive and disgusting, while their wicked hearts delighted in upholding evil. Given the accusations of chapter 2, much of this probably had to do with collaborating and profiting with those who oppressed and despoiled the common people for the sake of gorging on riches and land.

We are plagued today by a similar calamity of ruling authorities who delight in evil and hate the good. Men and women seated as judges over our courts and trusted with determining our laws have shown themselves to delight in overthrowing every standard of justice and decency. They preserve the "right" of mothers to have their unborn children killed for the sake of a lifestyle of freedom. Under the authority of our courts, Bibles are ripped from the hands of boys and girls in public schools. Standards of sexual decency and family order upheld since the dawn of civilization are overturned. All the while, the greatest delight is taken in money raised through the gambling addictions fostered by our state lotteries, tolerance is shown for the degradation of women by pornography, and many in power exult in the opulent lifestyles financed by those who purchase their influence.

Through Micah, God called the heads and rulers of Judah to account, and he will hold our leaders to account as well. The condemnation on our wicked rulers, however, will be shared by those whose votes placed them in power.

SHEEP-EATING WOLVES

Micah does not settle for a general condemnation of evil, however. He proceeds to describe these rulers installed to shepherd the flock of God's people as ruthless wolves who rip them apart. Micah sees them "tear[ing]

---

2. Theodoret of Cyr, "Commentary on Micah," in Alberto Ferreiro, ed., *The Twelve Prophets*, Ancient Christian Commentary on Scripture, Old Testament XIV (Downers Grove, Ill.: InterVarsity, 2003), 156.

the skin from off my people and their flesh from off their bones" (Mic. 3:2). They then "eat the flesh of my people, and flay their skin from off them, and break their bones in pieces and chop them up like meat in a pot, like flesh in a cauldron" (Mic. 3:3).

Here is a blood-curdling depiction of indifference to human suffering and exploitation of the weak. In utmost outrage, God charges that "these leaders . . . tear, eat, flay, break, and chop 'my people' as one would slaughter an animal to be eaten."[3] Peter Craigie summarizes: "They were hungry butchers, skinning the flesh of the weak for a tasty morsel to eat, breaking their bones and popping them into the stock pot to prepare a tasty soup. The officers of the court had no concern for others, no passion for justice; the horizon of their ambitions was merely to fulfill their own hungers and desires."[4]

Of course, Micah did not mean that Judah's wicked rulers were literally eating the people: he employs the gruesome metaphor of cannibalism to depict the severity of the violent injustice they perpetrated. How else could he describe the casting of widows and their children from their homes, the wrongful seizure of lands bequeathed by God to families and their heirs, and the deploying of bully squads to intimidate and crush all who opposed their will? Undoubtedly, Micah's outrage was fueled by faces in his mind of people he knew from back home in Moresheth who were so victimized, and from personal encounters with the poor, homeless victims who came to Jerusalem.

Doubtless the magistrates resented Micah's scathing description. Micah was being melodramatic, they would have argued. Jewish society was merely undergoing a long-awaited updating according to the latest economic theory. The concentration of wealth and power would bring efficiencies and allow Judah to achieve greater strength. Admittedly, there were short-term costs for the common people. But the rabble would get used to minor inconveniences so those more fit might channel the results of their labor. If the small number of elites enjoyed new heights of luxury as a result of their leadership, well, that was just the way of the world. This is how similar predators reason today, and presumably it is how the heads and rulers of Israel reasoned then.

Their problem was that God, speaking through the prophet, did not share their view. A quick perusal of the Ten Commandments will show that God

---

3. James Limburg, *Hosea–Micah*, Interpretation (Atlanta: Westminster John Knox, 1988), 175.

4. Peter C. Craigie, *Twelve Prophets*, Daily Study Bible Series, 2 vols. (Louisville: Westminster John Knox, 1985), 2:27–28.

requires us to preserve the life and well-being of our fellow man, to respect the property that God has given to others, and not to covet the blessings enjoyed by our neighbors. This alone shows that if the actions of the rulers were in keeping with worldly standards of the time, they were not in keeping with God's requirements. The argument, "This is how the world works, so I might as well make sure I come out on top," is always refused by God. As Micah later summarizes, God requires us "to do justice, and to love kindness, and to walk humbly with [our] God" (Mic. 6:8).

But it is not just the evil rulers of Jerusalem who need to consider God's perspective on sin. However lightly we take our sins, God takes them with the most intense seriousness. Anyone who had visited Jerusalem's temple should have known this, having watched the daily sacrifices for sin in which a bleating animal had its life torn out in place of the transgressing people. The message was that God detests our sin and must slay the wicked. It is the same in the New Testament's repeated teaching that the penalty for unforgiven sin is an eternity of judgment. According to the Bible, hell is the destination for all who sin, and a place where "the smoke of their torment goes up forever and ever, and they have no rest, day or night" (Rev. 14:11). What does this show but that our holy God violently detests all sin?

The good news of the gospel of Jesus is that he came to deliver us from this appalling (but just) condemnation. Jesus died on the cross for sins that he did not commit, but we did. Paul delivers the glorious message, "In him we have redemption through his blood, the forgiveness of our trespasses, according to the riches of his grace" (Eph. 1:7). But this gives us no reason to excuse our sins. Anyone who can consider the torments suffered by the holy and innocent Jesus Christ on the cross—chief among which were the torments of his soul under the wrath of God—and continue to take sin lightly, must be possessed of a calloused conscience which is repugnant to God. Of course, we are exactly such people, casually excusing sins that revolt the heart of God. Having been forgiven through faith in the blood of Christ, we are now commanded to turn our hardened hearts to be renewed by God in holiness and truth.

ABANDONED BY GOD

Heartlessly betraying God's righteous calling, the men clothed and appointed as shepherds descended on God's people, baring wolves' teeth.

But God reminds them that this is the "house of Israel" (Mic. 3:1), God's holy nation, and that their victims are "my people" (Mic. 3:2). God has loving sympathy with those he placed under their authority, just as God's heart inclines toward wives under the authority of husbands, children under parents, church members under pastors and elders, and citizens under civil leaders. If the shepherds will not provide justice and mercy to the people, then God will deal with the shepherds. Micah thus pronounces: "Then they will cry to the LORD, but he will not answer them; he will hide his face from them at that time, because they have made their deeds evil" (Mic. 3:4).

This threat presupposes the judgments already prophesied by Micah's earlier sermons. Disaster was coming from the Lord to the gates of Jerusalem (Mic. 1:12), in the form of an invasion of the mighty Assyrian army. When that happened, Micah says, when God gave them a measure of the same violence Jerusalem's rulers had inflicted on their own people, then they would turn their hearts to the Lord for help. "Then they will cry to the LORD, but he will not answer them" (Mic. 3:4).

It is God's glory that he is faithful to hear the cries of his people in distress. Psalm 107:6 celebrates God's readiness to answer prayers: "Then they cried to the LORD in their trouble, and he delivered them from their distress." But this would not happen when Jerusalem's rulers cried their prayers to God. John Mackay explains: "Those who have despised their covenant obligations will not be able to avail themselves of their overlord's assistance in the day of calamity. Their sin separates them from their God."[5]

The question may be asked whether Christians need to fear this warning. The answer is, "Yes." The issue here concerns those who systematically abuse their God-given authority, causing harm to those placed by God under their care. An example is that of a husband's covenantal obligation to his wife. In a later generation, the priests of Israel complained that God did not answer their prayers. "Why does he not?" replied the prophet Malachi. "Because the LORD was witness between you and the wife of your youth, to whom you have been faithless, though she is your companion and your wife by covenant" (Mal. 2:14). This principle is explicitly carried forward into the New Testament by the apostle Peter, who commands husbands to love and cherish their wives "so that your prayers may not be hindered" (1 Peter 3:7).

---

5. John L. Mackay, *Jonah, Micah, Nahum, Habakkuk and Zephaniah: God's Just Demands*, Focus on the Bible (Ross–shire, UK: Christian Focus, 1998), 86.

Proverbs 21:13 applies this principle generally: "Whoever closes his ear to the cry of the poor will himself call out and not be answered."

The wolves of Jerusalem will not only be deprived of God's deliverance in the day of their trouble, but will have to make do without the inward peace and comfort that come through communion with God. Micah adds, "he will hide his face from them at that time" (Mic. 3:4). This recalls the great Aaronic blessing: "The LORD bless you and keep you; the LORD make his face to shine upon you and be gracious to you" (Num. 6:24–25). To have God's "face to shine upon you" is to be conscious of God's favor and love. G. Wehmeier comments, "As the turning of the face is a sign of friendship and favor, so the turning away of the covering of the countenance is a sign of no mercy."[6] Bruce Waltke observes, "The worst form of judgment for Israel is not the affliction itself but the absence of God in it."[7]

This is something Christians may experience as God's chastisement when we "grieve the Holy Spirit" (Eph. 4:30) through persistent or gross sins. Indeed, when we feel an absence of God from our lives, and a corresponding lack of the grace of his Spirit within us, we should investigate the pattern by which we have been living, the sins we have been accommodating, and our faithfulness (or lack thereof) to the obligations God has given us for those under our care.

Why would God so abandon the rulers of Jerusalem? His answer was plain and clear: "because they have made their deeds evil" (Mic. 3:4). They had violated every pretense of justice, so God had afflicted them with calamity, refused to hear their prayers, and turned his face away from them—and God had done this justly as the penalty for their terrible sins. Their poor example urges us to give heed to our own manner of living and especially to our faithfulness in God-given authority. Paul made the issue clear: "Do not be deceived: God is not mocked" (Gal. 6:7).

THE OPEN DOOR OF GRACE

The only way for us to apply this passage honestly is to realize our own kinship with the ruthless rulers of Jerusalem. We might not have their opportunity for such widespread evil. But in the positions God has given us, we

6. Cited from Waltke, *A Commentary on Micah*, 151–52.
7. Ibid., 152.

have acted in a similar spirit. We have been preoccupied with our own well-being so as to act cruelly to others. We have turned our faces from the needy. We have caused harm to others in our behavior as parents and as children, as husbands and as wives, as bosses and as employees, as pastors and elders and as church members. We have imbibed of the spirit of the "heads of Jacob and rulers of the house of Israel" (Mic. 3:1). By our actions, we have shown hatred for good and love for evil. If God should visit us with calamity, refuse our prayers, and turn his face from us, we will have deserved it. If God should cast us forever into the torments of hell, we will have deserved that, too.

What hope is there for Micah's listeners, then and now? The answer is implied by the mere fact that God has graciously provided us this warning. We can turn our hearts from evil and convict ourselves before God, fully confessing our sins and the evil of them. We can seek the grace of our God who, Micah says, "delights in mercy" (Mic. 7:18, NKJV). We can turn our ears to the good news that God has acted in mercy by sending his Son to die on the cross for our sins.

One of Micah's original hearers who responded in this way was the highest official in the land, the one entrusted with authority over all the heads and rulers of the house of Israel, King Hezekiah. As I mentioned, Jeremiah records that Hezekiah did not lash out against Micah and his rebukes. Instead, Jeremiah says, "Did he not fear the LORD and entreat the favor of the LORD . . . ?" (Jer. 26:19). Hezekiah did exactly this, and when he prayed in true repentance and faith, God heard his plea, showed the king his face, and relented of the disaster he had brought.

An even greater example concerns Hezekiah's son and successor, King Manasseh. Manasseh was probably Judah's most wicked king, leading the people into abject idolatry, filling Jerusalem with innocent blood, and even instituting child sacrifices in the valley beneath the temple mount, starting with his own son (2 Kings 21:2–16). Predictably, God brought severe penalties upon Manasseh; but when he did, the evil king sincerely repented. The Bible records: "When he was in distress, he entreated the favor of the LORD his God and humbled himself greatly before the God of his fathers. He prayed to him, and God was moved by his entreaty and heard his plea and brought him again to Jerusalem into his kingdom" (2 Chron. 33:12–13). This is one prayer that God always hears and loves to answer: the sincere confession of sin and humble plea for God's grace. When Manasseh returned to Jerusalem, he removed the idols, cleansed the city of sin, and restored true worship, thus beginning the sweeping reformation that would be completed under his godly grandson, King Josiah, under whom Jerusalem enjoyed its last godly reign before God's judgment.

How could God forgive such grotesque sins as those committed by Manasseh—including child sacrifice? Only through the infinitely precious blood of his own divine Son. God is willing and able to forgive your sin, to the glory of his grace. Then God calls us to the kind of reformation that sweeps out the idols of our hearts and restores the principles of God's justice, through the power of the Holy Spirit that he sends. But God also calls you to be smitten by the prophetic rebuke, as Hezekiah was, to confess your sin and look humbly in faith to the Savior Jesus Christ: "For God so loved the world, that he gave his only Son, that whoever believes in him should not perish but have eternal life.... Whoever believes in him is not condemned, but whoever does not believe is condemned already, because he has not believed in the name of the only Son of God" (John 3:16, 18).

21

True-False Test

Micah 3:5—8

Thus says the LORD concerning the prophets who lead my people astray, who cry "Peace" when they have something to eat, but declare war against him who puts nothing into their mouths. (Mic. 3:5)

When making up exams, teachers have a number of options available. The easiest exam questions are multiple choice or matching: the answers are provided, and students merely have to line them up with the right questions. The next most difficult questions, however, are fill-in-the-blank. Here, the student has to know the correct answer. The most difficult questions are true-false, in which students often must make fine distinctions and exercise a high degree of discernment.

The situation of Old Testament Israel was similar to this. Perhaps the greatest challenge for God's ancient people was in distinguishing between false and true prophets. A prophet served as God's mouthpiece. The problem was that false prophets claimed to speak for God, when they did not. This was of vital importance in an age when God's revelation to his people was still unfolding. To follow a false prophet was to be led away from the truth, whereas true prophets guided their hearers in the way of the Lord.

How to Recognize a False Prophet

Moses was so concerned that the people be able to discern between true and false prophets that he gave clear instructions about this in his parting message. First, Moses noted that a true prophet must be able to make accurate predictions: "when a prophet speaks in the name of the LORD, if the word does not come to pass or come true, that is a word that the LORD has not spoken" (Deut. 18:22). But there was a second and vital test. The prophet must also speak in accordance with God's prior revelation; he must not lead the people astray. Moses taught, "If a prophet or a dreamer of dreams arises among you and gives you a sign or a wonder, and the sign or wonder that he tells you comes to pass, and if he says, 'Let us go after other gods,' which you have not known, 'and let us serve them,' you shall not listen to the words of that prophet or that dreamer of dreams" (Deut. 13:1–3). Even if a prophet could display apparently divine power in prophesying, the people were to be faithful not to betray what they knew to be true of the Lord.

Prophetic truth is Micah's concern as he delivers God's condemnation: "Thus says the LORD concerning the prophets who lead my people astray" (Mic. 3:5). Notice that Micah refers to these false teachers as "prophets." It is evident from this passage that in some sense these were genuine prophets; that is, they were probably card-carrying members of the prophetic community once led by Elijah and Elisha. In this capacity they had some access to true divine revelation. The earliest books of the Bible had been written, but it is doubtful that average Israelites could consult them. So when a layperson wanted to consult God's will, the first place for him to go was to the prophets, of whom there were a great many.

What made these teachers false prophets was not their lack of access to God's Word but rather what they did with God's Word. Micah charges them with leading God's people astray. They were not the kind of false prophets who openly taught the people to worship pagan idols, as was so often a problem. But they manipulated their message for selfish gain nonetheless. Instead of ministering God's true Word to their hearers, they trimmed their message depending on who was listening. Instead of representing God's opposition to injustice and moral corruption, they collaborated with the greedy rich in exploiting the people, encouraging the tolerance of sin. As Jeremiah would complain to a later generation: "Your prophets . . . have

209

not exposed your iniquity to restore your fortunes, but have seen for you oracles that are false and misleading" (Lam. 2:14). The word Micah uses for "lead astray" (Hebrew, *hammatyim*) has the connotation of the wandering of a lost person or the stupor of a drunk.[1] This was the moral effect of the prophets' false teaching.

The prophets were leading the people astray by adjusting their message according to what the recipients could do for them. They gave positive messages only to those who paid them well. Micah says they "cry 'Peace' when they have something to eat" (Mic. 3:5). The Hebrew word for peace, *shalom*, signifies a right relationship with God, with all the blessings of harmony and well-being that result. Micah charges that the false prophets were granting assurances of *shalom* to the very sinners who were most violently oppressing God's people and most flagrantly transgressing God's law. Michael Bentley comments:

> These false prophets were telling the inhabitants of Judah that everything was all right. Of course that was what they wanted to hear. We all love to hear good news. We long to be assured that everything is well. We desire an easy pathway through life. No wonder the people listened with pleasure when the false prophets said that everything was peaceful.[2]

But the prophets were not telling everyone good news: Micah charges that they "declare war against him who puts nothing into their mouths" (Mic. 3:5). You could get a positive message from the prophets if you paid well; but if you did not, their message would be one of woe and doom. David Prior writes: "The people who ought to have been told about war had peace preached to them. The people who ought to have heard about peace found that the religious authorities, like the rest of those in authority, had declared war on them."[3]

Micah's main accusation concerns the relationship between the false prophets' message and their motive. They were supposed to be driven by a zeal for God's glory and a holy concern for faith and godliness. Instead, they cared only about their own bellies. "Selfish expediency had become

---

1. Bruce Waltke, *A Commentary on Micah* (Grand Rapids: Eerdmans, 2007), 158.
2. Michael Bentley, *Balancing the Books: Micah and Nahum Simply Explained* (Durham: Evangelical Press, 1994), 46.
3. David Prior, *The Message of Joel, Micah & Habakkuk*, The Bible Speaks Today (Downers Grove, Ill.: InterVarsity, 1998), 140.

their criterion for the content of their oracles, on the principle that he who pays the piper calls the tune."[4] As Hans Wolff put it, "What came out of the mouth of those prophets depended on what was put into it."[5] This is what Paul said about his theological opponents: "their god is their belly, and they glory in their shame, with minds set on earthly things" (Phil. 3:19).

It is not that the prophets were wrong for receiving money. The Bible says that preachers are to be paid for their work. Paul instructed, "The Lord commanded that those who proclaim the gospel should get their living by the gospel" (1 Cor. 9:14), and, "You shall not muzzle an ox when it treads out the grain" (1 Cor. 9:9). Then, as now, those who labor in God's Word are to be provided for by the church. Yet a minister's motivation should never be to accumulate worldly gain through his ministry. He ministers for the good of the flock, speaking God's truth as received from God's Word. Whenever preachers become more concerned with their paychecks, their popularity, or their comfort, they will always be tempted to suit their preaching to the ear of the consumer in the pew. It is not a coincidence that some of the largest and wealthiest churches today are those that preach the so-called "prosperity gospel." "Peace, peace!" they cry. "God wants only to bless you and fill your life with earthly things!" Yet they seldom point out God's holy anger against sin and they suppress the message of the cross, since it implies that God might be more serious and demanding than churchgoers are interested in paying to hear.

An application of this charge against false prophets is that God's people need to be competent enough in the Scriptures to recognize false teaching. These lying prophets were credentialed spokesmen for God, members of a once-glorious prophetic college. People believed what they said, either rejoicing that all was well with God (when it was not) or suffering under spiritual torment when they were too poor to pay. God has provided teachers of his Word, to whom his people are to listen (Eph. 4:11). But in Micah's time, when the Bible was being written, and especially now when the completed Bible is widely available, God expects his people to discern between true and false prophecy.

4. Leslie C. Allen, *The Books of Joel, Obadiah, Jonah, and Micah*, New International Commentary on the Old Testament (Grand Rapids: Eerdmans, 1976), 311.
5. Cited in Waltke, *A Commentary on Micah*, 172.

John Mackay sagely comments, "History has certainly shown that no institutions can degenerate so quickly as theological colleges."[6] It is not sufficient for a preacher to be credentialed by an impressive seminary. Church members are to insist on teaching that faithfully sets forth the whole counsel of God from the Scriptures, and on ministers whose aims are demonstrably spiritual and God-honoring. Those who prefer preaching that treats sin lightly and promotes novelty or intellectual fashion are convicted along with the false prophets they love. Moses warned the people about false prophets, saying, "The LORD your God is testing you, to know whether you love the LORD your God with all your heart and with all your soul" (Deut. 13:3). Likewise, Christians' love for God today is seen in the kind of preaching for which they have an appetite.

THE CONSEQUENCES OF FALSE PROPHECY

All through the book of Micah, God reacts to sin with punishments suited to the crimes. So it is with the false prophets who enriched themselves through the abuse of their gifts and calling. "Therefore," Micah replies, "it shall be night to you, without vision, and darkness to you, without divination. The sun shall go down on the prophets, and the day shall be black over them" (Mic. 3:6).

Prophetic visions were usually received at night, but now their nights would pass without illumination. The word for *divination* designates occult practices forbidden by God but apparently practiced by these prophets, to include examining livers and consulting astrology charts. God will not permit any of these superstitious efforts to produce heavenly insight, and these prophets will be left in the dark. Bruce Waltke comments, "Like Samson, who lost his gift for abusing it and was plunged into darkness, so also these prophets who should have been the moral eyes of the nation would lose their gifted insight."[7]

The result will be the prophets' disgrace before the people: "The seers shall be disgraced, and the diviners put to shame" (Mic. 3:7). Left to their own wits, the prophets will fail to impress their moneyed clients and their public

6. John L. Mackay, *Jonah, Micah, Nahum, Habakkuk and Zephaniah: God's Just Demands*, Focus on the Bible (Ross–shire, UK: Christian Focus, 1998), 87.

7. Waltke, *A Commentary on Micah*, 173.

212

stature will suffer. Through them, the people will experience what Amos had predicted: "a famine . . . of hearing the words of the LORD" (Amos 8:11).

Apparently, God had graciously been providing revelation even to these false prophets. But now "there is no answer from God" (Mic. 3:7). The prophets "shall all cover their lips." They will be like the prophets of Baal in Elijah's time, who cried out, "O Baal, answer us!" But, the Bible records, "there was no voice, and no one answered" (1 Kings 18:26). The prophets of Baal were taken and slaughtered for their failure; the false prophets of Judah would suffer disgrace because God was no longer speaking to them.

Something similar happens today in churches where God's Word no longer is faithfully taught. In liberal churches, worldly theories about the Bible spread from academia into the smooth rhetoric of pulpits. The people are taught that the Bible must be interpreted to fit with current ideas of God, truth, morality, and salvation. In increasing numbers of evangelical churches, a man-centered or political agenda takes the place of the biblical gospel. In either case, the pulpit inevitably loses its power to effect true salvation, becoming a place for displays of personality rather than divine proclamation. The church becomes increasingly irrelevant, saying nothing different from what is heard elsewhere in the world. No longer able to rely on the Holy Spirit to draw believers to God's Word, such churches suffer the shame of having to market their music programs, exciting worship experiences, and other worldly goods and services. The prevalence of this trend has accelerated the disgrace of the whole church in society so that a land filled with Christian institutions suffers a famine for hearing the Word of the Lord.

HOW TO RECOGNIZE A TRUE PROPHET

The key to true-false tests is recognizing the crucial defect of a false answer or the ring of truth in the other. Micah's message has so far made clear what marks false prophets: they lead people astray by manipulating their message in order to enrich themselves. The false prophet, like the false preacher today, thought first about his own well-being before opening his mouth. But Micah concludes with a picture of the true prophet, offering himself as an exhibit. Micah is not boasting; rather, just as the apostle Paul frequently set forth his apostolic credentials in order to authentic his message, Micah points to the evident signs of spirituality in his preaching. "But as for me," he says, "I am filled with power, with the Spirit of the LORD, and with justice and might, to declare to Jacob his transgression and to Israel his sin" (Mic. 3:8).

Whereas the false prophet is disgraced by his impotence, the true prophet displays divine power through the Holy Spirit. Bruce Waltke says, "The spirit of [the Lord] gives Micah the supernatural courage to stand up, at the peril of his very life, to address wrongdoers."[8] Just as Micah's message comes from God, the strength to preach it in the face of opposition comes from the Lord. The true prophet is motivated not by personal gain or fear of loss, not by popularity, and not by the whims or felt needs of his hearers, but by the compulsion of God's Spirit working in and through him. Leslie Allen writes of Micah, "He is conscious of a power compelling him to speak."[9] He is like Jeremiah, who declared, "There is in my heart as it were a burning fire shut up in my bones, and I am weary with holding it in, and I cannot" (Jer. 20:9).

Micah's distinction between a Spirit-led prophet and one motivated by selfish greed exerts a decisive influence on the kind of ministry a preacher will have today. The true minister of God's Word relies not on oratory or zeal, not on verbal manipulation or emotional sentiment, not on scholarly authority or trendy insight, but on the powerful working of the Holy Spirit attending on God's Word. This was the apostle Paul's conviction when he set forth his philosophy of ministry: "We have renounced disgraceful, underhanded ways. We refuse to practice cunning or to tamper with God's word, but by the open statement of the truth we would commend ourselves to everyone's conscience in the sight of God" (2 Cor. 4:2).

This is the Spirit we need to animate our pulpits. With this in mind, John Calvin writes:

> Let those who are charged with preaching the Word of God acknowledge their insufficiency. May they realize that however gifted mankind on their own may be with the might of all that is treasured, or however confident in their endowed good sense and intelligence, all that amounts to nothing, unless God grants us his Holy Spirit. . . . No one is able on his own to serve God until God has strengthened him with his power, which must come from above.[10]

---

8. Ibid., 166.
9. Allen, *The Books of Joel, Obadiah, Jonah, and Micah*, 313.
10. John Calvin, *Sermons on the Book of Micah* (Phillipsburg, NJ: P&R Publishing, 2003), 165.

The power of the Holy Spirit exerted a decided influence not only on the manner, but also on the matter, the content, of Micah's preaching. He preached "with justice" (Mic. 3:8). Instead of having his perspective controlled by bribes, Micah was directed by God's standards of right and wrong. Included are the themes of God's mercy for the weak and God's anger against proud oppressors. Micah did not believe that standards of morality are adaptable to the fashions of the time, nor that the obligations of justice, charity, and love may be set aside when it comes to those in power. On the contrary, "His sole motive is to encourage right and discourage wrong."[11]

Micah says that a true prophet is motivated by a divine compulsion to speak truth from God, is stalwart in setting forth God's standards of justice, and, thirdly, stands firm in the Holy Spirit and in "might" (Mic. 3:8). The connotation of the word for "might" is that of a firm resolution and mighty deeds. Micah was prepared to suffer for God's truth and to raise his voice among the people like a valorous champion striding forth against the foe. Matthew Henry comments, "Those who are sure that they have a commission from God need not be afraid of opposition from men."[12] "Let them not yield," wrote Calvin, "to any gales that may blow nor be overcome by threats and terrors; let them not bend here and there to please the world; in a word, let them not succumb to any corruptions."[13] This is the spirit of "might" to which Micah refers.

The history of the Christian church is largely written by heroic figures empowered with the Spirit set forth here by Micah. We think of Polycarp, the aged bishop of Smyrna, who refused to recant his faith in Christ in the face of Roman lions: "Eighty and six years have I served [Christ]," he said, "and he never did me any injury: how then can I blaspheme my King and my Savior?"[14] We think of Martin Luther, who refused to compromise the teaching of God's Word when threatened with flames by the pope. "Here I stand," Luther declared. "I cannot do otherwise."[15] We think of the English preachers,

11. Ibid., 314.

12. Matthew Henry, *Commentary on the Whole Bible*, 6 vols. (Peabody, Mass.: Hendrickson, n.d.), 4:1035.

13. John Calvin, *A Commentary on the Twelve Minor Prophets*, 5 vols. (1559; repr. Edinburgh: Banner of Truth, 1986), 3:235.

14. Cited from *The Ante–Nicene Fathers: Translations of the Writings of the Fathers Down to 325 A.D.*, vol. 1, *The Apostolic Fathers, Justin Martyr, Irenaeus*, ed. Alexander Roberts and James Donaldson (1885; repr. Peabody, Mass.: Hendrickson, 1999), 41.

15. Roland H. Bainton, *Here I Stand: A Life of Martin Luther* (New York: Penguin, 1955, reprint 1995), 144.

Latimer and Ridley, during Bloody Mary's persecution. Chained to the stake, awaiting the flames, Latimer called out, "Be of good comfort, brother Ridley, and play the man; we shall this day light such a candle, by God's grace, in England, as I trust never shall be put out."[16] We think of Chinese house-church pastors such as Allen Yuan and Samuel Lamb, both of whom were imprisoned in labor camps for over twenty years but resumed preaching about Jesus as soon as they were released. "The more persecution, the more the church grows," Lamb states. Yuan has said: "We have a saying in Beijing. If you dare to preach, people will believe."[17] Their spirit will triumph over all the powers of earth and hell, by the Word of the Lord and the strength of his might. Of such stalwart believers, Hebrews 11:16 says, "God is not ashamed to be called their God," and "he has prepared for them a city."

Lastly, Micah defines the mandate of the true and Spirit-empowered prophet: "to declare to Jacob his transgression and to Israel his sin" (Mic. 3:8). This was the chief failing of the false prophets: they treated sin lightly and promised peace with God despite rebellion and sin. Jeremiah railed against a similar failing in his generation: "They have healed the wound of my people lightly, saying, 'Peace, peace,' when there is no peace" (Jer. 6:14). By contrast, the true prophet would highlight the sins of his generation, calling people to repentance for the sake of their true healing and for genuine reconciliation with God. Micah railed against transgression and sin from the beginning of his book (1:5), not because of some perversity in his own spirit, but because he knew that only when sin is confessed and renounced, when God's favor is sought through the blood of his covenant, will sin be forgiven and God's acceptance be gained.

THE BATTLE FOR TRUTH

Like Micah, we live in a generation when truth is for sale and when the voice of the pulpit is too often bent by the winds of fashion or influence. The words of Pontius Pilate to our Lord Jesus are practically a motto for our age: "What is truth?" (John 18:38). But Jesus declared, "I have come into the world—to bear witness to the truth" (John 18:37). Prior to Jesus, God sent the prophets to battle for truth. Since the resurrection of Jesus, God sends

16. J. C. Ryle, *Light from Old Times* (1890; repr. Moscow, Ida.: Charles Nolan, 2000), 158.
17. Cited from David Aikman, *Jesus in Beijing* (Washington, DC: Regnery, 2003), 57–65.

not only preachers but every Christian to stand up for truth. We must believe that there is truth and that God has revealed it in his Word. We must insist that truth matters even above our lives, that salvation comes only through belief in the truth, and that true unity is attained only in the truth. Like the prophets, we must battle for truth today. Indeed, Micah erects a standard that must be sought by all servants of God and coveted by every church: "I am filled with power, with the Spirit of the Lord, and with justice and might" (Mic. 3:8).

Especially we must be concerned for the truth of the Bible's teaching on sin: "to declare to Jacob his transgression and to Israel his sin"(Mic. 3:8). The carnal heart is not warmed to the thought of a holy God, but we must preach this. The sinful nature is offended by the notion of God's wrath versus all sin. The lustful human heart resents it when cherished sins are condemned as evil. Man's self-righteous heart is repelled by the idea that sin must be atoned for by blood. The relativist is outraged by the insistence that salvation comes only through faith in Jesus. But we must battle for all these things, like Micah and the true prophets, in the Spirit of the Lord, with justice and might. We do not battle for truth so that sinners will be condemned, since that will happen without our preaching. We battle for truth so that sinners might be saved—by confessing their sin, repenting, and believing in the Savior Jesus Christ, whose blood alone redeems our transgressions and sins.

22

THE MALADY OF SPIRITUAL PRESUMPTION

Micah 3:9–12

Therefore because of you Zion shall be plowed as a field;
Jerusalem shall become a heap of ruins, and the mountain of
the house a wooded height. (Mic. 3:12)

One of the most dramatic and telling scenes in Bible history took place at a likely place, but involved the most unlikely message. The place was the temple, in the holy city of Jerusalem. The event was a sermon about the temple building: the temple built by King Solomon as a place for God's name, where the holy priesthood served and the sacrificial offerings were made. There the prophet Jeremiah preached, "Do not trust in these deceptive words: 'This is the temple of the LORD, the temple of the LORD, the temple of the LORD'" (Jer. 7:4). "Stop trusting in the temple!" Jeremiah was warning. What an unlikely message for such a likely place! What could possibly be wrong with a faith that centered on the very house of God?

The problem Jeremiah faced was that so many people led godless lives yet sought to claim God's saving promises. In his day, the vices of theft, murder, adultery, blasphemy, and idolatry characterized the behavior of the people. Yet the people committing these sins still had the audacity to come before God's presence at the temple and claim his salvation. The prophet's point was that, as John Calvin comments, "Sacrifices are of no importance or value before God, unless those who offer them wholly devote themselves to God with a sincere heart."[1] While the Jews of Jeremiah's time were trusting in a building with its traditions and rituals, God was interested only in seeing the inward religion that reaps a harvest of godly behavior.

Spiritual Presumption Diagnosed

To show that this is not only an occasional problem, we turn back in time to the days of the prophet Micah, roughly a century before Jeremiah, and we find the same situation. Micah charged the leaders of his day: "Hear this, you heads of the house of Jacob and rulers of the house of Israel, who detest justice and make crooked all that is straight, who build Zion with blood and Jerusalem with iniquity. . . . yet they lean on the LORD and say, 'Is not the LORD in the midst of us? No disaster shall come upon us'" (Mic. 3:9–11). Here was another sermon about the temple and empty outward religion, focusing on the people's *ethics*, *religion*, and *presumption* on the Lord.

Micah begins his "temple sermon" with a catalogue of the evils and injustices perpetrated by Jerusalem's ruling elite. Many of these sins have already been cited by the prophet, which indicates the severity of his concern. "Hear this," he begins, using his now-familiar call for attention, "you heads of the house of Jacob and rulers of the house of Israel" (Mic. 3:9). Recalling for Judah's leadership the legacy of their forefather, Jacob/Israel, he summarizes his complaint: "You . . . who detest justice and make crooked all that is straight, who build Zion with blood and Jerusalem with iniquity" (Mic. 3:9–10).

During the reign of Hezekiah, Jerusalem experienced a significant economic boom, resulting in vast improvements to the city. Swelled by refugees from the conquered northern kingdom of Israel, and having enjoyed a long run of relative prosperity, the city grew three- or fourfold, as has

---

1. John Calvin, *A Commentary on Jeremiah*, 5 vols. (Edinburgh: Banner of Truth, 1989), 4:366.

been confirmed by archaeological studies.[2] King Hezekiah undertook public works of great size, including the Siloam tunnel that brought flowing water into the city.

But Micah was not captivated by the new towers and palaces. Once more condemning Jerusalem's leaders for injustice and corruption (see 2:1–2; 3:1–2), he adds that the city's expansion was achieved "with blood and . . . with iniquity" (Mic. 3:10). Remembering how God's people had built great structures in Egypt with their slave blood, Micah is appalled at the injustice involved in Jerusalem's civic growth. The situation was probably similar to what Jeremiah would condemn a century later: "Woe to him who builds his house by unrighteousness, and his upper rooms by injustice, who makes his neighbor serve him for nothing and does not give him his wages" (Jer. 22:13). Leslie Allen comments: "An eviction order here, a whisper there to arrange compulsory purchase, drafting 'volunteers' into forced labor squads—in these and doubtless other more murderous ways the men with the whip hands held cheap the God-given rights of property, liberty, and life."[3]

Moreover, the lust for money corrupted every branch of leadership, starting with the judges. Micah charges, "Its heads give judgment for a bribe" (Mic. 3:11). The guilty could get off through cash on demand, but the poor would find their appeals squeezed off the docket. As Isaiah complained, the Jewish courts "acquit the guilty for a bribe, and deprive the innocent of his right!" (Isa. 5:23). The spiritual leaders were no better: "its priests teach for a price; its prophets practice divination for money" (Mic. 3:11). This means the ministers in the temple were willing to teach God's law only when large honorariums were offered, and the prophets who gave God's will required that their palms first be greased. We see why the apostle Paul warned his protégé Timothy: "The love of money is a root of all kinds of evils" (1 Tim. 6:10). John Calvin summarizes the moral problem underlying Jerusalem's apparent prosperity: "No vice is more pernicious to the public good than to have its officers affected by greed, since it results in the loss of justice and equity. As for ministers of the Word, if their only desire is to enrich

2. See John L. Mackay, *Jonah, Micah, Nahum, Habakkuk and Zephaniah: God's Just Demands*, Focus on the Bible (Ross–shire, UK: Christian Focus, 1998), 89.

3. Leslie C. Allen, *The Books of Joel, Obadiah, Jonah, and Micah*, New International Commentary on the Old Testament (Grand Rapids: Eerdmans, 1976), 317–18.

themselves, then they become guilty of . . . misusing the Word of God and corrupting the doctrine of salvation."[4]

If we think this is a remote problem, found only in ancient times or in distant regions of the globe, we need only pick up today's newspaper. We will read of a justice system that often works only for those who can pay for it, of lawmakers who are purchased by political contributions, and of churches and ministries whose only discernible purpose is to fleece the needy sheep who wander into their pasture. All of us are susceptible to selfish greed, which is why the Bible warns us against it. Calvin counseled, "The truest means of remedying and checking this evil inclination that lies within us, is to show charity towards our neighbors."[5] The practice of generosity not only pleases God, but guards our hearts against the corruption of money.

Having laid bare the Jewish leaders' *ethics*, Micah turns to their *religion*: "Yet they lean on the LORD and say, 'Is not the LORD in the midst of us? No disaster shall come upon us'" (Mic. 3:11).

It is good to "lean" on the Lord. This means to place our confidence in God and rely on his salvation. This statement indicates that the immoral Jewish leaders taught and believed salvation by grace. They were counting on God's sovereign favor toward his chosen people, Israel, and his chosen city, Jerusalem. After all, was not Jerusalem the site of God's own temple and his holy service? Theirs was what we might call a "Psalm 46 faith," based on the psalm that celebrates "the city of God, the holy habitation of the Most High. God is in the midst of her; she shall not be moved; God will help her when morning dawns" (Ps. 46:4–5). They would have sung the psalm's great refrain with gusto: "The LORD of hosts is with us; the God of Jacob is our fortress" (Ps. 46:7).

The problem was not their doctrine, so far as it went, but the incongruity between their ethics and their religion. Instead of *trusting* in God's grace, they were *presuming* on God's grace. So confident were the Jews of Micah's time that God would protect and preserve them that they gave themselves liberty to abuse and oppress their neighbors. Paul warned of such people, "They profess to know God, but they deny him by their works" (Titus 1:16). But this is not the religion revealed by God in the Bible. Philip Ryken explains: "God has saved you *from* sin, not *for* sin. If you are unrepentant about lust,

---

4. John Calvin, *Sermons on the Book of Micah* (Phillipsburg, NJ: P&R Publishing, 2003), 176.
5. Ibid., 174.

bitterness, greed, anxiety, or any sin whatsoever, you are presuming upon God's grace."[6]

It is for fear of such presumption that some Christians think it dangerous to teach the Bible's doctrine of salvation by grace alone. "People will think they can live any way they want to," they complain. But the Bible's doctrine of saving grace opposes this way of thinking. The apostle Paul was concerned about this in his letter to the Romans. Having extolled God's grace for abounding over and above our sin, he then asked the important question: "What shall we say then? Are we to continue in sin that grace may abound? By no means! How can we who died to sin still live in it?" (Rom. 6:1–2). Paul reasoned that the very grace that frees us from the guilt of sin also frees us from the love of sin. Therefore, those who sin without repentance merely demonstrate the absence of saving grace from their lives. This is what Jeremiah stressed in his version of Micah's temple sermon:

> Behold, you trust in deceptive words to no avail. Will you steal, murder, commit adultery, swear falsely, make offerings to Baal, and go after other gods that you have not known, and then come and stand before me in this house, which is called by my name, and say, "We are delivered!"—only to go on doing all these abominations? (Jer. 7:8–10)

Thus those who preach the Bible's doctrines of grace must also exhibit the power of God's grace in the manner of their lives.

SPIRITUAL PRESUMPTION ANALYZED

Spiritual presumption is such a pernicious problem that we can profit from a thorough analysis of it.

One form of spiritual presumption presumes upon God's *power*. This was part of the Jews' problem in Micah's time, as they trusted in a spiritual power that they thought automatically emanated from God's temple in their city. This form of presumption had been a snare to Israel many times before, particular in the days of the prophet Samuel.

For generations, Israel's armies had triumphed over their enemies by God's power, as symbolized by the ark of the covenant that was carried

---

6. Philip Graham Ryken, *Jeremiah & Lamentations: From Sorrow to Hope*, Preaching the Word (Wheaton, Ill.: Crossway, 2001), 122.

before them into battle. As a result of earlier successes, the idea developed that the ark was a kind of spiritual power generator. By Samuel's time the people allowed themselves to lead the most sinful lives, but nonetheless to expect victory so long as they had their "God box." On one occasion, when the Israelites suffered a defeat at the battle of Ebenezer, they sent back for the ark. "Let us bring the ark of the covenant of the LORD here from Shiloh," they cried, "that it may come among us and save us from the power of our enemies" (1 Sam. 4:3). Notice that they were relying on "it" rather than on "him," that is, God. Because of this, God allowed them to suffer a defeat with great slaughter, including the capture of the ark by the Philistines and the death of the high priest's sons who were carrying it (1 Sam. 4:10–11).

This same form of spiritual presumption takes place today, especially with the many believers who have compartmentalized their lives. I was recently seated on a plane next to a man who had served as a preacher but who now worked in the business world. I asked him, "What is the biggest thing you have learned from the transition?" He answered, "The vast difference between the conduct of Christians on Sunday and their conduct from nine to five from Monday to Friday." But the sermon Christians hear on Sunday morning is not designed to be merely a battery recharge that will empower them for the week. Rather, it is intended by God to bring our whole lives under the authority of his Word.

At the heart of such presumption is an idolatrous view of God. David Prior writes: "Instead of choosing to humble ourselves and bow the knee to [God] as Lord and Master, we want to have him endorse and bless what we are doing and want to do. . . . In a word, it is an attempt to control God and make him play along with us, instead of gladly submitting to his control."[7] God calls for a living, Sunday-to-Saturday obedience to his Word. God is not a willing tool, and those who presume on his power will find themselves impotent before the onslaughts of the world.

A related form of spiritual presumption is that which falsely relies on God's *covenant promises*. Micah's generation loved to sing about their covenant privileges. They would have loved the hymn that begins: "We are God's people / the chosen of the Lord." Should they not celebrate, after all, the fact that God had made his covenant with their ancestors and that God's

---

7. David Prior, *The Message of Joel, Micah & Habakkuk*, The Bible Speaks Today (Downers Grove, Ill.: InterVarsity, 1998), 145–46.

covenant promises rested upon their nation? Micah quotes their creed: "Is not the LORD in the midst of us? No disaster shall come upon us" (Mic. 3:11). In an important sense they were right, for God had chosen Israel and given them precious promises. But they had forgotten that while God would achieve his covenant purposes through the nation of Israel, he could do so either by blessing or judging them. Israel would be saved and God's promises fulfilled whether or not individual members of Israel were saved through a right relationship with him.

Jeremiah made this point in his temple sermon with a history lesson: "Go now to my place that was in Shiloh, where I made my name dwell at first, and see what I did to it because of the evil of my people Israel" (Jer. 7:12). Jeremiah invited them to visit Shiloh precisely because there was nothing there to see. Shiloh is where the temple *used* to be, or at least the tabernacle that was its predecessor. This is where the ark was kept before God allowed the Philistines to capture it, and where the priests once conducted their ministry.

What happened to Shiloh? The people presumed upon their covenant relationship with God and ceased to obey his commands. So God removed not only his power but also his presence. What a warning this was to the spiritual presumers of Micah's day, who relied on God's presence in the temple. Psalm 78:58–60 put it this way: "For they provoked him to anger with their high places; they moved him to jealousy with their idols. When God heard, he was full of wrath, and he utterly rejected Israel. He forsook his dwelling at Shiloh, the tent where he dwelt among mankind."

This is a warning to people today who rely on their church membership to grant them God's favor, apart from a living and obedient faith. It warns Christian youths who go along with their parents to church and observe an outward faith but engage in no true discipleship to Christ. It is a warning to nations such as America, which glibly assumes God's favor because of past spiritual achievements, yet now embraces the grossest perversions and the most despicable sins. Most of all, it is a warning to churches that observe Christian traditions but neither teach true doctrine nor promote godly living.

This warning was vividly displayed to me when I ministered in downtown Philadelphia, which is practically filled with Shilohs. All around are cathedrals and preaching palaces built in former times, most of them immaculately maintained by financial endowments from prior days but now empty on Sundays. I was regularly confronted by one Shiloh, because I bought gas for my car at the service station that occupies its former location. The wall next door bears a mural of the lovely church that used to be there, but now is just "a shadow in the city."[8] Shiloh reminds us all not to presume on church membership, on baptism, on family reputations, or on prior spiritual experiences, but to practice true religion by walking in the ways of the Lord.

I want to mention one more kind of spiritual presumption, because it applies not only to false professors of religion but also to nonprofessors of religion. This is presumption not on God's power or God's covenant, but on God's *patience*. This kind of false religion presumes that there is plenty of time to get right with God, or that God will always give us one more chance so that we can put off the spiritual reformation our lives really need.

This seems to be the false lesson Jerusalem's leaders gleaned from God's deliverance from the Assyrian invasion, which Micah predicted in 2:12–13. They had been warned and God had spared them, so surely, they presumed, there was no urgency in responding to the prophet's further warnings. So it is today with many who hear the message of God's grace in Jesus Christ, with its call to a living discipleship of biblical obedience. "It can wait," they think, while they go on enjoying the deadly pleasures of sin. But the same gospel that promises grace to those who believe also warns of judgment on those who put off repentance and faith. The writer of Hebrews warns, "How shall we escape if we neglect such a great salvation?" (Heb. 2:3). We never know which instance of unbelief will finally harden our hearts, which breath will be our last in this world, or what moment it will be when God pulls down the curtain of history and begins his final judgment. The Bible warmly speaks of God's long-suffering patience, but to presume on God's patience is one of the greatest follies of all.

SPIRITUAL PRESUMPTION REMEDIED

Micah concludes his message with just such a warning. He has diagnosed Jerusalem's spiritual presumption and we have analyzed this problem. But Micah's sermon does not conclude until he deals with God's remedy for

8. Ryken, *Jeremiah & Lamentations*, 126.

spiritual presumption, beginning with the remedy of deadly and terrible judgment: "Therefore because of you Zion shall be plowed as a field; Jerusalem shall become a heap of ruins, and the mountain of the house a wooded height" (Mic. 3:12).

Zion is the mount on which the temple rested: it would be "plowed as a field." The building projects so proudly erected in Jerusalem would be reduced to "a heap of ruins." The walls, palaces, and civic glories were an impediment to God's plans because of the oppression with which they were raised, so they would all have to come down. This proves the saying, "Unless the LORD builds the house, those who build it labor in vain" (Ps. 127:1). Leslie Allen comments that "the skyline of the sacred city [would] be broken by buildings erected on morally weak foundations. . . . On that hill where the temple now stood in awesome splendor would spread a wilderness of bushes and brambles."[9]

However unlikely Micah's prophecy may have seemed to some of his hearers, God's threatened judgment finally came to Jerusalem in 587 B.C. The first step was the withdrawal of God's Spirit from the temple, so the sinful people could no longer boast of "the LORD in the midst of us" (Mic. 3:11; see Ezek. 10). Then, with Jeremiah as his weeping witness, God gave Jerusalem over to the marauding bands of Nebuchadnezzar. After the people were slain or enslaved, the temple was torn down, great stone by great stone: "He burned the house of the LORD, and the king's house and all the houses of Jerusalem; every great house he burned down" (Jer. 52:13).

The key words to Micah's warning are "because of you" (Mic. 3:12). Those who presume on God's grace and covenant become the cause of their own downfall, and often the downfall of many others. Jerusalem's fall was not caused by the Lord, though he was judging the city, but by those who spoke praises with their lips and worked evil in their hearts. Unless the sinful people heeded the warning, "because of you," the fall of their city would be certain.

But judgment was not the first of God's remedies, as Micah's message makes clear. Before the judgment was the remedy of preaching. The preaching of God's Word—both its promises and its warnings—is a means of God's grace to the spiritually presumptuous. It sounds a call to respond not

9. Allen, *Joel, Obadiah, Jonah, and Micah*, 320.

merely with the lips but with the heart. This is why it is so important that we preach God's Word today, not some more appealing message to tickle worldly ears, and even more important that we give heed to God's Word when it is preached.

One instance of God's Word overcoming spiritual presumption and forestalling judgment was the preaching of Micah in this passage. We do not always know how the prophets' messages were received, but in this case we do. We know because when Jeremiah preached a century later, and the authorities responded by arresting him and threatening him, "certain elders" spoke up on behalf of his message. Here is what they remembered:

> Micah of Moresheth prophesied in the days of Hezekiah king of Judah, and said to all the people of Judah: "Thus says the LORD of hosts, 'Zion shall be plowed as a field; Jerusalem shall become a heap of ruins, and the mountain of the house a wooded height.'" Did Hezekiah king of Judah and all Judah put him to death? Did he not fear the LORD and entreat the favor of the LORD, and did not the LORD relent of the disaster that he had pronounced against them? But we are about to bring great disaster upon ourselves. (Jer. 26:18–19)

This tells us that King Hezekiah, at least, responded to Micah's preaching with a convicted heart. He went to his knees with prayers of confession and pleas for mercy, and God received him. God's grace for his people is that whenever they turn and repent from their presumption and sin, he forestalls his judgment and helps them. Hezekiah went on to lead the people in one of the great reformations of Old Testament history, so that God's presence was maintained in the city and God sent his saving power in their defense. This, then, is the remedy we should undertake for our presumptuous sinning, by responding to the preaching of God's Word in sincere repentance, with prayers for grace, and with fresh resolve for new obedience to God's Word.

REPENTING OF SPIRITUAL PRESUMPTION

The fall of Jerusalem poses a warning to Christians. Jeremiah, speaking on behalf of Micah and all the prophets, summed up God's call to us: "I have sent to you all my servants the prophets, sending them persistently, saying, 'Turn now every one of you from his evil way, and amend your deeds, and do not go after other gods to serve them, and then you shall dwell in the land that I gave to you and your fathers'" (Jer. 35:15). The biblical term for this is reformation. It involves remembering God's Word, repenting of our sin, and returning to God for the grace we need to be renewed in faith and obedience.

Jesus Christ, the last and greatest of the prophets, brought this very message to Jerusalem and its rebuilt temple. But he put it this way: "Destroy this temple, and in three days I will raise it up" (John 2:19). Jesus predicted that after Jerusalem rejected him and handed him over to the cross, the city would be destroyed and its temple finally dismantled, never to be rebuilt. But when he said that "in three days I will raise it up," he was speaking of the new temple that he would build: the temple that is his body (John 2:21). When Jesus rose from the grave, having died on the cross for our sins, he lay the cornerstone of the true temple that will never be destroyed. Whenever a sinner repents and believes in Jesus, he or she becomes part of that spiritual body. The apostle Peter wrote: "As you come to him, a living stone rejected by men but in the sight of God chosen and precious, you yourselves like living stones are being built up as a spiritual house, to be a holy priesthood, to offer spiritual sacrifices acceptable to God through Jesus Christ" (1 Peter 2:4–5).

If this is true of us, then how can we go on in the sin of spiritual presumption? As people of the resurrection and the new temple that can never be destroyed, let us hear God's Word and like Hezekiah fall on our knees before God. Let us appeal again to the cleansing blood of Christ. Let us rise up in pursuit of the true spirituality of holiness. Let us continually reform our lives—by God's grace and in accordance with God's Word—so that we would present to God the Sunday to Saturday worship that is so acceptable and pleasing to him.

23

THE MOUNTAIN OF THE LORD

Micah 4:1–5

It shall come to pass in the latter days that the mountain of the house of the Lord shall be established as the highest of the mountains, and it shall be lifted up above the hills; and peoples shall flow to it. (Mic. 4:1)

The fourth chapter of Micah's prophecy presents us with one of the most striking contrasts in the Bible. The previous chapter concluded with a warning that Jerusalem "shall be plowed as a field" (Mic. 3:12). There could hardly be a more depressing picture of what would become of Mount Zion. Yet chapter four looks beyond the judgment to a more glorious restoration. The mountain would be laid low by God's judgment, but God's grace would have the final word: "It shall come to pass in the latter days that the mountain of the house of the Lord shall be established as the highest of the mountains" (Mic. 4:1).

This will happen, Micah says, in "the latter days," or as some versions put it, in "the last days." Because of the emphasis of much popular literature, many Christians think this phrase refers only to a narrow slice of time immediately before the return of Christ. But a careful study of the Bible shows that the prophets used this expression to denote a variety of future interventions when God would set things right and restore his people. Included in such "latter days" are the restoration of the Jews from their Babylonian captivity, the birth of Jesus the Messiah, and the final judgment followed by the eternal state of glory when Christ returns.

HIGHEST OF THE MOUNTAINS

Even though Israel's sin ensured that Mount Zion would be devastated, it was not just their mountain. It was also "the mountain of the house of the LORD." It was not just their name that was at stake in Jerusalem, but also God's name. Yet God's saving work would not be thwarted even by human sin. Micah thus declares, "It shall come to pass in the latter days that the mountain of the house of the LORD shall be established as the highest of the mountains, and it shall be lifted up above the hills" (Mic. 4:1).

In the ancient world, temples were either built atop mountains or else they were themselves designed to look like mountains. A temple was where heaven met earth; Babylonian ziggurats were conceived as stairways to heaven. A temple was where a god resided on earth, and from high on the mountain the god exercised his rule over the region. The idea was that the higher the mountain, the greater the god. Although Israel's temple was on a comparatively small mountain, only 2400 feet above sea level, Micah insists that history would show Israel's God to be the great and true God, exalted above all pretenders to deity. So important was this prophecy that it was repeated practically verbatim by Micah's contemporary, Isaiah (Isa. 2:2–5). The prophets were asserting that, as John Oswalt writes, "One day it would become clear that Israel's religion was *the* religion; that her God was *the* God."[1] As a cataclysmic earthquake is to the physical realm, so the victory of God's saving plan will cause a sudden and shocking reordering of apparent spiritual realities.

The highest peak always draws people—not merely to see it, but also to climb it. Every spring, hundreds of adventurers make the trek to Mount Everest, seeking their chance to stand on the top of the world. So it will be for Mount Zion, Micah foretells, that "peoples shall flow to it" (Mic. 4:1). This river of peoples ascending the exalted mountain of God is remarkable

1. John N. Oswalt, *The Book of Isaiah, Chapters 1–39* (Grand Rapids: Eerdmans, 1986), 117.

in that it flows uphill. It is the result of a supernatural working, contrary to the normal flow of nature. So it is when God's Word is lifted up among the people that God draws them by the irresistible power of his grace. Jesus spoke this way of his cross: "I, when I am lifted up from the earth, will draw all people to myself" (John 12:32).

This prophecy makes clear that the religion of the Bible is not compatible with other religions. Michael Bentley observes, "How foolish it is, then, for 'the church' to hold multifaith services, because all those who seek God through any means other than by faith in the Lord Jesus Christ are deluded. There is no other way to God."[2] Christians are not to synthesize their faith with other religions, but to advance the one true faith through the spread of the gospel. For the true God would have his mountain lifted up above the hills, his true faith neither corrupted nor diluted by mixture with counterfeits.

The subsequent history of Jerusalem does not encourage us to expect a literal fulfillment of this prophecy in the physical elevation of Mount Zion. The Bible records that after the Babylonian exile, God restored a remnant of his people to Jerusalem to rebuild his temple. But so greatly did the second temple pale in comparison with the glory of the first that the oldest men, who had seen Solomon's original temple in their childhood, wept with sorrow (Ezra 3:12). Today an Islamic mosque sits atop Israel's holy mountain. So should we look for some future event in which God will cause the Jewish temple to be rebuilt and Mount Zion is literally raised above Mount Everest?

The answer to this question was given by Jesus on the day of his resurrection from the grave. Walking alongside some forlorn disciples on the road to Emmaus, Jesus opened up the Scriptures and, Luke records, "beginning with Moses and all the Prophets, he interpreted to them in all the Scriptures the things concerning himself" (Luke 24:27). Those who do not foresee a literal fulfillment of prophecies like Micah's are often criticized for "spiritualizing" biblical truth. But it would be more accurate to speak of a Christ-centered fulfillment of the Old Testament. According to Jesus himself, the Old Testament from Moses through the prophets—the whole of it—is fulfilled in his own coming. Therefore, writes John Calvin:

2. Michael Bentley, *Balancing the Books: Micah and Nahum Simply Explained* (Durham: Evangelical Press, 1994), 53.

The real meaning of the Temple's grandeur and glory lies in its connection with the coming of our Lord Jesus. For that is when God would be revealed to all the world, resulting in a common assent and a common accord of faith. . . . The truth, which had previously been known only in the country of Judah, would now be published everywhere, that Christ might be manifested to the ends of the earth and the world called to the knowledge of salvation. That is how our Lord "magnifies" the mountain of Zion, since it is the source of our doctrine of truth and salvation.[3]

The fulfillment of Micah's prophecy therefore began when Jesus came into the world. It advanced dramatically when he rose from the grave, ascended into heaven, and poured out his Spirit on the church. It is not without significance that the church age began with representatives from a multitude of nations united as one in the Spirit of Christ including, Luke records, "Parthians and Medes and Elamites and residents of Mesopotamia, Judea and Cappadocia, Pontus and Asia, Phrygia and Pamphylia, Egypt and the parts of Libya belonging to Cyrene, and visitors from Rome, both Jews and proselytes, Cretans and Arabians" (Acts 2:9–11). If the Pentecost gathering had a theme verse, it could well have been Micah 4:1–2! The fulfillment of Micah's prophecy continues today through Christian missions, as the flowing river grows stronger, with more and more nations ascending to the house of the Lord through faith in Christ.

Learning the Law of Peace

The converts in Micah's vision are drawn not by any outward compulsion but by a powerful inward motivation. Micah writes: "Many nations shall come, and say: 'Come, let us go up to the mountain of the Lord, to the house of the God of Jacob, that he may teach us his ways and that we may walk in his paths'" (Mic. 4:2). Not only do the new converts come willingly, but they also call on others to join them in their ascent to God's house. This confirms that one of the surest signs of a truly converted heart is the desire to bring as many others along to salvation as possible.

Whereas in the old covenant it was only the Jews who went up Mount Zion singing joyful psalms, in the new age to come people from all over the world

---

3. John Calvin, *Sermons on the Book of Micah* (Phillipsburg, NJ: P&R Publishing, 2003), 190.

will take up the pilgrimage to God. Here we see the power of sin broken in the world. Whereas rebellious men built the Tower of Babel in a vain attempt to usurp God, so that God judged them with confusion and division, now God raises up his own mountain and draws people of all kinds together in humble adoration.

It is of special importance to note the purpose for which God is drawing peoples and nations to himself: "that he may teach us his ways and that we may walk in his paths." This is why we are to come eagerly to church: not only to bring praise to God but also to be taught of God. Is each of us willing to have our ideas about God, ourselves, and the priorities of life changed and molded by the Bible? Are we seeking revelation simply for the sake of our doctrinal correctness, or do we realize, as Micah did, that the ultimate purpose of biblical teaching is "that we may walk in his paths" (Mic. 4:2)?

This prophecy was an implied rebuke to the Jerusalem of Micah's time. How the people loved to attend the temple services. But they did not come humbly to be taught of God, nor did they depart resolved to walk in God's ways. It was precisely because of their presumptuous misuse of God's ordinances that the temple building was taken from them. Likewise, if Christians today who venerate the Bible do not learn truth from it or walk according to it, they should not be surprised when God removes it from them by giving unfaithful teachers. David Prior comments, "Unless worship involves teachability and issues in practical obedience, it is not worship at all; this was exactly the condemnation leveled by Micah at the current leadership of the city and the nation."[4]

Micah's vision of the exaltation of God's mountain is closely tied to the going forth of God's Word: "For out of Zion shall go forth the law, and the word of the LORD from Jerusalem" (Mic. 4:2). By God's law, Micah does not restrict the message to the Ten Commandments or even to the Old Testament law generally. Rather, he means, "The law as the rule of a godly life . . . or the word of revelation as the source of salvation."[5] No longer would Israel alone possess the oracles of God, for the teaching of the Scriptures would be published worldwide. This is the work of the Christian church and, indeed, of every Christian: to be taught of God's Word and to declare God's Word to the world.

4. David Prior, *The Message of Joel, Micah & Habakkuk*, The Bible Speaks Today (Downers Grove, Ill.: InterVarsity, 1998), 150.

5. C. F. Keil and F. Delitzsch, *Commentary on the Old Testament*, 10 vols. (Peabody, Mass.: Hendrickson, 1996), 10:310.

It was the special delight of the early Christians to point out how this prophecy was fulfilled through the work of Christ's apostles. Justin Martyr wrote in the second century: "We can show you that this has really happened. For a band of twelve men went forth from Jerusalem, and they were common men, not trained in speaking. But by the power of God they testified to every race of humankind that they were sent by Christ to teach to all the Word of God."[6] Theodoret of Cyr added, "This evangelical law and apostolic preaching began with Jerusalem as with a fountain and traveled across the whole world, offering irrigation to those who made their approach with faith."[7]

When the nations come to the house of God and the Word of the Lord goes forth, the effect is revolutionary. Micah declares: "He shall judge between many peoples, and shall decide for strong nations afar off; and they shall beat their swords into plowshares, and their spears into pruning hooks; nation shall not lift up sword against nation, neither shall they learn war anymore" (Mic. 4:3). With God as their ruler, the nations will not merely sign the temporary peace treaties familiar today, but will find it best to destroy their weapons and transform them into instruments of agriculture.

This is a famous prophecy, oft-quoted by those who long for peace. The United Nations building in New York bears this verse on a wall mounting, expressing the hope that diplomacy may bring this promised peace. Yet Micah does not envision any such peace among people until they first come humbly in faith to the Lord. The only basis for true peace in the home, society, and world is a shared bond in the rule of God through his Word. It is only when former enemies become brothers and sisters in Christ, having their sins put away at the cross and their hearts transformed by God's Spirit, that the motivations for conflict are done away. As Oswalt says, "Until persons and nations have come to God to learn his ways and walk in them, peace is an illusion."[8] This is why the church best serves the cause of peace not through political agitation, but by preaching God's Word so that sinners may be reconciled to God through Christ.

The power of the gospel brings peace to the hearts of hate-filled men. One example is Jacob DeShazer, an airman in the Doolittle bombing raid of

6. Justin Martyr in Alberto Ferreiro, *The Twelve Prophets*, Ancient Christian Commentary on Scripture, Old Testament XIV (Downers Grove, Ill.: InterVarsity, 2003), 160.

7. Theodoret of Cyr, in Ferreiro, *The Twelve Prophets*, 161.

8. Oswalt, *Isaiah*, 118

Japan in April 1942. The plan was for the pilots to take off from an aircraft carrier, fly briefly over Tokyo dropping bombs, and then ditch their planes over neutral China. But two of the planes, including DeShazer's, ended up in Japanese-occupied lands. Along with seven other airmen, DeShazer was captured and taken to Tokyo, where they were subjected to public scorn and torture. This was followed by the long years of the war spent in the most deplorable conditions.

In May 1944, DeShazer was in solitary confinement, with only a sliver of light sneaking in through an air vent. But a guard had provided him with a Bible, and by that dim light DeShazer eagerly read. First he read the Old Testament, and when he arrived in the New Testament, he recalls,

> I . . . read of the birth of Jesus Christ, the one who actually fulfilled the very prophecies of Isaiah, Jeremiah, Micah and the other Old Testament writers. My heart rejoiced as I found confirmed in Acts 10:43: "To him give all the prophets witness, that through his name, whosoever believeth on him shall receive remission of sins."

DeShazer's heart was changed by the Word of the Lord, his entire attitude transformed.

> I discovered that God had given me new spiritual eyes, and that when I looked at the Japanese officers and guards who had starved and beaten me . . . I found my bitter hatred for them changed to loving pity. . . . I read in my Bible that while those who crucified Jesus on the cross had beaten him and spit upon him . . . he tenderly prayed in his moment of excruciating suffering, "Father, forgive them for they know not what they do." And now from the depths of my heart, I too prayed for God to forgive my torturers.[9]

Another example of the peace of Christ is Mitsuo Fuchida, commander of the Japanese air forces in the attack on Pearl Harbor, giving the famous assault order, "Tora, Tora, Tora." Fuchida fought valiantly throughout the war, only narrowly escaping death, and was present for the Japanese surrender aboard the USS Missouri. With most of his friends dead and his nation humiliated, he fell into depression and heavy drinking. But in 1948, a Christian missionary handed Fuchida a tract at the Tokyo rail station. It was about how

---

9. The stories of Jacob DeShazer and Mitsuo Fuchida are told in Don Stephens, *War and Grace: Short Biographies from the World Wars* (Darlington, UK: Evangelical Press, 2005), 117–52.

Jacob DeShazer found grace to forgive his Japanese tormentors by receiving Jesus as his Savior. As a result, Fuchida bought a New Testament and began reading it. In Luke's Gospel, he encountered Christ praying from the cross, "Father, forgive them" (Luke 23:34). He later wrote, "Right at the moment I read that prayer, I seemed to meet Jesus for the first time. I understood the meaning of his death as a substitute for my wickedness, and so, in prayer I requested him to forgive my sins and change me from a bitter disillusioned ex-pilot into a well-balanced Christian with purpose in living."

Because of his notoriety and anti-American feelings among former soldiers, Fuchida was at first persecuted for his faith. Later, Japan offered Fuchida command of the postwar Self-Defense Air Force, but he turned it down to launch a worldwide ministry of evangelism. He especially delighted in preaching the gospel at Pearl Harbor, where his leadership had resulted in so many deaths. Once, when Jacob DeShazer was in Japan, the two arranged to meet, rejoicing in the bond of love that had replaced their former enmity, as God's direct answer to DeShazer's prison-cell prayers. Agreeing to join together in evangelism, their swords were truly beaten into plowshares for the kingdom of God. It is in this way, through God's supernatural spreading of the gospel, that Micah's prophecy of peace is being fulfilled today.

The Shalom of the Fig Tree

The name Jerusalem means "City of Peace." But, as Micah laments, the city was anything but peaceful in his time. It was a place of oppression and injustice, so that hardly anyone possessed the blessings of abundance and security. Yet Micah foresees that when God's Word has gone forth and the nations have come to learn, then there will be peace with all its blessings. He prophesies this with a classic expression of the full-orbed *shalom* (the Hebrew word for peace and well-being) that would come to everyone: "They shall sit every man under his vine and under his fig tree, and no one shall make them afraid, for the mouth of the LORD of hosts has spoken" (Mic. 4:4).

Fig trees were prized in Israel for their fruit and shade; along with the vine, the fig tree was a symbol of prosperity and security. No longer, Micah writes, would the greedy land barons gather all wealth to themselves, leaving others in poverty and subjecting everyone to fear. With God's blessing on the people, the land would burst forth in abundance. In the place of insatiable craving for more, each will be content with God's good provision. Bruce Waltke sums up the picture as "the full enjoyment of God's abiding peace and prosperity without fear or danger."[10]

Such blessing is the end result of Micah's prophecy: satisfaction of soul arising from peace with God and man, resulting from the Word of the Lord going out from his church, and all this because God has exalted his gospel with the coming of the Savior Jesus Christ. Waltke comments, "Those who live by war will die in war (Matt. 26:52), and those with 'swollen appetites' cannot anticipate peace."[11] But those who learn contentment in the peace of God will know the *shalom* of the fig tree, with nothing to covet and no one to fear.

So certain is this future that Micah adds, "for the mouth of the LORD of hosts has spoken." God's peace will come to God's people despite the scheming of unjust rulers and the threat of foreign armies, for the Almighty Lord will secure it. But when should we anticipate its coming?

Again, there is a temptation to a literal reading of these verses, so that we look for a coming age when Old Testament Jerusalem will be rebuilt in perfected form. Thus those committed to a premillennial view of Christ's second coming look on this verse as a simple proof text. When Christ comes again, they believe, he will establish a thousand-year epoch when the faithful literally will rest beneath the fig trees of Israel. John Sailhammer writes, "It is hard to understand Israel's prophets any other way than that they longed for a physical, that is, earthly, reestablishment of the Davidic monarchy."[12]

But this interpretation fails to appreciate the teaching of both the Old and New Testaments. As for the Old Testament, it was typical for the prophets to "represent the New Age under the symbols of the Old."[13] In other words, they presented future blessings in the terms of present realities their hearers could understand. As for the New Testament, Jesus insisted that his coming has effected a permanent change, so that "neither on this mountain nor in Jerusalem will you worship the Father," as he told the Samaritan woman.

10. Bruce Waltke, *A Commentary on Micah* (Grand Rapids: Eerdmans, 2007), 213.

11. Ibid., 212.

12. Cited in Kenneth L. Barker and Waylon Bailey, *Micah, Nahum, Habbakuk, Zephaniah*, The New American Commentary (Nashville: Broadman & Holman, 1999), 87.

13. Waltke, *A Commentary on Micah*, 206.

Instead, we worship God everywhere "in spirit and truth" (John 4:21, 23). For Jesus to return and reestablish the old covenant Davidic arrangement would be to overturn his own teaching about the effect of his coming.

So when will the mountain of God be exalted and the *shalom* of the fig tree come to earth? The answer is that it arrived with the coming of Jesus Christ. It was with God's peace that Jesus stilled the winds and the waves upon the sea and with God's plenty that he fed the five thousand with only a few loaves and fish. And it was with the words of Christ, which he brought from the mount of God's heavenly throne, that he brought peace to the souls of sinful men and women.

Another answer is that Micah's promise, having arrived with the coming of Christ, is being fulfilled now, in the age of the gospel, as his word of grace spreads throughout the world. Jesus brings peace to hearts, peace to homes, and peace to nations that come under the reign of his gospel. He brings an end to the envy, hatred, and greed that are the cause of our strife, so that bitter enemies like Jacob Deshazer and Mitsuo Fuchida may embrace as brothers in Christ. Thus, while we live amid trials in a world inflamed in unholy passions, we yet possess what Paul described as "the peace of God, which surpasses all understanding," which guards our hearts and minds in Christ Jesus (Phil. 4:7).

But Micah's prophecy of God's perfect *shalom* will be fully realized when Christ returns to usher in the eternal age of glory and peace, for which we patiently wait. The book of Revelation tells us:

> And I heard a loud voice from the throne saying, "Behold, the dwelling place of God is with man. He will dwell with them, and they will be his people, and God himself will be with them as their God. He will wipe away every tear from their eyes, and death shall be no more, neither shall there be mourning nor crying nor pain anymore." (Rev. 21:3–4)

Believing this promise, how should we resolve to conduct our lives? Micah answers by setting before his own generation a holy resolve to live in the light of the day that is sure to come: "For all the peoples walk each in the name of its god, but we will walk in the name of the LORD our God forever and ever" (Mic. 4:5). As God's Word dwells in us and as we live according to our faith in his promise and in obedience to his teaching, our hearts are made secure and our souls are filled with his grace.

These Last Days

The words of Micah's prophecy are among the most exciting that a Christian can ever read. They remind me of some of the most thrilling times I have had as a Christian. One took place on a red clay hill outside the city of Kampala, Uganda, where I had gone to teach at the African Bible College. One evening, the principal of the college, Dr. O. Palmer Robertson, invited us over for a Bible study. The text was Micah 4:1–5. As he read the prophet's words describing the lifting up of God's reign over all the world's false gods and the inbringing of all peoples to the house of the Lord, I felt my skin almost tingling. We had spent that day in African villages spreading the good news of Jesus Christ. Men and women from Muslim, animist, and irreligious backgrounds had professed their faith in the gospel of God's grace. What the prophet had written was happening right before us, and even through our ministry: the mountain of the house of the Lord was lifted up above the hills and the nations were streaming in.

This passage also came to my mind one evening after I had preached in a small Presbyterian church in the village of Messailler, Haiti. Here were people from yet another distant land streaming up to the heavenly mount as God's Word was going forth. Meeting for prayer afterward, several of us reflected on Micah's prophecy and marveled that God should use us to send forth his Word among the nations.

The thrill is that we are living in the latter days spoken of by the prophet Micah. Indeed, the ingathering of the nations that he spoke of—the work of gospel missions and the spread of Christ's blessing at home and around the world—is the great work of our age. The latter days Micah foresaw are *these days* in which we live. Therefore, God will use your voice, your prayers, your financial contributions, and your witness so that many people—one at a time or many together—will see the glory of the Lord exalted in Jesus Christ, will come to God through faith in the gospel, will learn of his ways, and will in turn say to their fellows: "Come, let us go up to the mountain of the Lord, to the house of the God of Jacob, that he may teach us his ways and that we may walk in his paths" (Mic. 4:2).

24

THY KINGDOM COME

Micah 4:6–8

*The lame I will make the remnant, and those who were cast off, a
strong nation; and the LORD will reign over them in Mount Zion
from this time forth and forevermore. (Mic. 4:7)*

Over the past century and more, a ferocious battle has raged
between the worldviews of Darwinism and Christianity. This
war is fought on many fronts. On the scientific front, evolu-
tionists battle against creation science and, more recently, the evidence for
intelligent design. On the political front, school boards and legislatures
battle over the content of public school textbooks. Often overlooked is perhaps one of the most significant battlegrounds, that of ethics. Evolution's
creed tells us that only the strong deserve to survive. In radical contrast is
the ethic of the Bible, which says that God "has pity on the weak and the
needy" (Ps. 72:13).

One high-profile combatant in this conflict is Princeton bioethics pro-
fessor Peter Singer. In his book *Rethinking Life and Death*, Singer seeks
to replace the Christian doctrine of the sanctity of life with a utilitarian
approach. Ruthlessly following evolutionary logic, he advocates the killing
of disabled children. "The fact that a being is a human being, in the sense

of a member of the species *Homo sapiens*, is not relevant to the wrongness of killing it," Singer writes; "it is, rather, characteristics like rationality, autonomy, and self-consciousness that make a difference." Infants, he asserts, lack these traits; "Killing them, therefore, cannot be equated with killing normal human beings, or any other self-conscious beings."[1] The same goes for noninfants with disabilities that reduce their utility for society and their capacity for Singer's definition of happiness. While such "ethics" may seem extreme, they are increasingly mainstream and are fully consistent with the logic of Darwinism.

The Bible's vision of a better world could not be more radically opposed to the evolutionary ethic. We see this in the prophet Micah's foretelling of the coming age in which God's rule will be finally established. "In that day," he asserts, "I will assemble the lame, and gather those who have been driven away . . . and the lame I will make the remnant, and those who were cast off, a strong nation" (Mic. 4:6–7).

Remnant of the Lame

Darwinists and Christians are agreed on one thing: the strong do survive. The Lord looks upon his weak and scattered people and declares, "I will make the remnant . . . a strong nation" (Mic. 4:7). The Bible constantly insists that God's people will be strong and victorious over history. Jesus said of his church: "The gates of hell shall not prevail against it" (Matt. 16:18).

Evolutionary theory conceives of strength mainly in terms of the ability to survive the rigors of a hostile and changing world. The church's strength is its ability to endure assault from within and without. The church endures not through the power to dominate and destroy, but because of God's preserving grace. Speaking of a power the world does not know, Nehemiah declared, "The joy of the Lord is your strength" (Neh. 8:10).

Micah preached on this theme in the midst of a great devastation among God's people. In 701 b.c., the Assyrian king Sennacherib invaded Judah, conquering the region surrounding Jerusalem and taking hundreds of thousands of Jews into captivity. In this scene of despair, the prophet assures the people that in the providence of God they would yet be made strong.

1. Peter Singer, *Practical Ethics*, 2nd ed. (Cambridge: Cambridge University Press, 1993), 175–217.

Peter Craigie states, "With the nation in ruins and the capital city hanging on grimly in its fight to survive, there must have been many honest souls in Jerusalem who thought that the reign of God in Judah had come to an end . . . but to such dispirited people, Micah offered a view of the future in which the 'former dominion' would return to Jerusalem."[2] This dominion would come in the "latter days" spoken of in Micah 4:1, that is, in the time of the coming Messiah.

To ensure that God's people know what kind of people are made strong, Micah says: "I will assemble the lame and gather those who have been driven away and those whom I have afflicted" (Mic. 4:6). Here, the prophet returns to the imagery of a flock of sheep, one that has been scattered and abused. Israel will become a strong nation not because of their own virtue, but through the path of judgment and conviction of sin that leads to the merciful extension of God's grace.

Some commentators see the reference to the "lame" as an allusion to God's striking Jacob on his thigh, when Israel's patriarch wrestled with the Lord beside the River Jabbok. As a result of his wounding, Jacob had a limp for the rest of his life. David Prior writes:

> The result of that wrestling-match was a different Jacob, someone who was teachable, humble, and able to be used by God. So now with "the house of Jacob": as God . . . moved to bring his people low, he would turn them into a strong nation. They would limp for the rest of their lives, but they would genuinely lean on the LORD and walk in his name.[3]

This was, in fact, the effect of the trials of Micah's day and the generations that followed. Through their devastation by Assyria, and their later conquest and enslavement by the Babylonians, they received a bitter wound. But, stripped of every other support, they put aside their idols and learned to walk in the strength of the Lord alone.

Micah's prophecy of the weak made strong offers several insights for Christians. First, just as Micah promised that the strong nation would be composed of the lame and the weak, the Christian church is composed of those who are spiritually needy and poor. Paul wrote: "Not many of you were

2. Peter C. Craigie, *Twelve Prophets*, Daily Study Bible Series, 2 vols. (Louisville: Westminster John Knox, 1985), 2:35.

3. David Prior, *The Message of Joel, Micah & Habakkuk*, The Bible Speaks Today (Downers Grove, Ill.: InterVarsity, 1998), 153.

wise according to worldly standards, not many were powerful, not many were of noble birth" (1 Cor. 1:26). The reason the church consists of lowly people is that those who consider themselves wise, powerful, and noble find it hard to humble themselves before a Savior. They are winners, so what salvation do they need? Likewise, many come to Jesus only when life has wilted their hopes and trials have brought them to despair. But there is another reason why the church consists of those lame and ignoble: God delights to glorify his grace in the salvation of the weak. Paul continues, "God chose what is foolish in the world to shame the wise; God chose what is weak in the world to shame the strong; God chose what is low and despised in the world, even things that are not, to bring to nothing things that are, so that no human being may boast in the presence of God" (1 Cor. 1:27–29).

Second, we should realize that the process of salvation described by Micah—the lame made strong, the scattered drawn in, and the afflicted blessed—is God's way of saving all who believe. As Paul preached, "Through many tribulations we must enter the kingdom of God" (Acts 14:22).

Believers suffer the trial of conviction for sin. We must know ourselves cursed before God for our sin before we may be blessed through faith in the gospel of forgiveness. Notice that God promises to gather not only "those who have been driven away," but also "those whom I have afflicted" (Mic. 4:6). It was God who afflicted them in judgment so that he might save them by grace.

This process continues after our conversion. Christian growth follows a path of discipline and trial. The writer of Hebrews tells us, "The Lord disciplines the one he loves, and chastises every son whom he receives" (Heb. 12:6). The purpose of this divine correction is our growth in godliness: "he disciplines us for our good, that we may share his holiness" (Heb. 12:10). Likewise, the apostle Peter tells us that it is through the crucible of trials that our faith grows stronger: "You have been grieved by various trials, so that the tested genuineness of your faith—more precious than gold that perishes though it is tested by fire—may be found to result in praise and glory and honor at the revelation of Jesus Christ" (1 Peter 1:6–7).

Third, God reveals himself through Micah as a loving shepherd who cares for his weak and afflicted sheep. All the verbs in this passage tell of God's merciful intervention for his needy people: "I will assemble . . . gather . . . I will make" (Mic. 4:6–7). This is the source of our salvation: the

243

sovereign compassion of God who fulfills his promises of grace to those who believe. Instead of simply allowing his chastened people to wander off to their destruction, God preserved them as a remnant. This means God ordained that they would be the seed of a future salvation, lovingly protecting them until the coming of Christ. Centuries after Micah, Matthew recorded that "when [Jesus] saw the crowds, he had compassion for them, because they were harassed and helpless, like sheep without a shepherd" (Matt. 9:36). What an encouragement this is to trust and rely on the grace of Christ, who sympathizes with our weakness (Heb. 4:15).

Fourth, since God cares for the weak and the needy, we should do the same. Instead of the Darwinian logic that says progress simply requires the trampling of the weak, God's example would have us show compassion on those in need, especially on God's children who are afflicted by doubt, temptation, or trouble. Gary Smith writes: "Our Lord did not abandon the wounded and weak who could not help themselves, and neither should we. Nor did he give up on those who deserved to be punished or write them off as hopeless cases of no value, and neither should we."[4]

This prophecy of the gathering and strengthening of lame sheep is part and parcel of the great prophecy that preceded it. "It shall come to pass in the latter days," Micah said, "that the mountain of the house of the LORD shall be established as the highest of the mountains . . . and peoples shall flow to it" (Mic. 4:1). But how will this marvelous situation come to pass? It will happen through the nation that had been wounded by God's judgment, a lame and scattered flock, when God assembled them back secure in their ancient home. The evident fulfillment of this prophecy was the restoration of the Jews from their Babylonian captivity and the re-inhabiting of Jerusalem, which was the precursor to its greater fulfillment in the coming of the Messiah, Jesus Christ.

THE LORD WILL REIGN

The first step in Israel's salvation would be their regathering in the land. But this was a prelude to a greater blessing: "The LORD will reign over them in Mount Zion" (Mic. 4:7). God promised not only to bring the people back

---

4. Gary V. Smith, *Hosea, Amos, Micah*, The NIV Application Commentary (Grand Rapids: Zondervan, 2001), 518.

and give them a second chance, but also to further remedy their situation by personally coming to reign as their king.

One of the tragic moments in Israel's history was their rejection of God as king and their insistence on having a human king like all other nations. The elders demanded of the prophet Samuel, "Give us a king to judge us" (1 Sam. 8:6). When Samuel lamented their foolish demand before the Lord, God answered, "They have not rejected you, but they have rejected me from being king over them" (1 Sam. 8:7). Henceforth, Israel was ruled by human kings. First there was wicked King Saul, whom God mercifully replaced with King David, "a man after [God's] own heart" (1 Sam. 13:14). Over the centuries, God's people were sometimes blessed with faithful kings who obeyed the Lord. But on the whole, the human kingship was a disaster, finally resulting in the breaking of God's covenant and the destruction of Jerusalem.

All along, of course, God had retained his sovereignty over the people. Thus a godly king was one who recognized the Lord's authority and obeyed his Word; ungodly kings went their own way, claiming an independent sovereignty. But there would be a difference in the latter days to come: God would openly rule as king over his people, and his reign would last forever: "The LORD will reign over them in Mount Zion from this time forth and forevermore" (Mic. 4:7).

This is a prophecy of the reign of the Lord Jesus Christ over his church, the new Mount Zion from which God's Word goes forth. The writer of Hebrews makes this very equation, telling believers that in Christ they "have come to Mount Zion and to the city of the living God, the heavenly Jerusalem" (Heb. 12:22). John Calvin comments on Micah's prophecy: "Now God himself will ascend the throne in a conspicuous manner, so that no one may doubt but that he is the king of his people. And this was really and actually fulfilled in the person of Christ. Though Christ was indeed the true seed of David, he was yet at the same time Jehovah, even God manifested in the flesh."[5]

This is the true glory of the Christian faith, that Jesus Christ, the heir of the house of David and the Son of God Most High, reigns over the church as its king. After his atoning death for our sins and his resurrection from the grave, Jesus ascended into heaven and took his heavenly seat of royal authority. Paul explains that God the Father "put all things under his feet and gave

---

5. John Calvin, *A Commentary on the Twelve Minor Prophets*, 5 vols. (1559; repr. Edinburgh: Banner of Truth, 1986), 3:277.

him as head over all things to the church, which is his body, the fullness of him who fills all in all" (Eph. 1:22–23). Christ reigns over his church by his Word, so that we honor his rule by teaching and obeying the Bible. Christ reigns in us by the Spirit he sends. And Christ rules over us with the same authority that God exercised over Israel in the Old Testament. Jesus therefore was worthy of the hosannas the people sang when he rode into Jerusalem on a donkey, the humble symbol of the Davidic kingship, just as he is worthy of our praise today:

> All glory, laud, and honor, to thee, Redeemer, King
> To whom the lips of children made sweet hosannas ring!
> Thou art the King of Israel, thou David's royal Son,
> Who in the Lord's name comest, the King and blessed One![6]

Christ's kingdom is perfect, not only because of his righteousness and mercy, but also because his reign will have no end, fulfilling Micah's prophecy. Hebrews 1:8–9 extols Christ: "Your throne, O God, is forever and ever. . . . You have loved righteousness and hated wickedness; therefore God, your God, has anointed you with the oil of gladness beyond your companions."

This was the hope that God gave his ancient people to sustain them in the long years of tribulation, exile, and anticipation of their Savior's coming. Isaiah foretold it: "For to us a child is born, to us a son is given; and the government shall be upon his shoulder. . . . Of the increase of his government and of peace there will be no end, on the throne of David and over his kingdom, to establish it and to uphold it with justice and with righteousness from this time forth and forevermore" (Isa. 9:6–7). Micah's prophecy went on to specify the birth of Christ the king: "But you, O Bethlehem Ephrathah, who are too little to be among the clans of Judah, from you shall come forth for me one who is to be ruler in Israel, whose origin is from old. . . . And he shall be their peace" (Mic. 5:2, 5). After the return to Jerusalem, Zechariah foretold the coming of Christ to the royal city on Palm Sunday: "Behold, your king is coming to you; righteous and having salvation is he, humble and mounted on a donkey, on a colt, the foal of a donkey" (Zech. 9:9).

6. Theodulph of Orleans, "All Glory, Laud, and Honor," c. 820, trans. John Mason Neale, 1854.

This was the hope of all those who waited on the promise of the Lord. Mary believed this promise in the angel's annunciation: "You will conceive in your womb and bear a son, and you shall call his name Jesus. He will be great and will be called the Son of the Most High. And the Lord God will give to him the throne of his father David, and he will reign over the house of Jacob forever, and of his kingdom there will be no end" (Luke 1:31–33). Finally, against the night sky of Bethlehem, the place prophesied by Micah, an angel heralded his birth: "Fear not, for behold, I bring you good news of a great joy that will be for all the people. For unto you is born this day in the city of David a Savior, who is Christ the Lord" (Luke 2:10–11). God's promise to reign was wonderfully fulfilled in the birth of his own Son, a king from the line of David, a Savior to reign as Lord forever.

Today, God's people look back on the coming of our King, receiving him as Savior and honoring him as Lord. Yet it was Jesus who taught us to look to the future and pray to the Father still to send his kingdom: "Our Father . . . Your kingdom come" (Matt. 6:9–10). We look not for the appearance of the King, but for the spread of his reign of grace and truth. We pray, "Your will be done, on earth as it is in heaven" (Matt. 6:10): this is our hope, and it is the calling we pursue in obedient faith by teaching and applying Christ's Word to our lives.

FORMER DOMINION RESTORED

Micah concludes this brief salvation oracle with a word-picture of the restoration that will result from God's reign amid his people: "And you, O tower of the flock, hill of the daughter of Zion, to you shall it come, the former dominion shall come, kingship for the daughter of Jerusalem" (Mic. 4:8).

These verses depict the restoring of security to the people of God. The "tower of the flock" probably refers to the watchtower near the sheep gate on the southeast side of the temple mount. From this high perch, the sentinels could oversee the flocks on their way to the city. The "hill of the daughter of Zion" literally refers to *Ophel*, the fortress mound where David's old citadel guarded the temple mount. The progression of Micah's sermon is thus that the Lord will gather his lame and scattered sheep, that he will personally reign over them in the coming of the God-man Jesus Christ, and that God will then establish secure fortresses around their salvation.

As a result of this all-sufficient salvation, the blessings attending to the former dominion will be abundantly restored. The highest ideals that God's ancient people ever thought to attain will be manifested in the Christian church, including the full forgiveness of our sins in Christ's blood, the inwardly transforming power of the Holy Spirit, the right of access to the Father as beloved children, the loving provision of all our needs, holy fellowship among the redeemed, and divine protection for our souls. Whenever Christians read of the spiritual achievements and blessings of ancient Israel, we should know that these are fully restored to the church over which Christ reigns forever as king, and they will be perfected eternally when he returns in glory. As Solomon was given wisdom, we have the Word of God to transform our minds to discern God's will (Rom. 12:2). As prophets prayed down the power of heaven, we have Christ's mediation and the interceding help of the Holy Spirit in our prayers (Rom. 8:26). And as God fed the tribes of Israel with manna in the desert, Paul assures us, "My God will supply every need of yours according to his riches in glory in Christ Jesus" (Phil. 4:19).

Micah thus declares, "The former dominion shall come, kingship for the daughter of Jerusalem" (Mic. 4:8). God never lapsed in his sovereignty, though sin seemed to reign on the earth for so long. This is why the sign heralding Israel's king was hung above the cross on which Christ died for sins: "Jesus of Nazareth, King of the Jews" (John 19:19). By his sin-atoning death, Jesus put an end to the reign of sin and death over us, and by his glorious resurrection he ascended to his heavenly throne, from which the blessings of his redemption and the power of his salvation will come to his blood-bought people forever.

The Saving Shepherd-King

How grateful we should be that our holy God, the High King of Heaven, does not subscribe to the ethics of Darwinian humanism. For what hope would we have if God granted us the right to life only on the basis of our utility to him and others? Instead, he is the saving Shepherd-King, who says, "I will assemble the lame and gather those who have been driven away and those whom I have afflicted; and the lame I will make the remnant, and those who were cast off, a strong nation; and the LORD will reign over them in Mount Zion from this time forth and forevermore" (Mic. 4:6–7). Let us, likewise, adhere to the ethics of his kingdom—the ethics of mercy, grace, and love—and let us declare them through the gospel to the world. For the lessons of Micah's prophecy are the lessons of the gospel, the message our King Jesus brought into the world and now sends us to live and proclaim.

The first lesson is that the key to life is not in attaining a certain measure of human power and status, but in receiving this Shepherd-King in faith. This is what saves God's people: the grace of the king who reigns over them. James Boice summarizes: "Micah is telling his readers that even in times of judgment it is good to be in the gentle care of Israel's good shepherd."[7] Is your soul under the care of Jesus Christ? Have you entered into his kingdom through faith in his saving reign? You can be saved simply by trusting him in your heart and calling on him with your mouth. The Bible says, "Everyone who calls on the name of the Lord will be saved" (Rom. 10:13).

The second lesson is that the strength of Christians flows from the promises of God's Word. Our hope is never in our own strength. But God says, "I will assemble the lame and gather those who have been driven away ... I will make the remnant ... a strong nation" (Mic. 4:6–7). God is able to keep his promises, and his own glory demands that he do so. Micah's original hearers could think back to numerous promises God had fulfilled, confirming his right to be trusted by them. But as we look back on the specific fulfillments of Micah's promises in the coming of Jesus Christ, how much greater hope ought we to have in the promises of God's Word. Paul taught, "All the promises of God find their Yes in [Christ]" (2 Cor. 1:20). Therefore, through our faith in Jesus, we give our "Amen" to the promises of God for us, and rest our souls securely in the citadel of his sovereign faithfulness.

Lastly, we need to respond to Micah's prophecy in a manner similar to that which he intended for the Jews of old. Hard times were coming. A storm of divine judgment was falling. But God promised light ahead for those who persevered in faith. How much more incentive have we, having seen the light of the coming of Christ, to press on in faith, in ministry to the church and the world, and in wholehearted devotion to our Lord. For Jesus is not a wolf who permits only the fittest to survive; rather, he is the good shepherd, who leads his sheep "in paths of righteousness for his name's sake," leading them all to dwell forever "in the house of the LORD" (Ps. 23:3, 6).

7. James M. Boice, *The Minor Prophets*, 2 vols. (Grand Rapids: Baker, 1986), 2:342.

25

Now and Then

Micah 4:9–5:1

Writhe and groan, O daughter of Zion, like a woman in labor, for
now you shall go out from the city and dwell in the open country;
you shall go to Babylon. There you shall be rescued; there the LORD
will redeem you from the hand of your enemies. (Mic. 4:10)

A complaint that some level against Christians is that our faith represents "pie-in-the-sky" religion. In other words, Christians are people who place their hopes in heaven because we cannot cope with life on earth. History disproves this claim, of course, since Christianity has had a most profound this-worldly effect for good. The spread of Christianity is typically accompanied by improved standards of education, health, government, and civil liberties.

The "pie-in-the-sky" complaint also misreads the Bible. An example is Micah's preaching at the end of chapter 4 and leading into chapter 5. Here we encounter the word "now" four times in six verses. Micah has given his hearers a hope for the future—and Christians make no excuse for this—promising that the time will come when God assembles his scattered people in strength and when royal dignity returns to Jerusalem. But does a hope for the future lead believers to avoid present realities? Not if Micah can help it. David Prior comments: "He drags himself and his listeners back into the harsh realities of their present situation. He faces up to this present darkness in the light of the glorious future just described."[1] Micah is determined for the present attitude of God's people to be profoundly shaped by his vision of a future hope.

THIS PRESENT DARKNESS

It is not possible to pinpoint the exact time of Micah's preaching, but it seems that this message was one of many given around the time of Sennacherib's devastating invasion in 701 B.C. Much of the Jewish nation was conquered by the Assyrians and a large portion of the population was forced into exile. God destroyed the Assyrian army in one of the miraculous deliverances of the Old Testament, with 185,000 enemy soldiers struck down in a single night by the angel of the Lord (cf. Isa. 37:36). But, even in victory, the people must have been horrified by the aftermath. Death and ruin were all around them, and the threat of continued danger still loomed. In order to raise their spirits, God commissioned Micah with the salvation promises of chapters 4 and 5. God would glorify his city in the age to come, and he would restore and strengthen his people.

With this having been said, the prophet addresses the people's present situation: "Now why do you cry aloud?" he asks. "Is there no king in you? Has your counselor perished, that pain seized you like a woman in labor?" (Mic. 4:9). The torment of Jerusalem was so intense that Micah compared it to a woman's labor in childbirth, which especially in times prior to modern painkillers was a very great physical anguish.

Micah may have been challenging the people's shaken confidence in King Hezekiah, whose reckless policies had brought about the invasion. But the text makes it clear that Micah is also speaking of the future, when the house of David would be overthrown. This took place a hundred years later, when the Babylonians captured Jerusalem, put the king to death, and led the people off in chains. Micah anticipates the great outpouring of grief over this loss because "such glorious promises were attached to the throne, the king being the visible representative of the grace of God, and his removal a sign of the

1. David Prior, *The Message of Joel, Micah & Habakkuk*, The Bible Speaks Today (Downers Grove, Ill.: InterVarsity, 1998), 154.

wrath of God and of the abolition of all the blessings of salvation."[2] Even though the Davidic kingdom had not yet fallen, this looming prospect was part of the "now" set before the Jews in Micah's time.

The second part of the dreadful "now" they faced involved the travail of captivity and exile. Micah preached: "Write and groan, O daughter of Zion, like a woman in labor, for now you shall go out from the city and dwell in the open country; you shall go to Babylon" (Mic. 4:10).

This was a most specific and remarkable prophecy, given when Babylon was not yet a world power capable of such a distant conquest. But Micah speaks from God, who foreknows and foreordains all things. Beginning in 605 B.C., the Babylonian deportation of the Jews followed the pattern Micah laid out. First they would be forced to "go out from the city." Then they were kept in deportation camps "in the open country." Finally, the Jews were taken into wicked Babylon for their captivity. The Babylonians were certainly known in Micah's time; Hezekiah received envoys from Babylon and courted their favor (cf. Isa. 39:1–8). But Micah's specific prophecy "goes so beyond the bounds of the political horizon of Micah's time, that it cannot be accounted for from any natural presentiment."[3] The only explanation for so remarkable a prophecy is that its origin was in God's plan for future history.

What a chilling prospect Micah held before the Jews! Micah is not merely warning them of the possibility of divine judgment; he also assures them of its certainty. This was the "now" of which he was writing, the chastening that loomed on the horizon of history. They will cry aloud for the loss of their kingship, and they will be taken from the city to Babylon. Micah wrote to prepare them for this great hardship. Calvin paraphrases the prophet's message: "For God has decided that the city of Jerusalem must be razed and that you shall be banished from the inheritance that he had assigned you. It shall come to pass. Thus resolve yourself to receive the punishment and to endure the chastisement."[4]

Not much comfort, is it? Yet all believers are told plainly by God's Word that we must prepare to endure hardship. This was a point the apostle Paul tried to make with the earliest Christians. An example comes from his first

2. C. F. Keil and F. Delitzsch, *Commentary on the Old Testament*, 10 vols. (Peabody, Mass.: Hendrickson, 1996), 10:315.

3. Ibid.

4. John Calvin, *Sermons on the Book of Micah* (Phillipsburg, NJ: P&R Publishing, 2003), 242.

letter to the Thessalonians. He sent his helper Timothy, "to establish and exhort you in your faith, that no one be moved by these afflictions. For you yourselves know that we are destined for this" (1 Thess. 3:2–3). According to Jesus, this suffering would be in part because of the world's hatred of him: "If the world hates you, know that it has hated me before it hated you. If you were of the world, the world would love you as its own; but because you are not of the world, but I chose you out of the world, therefore the world hates you" (John 15:18–19). Everyone can expect hostility because of his vices, but Christians alone can expect opposition because of our virtues, which testify to the Savior whom the world hates.

This is the reality of our present, just as loss of kingship and coming exile were the present reality facing Jerusalem. How are God's people to face such daunting challenges? The answer to "now," Micah says, is "then." The key to persevering with joy in present difficulty is the knowledge of a certain and glorious salvation to come. With this in mind, he turns to the future: "There you shall be rescued; there the LORD will redeem you from the hand of your enemies" (Mic. 4:10). Yes, they would be taken off in chains into pagan darkness, and it is there that they would see God's salvation.

There are important lessons for us to learn from this prophecy. The first is that God's people are never without a saving king. Micah's statement in verse 9 is highly suggestive of the promise given by his contemporary, Isaiah: "For to us a child is born, to us a son is given; and the government shall be upon his shoulder, and his name shall be called Wonderful Counselor, Mighty God, Everlasting Father, Prince of Peace" (Isa. 9:6). This unquestionably directs us to the Lord Jesus Christ, God's own Son, whom God has made king forever for his people. Of his reign, "there will be no end," and he will sit on the throne of David "from this time forth and forevermore" (Isa. 9:7). Moreover, Jesus upholds his reign "with justice and with righteousness" (Isa. 9:7), so the people of Christ need never fear God's wrath.

Expecting the people to know that the Lord is their true king, Micah speaks with sarcasm to his afflicted people: "Now why do you cry aloud? Is there no king in you?" (Mic. 4:9). Yes, their earthly king would be taken away, but not their true Sovereign. In this light, the removal of Judah's kings was a step forward in salvation, so that the people would be prepared for the true King, who faithfully performs God's will and brings his saving plans to loving fulfillment. We, likewise, need to have our false supports removed, so that we will trust the only true Savior. Ever ruling for us, Christ the King works in us by God's Holy Spirit to bolster our flagging strength and encourage our weary hearts.

Second, note the manner by which God's people will be delivered: by redemption. "There you shall be rescued," Micah insists; "there the Lord will redeem you from the hand of your enemies" (Mic. 4:10). This means God will deliver his people from their strong foe by the power of his own might. Micah's language would remind his hearers of the exodus from Egypt. Israel was redeemed from bondage to Pharaoh by God's might and by the blood of the Passover lamb, which protected them from the angel of God's wrath.

Ultimately, the Israelites' redemption is not merely from the might of Babylon but from the guilt and power of their sins. This is why in the fullest sense the redemption of God's people has always been through the cross of their promised Messiah. Paul writes: "In him we have redemption through his blood, the forgiveness of our trespasses" (Eph. 1:7). As the hymn puts it:

He breaks the power of reigning sin; he sets the prisoners free
His blood can make the foulest clean; his blood availed for me.[5]

Looking forward to the same deliverance as Micah, and through it to our true redemption from sin, Isaiah spoke of the Servant-King to come: "he was wounded for our transgressions; he was crushed for our iniquities; upon him was the chastisement that brought us peace, and with his stripes we are healed. All we like sheep have gone astray; we have turned every one to his own way; and the Lord has laid on him the iniquity of us all" (Isa. 53:5–6). Our true bondage is to sin and its guilt, so the true redemption is by the death of Christ, whose blood paid the penalty our sins deserve.

Third, throughout the Bible, God's people find the light of salvation in the darkness of trial and loss. Another way to say this is that God designed for Israel to find its salvation through death and resurrection in Christ. Just as Jonah was swallowed by the great fish, there to cry out to God and find life, Israel required the purging of being swallowed up inside the utter paganism of Babylon in order to see the light of God's grace. Their characteristic sin prior to the exile was idolatry, so into the deepest hell of idolatry they would

5. Charles Wesley, "O for a Thousand Tongues to Sing", 1739; alt. 1961.

go. There, they would experience both punishment and liberation; for when they cried out to God, he rescued them.

The same pattern will hold true for us, for only by dying to idols, to sin, and to self can we lay hold of the redeeming blood of Christ as our rescue. The death that is conviction of sin becomes for us the place of liberation and redemption. When we, like the Jews in Babylon, are helpless and beyond human hope, God intervenes to rescue us by the grace of the cross of Christ.

DARKENED IN UNDERSTANDING

With that hope for the future in his hearers' minds, Micah returns to the present. "Then" is the time of their salvation, but "now" is the difficult time in which they must exercise their faith. Micah has assured them that God had ordained the end to their earthly kingship and even the end of their security in Jerusalem. The reality was that, as anyone could see, Judah's political and military situation was fundamentally compromised. The violent empires of their world were on the rise, with mighty armies constantly on the march. Micah summarizes, "Now many nations are assembled against you, saying, 'Let her be defiled, and let our eyes gaze upon Zion'" (Mic. 4:11).

The imperial powers were well aware of the holy city on Mount Zion; they were all too eager to overthrow the strange God who had disrupted so many of their evil plans. They hungered to defile the sacred precincts of the God of Israel. David Prior observes, "Godless people always take a perverse delight in the downfall of those who have been held up as God-fearing and distinctive."[6] Kenneth Barker notes, "Those who are unholy desire to render the holy also unholy, like themselves, then to gloat over it."[7] This is a present reality in our world, just as it was in Micah's, so that Christianity is not merely opposed in popular culture but is often mocked, while the failures of every Christian are celebrated with hilarity and scorn.

How important it is, then, for God's people to have a divine perspective not only on the future, but also on the present. Micah highlights one key

---

6. Prior, *The Message of Joel, Micah & Habakkuk*, 156.
7. Kenneth L. Barker and Waylon Bailey, *Micah, Nahum, Habakkuk, Zephaniah*, The New American Commentary (Nashville: Broadman & Holman, 1999), 93.

piece of information: for all their clever schemes, there is something essential that the nations do not know. Micah writes: "they do not know the thoughts of the LORD; they do not understand his plan" (Mic. 4:12).

However determined and equipped the wicked may be to assail God's people of faith, they are nonetheless ignorant of God's working in history. They do not realize that the God of the Bible is sovereign over all things, with a plan to glorify himself by saving his people. This ignorance about God and his plan is one of the worst byproducts of unbelief. Paul says: "They are darkened in their understanding, alienated from the life of God because of the ignorance that is in them, due to their hardness of heart" (Eph. 4:18). For this reason, all their plotting is utterly in vain, as the psalmist celebrates:

> Why do the nations rage
> and the peoples plot in vain?
> The kings of the earth set themselves,
> and the rulers take counsel together,
> against the LORD and against his anointed, saying,
> "Let us burst their bonds apart
> and cast away their cords from us."
> He who sits in the heavens laughs;
> The Lord holds them in derision.
> Then he will speak to them in his wrath,
> and terrify them in his fury. (Ps. 2:1–5)

The New Testament applies this text to the crucifixion of the Lord Jesus Christ (cf. Acts 4:25–26). Paul writes: "We impart a secret and hidden wisdom of God, which God decreed before the ages for our glory. None of the rulers of this age understood this, for if they had, they would not have crucified the Lord of glory" (1 Cor. 2:7–8).

Believers are to rely on God's plan, revealed to us in the Bible, especially in times of darkness. Thus it was at the beginning of their captivity that Jeremiah wrote on God's behalf to the exiles in Babylon: "I know the plans I have for you, declares the LORD, plans for wholeness and not for evil, to give you a future and a hope" (Jer. 29:11).

But what of the unbelieving nations, who assemble in lust against God's city? What is God's plan for them? Micah continues: "he has gathered them as sheaves to the threshing floor" (Mic. 4:12). The ungodly exult in defying God's will, when in fact it is God who has gathered them for destruction.

We remember that the land on which the temple was built, purchased by King David, was previously a threshing floor (2 Sam. 24:24). This was a place where wheat was first ground into small bits and then separated from the chaff. Not knowing this, the nations conspired to bring themselves to this very place. But God remembered; indeed, his design was set in place from eternity past. Bruce Waltke comments:

> The pagan throng do not understand that they are in [the Lord's] hands the unwitting tools of their own destruction .... They willfully conspired to break into the temple precincts, but in [the Lord's] comprehensive will they brought themselves of their own accord to his threshing floor where they are about to be pulverized; they came to Jerusalem to strip its temple, but precisely there they will be stripped; where they conspired to desecrate [the Lord's] name and sanctuary, their filthy loot will be consecrated to [the Lord] for destruction; where they hoped to rid the earth of the transcendent and holy God, the Lord of all the earth will rid the earth of them.[8]

This was precisely what happened during Sennacherib's invasion in Micah's day. The Assyrians assembled before God's city and God destroyed them there. But the principle finds its chief fulfillment at the cross of Christ. It is obvious that behind the pagan nations was the will of the devil. And at the cross, the greatest triumph of Satan's perverse will resulted in the overthrow of his kingdom, the release of his captives, and the highest glorification of God. The same principle operates whenever the world assails the church and the ungodly afflict individual Christians. Through our faith in God and his saving plan, not only do we find deliverance but the wicked are overthrown.

GOD'S THRESHER-CHURCH

Finally, Micah prophesies that God will use his church as his instrument for overthrowing the powers of the world. He concludes: "Arise and thresh, O daughter of Zion, for I will make your horn iron, and I will make your hoofs

8. Bruce Waltke, *A Commentary on Micah* (Grand Rapids: Eerdmans, 2007), 259.

bronze; you shall beat in pieces many peoples; and shall devote their gain to the LORD, their wealth to the Lord of the whole earth" (Mic. 4:13).

First, God summons and equips his people. So it is today, that Jesus calls his own out of the world and strengthens them with the bread of his Word. Matthew was sitting in the sin of his tax collector's booth, but Jesus called him, saying, "Follow me," and the new disciple "rose and followed him" (Matt. 9:9). Equipped by the Spirit to declare God's Word, Matthew became one of the twelve apostles whose gospel preaching overturned the world. Likewise, every Christian is called not only to salvation through faith in Jesus, but to grow strong through the Word and prayer. "Arise and thresh," God calls us, sending us to wage spiritual conquests in the power of truth and love, with the gospel message of God's grace, "We destroy arguments and every lofty opinion raised against the knowledge of God, and take every thought captive to obey Christ" (2 Cor. 10:5).

Second, the church is used by God as an instrument for judging the world. The gospel witness of Christians is the means by which God separates the wheat from the chaff, as the Word of Christ is either accepted or rejected. At the threshing floor, bulls and heifers stamped the wheat into fine pieces, so that the harvester could take the threshing fork, cast the bits into the wind, and separate the wheat from the chaff. God's people are equipped with bronze hooves for this work of threshing, and iron horns, correlating to what Paul called "the sword of the Spirit, which is the Word of God" (Eph. 6:17). By the gospel message that we preach, the light that we shine into darkness, and the good works we perform to the glory of God, Christians are used by God for the judgment of those who will not repent and believe. Thus the book of Revelation celebrates the victory of the redeemed over Satan and his powers: "they have conquered him by the blood of the Lamb and by the word of their testimony, for they loved not their lives even unto death" (Rev. 12:11).

Third, the victory of God's people delivers the wealth of the world into their hands. When the exodus generation departed from Egypt, they took with them the spoils of the Nile. And when Joshua conquered Jericho, its great riches came into the Israelites' possession. All this was dedicated to the Lord for the display of his glory. And what is the true wealth of the world, but the precious souls of men and women? We have the privilege of living in the days foreseen by the prophets, when the spoils of the earth are gathered in by the preaching and witness of the gospel, as pagans like us are converted by the Word of God's power, to display the triumph of the God who is Lord of all the earth. Thus the aim of our labor is never the accumulation of power for our own purposes or for the glory of our churches and ministries, but always for the display of the glory of God.

This was the future—the "then" of which Micah's generation was to be aware. So what did this mean for the "now"? Micah concludes his oracle with a call to arms: "Now muster your troops, O daughter of troops; siege is laid against us; with a rod they strike the judge of Israel on the cheek" (Mic. 5:1). Now is the time for readiness to enter spiritual battle. God's people must be made aware of what God was bringing: their city would fall and their king would be removed. But this was only the opening stage of a greater spiritual contest. They were to trust the Lord's plan for their salvation and for the overthrow of evil, all for the display of the manifold glories of God.

This is our calling in the midst of today's present darkness. Having been called to faith by the Word of Christ, we are to equip ourselves with what Paul described as "the whole armor of God" (Eph. 6:13): with the belt of truth, the breastplate of righteousness, shoes shod with the gospel of peace, the shield of faith, the sword of God's Word, and, not least, the mighty power of prayer (Eph. 6:14–18).

THE COST OF VICTORY

In every great battle, the cost is great even to the victors. How great is the cost in God's triumph over the evil powers in history! The cost to God is immeasurably great, in giving his only Son to die for our sins. The cost to Jesus, our Savior-King, is beyond comprehension: "the precious blood of Christ" (1 Peter 1:19). While we receive our salvation by faith alone, as a free gift of God's grace, still it costs us everything else. We surrender our self-righteousness, confessing our sins and need of forgiveness. We cede lordship over our lives, yielding to Christ. He calls us to take up the cross, the instrument of death where he died for our sins. He insists, "Any one of you who does not renounce all that he has cannot be my disciple" (Luke 14:33).

This means that the Christian life cannot be lived at leisure under peaceful skies. Christianity is the farthest thing from pie-in-the-sky escapism. It is life in the storm, bearing the peace of God; it is a battle in the darkness, shining the light of Christ. Now is the time for warfare in our hearts to remove the vestiges of sin, for labor in God's Word for the renewing of our minds, and for ministry in the wicked world with the love and truth of Christ. "Now muster your troops" (Mic. 5:1), God calls to his daughter-church, the warrior-bride of his royal Son. Now is the time of our struggle, strife, and pain for the gospel. But then, when Christ returns in the glory of the everlasting age, the joy of our redemption will remove even the memory of pain, just as the delivery of the child makes the laboring mother forget her birthing struggle. "For this slight momentary affliction," Paul writes, "is preparing for us an eternal weight of glory beyond all comparison" (2 Cor. 4:17).

26

O Bethlehem Ephrathah!

Micah 5:2–6

But you, O Bethlehem Ephrathah, who are too little to be among
the clans of Judah, from you shall come forth for me one who is to
be ruler in Israel, whose origin is from of old, from ancient days.
(Mic. 5:2)

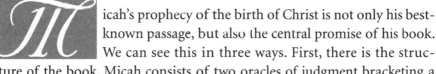icah's prophecy of the birth of Christ is not only his best-known passage, but also the central promise of his book. We can see this in three ways. First, there is the structure of the book. Micah consists of two oracles of judgment bracketing a great salvation oracle. The prophecy of a Savior from Bethlehem is the chief promise of the salvation oracle, and thus occupies the theological center of Micah's book. Second, Micah here offers the solution to the chief problem against which he has been preaching. Jerusalem's crisis resulted from corrupt and unfaithful leadership. God's answer is one who "shall come forth for me . . . who is to be ruler in Israel" (Mic. 5:2).

Third, this prophecy of the Messiah's birth in Bethlehem is the most remarkable of Micah's predictions. Chapter 1 prophesied the details of the Assyrian invasion under Sennacherib. Skeptics reject this as a true prediction. Because the events took place during Micah's lifetime, it is not possible to prove that he told of them in advance. In Micah 4:10 he predicts Judah's Babylonian captivity, which would not happen for over a hundred years. This, too, is rejected by critical scholars, who insist that prophecy of the future is not possible, and assert that Micah's prophecy must have been inserted in the text after the fact.

No such quibbles can be made about Micah 5:2, which accurately predicts the Messiah's birth *seven hundred* years beforehand, copies of which exist from before the time of Christ. Micah's prophecy of Christ's birth was so well known that when King Herod sought the location of the Savior's birth, his royal scholars referred to it without hesitation: "In Bethlehem of Judea, [who] are by no means least among the rulers of Judah, for from you shall come a ruler who will shepherd my people Israel" (Matt. 2:5–6).

This prophecy of the birth of Jesus Christ, the Savior-King of Israel, is the chief message that God gave to Micah for the hope of his people. But it is more than a prediction: it is a sermon outlining the chief features of the Savior's coming and unfolding God's mysterious plan for history, centered on the victory of the true king, Jesus Christ.

A SMALL TOWN LAUDED

Micah announces this prophecy against the backdrop of Jerusalem's dire situation around 700 B.C. Assyria had ravaged the country, and though God had miraculously saved the city, Jerusalem faced the bleak prospect of ineffective leadership. In chapter 4, Micah promised a future time of strength and glory in a revived kingship. He called the people to look forward to "that day" (Mic. 5:10) to come. But where should they look for this new day of hope?

Micah answers in a way that is both remarkable and wonderful. The people are not to look to the high hills of privilege and power, but to a small town in the country: "But you, O Bethlehem Ephrathah, who are too little to be among the clans of Judah, from you shall come forth for me one who is to be ruler in Israel" (Mic. 5:2).

Bethlehem was a remarkable place to bring forth a great king because of its obscurity and insignificance. This is seen from Micah's need to cite not only the name of the town, Bethlehem, but also the district, Ephrathah, so people would not confuse it with another Bethlehem in the region of Zebulun. An important city such as New York, London, or Paris does not require its state or even national affiliation, but Bethlehem (being so easily overlooked) did.

Moreover, Micah observes that Bethlehem was so small as to be "too little to be among the clans of Judah" (Mic. 5:2). When Joshua allotted towns for the tribe of Judah, Bethlehem was not large enough to be among the 115 cities and towns on the list (cf. Josh. 15:20–63). In modern terms, Bethlehem wouldn't merit a single traffic light or sport a single radio station. By referring to Bethlehem as "too little to be among the clans of Judah," Micah makes a point about its political and military insignificance. The word for "clans" is literally "thousands" (Hebrew, *eleph*). This refers to the basic unit of the Israelite army, which each clan was to raise when its tribe went to war. Bethlehem could not raise any such force, so it did not warrant even the modest designation of a clanhold.

But just because Bethlehem lacked political or military importance does not mean the town lacked any significance at all. Indeed, when we consider Bethlehem's biblical significance we see this as not only a remarkable but also a wonderful prophecy. This is first indicated by its name—remember that Micah takes the names of towns very seriously (cf. Mic. 1:10–16)—which means "house of bread." Likewise, the name Ephrathah means "bountiful." Unlike other towns Micah has mentioned, which will not live up to their names, Bethlehem Ephrathah will: she will provide for Israel by bringing forth a king.

Bethlehem had already played a prominent role that belied its secular insignificance. The love story of Ruth, the humble Moabite believer, and Boaz, the kinsman-redeemer, took place in Bethlehem. More importantly, Bethlehem was the hometown of Ruth and Boaz's descendant, King David. When the prophet Samuel sought a king after God's own heart, God directed him to this small town: "I will send you to Jesse the Bethlehemite, for I have provided for myself a king among his sons" (1 Sam. 16:1). James Boice comments: "Bethlehem was a small town among the many towns of Judah, but with a great history. And yet, the history of Bethlehem was to become even greater, for it was out of Bethlehem that he who was to be a divine and everlasting ruler over Israel would come."[1]

There are several lessons involved in Micah's prophecy. The first is that *God's way of salvation is contrary to the expectations of men.* Consider the

1. James Montgomery Boice, *The King Has Come* (Ross–shire, UK: Christian Focus, 1992), 40.

choosing of David. When Samuel arrived in Bethlehem, he asked Jesse to present his sons. Jesse brought out seven fine-looking young men, but little David was not taken seriously enough to be summoned. Yet contrary to all human expectations, David was the one God would use to launch his kingdom. Now, amid the dying embers of David's line, God promises something even more unexpected. "In these days of royal weakness Yahweh reaffirms through Micah that his will is not to sweep aside a worn-out, dying institution. It will flourish again in all its pristine beauty. The sacred promise of old will come true in a new demonstration of divine blessing."[2]

A second lesson is that *God delights to use unlikely instruments so as better to display his glory.* A new ruler would not come from a likely place such as Jerusalem, but from little, faithful Bethlehem. Bruce Waltke writes, "The focal point in redemptive history is none other than the insignificant town of Bethlehem, showing that Israel's future greatness does not depend on a great human king but on divine intervention to bring greatness out of nothing."[3] Likewise, today, God does not achieve his works through the fleshly appeal of charismatic personalities, but through the hands and lips of humble believers committed to doing his will. The greatest example is Jesus Christ, who was born not into prominence but obscurity, not into wealth but poverty, not into power but weakness. Paul stated that the same was true of the early church, which God used to turn the entire world upside down:

> Not many of you were wise according to worldly standards, not many were powerful, not many were of noble birth. But God chose what is foolish in the world to shame the wise; God chose what is weak in the world to shame the strong; God chose what is low and despised in the world, even things that are not, to bring to nothing things that are, so that no human being might boast in the presence of God. (1 Cor. 1:26–29)

Third, Micah shows that *the true hope of believers lies in God's sovereign grace.* The last thing anyone could say about King David was that he was a self-made man. No, David was a God-made man! Only by God's sovereign appointment and through the mighty working of God's grace could a shepherd boy accomplish all that David did. David's defining

---

2. Leslie C. Allen, *The Books of Joel, Obadiah, Jonah, and Micah,* New International Commentary on the Old Testament (Grand Rapids: Eerdmans, 1976), 344.

3. Bruce Waltke, *A Commentary on Micah* (Grand Rapids: Eerdmans, 2007), 272.

attribute was faith in the greatness and power of God. So it must be for all God's people, Micah indicates. The only way for little Bethlehem to dominate world history is by God's sovereign grace. So it would be for Bethlehem's greatest son, Jesus Christ, the Savior promised by Micah. Waltke comments:

> The Messiah's success depends on sovereign grace: God's election, intervention, and empowering. He renounces all human pomp and circumstance and power so that it might be evident to all that [the Lord] elected him and his strength is in [the Lord]. His rise to universal and eternal significance defies man's ways and thoughts and can best be accounted for by divine intervention and enablement. Indeed, he triumphs . . . by committing himself in faith and obedience to his God who elected him and delighted in him.[4]

This was Micah's message to his troubled generation. What hope was there to escape from their troubles? They were looking for some worldly strategy, compromise, or alliance that would enable them to survive. Micah replies, "Remember little Bethlehem. Remember little David. He trusted the power of God and prevailed." Waltke sums up the message: "History mutely bears witness that human ways to greatness lead finally to humiliating defeat (4:14 = 5:1 in English translations), whereas God's ways lead ultimately to triumph (cf. Isa. 55:8–9)."[5]

A Great Savior Promised

Believers triumph not because of their own strength, but because God has provided them a mighty Savior. This was the good news Micah preached to his generation: "From you shall come forth for me one who is to be ruler in Israel, whose origin is from of old, from ancient days" (Mic. 5:2). From Bethlehem will come a Savior who is great in his person, his calling, his ministry, and his salvation.

This promised Savior is *great in his person*. Micah says that his "origin is from of old, from ancient days" (Mic. 5:2). Scholars debate the meaning of this expression. Some point out that the words translated "from

4. Ibid., 300–1.
5. Ibid., 301.

of old" are used in the Bible to speak of God's eternity (Hebrew, *mime olam*). For instance, Deuteronomy 33:27 uses *olam*, saying, "The eternal God is your dwelling place, and underneath are the *everlasting* arms" (emphasis mine). In this view, the ruler that Micah foretold will arise from eternal, and therefore divine, origins. Based on this reading, some commentators see this as a direct reference to the eternal and divine being of Jesus Christ.

While the New Testament most certainly teaches Christ's eternal being (cf. Luke 1:32–33; 1 Tim. 6:16; Heb. 1:10), many scholars believe Micah is referring more directly to Jesus' ancient human lineage. They argue that the contextual link with Bethlehem indicates that "from of old" highlights Jesus' ancestral origin from the royal house of David. This view better reflects Micah's immediate context. But Isaiah, in foretelling the same event, ascribes blatant divinity to the promised Savior: "For to us a child is born, to us a son is given; and the government shall be upon his shoulder, and his name shall be called Wonderful Counselor, Mighty God, Everlasting Father, Prince of Peace" (Isa. 9:6).

In those days when the house of David teetered on the brink of despair, Micah having already predicted its utter ruin (cf. 4:9; 5:1), God prophesied a new David who would never fail. When Micah adds, "And he shall stand" (5:4), the prophet indicates that this royal Son will do what David's other descendants could not achieve: the promised Messiah would establish his throne eternally. Isaiah foretold, "Of the increase of his government and of peace there will be no end, on the throne of David and over his kingdom ... from this time forth and forevermore" (Isa. 9:7).

The promised Savior is also *great in his calling*. He comes forth not primarily for the people's sake but for God's: from Bethlehem "shall come forth *for me*" (italics added). Here stands the One who comes to achieve God's purpose in history; he is, as Isaiah designates him, the "Servant of the LORD." Isaiah's first servant song says: "Behold my servant, whom I uphold, my chosen, in whom my soul delights; I have put my Spirit upon him; he will bring forth justice to the nations" (Isa. 42:1). These words were deliberately echoed by the voice that John the Baptist heard from heaven when Jesus was baptized: "This is my beloved son, with whom I am well pleased" (Matt. 3:17). Walter Kaiser comments, "The Messiah was to be first of all for the Lord's benefit and His plans, and only secondarily in response to Israel and her distress."[6] Jesus himself asserted this: "My food is to do the will of him who sent me and to accomplish his work" (John 4:34).

Moreover, the promised Messiah would be *great in his ministry*. Micah adds: "And he shall stand and shepherd his flock in the strength of the LORD, in the majesty of the name of the LORD his God" (Mic. 5:4). Jesus took up this prophecy, teaching: "I am the good shepherd. The good shepherd lays down his life for the sheep. . . . I know my own and my own know me . . . and I lay down my life for the sheep" (John 10:11, 14–15). Unlike the false shepherds of Micah's day, corrupt leaders who betrayed and oppressed the people, God's promised Savior tends the flock "in the strength of the LORD." Like the shepherd boy David, who slew giant Goliath with a hand strengthened by God, Jesus came to overthrow the power of Satan and the curse of sin (cf. 1 John 3:8). David stood before Goliath, boasting: "You come to me with a sword and with a spear and with a javelin, but I come to you in the name of the LORD of hosts, the God of the armies of Israel, whom you have defied" (1 Sam. 17:45). Jesus overcame our true and greatest enemy, submitted his body to the nails and the cross conquering sin "in the majesty of the name of the LORD his God" (Mic. 5:4). "Father, into your hands I commit my spirit!" (Luke 23:46) he cried as he died for our sins.

The best known of Isaiah's servant songs highlights the very heart of Jesus' shepherding ministry. Jesus said, "The good shepherd lays down his life for the sheep" (John 10:11). Isaiah had foretold this, using words that Micah likely would have known: "He was wounded for our transgressions; he was crushed for our iniquities; upon him was the chastisement that brought us peace, and with his stripes we are healed. All we like sheep have gone astray; we have turned every one to his own way; and the Lord has laid on him the iniquity of us all" (Isa. 53:5–6). The only hope for wayward Israel, as for every sinner, is that God would send his own Son to suffer the penalty of our sins.

Finally, Micah's promised Savior would be *great in his salvation*: "And they shall dwell secure, for now he shall be great to the ends of the earth. And he shall be their peace" (Mic. 5:4–5). Here was Israel's only hope: a new David would come in the strength of the Lord, to shepherd them into green pastures. Jesus would offer a security scarcely imagined: the assurance of God's

6. Walter C. Kaiser Jr., *Micah–Malachi*, The Communicator's Commentary (Dallas: Word, 1992), 64.

blessing through the forgiveness of our sins. Michael Bentley writes: "Those who have the assurance that their sins have been forgiven, and who have dedicated their lives to the service of the Lord, experience many spiritual blessings. They know security from all their fears, and they are aware of the peace of God in every area of their lives."[7] This is the blessedness of which David sang of old:

> The LORD is my shepherd; I shall not want.
> . . .
> He restores my soul.
> He leads me in paths of righteousness
>   for his name's sake.
> Even though I walk through the valley of the shadow of death,
>   I will fear no evil,
> . . .
> Surely goodness and mercy shall follow me
>   all the days of my life,
> and I shall dwell in the house of the LORD
>   forever. (Ps. 23:1, 3–4, 6)

A MARVELOUS PLAN REVEALED

Micah's prophecy answers many urgent questions facing his generation. Who? A descendant of David. What? A ruler in Israel. Where? From Bethlehem. Why? For me, says God. This leaves only one question: When? Here the answer is not so simple, nor so comforting. Micah gives an answer, and in so doing offers a glimpse at God's marvelous and inscrutable plan for history. He begins: "Therefore he shall give them up until the time when she who is in labor has given birth" (Mic. 5:3).

Micah foretold that the coming years—centuries, in fact—would involve such hardship for the Jews that could only be compared to a woman in the travails of childbirth. This would happen because God would "give them up." Israel would be handed over by God to suffer and be purified. They had turned their hearts to idols, so in the care of idols they would fall into

---

7. Michael Bentley, *Balancing the Books: Micah and Nahum Simply Explained* (Durham: Evangelical Press, 1994), 64.

ruin. God would no longer tolerate their empty worship and false hearts. Isaiah wrote: "When you spread out your hands, I will hide my eyes from you; even though you make many prayers, I will not listen; your hands are full of blood" (Isa. 1:15).

Abandoned by God, over the coming centuries Israel would experience the full fury of her greatest fears, including Jerusalem's fall, the destruction of the temple, slaughter, and exile. Even after God restored a remnant to the city and caused the temple to be rebuilt, the centuries that followed would include subjugation to pagan empires, the desecration of the new temple, and occupation by foreign armies. God's people would have to learn the bitter wages of sin so as to ready themselves for Christ's coming. Jesus' first message related to this chastisement: "The kingdom of God is at hand; repent and believe in the gospel" (Mark 1:15). Micah's "therefore" in verse 3 relates directly to Christ's appearance: God would give the people up to all the travails of bondage and affliction, for the purpose of readying Israel's heart for the Savior.

When Jesus was born, the remnant of God's faithful people was in fact ready and waiting. One of these people was Zechariah, father of John the Baptist. He responded to the news of the coming birth by reflecting on prophecies such as Micah's: "Blessed be the Lord God of Israel, for he has visited and redeemed his people and has raised up a horn of salvation for us in the house of his servant David, as he spoke by the mouth of his holy prophets of old, that we should be saved from our enemies" (Luke 1:68–71). We hear similar words of faith from the lips of Jesus' mother, Mary, and from aged Simeon and Anna, who were waiting for the Messiah in the courts of the temple (cf. Luke 2:22–38).

Consider the marvelous providence involved in the fulfillment of Micah's prophecy, signaling the end of Israel's divine abandonment. Joseph the carpenter was betrothed to the maiden Mary in Nazareth of Galilee. An angel appeared to each of them, foretelling that by the Holy Spirit's power, God's Son would be born through her virgin womb. Meanwhile, in far-away Rome, Emperor Caesar Augustus had an argument with King Herod, and as a result decreed that Judea would be levied with a tax. To emphasize his authority, Augustus took the unusual measure of requiring all the Jewish people to be registered in their hometowns. This occurred during the very month that Mary was expecting to bear her son. So Joseph and Mary made the arduous journey to the place of Joseph's origin, which as a descendant of David was Bethlehem. There—not by Caesar's will but by the sovereign decree of God, in fulfillment of his ancient prophecy—the virgin spoken of by Isaiah gave birth to God's Son, and it was out of Bethlehem that Israel's Savior-King was brought forth. The world was sleeping when the sign of salvation was given; as Phillips Brooks wrote in "O Little Town of Bethlehem": "Yet in thy dark streets shineth the everlasting Light; the hopes and fears of all the years are met in thee tonight."[8]

This ended the first phase of God's marvelous plan for his people. Micah then notes two features of the phase that would follow. He states, "then the rest of his brothers shall return" (Mic. 5:3), and adds, "now he shall be great to the ends of the earth" (Mic. 5:4). Both of these prophecies refer to the ingathering of the Gentiles through the missionary spread of the gospel to all nations.

This is God's plan for rescuing his people from their foreign enemies, by gathering believers from all nations as members of one spiritual family through faith in Christ. The Jews were burdened only for their own brothers—Israelites who had been lost to captivity. But Micah speaks of the return of "his" brothers—the Messiah's brothers—to include both lost Israelites and lost Gentiles. Jesus foretold this in his good shepherd discourse: "I have other sheep who are not of this fold. I must bring them also, and they will listen to my voice. So there will be one flock, one shepherd" (John 10:16). Paul, quoting from Micah's prophecy, states that in the spiritual bond of faith the enmity between Jew and Gentile is finally removed: "Now in Christ Jesus you who once were far off have been brought near by the blood of Christ. For he himself is our peace, who has made us both one and has broken down in his flesh the dividing wall of hostility" (Eph. 2:13–14). Bruce Waltke comments, "In this way Messiah's rule will become great, even to the ends of the earth, and so Israel will live securely."[9]

Lastly, Micah presents a vision that is among the most difficult to interpret in the entire book: "When the Assyrian comes into our land and treads in our palaces, then we will raise against him seven shepherds and eight princes of men; they shall shepherd the land of Assyria with the sword, and the land of

8. Phillips Brooks, "O Little Town of Bethlehem," 1868.
9. Waltke, *A Commentary on Micah*, 303.

Nimrod at its entrances; and he shall deliver us from the Assyrian when he comes into our land and treads within our border" (Mic. 5:5–6).

Because these verses speak specifically about the Jews' defeat of Assyria and Babylon, some scholars conclude that this promise must be fulfilled after the return of Christ, when Israel is thought to be regathered in its ancient land against its former foes. But such a view fails to appreciate the prophets' common practice of presenting distant realities in present-tense form. The substance of the promise is the same for all generations—triumph over evil—but to make sense to their original hearers, the prophets necessarily garbed the future fulfillment in the clothes of their present situations.

The threat in Micah's time came from Assyria, with danger looming from Babylon ("the land of Nimrod"), so Micah dresses his message of future victory in terms of their defeat. Micah says, "We will raise against him seven shepherds and eight princes of men; they shall shepherd the land of Assyria with the sword" (Mic. 5:5–6). The numbers seven and eight speak of an adequate (indeed, more than adequate) supply of holy leaders, who under the promised Messiah would defend their territory and strike back with great effect.

Living in Micah's future, we see this promise fulfilled in Christ's provision for the security of his church. As Micah foresaw, Christ raises up gifted shepherds and leaders to protect the truth and cast back the enemies of our faith. The sword we wield today, shepherding more and more of Christ's sheep and defending the doctrines of the gospel, is the Word of God. And redeemed by Christ's blood, we enjoy "the peace of God, which surpasses all understanding" (Phil. 4:7).

DYING TO LIVE

So Israel would suffer years of travail to chasten them for their sins. Then the Savior, a new and greater David, would appear. He would shepherd not only Israel but all the nations, giving peace and making his name great throughout the earth. His kingdom would stand against all foes, because "he shall deliver us from the Assyrian when he comes into our land and treads within our border" (Mic. 5:6).

Does this plan seem familiar? It should, because its outline mirrors the story of Jesus himself: death, resurrection, exaltation, and eternal peace.

Israel must die to sin, finding new life from God, walking in his power, and patiently awaiting his salvation.

So it is for every believer. To be a Christian is to have the story of our former life ended with the words, "And then he died." Then a new book begins, telling of a new life in Christ, with God's power working in us and a sure hope of glory. Are you ready to die with Christ? By this, the Bible means a death to sin and self. Paul said of Jesus, "the death he died he died to sin, once for all, but the life he lives he lives to God" (Rom. 6:10). But this daily death of the Christian life is accompanied by a daily coming to new and eternal life with Christ. If you are ready to die with Jesus, he is ready to grant you life, and he will be your peace.

27

THE RESURRECTION CHURCH

Micah 5:7–15

Then the remnant of Jacob shall be in the midst of many peoples
like dew from the LORD, like showers on the grass, which delay not
for a man nor wait for the children of man. (Mic. 5:7)

*A*ccording to the Bible, the event in history that has most defined our present age is not Gutenberg's invention of the printing press, or the establishment of the Western democracies, or the Second World War. Rather, it was a gathering for prayer of 120 disciples of Jesus Christ in a room in Jerusalem almost two millennia ago. As Jesus had promised (Acts 1:8), and as the Old Testament had prophesied (Joel 2:28), the Holy Spirit fell upon that primeval church. It was the culminating act of God's Son in his first coming to our world. Jesus came to live a perfect life, die an atoning death, rise from the grave, ascend to heavenly authority, and pour out his Spirit on the church. Thus Pentecost, the final event in this sequence, is the historical event that defines this age of grace. Jesus, having died for our sins, poured out his Spirit on the church. Henceforth the Christian life is life in the Spirit of God.

The Pentecost outpouring has two great implications for the church of the resurrection age, the age of the Holy Spirit, as well as for all believers who are called to resurrection life. First, it means the church is imbued with power from on high for ministry in the world. John writes, "He who is in you is greater than he who is in the world" (1 John 4:4). But this brings a corresponding responsibility for holiness among God's people. Paul explains: "By sending his own Son in the likeness of sinful flesh and for sin, [God] condemned sin in the flesh, in order that the righteous requirement of the law might be fulfilled in us, who walk not according to the flesh but according to the Spirit" (Rom. 8:3–4).

As he ministers to his generation in darkness, the prophet Micah looks forward to our present age, the resurrection age of the Spirit. The prophecy of chapter 5 begins with a focus on the coming of Christ, who would be born in Bethlehem. But now Micah's vision extends beyond Christ's first advent into the age of the gospel. John Mackay writes: "Its position in this chapter places it after the appearance of the Messiah, and it is therefore a consequence of his rule."[1] Micah's prophecies of strength for God's people look forward to the new covenant, in which the aims of the old covenant are fulfilled. The prophet foresees an age of power for the church in the world, but also a divine mandate for holiness that exceeds even that of the old covenant.

The Church: God's Blessing for the World

At the very beginning of the history of God's ancient people, it was made clear that God intended them to be a blessing to the world. We see this as far back as the calling of Abraham, father of the Old Testament people: "I will make of you a great nation, and I will bless you and make your name great, so that you will be a blessing . . . and in you all the families of the earth shall be blessed" (Gen. 12:2–3). This promise is especially fulfilled as the bud of Israel has bloomed in the church, just as Jesus commanded in the Great Commission: "Go therefore and make disciples of all nations, baptizing them in the name of the Father and of the Son and of the Holy Spirit" (Matt. 28:19).

Yet it would never be because of size or strength in worldly terms that the church would wield God's power. Micah says, "the remnant of Jacob shall be among the nations" (Mic. 5:8). Just as in his own time, when the small nation of Israel was beset by greater world powers, the church of God's people

1. John L. Mackay, *Jonah, Micah, Nahum, Habakkuk and Zephaniah: God's Just Demands*, Focus on the Bible (Ross–shire, UK: Christian Focus, 1998), 109.

is always a remnant in the world. Whenever the church has tried to seize earthly power, it has lost its spiritual influence. Bruce Waltke writes, "Like the Messiah, [God's people] step forth small and lowly among the nations and become great by the divine initiative."[2] Although it is comparatively small in numbers and lacking in earthly power, God intends for his true church to play a decisive role in the world.

But what is the nature of the church's influence in the world? Micah provides two answers. First, he writes: "Then the remnant of Jacob shall be in the midst of many peoples like dew from the LORD, like showers on the grass, which delay not for a man nor wait for the children of man" (Mic. 5:7).

This is a lovely expression of the blessing God's remnant is to bring to the world. Leslie Allen writes, "Men's heavy hearts must have been lightened by the very mention of the dew and rain falling on thirsty grass."[3] The reason for the blessedness of dew was the lack of rainfall in Palestine during the important summer months. The heavy dews resulting from the condensation of air laden with moisture from the Mediterranean Sea were of vital agricultural importance. Thus the patriarch Isaac blessed his son Jacob: "May God give you of the dew of heaven and of the fatness of the earth and plenty of grain and wine" (Gen. 27:28). In a parched land like theirs, dew was often the only refreshment and thus was considered a literal godsend.

Similarly, Micah continues, God's people are to be "like showers on the grass, which delay not for a man nor wait for the children of man" (Mic. 5:7). Summer showers gave hope for a good harvest, and the church likewise brings life to the world and gives hope for eternity. David spoke this way about those who rule in godly fear and thus spread a heavenly influence: "he dawns on them like the morning light, like the sun shining forth on a cloudless morning, like rain that makes grass to sprout from the earth" (2 Sam. 23:4).

This is to be the effect of Christians in our world today, bringing life and renewal. Ours has become a wilderness world, despite our material abundance. Consider the state of morality in our society and the sheer misery induced by godless living. Christians are to be like dew that falls from heaven, a breath of morally pure fresh air. Consider the craven attitude toward sexuality today: the sexual purity of Christians is not only to be a stirring reminder

2. Bruce Waltke, *A Commentary on Micah* (Grand Rapids: Eerdmans, 2007), 315.
3. Leslie C. Allen, *The Books of Joel, Obadiah, Jonah, and Micah*, New International Commentary on the Old Testament (Grand Rapids: Eerdmans, 1976), 353.

of moral truth, but also to invoke aspirations of nobility that our society has all but lost. Or consider the state of our communities. Real communities where people know and care for one another are increasingly rare. But when a Christian family moves to the neighborhood, the effect should be blessing for all, as God's people take a redemptive interest in their neighbors, as children are treated with godly nurture, and as a loving concern is shown to those in need.

Of course the greatest refreshment Christians bring is the light of the gospel. What will our neighbors do when sickness and death knock on their door? Who will give an answer to the great questions that keep so many lying awake at night: questions about the meaning of life, the judgment of God, and life after death. "You are the light of the world," Jesus said. "Let your light shine before others, so that they may see your good works and give glory to your Father who is in heaven" (Matt. 5:14, 16).

THE CHURCH: GOD'S CONQUEST OF THE WORLD

The presence of God's people in the world has a second effect, one that at first seems antithetical to the first: "And the remnant of Jacob shall be among the nations, in the midst of many peoples, like a lion among the beasts of the forest, like a young lion among the flocks of sheep, which, when it goes through, treads down and tears in pieces, and there is none to deliver" (Mic. 5:8). The lion is not a domesticated animal, and the church is not to be domesticated by the world. The lion rules his domain and is utterly able to defend his prerogatives.

This, too, is to be the relationship of the church to the world. Leslie Allen explains: "The imagery of Israel as a lion is an ancient one, which stands for the irresistible conquest of all opposition. The prophet is recalling a traditional role associated with holy war. . . . Here there is an application to Israel as the earthly representative of the divine Victor. God's cause, with which Israel is identified, must triumph."[4]

The triumph of God's cause in the world is also, of course, for the benefit of the world, though many in opposition will be crushed. God places his church in the world in order to bless the world. But the world is not permitted

4. Ibid., 354.

to overcome the church and, for those who try, the results will be disastrous. Paul expressed this dichotomy in this way: "We are the aroma of Christ to God among those who are being saved and among those who are perishing, to one a fragrance from death to death, to the other a fragrance from life to life" (2 Cor. 2:15–16). It is natural for Christians to desire to bless the world and the people around them, but the reality is that those who reject our gospel will suffer destruction for their unbelief, even as those who believe will be saved.

If it is a shame when Christians fail to bring refreshment and blessing to the world, it is equally a rejection of our calling when we are intimidated by worldly powers. We see this today as many churches adopt a worldly message, worldly priorities, and worldly methods. The apparent logic is that since the world cannot be beaten, it must be joined. But this is false. Jesus said that he would build his church on the rock of the gospel, "and the gates of hell shall not prevail against it" (Matt. 16:18). Notice that it is hell's gates that are under assault, not the church's gates; hell's gates cannot withstand the church. This means that the presence of God's people is designed to inhibit sin and to force back worldliness by the presence of godliness, all for the ultimate blessing of the world. So it has been in history, as Christian values and ideas have pushed back the darkness of barbarism, bringing light in the realms of government, education, science, culture, and the arts.

Micah concludes this description of God's blessing to the nations, saying, "Your hand shall be lifted up over your adversaries, and all your enemies shall be cut off" (Mic. 5:9). What a promise this is of power for the church in the world. Opposition to Christianity is growing in the West today, as seen in the success of best-selling books not merely opposing Christian truth but appealing for society no longer to tolerate God's people. What will happen? Micah gives the answer. I think it likely that the atheistic best sellers will merely spur Christian thinkers to speak more boldly and effectively to the culture. In any case, despite whatever temporary success God's enemies may enjoy, they will in time be cut off, and the hands of God's people will be lifted up over their foes.

In our generation, this prophecy has been especially fulfilled in the developing world. In China, for instance, it is widely acknowledged that the gravest threat to the tyranny of communism is the growing Christian church. Journalist David Aikman, for many years the *Time* magazine bureau chief in Beijing, argues that it is more than feasible that Christianity will become the dominant worldview of the emerging China. He writes of meeting highly educated Chinese "who were not satisfied that either the Marxist interpretation of religion or the standard Western Darwinian understanding of life adequately explained the human condition in general and the Chinese condition in particular," so they are open-minded to the gospel. He records a Beijing dinner party attended by the then-president and leader of China's Communist Party, Jiang Zemin. "Comrade Jiang," a guest asked, "if, before leaving office, you could make one decree that you know would be obeyed in China, what would it be?" Jiang quietly reflected, then answered, "I would make Christianity the official religion of China."[5]

The opportunity before us calls Western Christians to a far greater boldness in our secular context. James Boice cites a column in the *New York Daily News* by William Reel, decrying the deplorable condition of New York City. Reel recounted the barbaric statistics regarding murder, rape, alcoholism, and pornography. But was his chief concern the failure of civic government? Reel wrote: "Of course, you gave up on New York politicians long ago. They are pathetic and embarrassing. But what is worse than the abdication of political leadership in New York is the abdication of spiritual leadership. There is no one willing to speak the truth, to call the Neros to account, to warn of the wrath of God." Then he asks, "When was the last time a Catholic leader said anything more forceful than 'God bless you'? New York needs a John the Baptist and Catholicism gives us Caspar Milquetoasts. The Protestant leadership is effete and insipid, debating Holy Orders for lesbians at a time when grandmothers are regularly and brutally assaulted by muggers and rapists."[6] How remarkable it is when secular columnists lament the influence of true Christianity, even though they personally have not embraced it. God has called us to be dew on the grass, a lion among the beasts, and he has promised to lift our hands against all those who oppose his reign in the church.

GOD'S HOLINESS IN THE CHURCH

The resurrection church, blessed with the power of God's Holy Spirit, is made mighty by God to be a blessing in the world. But that same church, by

5. David Aikman, *Jesus in Beijing* (Washington, DC: Regnery, 2003), 17–18.
6. James M. Boice, *The Minor Prophets*, 2 vols. (Grand Rapids: Baker, 1986), 2:347–48.

virtue of the presence of the same Holy Spirit, is under a high obligation to holiness. So it always is when God dwells amid his people: the people must be made a fitting home for God and a holy vessel for his sacred service.

With this in mind, Micah casts his eye forward and sees God acting as vigorously in the church as he does in the world through the church: "And in that day, declares the LORD, I will cut off your horses from among you and will destroy your chariots; and I will cut off the cities of your land and throw down all your strongholds; and I will cut off sorceries from your hand, and you shall have no more tellers of fortunes; and I will cut off your carved images and your pillars from among you" (Mic. 5:10–13). Here God promises to "cut off"—effectively remove—four kinds of worldliness and sin that would keep his people from bearing his resurrection power. James Boice comments: "Micah writes of a day when the nation would be purified of its sin and maintained in an attitude of pure and intense devotion to God."[7]

The first of these warnings pertains to the displacing of the church's faith from a reliance on God to a trust in the weapons of worldly warfare: "I will cut off your horses from among you and will destroy your chariots" (Mic. 5:10). In Micah's day, horses and chariots were the ultimate in military technology. God's design was not to render Israel defenseless but rather to defend Israel himself. The attitude he desired is that expressed by David in Psalm 20:7: "Some trust in chariots and some in horses, but we trust in the name of the LORD our God." Instead of trusting in false means and giving glory to false champions, God desires his people to rely on his might alone. So it is today. However foolish it is for any nation to rely on military technology instead of trusting in God alone, it is utterly lamentable in the church. And how vulnerable the church becomes when the wisdom of marketing and worldly entertainment is taken up as the way of success, instead of humble reliance on prayer and the Word of God.

In a related statement, Micah adds: "I will cut off the cities of your land and throw down all your strongholds" (Mic. 5:11). We remember from earlier in Micah how easily Sennacherib was able to overthrow the Judean stronghold of Lachish. God says of fortress-cities like this: "it was the beginning of sin to the daughter of Zion" (Mic. 1:13). So it always is when the church no longer

---

7. Ibid., 2:349.

sings "A Mighty Fortress Is Our God," but becomes proud in its fortress stockpiles of numbers, money, and worldly influence.

Thirdly, the Lord declares, "And I will cut off sorceries from your hand, and you shall have no more tellers of fortunes" (Mic. 5:12). In the pagan nations of Micah's day, rulers eased their anxiety for the future by appeal to occult diviners of all kinds; it seems that this sin had made its way into the councils of Jerusalem. How easily this vanity makes its way into the council chambers of churches today. Walter Kaiser insightfully observes, "whenever the word of God is scarcely heard because of a widespread disregard for it, or boredom with it, then [people] will have to seek out the netherworld."[8] Thus the rapid spread of fortune-tellers and similar occultists in Western society today can only reflect the lost confidence in God's Word in the church. Isaiah diagnosed this problem in the Jerusalem of Micah's time: "When they say to you, 'Inquire of the mediums and the necromancers who chirp and mutter,' should not a people inquire of their God?" (Isa. 8:19). God intends our anxiety over the future to be relieved in prayer and through the study of God's Word, the very means of grace so greatly neglected in today's churches. Isaiah's remedy then is of the greatest relevance: "To the teaching and to the testimony!" (Isa. 8:20).

Lastly, God promises to eradicate idolatry among his people: "I will cut off your carved images and your pillars from among you, and you shall bow down no more to the work of your hands; and I will root out your Asherah images from among you and destroy your cities" (Mic. 5:13–14). The religion of idols addressed mankind's need of divine power. Worship of an image was a way of gaining that god's favor and intercession. The Baal pillars and the Asherah poles pertain most directly to fertility, which explains why they were the greatest temptation to a society dependent on dew and rain for their agricultural survival. Rather than rely on prayers to the Lord for the rains needed for a fertile harvest, the Israelites were tempted to take matters into their own hands by visiting the local shrine to Baal or Asherah, whose advertised powers promised fast results.

Idolatry is cited by the Old Testament as the chief cause of Jerusalem's downfall when God gave the city over to the Babylonian invaders (Jer. 3:2–3). God not only punished idolatry, but delivered his people from the worship

8. Walter C. Kaiser Jr., *Micah–Malachi*, The Communicator's Commentary (Dallas: Word, 1992), 66.

of idols by forcing them to live in the heart of pagan Babylonia. The fact that the Bible makes no mention of the problem of idolatry after the exile indicates the success of God's resolution: "You shall bow down no more to the work of your hands" (Mic. 5:13).

God is equally earnest in demanding that Christians repudiate the prevailing idolatries of materialism, sensualism, and egoism today. One defining characteristic of idolatry is always licentiousness, since one of the main reasons to serve pagan gods was that they made no moral demands on their servants. So it is that in America today those who achieve success, wealth, and political power are seldom expected to conduct themselves with moral uprightness. The logic of idolatry and licentiousness should be alien to the people of God, who turn to him for their needs and live in the midst of his holy presence.

Taken together, the four sinful tendencies that God promises to eliminate give us a good understanding of holiness, cast primarily in terms of the believers' devotion to and reliance on God. What does God want removed from his people? God hates a reliance on worldly means instead of the holy weapons of prayer and the Word. God hates the pride and self-reliance signified by Israel's fortress cities; instead, God's people are to seek their only shelter in the name of the Lord. Moreover, God's people are to take their guidance from God's Word, relying neither on social prognosticators nor occult fortune-tellers. Lastly, God's people are to repudiate the idols of their age—idols who repay allegiance with an open door to sinful pleasure—but instead worship only the Lord their God and pursue the holiness he requires.

If any Christian doubts the zeal of God's insistence on this approach to holiness, he need only consider the last verse of Micah's oracle: "In anger and wrath I will execute vengeance on the nations that did not obey" (Mic. 5:15). God has settled his wrath upon all ungodliness and unrighteousness (cf. Rom. 1:18). In his patient working in history, God declares that he gives unbelieving idolaters over to wallow deeper in their sin: "Since they did not see fit to acknowledge God, God gave them up to a debased mind to do what ought not to be done" (Rom. 1:28). So it was in the Roman Empire of Paul's time, and so it is today in the rapid decay of the decadent West. How insistent is God's calling that his people are to be different! Indeed, only in the pursuit of Christ-like holiness can any person or any church seriously claim the name of Christian or hope to have the influence for blessing and salvation that God desires us to have in the world. In the end, the day of judgment will come and the righteous wrath of God will be revealed: "In anger and wrath I will execute vengeance on the nations that did not obey," says the Lord (Mic. 5:15).

REFORMATION AND REVIVAL

Micah's prophecy applies to our situation today with compelling force. In the two halves of this prophecy—to bless and to smite the world—we may discern God's mandate for the church. God calls the church to reformation, and he promises power and life to the church that renounces worldliness and turns wholeheartedly to God. The church must pursue reformation according to the Word of God, and God promises revival power in response, so the church may fulfill her calling in the world.

Reformation begins with repentance for our sin and disobedience. This is how Hezekiah, Jerusalem's king in the time of Micah, responded to the preaching of the messages we are studying. A century later, Jeremiah exhorted the people with Hezekiah's example: "Did he not fear the LORD and entreat the favor of the LORD, and did not the LORD relent of the disaster that he had pronounced against them?" (Jer. 26:19). Second Chronicles records that Hezekiah restored the priesthood and true worship in the temple and sent Bible teachers throughout the country to instruct the people in the truth and way of the Lord (cf. 2 Chron. 29:1–36). This is the second step in reformation: having repented of sin and worldliness, to return to the ways of the Lord as taught in his Word. The result of Hezekiah's reformation was the blessing of God through the renewal of national spiritual life. People began to humble themselves and to come before God in his temple: "The hand of God was also on Judah to give them one heart to do what the king and the princes commanded by the word of the LORD" (2 Chron. 30:12).

Reformation will take on a similar form today. We must return to the ways of the Lord as taught in Scripture. We must reform ourselves and our church by the Word of God. This will mean a reformation of our worship, a reformation of our approach to ministry, a reformation of our teaching, and, indeed, a reformation of our lives. Is such a reformation possible today? And if we reform according to God's Word, will it make a difference?

The entire record of church history says that reformation is possible and that, while revival is always a sovereign act of God that can only come at times of his choosing, reformation makes a vital difference in the life of the church. One of the great examples is the reformation of the city of Geneva under the ministry of John Calvin. In 1535 the Geneva city council elected to break with Roman Catholicism and align with the Protestant Reformation, hoping to help curb the city's social ills. But this political move brought no real change. In the next year, John Calvin was persuaded to take up a pulpit ministry in Geneva. At first Calvin was ignored. By 1538 his preaching was so unpopular that he was dismissed and he departed to live in Strasbourg. But as conditions deteriorated in Geneva, Calvin was summoned to return and, driven by his sense of duty, he resumed his ministry on September 13, 1541. James Boice tells what happened:

> Calvin had no weapon but the Bible. From the very first, his emphasis had been on Bible teaching, and he returned to it now, picking up precisely where he had left off three and a half years earlier. Calvin preached from the Bible every day, and under the power of that preaching the city began to be transformed. As the people of Geneva acquired knowledge of God's Word and were changed by it, the city became, as John Knox called it later, a New Jerusalem from which the gospel spread to the rest of Europe, England, and the New World.[9]

The effects of this spiritual revival, brought on by the reforming effects of God's Word, reached into every area of Geneva's life. Efforts were made to improve cleanliness in order to combat disease. Markets were supervised for fairness and beggars were provided for in safe poorhouses. Hospitals were built, and for the first time in Geneva provision was made for the education of all classes. Realizing that good jobs were needed, the cloth and silk industry was imported. The spread of biblical religion even improved government. Historian Marcellus Kik observed, "It is no mere coincidence that religious and political liberty arose in those countries where Calvinism had penetrated most deeply."[10]

The lesson of this example is that resurrection life comes to churches, Christians, and even cities that reform out of sincere devotion to God's Word.

---

9. James Montgomery Boice, *Whatever Happened to the Gospel of Grace?* (Wheaton: Crossway, 2001), 83–84.

10. Cited in Boice, *Whatever Happened to the Gospel of Grace?* 84.

But reformation is not merely God's advice; it is also his demand. So it was revealed in the seven letters that the risen and exalted Jesus directed to the churches in the book of Revelation. In the first of these letters, to the church in Ephesus, Jesus spoke:

> I have this against you, that you have abandoned the love you had at first. Remember therefore from where you have fallen; repent, and do the works you did at first. If not, I will come to you and remove your lampstand from its place, unless you repent (Rev. 2:4–5).

Do we see the importance of the church's godliness? Do you see the importance of your personal devotion to Christ? If we will repent, reforming ourselves by God's Word, Christ will revive us with life—in fact, reformation will show that Christ has already been graciously among us bringing life. Then we will be the blessing to the world we are meant to be, like dew on the summer grass. We will have nothing in the world to fear, for God will make us like a lion in the midst of beasts. He will raise up our hands so that the gospel of his salvation may have its victory in the world.

28

THE GIFT THAT GOD REQUIRES

Micah 6:1–8

He has told you, O man, what is good; and what does the Lord
require of you but to do justice, and to love kindness, and to walk
humbly with your God? (Mic. 6:8)

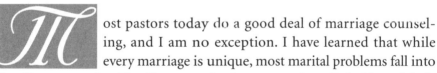ost pastors today do a good deal of marriage counseling, and I am no exception. I have learned that while every marriage is unique, most marital problems fall into familiar categories. Usually one or both partners have little idea of their biblical calling in marriage, or have expectations that are not reasonable. It is especially common in marriage for spouses to take one another for granted: amid the busyness of life, they do little to convey their appreciation or affection. When this has been going on for a long time, emotional coolness and hard feelings may easily damage their relationship.

In Micah 6 God has a quarrel with his people Israel along these very lines. Not that the Lord has grown distant toward them, but rather that his people have taken him for granted and distanced their hearts. As God summons the prophet to plead his case, the scene is that of the courtroom. But it is family court, not criminal court. God has a grievance against his people, and the result he seeks is the renewal of the ancient covenant faithfulness and love.

As he ministers to his generation in darkness, the prophet Micah looks forward to our present age, the resurrection age of the Spirit. The prophecy of chapter 5 begins with a focus on the coming of Christ, who would be born in Bethlehem. But now Micah's vision extends beyond Christ's first advent into the age of the gospel. John Mackay writes: "Its position in this chapter places it after the appearance of the Messiah, and it is therefore a consequence of his rule."[1] Micah's prophecies of strength for God's people look forward to the new covenant, in which the aims of the old covenant are fulfilled. The prophet foresees an age of power for the church in the world, but also a divine mandate for holiness that exceeds even that of the old covenant.

God's Covenant Lawsuit

In our day, such a quarrel would take place in a counselor's office or pastor's study. But the Old Testament form for God's appeal to his people was the covenant lawsuit. This kind of proceeding was designed to protect and vindicate one who has been wrongfully used in a covenant relationship. Since in this case it is God who calls for redress, it is an extremely public affair: he summons his prophet to stand before the people on his behalf. He calls the very mountains to witness what will be said between the Lord and his betrothed covenant nation. "Arise," God calls to Micah, "plead your case before the mountains, and let the hills hear your voice" (Mic. 6:1). It is not unlikely that Micah delivered God's message in the temple courts, where many of Jerusalem's leaders would be present. Moreover, his speech might well have been given during one of the great feasts when the whole nation was assembled, especially the Passover, with its remembrance of the historical events Micah recounts.

The prophet summons the long-standing mountains to bear testimony, since they have borne witness to Israel's long record of misdeeds. There is likely an intended contrast between the immovable mountains and the fickle hearts of Israel. Furthermore, "Calling such important witnesses stresses the seriousness of the case and its epoch-making quality. Who can be the guilty party at so awesome a court hearing?"[2]

---

1. John L. Mackay, *Jonah, Micah, Nahum, Habakkuk and Zephaniah: God's Just Demands*, Focus on the Bible (Ross–shire, UK: Christian Focus, 1998), 109.
2. Leslie C. Allen, *The Books of Joel, Obadiah, Jonah, and Micah*, New International Commentary on the Old Testament (Grand Rapids: Eerdmans, 1976), 365.

Most importantly, this reference to the witness-mountains locates the protest within the covenant that God made through Moses. Micah cries, "Hear, you mountains, the indictment of the LORD, and you enduring foundations of the earth" (Mic. 6:2). The mountains were the very witnesses summoned to observe God's making of his covenant with Israel. Three times during his covenant-making with Moses, God said, "I call heaven and earth to witness" (Deut. 4:26; 30:19; 31:28). Only if the mountains could be moved and their foundations dug up would God's covenant obligations suffer a lack of testimony before his people. The mountains knew that in entering God's covenant, Israel had promised obedience to his commands, and in return had received God's promise to bless them as his own beloved people. The ancient hills had also witnessed Israel's infidelity to these marriage vows.

With this august assembly gathered, Micah explains the purpose of his message: "for the LORD has an indictment against his people, and he will contend with Israel" (Mic. 6:2). The charge is a breach of covenant, and thus spiritual adultery: Israel has not fulfilled her marriage vows to the Lord. His rightful expectations as husband have not been met. Israel has lost interest in God, taking his blessings for granted, and has gone its own way. The indictment has the purpose not of dispensing punishment but of pleading renewed loyalty and love. David Prior notes: "The language here is personal and passionate, far more like a father's pleas to his child or a husband pleading with his wife. . . . This is the plea of a loving God, whose heart has been broken by his people's rejection of him."[3]

GOD'S CASE VINDICATED

God's passion is seen in the opening words of his complaint: "O my people" (Mic. 6:3). God reaches out to Israel with tender love. Then he goes on to invite complaints against his own marital performance: "O my people, what have I done to you?" (Mic. 6:3). The implication is that Israel has acted as if God had let them down. They have grown tired and bored with God. But what has God done to merit this emotional distance? Has the Lord failed to uphold his end of the covenant? Israel is invited to explain. God queries, "How have I wearied you? Answer me!" (Mic. 6:3).

3. David Prior, *The Message of Joel, Micah & Habakkuk*, The Bible Speaks Today (Downers Grove, Ill.: InterVarsity, 1998), 170.

Israel, it seems, found it tiresome to be God's people. Like many believers in Christ today, they were weary of having to live a certain way and of being forbidden the world's sinful pleasures. But has God deserved this attitude? His complaint here is similar to the one in his song of the vineyard in Isaiah: "What more was there to do for my vineyard, that I have not done in it? When I looked for it to yield grapes, why did it yield wild grapes?" (Isa. 5:4).

God's complaint could easily be repeated today. It is especially telling for those who reject his salvation altogether: what has God done to deserve such rejection? It is also a valid complaint for any of God's covenant people, who should turn their hearts away from God and back to the world. George Hutcheson gives a universal assessment: "There can be no true cause shown why any should choose to forsake God. Yea rather, all should cleave unto him, since his commands are not grievous, his yoke easy, his trials not above measure, his punishments not above deserving, and a Mediator ready to undertake for his people in all exigencies."[4]

"Answer me!" God demands, but Israel had no answer. So it will be on the day of judgment when all mankind stands before the Lord, and many discover too late that they have no reply to God's indictment. If God's faithful love for Israel formed the basis for Micah's complaint, God's mercy in Jesus Christ for all mankind will stand behind God's angry condemnations at the end of history. Bruce Waltke comments: "He dealt with them in the grace of the cross of Jesus Christ, but they responded unnaturally in unthankful apathy and neglect, and so their mouths will be silenced, and they will be held accountable before him (cf. Rom. 3:19)."[5]

Hearing no explanation for Israel's lack of devotion, the Lord calls his people to consider the evidence of their history. This reminds us that Christianity is a historical religion: our salvation rests on God's great saving acts, especially the gift of his Son Jesus to die on the cross for our sins. Looking into Israel's past, Micah demands that they consider God's deliverance of Israel in the exodus from Egypt. This was the greatest saving event of the Old Testament, serving as a paradigm for the greater deliverance in Christ.

God recounts the exodus in four stages, beginning with his freeing of Israel from their bondage in Egypt: "For I brought you up from the land

4. George Hutcheson, *Exposition of the Minor Prophets* (Lafayette, Ind.: Sovereign Grace Publishers, 2001), 148.
5. Bruce Waltke, *A Commentary on Micah* (Grand Rapids: Eerdmans, 2007), 379.

of Egypt and redeemed you from the house of slavery" (Mic. 6:4). The language is provocative: not only has God not let Israel down, but he brought them up from the mud pits of the Nile. The God they had spurned with their hearts is the saving God who rescued them from their helpless, hopeless bondage under Pharaoh's whip.

Every believer can see a similar redemption in the cross of Christ. We were slaves in bondage to sin, held fast in its power, condemned by its guilt. But God had mercy and sent his Son to receive sin's punishment in our place on the cross. Remembering this great salvation, how can we ever grow bored with God or resent our discipleship to Jesus? God has not let us down, but rather has lifted us up from our sin.

But God did not stop with Israel's departure from Egypt. He adds, "and I sent before you Moses, Aaron, and Miriam" (Mic. 6:4). In other words, God raised up Spirit-anointed leaders to guide Israel to the Promised Land. Moses was the lawgiver who met with God. Aaron was the high priest who made atonement for their sins. Miriam, their sister, was the prophetess who led the women in singing of God's victory on the banks of the Red Sea (Ex. 15:20–21). It might be true that in Micah's time Israel's leaders fell far short of their forebears in the exodus, but this was the result of the people's lack of devotion to the Lord. Likewise, we can be sure that if we seek the Lord to be our Savior and Shepherd, he will provide faithful preachers, pastors, and lay leaders whose instruction and example will serve us in the pilgrimage of our lives.

God not only sent his people on their way to freedom, but also intervened on their behalf along the way: "O my people, remember what Balak king of Moab devised, and what Balaam the son of Beor answered him" (Mic. 6:5). As the tribes of Israel drew near to the Promised Land, the king of Moab plotted to deter them. Summoning Balaam, who possessed unspecified mystic powers, they employed him to utter a curse on Israel, which at least would have had the effect of making many Israelites believe they were cursed. But each time Balak summoned Balaam to curse, God "resisted the ungodly king and his hireling prophet, and instead put a word in the pagan prophet's mouth that blessed Israel."[6] Thus the Lord, having delivered Israel out from Egypt, also oversaw the successful journey to Canaan. Believers in Christ will

---

6. Ibid., 384.

likewise be able to think of times in which God savingly intervened in the course of our journey through this world, and we may face the challenges ahead with confidence in his vigilant care.

Micah wraps up the account by saying, "and what happened from Shittim to Gilgal" (Mic. 6:5). This refers to the passage of the Jordan River, completing the exodus journey. Shittim was that last stop on the east bank of the Jordan and Gilgal was the first camp on the west side. In this crossing, the Lord continued to help Israel, even drying up the Jordan waters, just as he had done at the Red Sea, to enable Israel to pass over with dry feet.

Taken together, this history lesson recalled Israel's deliverance from bondage, God's provision of spiritual leadership, God's intervention along the way, and God's oversight of the journey's successful conclusion. God did not leave his people to fend for themselves, either in the slavery in Egypt or on the long journey to Canaan, but provided his saving grace at every point of their need. Christians likewise may look to God with thanks for his every provision for our journey through this life into heaven, being sure, with the apostle Paul, "that he who began a good work in you will bring it to completion at the day of Jesus Christ" (Phil. 1:6).

Yet God's great works in history will only impact our present faith if we remember them! This was God's purpose: "that you may know the saving acts of the LORD" (Mic. 6:5). The Hebrew text literally states that history reveals the "righteousnesses" of the Lord. In other words, God's saving acts vindicate him before his people. This is why the essential work of each generation is to recount and pass on the good news of what God has done all through history, especially in the gift of his Son Jesus to deliver us from sin. God had instructed Israel, "Remember the whole way that the LORD your God has led you these forty years in the wilderness" (Deut. 8:2). Likewise, the chief purpose of preaching today is to hold before the church the good news of God's salvation in Jesus Christ. It was for this same reason that Jesus instituted the sacrament of the Lord's Supper, signifying his atoning death, instructing us, "Do this in remembrance of me" (Luke 22:19). By word and sacrament together, Christ's church is reminded of God's "righteousness" in providing his Son to redeem us from our sin by his own blood.

Micah's point is that God's people are to be drawn to him in a bond of grateful devotion. Our motivation to worship and serve God is chiefly our thanksgiving for his salvation blessings. In the gospel we see proof of his faithfulness to his promises and evidence of his redeeming love. Believers are to reason, "The God who did all this for me will not fail to meet my present or future needs." As Paul urges, after detailing God's gospel salvation in the first eleven chapters of Romans, our only reasonable response to such abounding grace is "to present your bodies as a living sacrifice, holy and acceptable to God, which is your spiritual worship" (Rom. 12:1). Leslie Allen observes that Micah's recital of God's blessing for Israel in the exodus "symbolizes not only the covenant love of God but also his claim upon the covenant loyalty of his people. . . . [It] was intended to create a permanent bond of allegiance between him and their descendants."[7] How much more ought Christians embrace this bond of gratitude in thanks for the redeeming blood of Christ.

"I SURRENDER ALL"

Many of us have wealthy friends or family members for whom it is almost impossible to buy gifts. Everything they might want they already have. How much more difficult was Israel's challenge: just what do you give the God who already has everything? "With what shall I come before the LORD, and bow myself before God on high?" (Mic. 6:6), the people ask. God desired his people to seek restoration with him, so what will it take? What evidence can they produce to prove their love? Micah's hearers know that God is far above them, so they come bowing. They also know they should not come empty-handed, so what gift should they bring to the Lord?

Immediately, the Israelites turn to the offering of sacrifices: "Shall I come before him with burnt offerings, with calves a year old?" (Mic. 6:6). Burnt offerings were completely consumed by fire, unlike fellowship offerings, a portion of which was returned to the giver. So the burnt offering was costly. The same was true of a year-old calf. Calves could be offered from seven days old, so a year-old calf was one in which a year's worth of labor and food was invested. Would God be satisfied with costly offerings like these?

From quality, the speaker turns to quantity: "Will the LORD be pleased with thousands of rams, with ten thousands of rivers of oil?" (Mic. 6:7). He thinks of the mammoth offerings made by Solomon and other kings.

7. Allen, *Joel, Obadiah, Jonah, and Micah*, 366.

Solomon used to offer a thousand burnt offerings at a time (1 Kings 3:4), and for the dedication of the temple he sacrificed 22,000 oxen and 120,000 sheep (1 Kings 8:63). Would something like that suffice, or oil offerings in the tens of thousands?

Taking this logic to its ultimate conclusion, he asks, "Shall I give my firstborn for my transgression, the fruit of my body for the sin of my soul?" (Mic. 6:7). Child sacrifice was, of course, an abomination to God, since it followed the despicable practice of the pagan god Molech. It is possible, however, that Abraham's willingness to offer his son Isaac is remembered here. But the idea is evident: I will give my greatest possession to the Lord if that is what he desires, even my own flesh and blood.

We are reminded here of Israel's namesake, the patriarch Jacob, when he returned to the land of his fathers to face his brother Esau. Jacob had wronged Esau twenty years earlier, stealing his father's blessing at the contrivance of his mother Rebecca. When Jacob fled, Esau promised to kill him in revenge (Gen. 27:41–42). Now Jacob was returning from distant lands with his wives, children, and vast flocks, dreading the reunion that would occur once he crossed the river Jabbok, the boundary of his father's old lands. Sending a servant ahead to scout the situation, the report came back: "[Esau] is coming to meet you, and there are four hundred men with him" (Gen. 32:6).

Jacob was now in dreadful fear, but he had a plan. He would appease Esau with a series of gifts. First, he sent forward two hundred female goats with a servant to present them as an offering to Esau. But, Jacob wondered, "What if that is not enough?" So then he sent another servant with twenty male goats. "I may appease him with the present that goes ahead of me," Jacob reasoned. "Perhaps he will accept me" (Gen. 32:20). But unsure of this, Jacob sent more of his flocks as gifts, then more, and then still more. Altogether, he sent servants to Esau with thirty female camels with their young, forty cows, ten bulls, twenty female donkeys, and ten male donkeys. Running out of animals, he then turned to offering his wives and children. First he sent Leah, his least favored wife, with her children, then Rachel, his beloved wife, with her children. Still, Jacob could not know that Esau was appeased. But now, with all his possessions, all his wives, and all his children having been offered to appease Esau's wrath, Jacob was alone.

If Jacob had known the old hymn, he could have sung it in the darkness by the river: "I surrender all . . . all the goats, all the sheep, all the camels, all the cows, all the bulls, and all the donkeys, with all my wives and children." But Jacob had not surrendered all, for he had not surrendered himself. Therefore God came and wrestled with Jacob in the darkness, and when Jacob gave himself to the Lord in faith, he finally knew that he was saved.[8]

This was the problem with Israel's attitude toward the Lord. They would offer burnt offerings, year-old calves, thousands of rams, and tens of thousands of rivers of oil. But they would not offer God what he asked for: themselves, their hearts, their undivided faith, their unfeigned devotion.

HE HAS SHOWN YOU, O MAN

So what *is* the gift that God requires? Micah answers, "He has told you, O man, what is good" (Mic. 6:8). It was not a mystery what God required, because he had revealed this clearly in his Word. Micah addresses himself to the individual worshiper—"you, O man"—asserting that God has already told him what is required. Consider the words of God to Moses so long before: "And now, Israel, what does the LORD your God require of you, but to fear the LORD your God, to walk in all his ways, to love him, to serve the LORD your God with all your heart and with all your soul, and to keep the commandments and statutes of the LORD, which I am commanding you today for your good?" (Deut. 10:12–13). God's people were to serve him by keeping the two tablets of the Ten Commandments, which Jesus summarized as follows:

> You shall love the Lord your God with all your heart and with all your soul and with all your mind. This is the great and first commandment. And a second is like it: You shall love your neighbor as yourself. On these two commandments depend all the Law and the Prophets. (Matt. 22:37–40)

What was the problem with the Israelites' desire to bring sacrifices? The problem was that the sacrifices were a picture of what God had promised to give to them, the true Lamb of God, his own Son, whose death would atone for their sins. The sacrifices were never intended to function as a way of buying off God. The question, then, is what those who have received God's priceless gift of salvation should then offer to him in return. The answer is

8. Taken from James Montgomery Boice, *Amazing Grace* (Wheaton, Ill.: Tyndale, 1993), 208–9.

our very selves: our hearts, our minds, our bodies, and our souls. The way we offer ourselves to God is by loving him with all that we are and loving our neighbor as ourselves.

Micah expresses this truth with one of the most succinct, lovely, and potent descriptions of a life offered in gratitude to God. Geerhard von Rad calls Micah 6:8 "the quintessence of the commandments as the prophets understood them."[9] J. M. P. Smith calls the verse "the finest summary of the content of practical religion to be found in the Old Testament."[10] Micah declares: "He has told you, O man, what is good; and what does the LORD require of you but to do justice, and to love kindness, and to walk humbly with your God?" (Mic. 6:8).

In these memorable words we see the prophetic summary of God's law. First, our duty to man is to "do justice" and "love kindness." The idea of justice is that we are to treat people fairly, giving them what is due to them. A person who "does justice" is one who treats people right, offering respect, integrity, and fairness. Secondly, loving our neighbor means to "love kindness." The word for "kindness" (Hebrew, *chesed*) is one of the hardest words in the Old Testament to translate with just one term. In different contexts it is translated mercy, faithfulness, and loving-kindness. It is the great description of God's faithful, kind, and merciful covenant love. As Peter Craigie explains: "it gives, where no giving is required, it acts when no action is deserved, and it penetrates both attitudes and activities."[11] To "love kindness" is to look on the weak and vulnerable with the eyes of God's love and give them not what they deserve, but what they need.

Justice and kindness summarize the second great commandment. Micah concludes with the first great commandment, summarizing our love for God: "to walk humbly with your God" (Mic. 6:8). To love God is to walk with him. This means a lifestyle wholly devoted to him, seeking his glory in all things and enjoying his pleasure in our lives. To walk with God is to live humbly. The Hebrew word more accurately means to walk "circumspectly" or "carefully"; that is, to act with an awareness of the holiness and grace of the Lord. Walter Kaiser writes, "Pride alone insists on taking first place, but

---

9. Cited from Kenneth L. Barker and Waylon Bailey, *Micah, Nahum, Habbakuk, Zephaniah*, The New American Commentary (Nashville: Broadman & Holman, 1999), 113.

10. Ibid.

11. Peter C. Craigie, *Twelve Prophets*, Daily Bible Study series 2 vols. (Louisville: Westminster John Knox, 1985), 2:46.

faith seeks to give God first place. . . . Living a circumspect lifestyle will bring one's life into conformity with God's will."[12] It is only a man or woman who is born again to a living faith who can walk humbly with God, and only one who walks with God is able truly to do justice and love kindness.

Corrie ten Boom tells a story about her father that exemplifies the god-liness Micah describes. Her father was a watchmaker, and the family was experiencing great financial hardship. A wealthy man came into his shop and decided to buy the most expensive timepiece available, the sale of which would provide for all the family's needs. As her father was putting the cash into the box, the man mentioned that he was buying it because a nearby competitor had been unable to fix his previous watch. At this, Corrie's father asked to see the broken watch. After a few minutes of tinkering, he handed it back, fixed. "There, that was a very little mistake," he said. "It will be fine now. Sir, I trust the young watchmaker. Someday he will be just as good as his father. . . . Now I shall give you back your money and return your watch."

Young Corrie was shocked by her father—by his justice, kindness, and humble walk before God. She complained that he had thrown away a golden opportunity for much-needed income. But he gently chided her, "Corrie, what do you think that young man would have said when he heard that one of his good customers had gone to Mr. ten Boom? Do you think that the name of the Lord would be honored? As for the money, trust the Lord, Corrie. He owns the cattle on a thousand hills and He will take care of us."[13] Corrie's father showed justice to the man whose watch needed fixing. He showed kindness to the young watchmaker whose reputation was at stake. And most importantly, his approach to business and life was humbly appropriate for one redeemed and cared for by the sovereign God of grace.

LOVE SO AMAZING, SO DIVINE

How much has God been willing to give to us? God has given himself in the covenant of grace, and while we were still sinners he gave his only Son to deliver us from our sins by the blood of his cross. What gift is appropriate for us to offer back to him? We can never match God's amazing gift of grace. But we can give him all that we have and all that we are. God does not want

---

12. Walter C. Kaiser Jr., *Micah–Malachi*, The Communicator's Commentary (Dallas: Word, 1992), 74.
13. Corrie ten Boom, "Trust the Lord," *Guideposts* (Aug. 1976): 7.

us to give ourselves to him in elaborate shows of rituals and sacrifices, but in the daily way we live, walking humbly with him and showing justice and kindness to our fellow man.

This leaves only one question: how do we wrap this gift that God desires? We wrap it in trusting faith, born of a grateful heart. As Isaac Watts immortalized in his hymn, the gift that God requires is our self-surrendering love in grateful wonder at the priceless gift of Jesus Christ:

> When I survey the wondrous cross
> On which the Prince of glory died,
> My riches gain I count but loss,
> And pour contempt on all my pride . . .
>
> Were the whole realm of nature mine,
> That were a present far too small;
> Love so amazing, so divine,
> Demands my life, my soul, my all.[14]

14. Isaac Watts, "When I Survey the Wondrous Cross," 1707.

29

GOD'S CALL TO THE CITY

Micah 6:9—16

The voice of the LORD cries to the city — and it is sound wisdom to fear your name: "Hear of the rod and of him who appointed it!" (Mic. 6:9)

ur cities teem with voices of all kinds. There are voices of laughter, excitement, sorrow, and suffering. Cities burst with the soundtrack of stores, schools, and entertainment venues. But of all the voices in a city, the one most needed is the voice of the Lord. In this final section of his prophecy, Micah takes his voice as public as possible. "The voice of the LORD cries to the city," he declares (Mic. 6:9). Nothing determines the fate and well-being of a city, he indicates, more than its attitude toward the voice of God. As goes the city, so goes the nation.

God did not leave himself without a witness in the streets of Jerusalem; Micah's voice goes forth as a plea to the city that lived in ignorance of God's ways. David Prior compares God to "a town crier, calling publicly for the attention of every citizen, because what he has to say is so important."[1] Even if no one else will listen, Micah answers, "it is sound wisdom to fear your name"

---

1. David Prior, *The Message of Joel, Micah & Habakkuk*, The Bible Speaks Today (Downers Grove, Ill.: InterVarsity, 1998), 178.

(Mic. 6:9). The city is deaf to the voice of the Lord, for the people have forgotten that it is the greatest privilege to hear God's Word. They have forgotten that "the fear of the LORD is the beginning of wisdom" (Ps. 111:10).

THE CITY JUDGED BY GOD

We can easily imagine the looks Micah must have received. He is an annoyance. He is a zealot who will not stay quiet, a disturber of the "peace." In a city that had known economic booms, the people are concerned only with getting their piece of the pie. In a city that had become a marketplace of the nations, the residents want only to hear the sound of clinking coins. In a city surrounded by fertile lands, the noise they desire is that of wagon wheels delivering produce. The city is deaf to the voice of God, but the prophet will not be silent. Micah is determined to remind the people of the inconvenient truth that *God will not go away.*

There are times that call for subtlety and nuance, and other times that call for frankness. Micah's time was the latter, so he answered the indifference of the city by proclaiming God's intent to judge: "Hear of the rod and of him who appointed it!" (Mic. 6:9). God had ordained chastisement for Jerusalem, and amid the clamor of the markets the people are summoned to face the reality of the God they had ignored. We are reminded of America in 2008, oblivious to signs of the looming stock market crash until finally it came. In the context of Micah's prophecy there can be little doubt that he refers to the marauding Assyrians. Isaiah made the connection explicit: "Ah, Assyria," he cried, "the rod of my anger; the staff in their hands is my fury!" (Isa. 10:5).

How common it is for men and women caught up in the affairs of the world to imagine that God is absent from the equation of their lives. They exercise liberties upon the patience of God, never realizing that the wages of sin must ultimately be paid. Yet God's patience, born of his tender heart, always has limits. He asks Jerusalem, "Can I forget any longer the treasures of wickedness in the house of the wicked?" (Mic. 6:10). He has granted them time to repent; all through Micah's prophecy he has cried out against the violently wicked pursuit of wealth. But the people and especially their leaders occupied that time in grabbing more wealth. Now the rod of judgment would enter God's hand and they would be reminded that God never goes away. "The fool says in his heart, 'There is no God'" (Ps. 14:1), warned David.

The people of Jerusalem, like those in our cities today, acted as if God had forgotten them, that they could safely write their own rules. But history bears stark testimony to the folly of forgetting the Lord.

Not only would God not go away, Micah insisted, but he is also *a God who will not change*. The same God who gave the Ten Commandments to Moses is still God today. As secular society rewrites its rules, God refuses to amend his own. Therefore the prophet, standing amid the merchants' booths, complains against "the scant measure that is accursed" (Mic. 6:10). God asks, "Shall I acquit the man with wicked scales and with a bag of deceitful weights?" (Mic. 6:11).

Here the prophet is commenting on the "tricks of the trade" in Jerusalem's commerce. The "scant measure" of verse 10 refers to the liquid and dry bushel (Hebrew, *ephah*) used to measure produce, roughly equal to five gallons. Buyers were dependent on the honesty of merchants, and unscrupulous sellers would make their measures slightly small so as to sell less than was agreed. A similar trick was to use dishonest scales or, literally, a "bag of deceitful weights" (Mic. 6:11). These were weighing stones whose mass did not correspond to their markings, so that more gold and silver would have to be paid into the scales by those making a purchase. The merchants were robbing their customers both coming and going: giving them less than promised and making them pay more than agreed.

Such corruption is "accursed" to God (Mic. 6:10). In the giving of his law, the Lord decreed: "You shall do no wrong in judgment, in measures of length or weight or quantity. You shall have just balances, just weights, a just ephah, and a just hin" (Lev. 19:35–36). God is just and true, and his people were to reflect this in their business dealings. Proverbs 20:23 states: "Unequal weights are an abomination to the LORD, and false scales are not good."

This reminds us that our true religion is displayed in our treatment of other people. Even our business practices—the way we treat customers and deal with market pressures—reveal which God we truly worship. God is present in the marketplace, and his ways are not malleable the way that corporate ethics are today. Gary Smith rightly comments: "God will judge those who do not conduct their business dealings with others honestly and without deception or lies."[2]

2. Gary V. Smith, *Hosea, Amos, Micah*, NIV Application Commentary (Grand Rapids: Zondervan, 2001), 559.

God determines our true religion not only in how we handle money, but also in how we handle matters of truth. He continues, "Your rich men are full of violence; your inhabitants speak lies, and their tongue is deceitful in their mouth" (Mic. 6:12).

Micah rebuked the violence of the greedy elites earlier in this book. The rich not only controlled the courts, so that they could cheat the common people, but they also employed gangs of thugs to impose their will. The prophet said, "They covet fields and seize them, and houses, and take them away; they oppress a man and his house, a man and his inheritance" (Mic. 2:2). But now he adds his disgust over the way this has caused corruption to spread all through society. It is because of the violence of the rich and powerful that "your inhabitants speak lies" and "their tongue is deceitful" (Mic. 6:12). David Prior writes, "the violence of a few leads to dishonesty by the many. A city where brutality and ruthlessness are the order of the day inevitably becomes a place where people lie and deceive for survival. Nobody can be trusted. No longer is peoples' word their bond."[3]

One need only consider the culture in many of our corporations today to witness the truth of this. When senior executives betray loyal employees, laying off thousands to realize short-term stock gains, the inevitable result is a workforce that no longer considers the company's well-being. If lawmakers are "on the take," granting favorable rules for those who make large contributions, it is inevitable that companies will no longer pursue the public good. In a land where once a handshake was enough, now lawyers must pore over contracts to examine the small print and the embedded loopholes.

In many African countries where bribery has become a part of civil survival, this presents a pressing issue to Christians. Uganda, for instance, was long known as one of Africa's most honest nations. But the violent years of Idi Amin's rule (1971–79) destroyed the culture of integrity, replacing it with one of corruption and deceit. Many of the church leaders there realize that if the nation is to return to uprightness, Christians must courageously lead the way. But Westerners are deceived if we think our societies are free from corruption, a reality that is highlighted in nearly every election cycle. Micah 6:8 laid out God's calling for his people: "What does the LORD require of you but to do justice, and to love kindness, and to walk humbly with your God?" God

3. Prior, *The Message of Joel, Micah & Habakkuk*, 180.

has not changed, and he still calls his own people to stand against violence and deceit, engaging only in fair, honest, and humane business practices, and refusing to embrace a culture of deceit.

The early church leader Tertullian discovered a member of his church who was engaged in fraudulent business. The man defended his practices, insisting that it was the only way he could stay afloat. He implored his bishop, "I have to live!" Tertullian famously replied, "Do you?"[4] Christians today need to embrace a similar attitude, being willing to fail in business by the world's standards before we are willing to engage in corruption, moral violence, or deceit.

In the long run, obeying God is the only practical choice, because not only is he a God who will not go away and a God who will not change, but he is *a God who will not stand aside.* He declared to Micah's Jerusalem: "Therefore I strike you with a grievous blow, making you desolate because of your sins" (Mic. 6:13). God does not strike sinners because of any harshness in his spirit—indeed, God's patience displays the opposite—but for one simple reason: "because of your sins."

God will not stand aside and allow sin to continue unchecked; a society perverted by lusts into moral violence and deceit must eventually face God's wrath. "This is his universe," writes James Montgomery Boice. "He is the holy God, and our sin has introduced a foul blemish into it. He is opposed to sin and is determined to stamp it out."[5] The Puritan William Gurnall warns us:

> Think not, sinners, that you shall escape thus; God's mill goes slow, but grinds small; the more admirable His patience and bounty now is, the more dreadful and unsupportable will that fury be which ariseth out of His abused goodness. Nothing smoother than the sea, yet when stirred into a tempest, nothing rageth more. Nothing so sweet as the patience and goodness of God, and nothing so terrible as His wrath when it takes fire.[6]

Observing how God's chosen people of old fell into such a settled state of depravity, we should realize how prone we are to doing the same. Let us

---

4. Tertullian, *On Idolatry*, ch. 5.

5. James Montgomery Boice, *Ephesians: An Expositional Commentary* (Grand Rapids: Baker, 2006), 53.

6. William Gurnall, cited in A. W. Pink, *The Attributes of God* (Grand Rapids: Baker, 1975), 86

prayerfully develop a habit of responding to the warnings of God's Word, quickly repenting of known sins, and asking God for a tender spirit that hears his voice of rebuke.

THE CITY CURSED

When Micah warns that God will make Jerusalem "desolate because of your sins," he no doubt refers to the threat of invasion and the destruction of the city, a threat that was made good by the Babylonians in 586 B.C. But realizing that at the time such a disaster seemed distant and unreal, he expands his threat to touch upon the affluent lifestyle so near and dear to his hearers' hearts. Drawing directly from God's ancient words to Moses, he utters a curse of futility on their cherished possessions:

> You shall eat, but not be satisfied, and there shall be hunger within you; you shall put away, but not preserve, and what you preserve I will give to the sword. You shall sow, but not reap; you shall tread olives, but not anoint yourselves with oil; you shall tread grapes, but not drink wine. (Mic. 6:14–15; cf. Deut. 28:30–31, 38–40)

First, Micah touches on the abundance of their food: while they would have plenty to eat, they would not enjoy satisfaction. Why? "There shall be hunger within you" (Mic. 6:14). Avarice is always the enemy of contentment, and those who are at odds with God experience a hunger of the soul that no food can satisfy. This curse probably indicates that God will impose a sickness of the body, such as dysentery, so that no matter how much is eaten the body will remain malnourished.

Next, they will store up goods but find that nothing is preserved. "And what you preserve," God warns, "I will give to the sword" (Mic. 6:14). The Bible commends the kind of frugality that saves against a rainy day (cf. Gen. 50:20–21). By contrast, worldly people respond to anxiety for the future by seeking to build an idolatrous rampart of stored-up wealth. But the future is truly secured only through a right relationship with God.

Jesus told a parable about a "rich fool" who greedily stockpiled his wealth in ever-larger barns, never giving a thought to the needy. But God intervened, saying, "Fool! This night your soul is required of you, and the things you have prepared, whose will they be?" (Luke 12:20). In Jerusalem's case, the stockpiled wealth would be taken by the invaders' sword. Jesus likewise condemned everyone "who lays up treasure for himself and is not rich toward God" (Luke 12:21); one way or another, in death if not sooner, money will fail to secure our souls.

Micah now turns to the produce of the field: "You shall sow, but not reap; you shall tread olives, but not anoint yourselves with oil; you shall tread grapes, but not drink wine" (Mic. 6:15). Prior explains: "They will put in all the effort and spend much time and many resources in production, but there will be nothing to show for it. Their hard work will prove useless. Worse than that, the benefits will be reaped by others; the profits will go to boost the revenues of their competitors."[7] Whereas once Israel through faith had eaten from fields others had planted, now in sinful unbelief the opposite will result. As God foretold to Moses: "A nation that you have not known shall eat up the fruit of your ground and of all your labors, and you shall be only oppressed and crushed continually, so that you are driven mad by the sights that your eyes see" (Deut. 28:33–34).

The futility envisioned by Micah is in large measure experienced by America today. We exert so much labor but experience so little joy. Our satiation fails to give satisfaction. Material prosperity does not secure peace. During one of my trips to East Africa, some Christian friends told me that "America is Africa's God." They meant that their countrymen coveted the material abundance and leisure lifestyle enjoyed by Americans. But I pointed out things they did not know, such as America's high rate of depression and the widespread dependence on mood-altering drugs. "How many people in your town committed suicide last year?" I asked them. Shocked, they replied that suicide was unknown among them. I then informed them that in the preceding year two people had taken their own lives on my own street in affluent America. America without God is experiencing a cursed futility, so that the idols of materialism and sensuality sap the very life out of our nation's soul. In a land that once boasted safe homes, good schools, plentiful jobs, and fair prices, we are now beset by social, moral, economic, political, and psychological crises on every side. What has happened? We suffer the curse of futility in cities and a nation that no longer has an ear for the voice of God.

7. Prior, *The Message of Joel, Micah & Habakkuk*, 184.

What was the missing ingredient in Jerusalem? Why would Jerusalem eat but still go hungry? Why would they store and yet preserve nothing? Why would they sow but not reap, tread olives but not anoint themselves with oil, and tread grapes but drink no wine? The missing ingredient was God's blessing. As Solomon taught, "Unless the LORD builds the house, those who build it labor in vain," and unless God's blessing rests upon you, "it is in vain that you rise up early and go late to rest, eating the bread of anxious toil" (Ps. 127:1–2). Only God can give satisfaction to life, peace to the soul, and security for the future. When our souls go unsatisfied, Calvin directs us back to Micah 6:8 and the way that pleases God:

> God has revealed how we can acquire the things we need in order to sustain ourselves, as well as how to find lasting nourishment for all our life, and even how our children after us can enjoy it, that is, by walking in fear and humility before God and in equity and righteousness with our neighbors. Therefore, if we conduct ourselves this way, he assures us that, even if he grants us only a little, we will still experience contentment, and if we enjoy plenty, he will cause it to prosper, not only for ourselves, but for others. But on the contrary, God threatens us if we think we can advance ourselves by means of fraud, rapine, and dishonest transactions, for all that we might gain this way will profit us nothing, but will run off like water.[8]

THE CITY CONVICTED AND CONDEMNED

Micah 6 began with Jerusalem's summons to the covenant lawsuit of God. The chapter ends with God's conviction and just condemnation. Practically the worst accusation God could level at Jerusalem was that it had fallen into the sin of its northern cousin, the wicked city of Samaria, which had fallen to the sword within the memory of his hearers. "For you have kept the statutes of Omri," God convicts them, "and all the works of the house of Ahab" (Mic. 6:16). Omri was the Israelite king who founded his reign in blood, establishing a strong but depraved dynasty. His son Ahab, infamous for his confrontations with the prophet Elijah, institutionalized the idolatries of his wicked queen Jezebel, leading the people into the worship of the pagan gods Asherah and Baal.

8. John Calvin, *Sermons on the Book of Micah* (Phillipsburg, NJ: P&R Publishing, 2003) 357–58.

The reigns of Omri and Ahab represented a wanton abandonment of Israel's God and all his ways. Their political, economic, and religious policy was that of unbridled worldliness and expediency. Most despicable were the practical effects of their idolatry: "That religion had nothing corresponding to the ethical requirements of the covenant of the Lord but rather introduced an outlook on life which thought nothing of trampling the rights of others."[9]

The signature event of Ahab's reign was the theft of Naboth's vineyard, in which an honorable and godly neighbor was slain so as to lay hold of his land (1 Kings 21). Now a similar idolatry of commercial profiteering had taken root in Jerusalem, so that however fervent their sacrifices at the temple of the Lord, their practical religion revealed an idolatry no less offensive than that of Omri and Ahab. Similarly today, God is not fooled by those who make a show of Christianity but betray idolatry in their love of money, their dishonesty in business, and their cavalier attitude toward truth.

Notice that God convicts Jerusalem in that the people "have walked in their counsels" (Mic. 6:16). Idolatry begins as an attitude we pick up from the world, a way of looking at the world along with its ideas of happiness. Think of the ideas coming out of our universities: that there is precious little truth, reality, or meaning, and no authority at all. Then there is Hollywood's enticing portrait of the happiness that supposedly comes by being free from shackles, by trying new things according to all one's desires, and particularly by immersing oneself in sensual practices that used to be shameful but no longer are. If you expose your mind to such counsel, you will be pulled into the cruel pragmatism of Omri, the cowardly compromises of Ahab, and the lurid violence of Jezebel. Their just end was the awful condemnation of a wrathful God, and so will be the end of all who walk in their counsel.

So it would be for Jerusalem: God promises to "make you a desolation, and your inhabitants a hissing; so you shall bear the scorn of my people" (Mic. 6:16). It is offensive to God when the world indulges in wickedness, but it is intolerably offensive when his people give themselves over to the evils of the world. The people who were intended by God to be "a light for the nations" (Isa. 42:6) will instead become a byword among all peoples. The ghastly fate of Jerusalem, when the sword of God's justice finally came, would dumbfound and horrify even the most hardened pagans. Jerusalem, the city

---

9. John L. Mackay, *Jonah, Micah, Nahum, Habakkuk and Zephaniah: God's Just Demands*, Focus on the Bible (Ross–shire, UK: Christian Focus, 1998), 124.

named for its calling to bear God's peace, would instead bear hissing jeers and mocking scorn for its once-proud claim to be the city of God. Elizabeth Achtemeier sagely applies this same condemnation to the religious sphere today: "Such scornful hooting is perhaps that same reaction that the secular world has to the church when the community that is supposed to be the body of Christ fails to live up to its covenant with the Lord."[10]

OUR CALLING TO THE CITY

God's warnings and threats always imply an invitation to grace. If God was finally resolved to deliver his wrathful vengeance, no warning need be given. Therefore God's warning constitutes a call to Christians to sound God's voice in the city. An example for a Christian mission to the city is given in Jeremiah 29:5–7, in the letter God had sent to the remnant of the Jews sent off to exile in Babylon. God presented them with a three-point agenda for the ministry of God's people in a violent and godless city like Micah's or like many of ours today.

First, God commanded them to *establish a presence in the city*: "Build houses and live in them; plant gardens and eat their produce. . . . multiply there, and do not decrease" (Jer. 29:5–6). Likewise, a Christian awareness of the importance and the depravity of our cities today will lead us to invest our lives in the city. There is a great need today for Christians to live in urban areas, to operate honest businesses in the city, and to spread the wholesome influence of godliness in the city streets. Ronald Sider writes:

> Evangelicals must reverse the continuing evangelical flight from the cities. . . . Tens of thousands of evangelicals ought to move back into the city. . . . If one percent of evangelicals living outside the inner city had the faith and courage to move in town, evangelicals would fundamentally alter the history of urban America.[11]

Second, God directed his people to *seek the peace of the city*: "seek the welfare of the city where I have sent you into exile" (Jer. 29:7). Philip Ryken

10. Elizabeth Achtemeier, cited in Kenneth L. Barker and Waylon Bailey, *Micah, Nahum, Habbakuk, Zephaniah* (Nashville: Broadman & Holman, 1999), 120.

11. Ronald Sider, cited from Philip Graham Ryken, *Jeremiah and Lamentations: From Sorrow to Hope*, Preaching the Word (Wheaton, Ill.: Crossway, 2001), 412.

comments: "Seeking the peace of the city means being a good neighbor. It means shoveling the sidewalk. It means cleaning the street. It means planting a tree. It means feeding the poor. It means volunteering at the local school. It means greeting people at the store.... It means shutting down immoral businesses. It means embracing people from every ethnic background with the love of Christ."[12] Above all, seeking the peace of the city calls us to introduce the city to the Prince of Peace, who brings an end to war with God through his blood of the cross. The Bible says, "We have peace with God through our Lord Jesus Christ" (Rom. 5:1), and only through the knowledge of Jesus and faith in his gospel can any person or any city truly know peace.

Third, God calls his people to *pray for the city*: "and pray to the LORD on its behalf" (Jer. 29:7). If the flight of evangelical families from the city is a problem today, how much greater is the flight of evangelical churches from the city! Our most important churches are those located in cities, and there is no higher calling for those churches than to pray for the city, exuding the aroma of Christian faith, hope, joy, and love. When Abraham was taken to witness the destruction of Sodom and Gomorrah, he did not gloat but pleaded with God for their salvation. So too must we plead with God to use us—as individuals, as families, and as a church—for the gospel work of salvation in the city, for, as God told the exiles in Babylon, "in its welfare you will find your welfare" (Jer. 29:7).

In one of the most touching scenes from the gospels, Jesus wept over Jerusalem, an unbelieving city that was doomed beyond redemption. But as James Boice urges us, "our cities are not necessarily doomed So long as the return of Christ in final judgment is postponed, we have always before us the possibility of a spiritual and moral resurrection."[13] Micah's ministry was an example, and he pled with his generation, saying, "The voice of the LORD cries to the city" (Mic. 6:9). God blessed that voice so that many repented and the nation experienced a general reformation. May the Lord's voice go forth into the city today, and may ours be the voices through which he speaks with truth, power, and grace.

12. Ryken, *Jeremiah and Lamentations*, 414.
13. James M. Boice, *The Minor Prophets*, 2 vols. (Grand Rapids: Baker, 1986), 2:352–53.

30

THE PROPHET'S LAMENT

Micah 7:1–7

But as for me, I will look to the LORD; I will wait for the God of my salvation; my God will hear me. (Mic. 7:7)

Jesus' last visit to the temple in Jerusalem ended up in a way that broke his holy heart. He had entered the city triumphantly, fulfilling many prophecies of the coming of Israel's king. But after an initially enthusiastic welcome, people began turning against him, as Jesus knew they would. There, in the courts of a building intended to represent God's loving communion with his people, God's Son concluded his last visit with a series of prophetic woes:

> Woe to you, scribes and Pharisees, hypocrites! . . . Woe to you, blind guides . . . . Woe to you, scribes and Pharisees, hypocrites! For you build the tombs of the prophets . . . . Thus you witness against yourselves that you are sons of those who murdered the prophets. (Matt. 23:13, 16, 29–31)

Knowing that with his crucifixion, the penalty for the righteous blood spilt in Jerusalem would doom the city, Jesus concluded with a mournful lament:

O Jerusalem, Jerusalem, the city that kills the prophets and stones those who are sent to it. How often would I have gathered your children together as a hen gathers her brood under her wings, and you would not! (Matt. 23:37)

The hardened unbelief of Jerusalem had been building over many years, even centuries. Thus Jesus is linked with the prophet Micah, who begins the last chapter of his prophecy with a similar lament. Micah understood that the situation Jesus later denounced was happening right before his eyes. The depravity of the people, especially the leaders, was causing a spiritual breakdown in society, leaving his soul bitter and his heart barren.

MICAH'S WOEFUL LAMENT

It says much about the intensity of Micah's emotional suffering that the expression he uses in verse 1 is found on the lips of Job: "Woe is me!" (Mic. 7:1). The Hebrew expression is identical in Job, although in that book it is translated "Woe to me!" (Job 10:15). While in Job it is a cry of agony, in Micah, it is a cry of desolation for the spiritual state of Jerusalem. Another counterpart can be seen in the mournful message of Jeremiah in the book of Lamentations. Micah wept over a city that was doomed for its sins; Jeremiah wept over the same city's ruin after the full extent of the promised doom had come: "How lonely sits the city that was full of people! How like a widow has she become, she who was great among the nations!" (Lam. 1:1). As a prophet of the holy God, Micah was required to pronounce woes upon the unrepentant wicked (see Mic. 2:1). But as a true prophet, Micah proclaimed God's judgment with tears. He feels the woe for his people's sin deep within his own soul.

Micah explains his distress with a simile, comparing himself to one who comes to the fields after the summer harvest but is bitterly disappointed by the absence of fruit: "For I have become as when the summer fruit has been gathered, as when the grapes have been gleaned: there is no cluster to eat, no first-ripe fig that my soul desires" (Mic. 7:1). Israel's law directed harvesters not to go back through the fields a second time to pick clean the fields (Lev. 19:9–10; Deut. 24:19–21). Instead, they were to leave gleanings for the poor. Micah compares himself to one who comes to the fields hungry, his stomach aching for the sweet fruit and the ripe figs he expects to find. Instead, he is shattered when his longings are unmet: there is no fruit for him to eat. There is not one cluster of grapes and not even one ripe fig left to satisfy his craving.

In such prophetic imagery, the vineyard represents Israel or, more specifically in this case, the city of Jerusalem. Micah leaves no doubt as to the significance of his lament for Jerusalem: "The godly has perished from the earth, and there is no one upright among mankind" (Mic. 7:2). The fruit for which Micah yearned was the "fruit of righteousness" (cf. Phil. 1:11).

We may surmise that this final chapter of the book of Micah reflects the culminating years of the prophet's long ministry, which included the reigns of Jotham, Ahaz, and Hezekiah. While God had granted a season of repentance and reformation under Hezekiah, the downward trend was only briefly checked. The Bible records that even Hezekiah indulged in the lust for riches that corrupted the city's leaders, and that his heart became proud (2 Chron. 32:24–25). Micah could discern the godless trends that would break forth in unimaginable decadence under Hezekiah's son Manasseh. His heart is broken that after a lifetime of ministry the city was worse than when he started and its doom only more assured. The quality most absent from Jerusalem was godliness: Micah could see no evidence that the people responded to God's blessing with a commitment to God's honor; in the lifestyles of the society he saw no faithfulness or obedience to the Lord. This was the fruit for which his hungry soul yearned, and the utter lack of godliness made him bitter and mournful.

Micah's lament depicts the broken heart of God over his rebellious people. Isaiah stated this in a parallel prophecy, in which he asked what more God could have done to make his vineyard Israel fruitful: "He dug it and cleared it of stones, and planted it with choice vines; he built a watchtower in the midst of it, and hewed out a wine vat in it: and he looked for it to yield grapes, but it yielded wild grapes" (Isa. 5:2). How bitter this was to the heart of the Lord! And how severe is God's just judgment on his unfruitful church: "And now I will tell you what I will do to my vineyard. I will remove its hedge, and it shall be devoured; I will break down its wall, and it shall be trampled down. I will make it a waste" (Isa. 5:5–6).

God's Desire for Righteousness

We should make at least three reflections from Micah's opening lament. The first is to realize that God is seeking the fruit of righteousness from his people. The church is not to occupy itself with temporal success. If it is God who provides success and security for his church, then God's people are not to embrace a worldly approach to gaining money, power, and influence. Instead, the church is to yield to God the sweet fruit of godly faithfulness. What God desires in our worship is not the carnal enthusiasm that attracts the ungodly, but holy affections that draw us near to him. God has provided all that his people need to abound in sweet and holy fruitfulness, and when he comes to his vineyard it is fidelity to his Word that he craves.

Second, Micah's lament raises a question for every member of the church. After God has invested in us through the ministry of his gospel, will he find sweet fruit in our lives? Is there a growing faith? Are we pressing on in sanctification and advancing in good works? Are we contributing positively to the work of ministry, evangelism, and missions? Paul wrote to the Philippians to tell of his yearning for them: "It is my prayer that your love may abound more and more, with knowledge and all discernment, so that you may approve what is excellent, and so be pure and blameless for the day of Christ, filled with the fruit of righteousness that comes through Jesus Christ, to the glory and praise of God" (Phil. 1:9–11). God longs for the fruit of love, truth, purity, and righteousness. Are we seeking to offer these to him, or are we preoccupied with the world's pleasures and tangled in the weeds of sin?

Thirdly, Micah shows us how difficult and painful it will often be for preachers of God's Word, and how the servants of God must persevere through trials. At the appropriate time God will cause the seeds of his Word to sprout and bear fruit. In the meantime, John Calvin reminds us,

> It is requisite that those of us who have been ordained of God to announce his Word, should faithfully fulfill our charge, rigorously endeavoring in our studies to lead mankind to salvation, attempting with all our effort to see that God is honored. . . . Inasmuch as God causes the doctrine which we proclaim to prosper, even if we never see its effects with our eyes, let us continue to perform our office and persevere in our calling.[1]

Sin in the City

As Micah continues his lament, he utters a prophetic description of sin that extends far beyond the walls of Jerusalem. In his frustration, Micah

---

1. John Calvin, *Sermons on the Book of Micah* (Phillipsburg, NJ: P&R Publishing, 2003), 368–69.

may not have been speaking the literal truth about Jerusalem when he said, "The godly has perished from the earth, and there is no one upright" (Mic. 7:2). Like Elijah who cried out in his depressed state in the days of Ahab and Jezebel, "I, even I only, am left" (1 Kings 19:10), when in fact there were still seven thousand faithful Israelites, Micah is so distressed that he imagines himself to be the lone remaining believer.

Nonetheless, Micah's description is perfectly accurate when it comes to man in his fallen state, apart from God's regenerating grace. "There is no one upright among mankind," Micah grieves. This lament echoes Psalm 14:3, which says, "They have all turned aside; together they have become corrupt; there is none who does good, not even one." If we doubt the universal scope of this observation, the apostle Paul cites this psalm in his teaching on the spiritual state of the entire human race in its fallen condition (Rom. 3:10). Micah means that his generation as a whole is no longer faithful in following the Lord, and none are righteous before God. So it is with every sinner apart from the grace of God in Christ.

Considered from a merely human perspective, there is no way we would come to this conclusion. There are always people we think are commendable; we even speak of "honor among thieves." But when we consider righteousness as God defines it—that is, in terms of the perfect standards of his moral law—then Micah's statement is completely accurate. There is not one single person alive who is fully righteous before God for the simple reason that every one of us violates God's law and thus is bound over to condemnation.

With the bonds of God's covenant severed in Micah's day, immorality was unrestrained in Jerusalem. The city had come to resemble the vicious society that is increasingly seen in our own post-Christian times. Leslie Allen writes: "Wherever the prophet looks he can see only the lamentable spectacle of hostility and internecine strife among a people who should have been bound together by strong ties of religion and race."[2]

To prove his case, the prophet gets specific about the moral climate of Jerusalem. He depicts the bloodthirsty way individuals relate to one another: "They all lie in wait for blood, and each hunts the other with a net" (Mic. 7:2). Life is now seen as a battle in which one can succeed only by plotting

---

2. Leslie C. Allen, *The Books of Joel, Obadiah, Jonah, and Micah*, New International Commentary on the Old Testament (Grand Rapids: Eerdmans, 1976), 385–86.

against his neighbor. Micah describes the state of human society in vivid terms: man in sin is like an animal crouching to spring for the kill, or like an assailant poised to attack. Instead of seeking the good of his neighbor, everyone is seeking to take advantage of others, even to the point of death. Allen writes: "Members of the covenant community of Israel treat one another like warring enemies and wild animals. Gone is the fellowship that was based on traditional ties and upheld conservative values. Society has disintegrated into a struggling mass of hostile individuals."[3]

This, too, Paul applies universally to the human condition in sin: "Their feet are swift to shed blood; in their paths are ruin and misery, and the way of peace they have not known" (Rom. 3:15–17). The situation that Micah laments in Jerusalem is a perfect illustration of Paul's teaching about sinful humanity. But we have illustrations all around us today as well. People are violent, as the newspaper testifies daily. Unable to live in harmony, we easily develop anger and malice toward others. If we can get away with it, we respond to threats with violence. It is only by the mighty working of God's grace that even Christians can live in harmony with the closest of our loved ones.

The problem of sin flowed from the top in Micah's Jerusalem. Micah had contended with corruption and vice among the city's leaders all through his ministry. But little progress had been made: "Their hands are on what is evil, to do it well; the prince and the judge ask for a bribe, and the great man utters the evil desire of his soul; thus they weave it together" (Mic. 7:3). Micah is describing a society riddled with corruption from top to bottom. How could it be different when the rulers and judges are on the take, and when those with power (e.g., "the great man" of v. 3) act so ruthlessly? In such a culture—the very culture to which sinful mankind typically descends when unrestrained by God and his Word—the only thing people are really good at is working evil. Micah speaks with bitter sarcasm when he names evildoing as the one remaining proficiency of his people: "Their hands are on what is evil, to do it well."

Micah wraps up his condemnation of Jerusalem's immorality with another comment that is wrapped in sarcasm: "The best of them is like a brier, the most upright of them a thorn hedge" (Mic. 7:4). Briers are prickly nuisances

---

3. Ibid., 386.

to those who brush against them, and thorn hedges are an obstruction to progress. This is Micah's way of saying what Paul later stated in Romans 3:12: "All have turned aside; together they have become worthless; no one does good, not even one." Paul's assessment reminds us of one other characteristic of briers and thorns, namely, that they are quick to burn as fuel in the furnace. Thus Micah's description of Jerusalem's depravity is a stern warning and a call for urgent repentance.

What can account for this sorry state of affairs, both in Jerusalem and throughout the human race? Paul gives the answer, concluding his description of man's total depravity: "There is no fear of God before their eyes" (Rom. 3:18). Humanity lives in rebellion against God, and the result is a downward spiral into decadence and evil. God made man somewhere between the angels and the beasts. Psalm 8 says: "You have made him a little lower than the heavenly beings and . . . have put all things under his feet, all sheep and oxen, and also the beasts of the field" (Ps. 8:5–7). Man was intended to look upward for his identity and his moral standards, not downward. But if we will not look to God in reverent faith, the inevitable result is a descent into bestial chaos and violence.

A DAY OF CONFUSION

At this point, we might well ask the prophet what God intended to do about this situation. We hear this frequently today, as unbelieving people blame God for the deplorable conditions throughout the world. "What is God going to do for us?" people rebelliously demand. Micah responds in a way that the wicked scarcely imagine: "The day of your watchmen, of your punishment, has come; now their confusion is at hand" (Mic. 7:4).

It is not obvious to what "the day of your watchmen" refers. It could refer to the prophets, who were the watchmen of Israel, warning against the judgment to come. This is how the term is used in Ezekiel 33:7, where God appoints the prophet as a watchman to pass on his warnings of judgment. On this interpretation, the meaning is that the punishment long foretold by the prophets was about to be loosed on Jerusalem. According to the other main interpretation, "the day of your watchmen" may indicate that the time has come for the watchmen of Jerusalem to be tested. In either case, the ultimate meaning is clear: "your punishment has now come." Year after year the prophets had given warning, and all the signs of impending judgment were evident, if only Jerusalem's sentinels had been watching. Now God would vindicate his servants and visit the rebel sinners with judgment.

The nature of Micah's lament indicates that the prophet probably preached this message toward the end of his long ministry. If so, it was long after the days of impending conquest from the Assyrian ruler Sennacherib. At the very latest, Micah's ministry ended around a century before the eventual fall of the city to the sword of the Babylonians. So what judgment does Micah have in mind? He insists that "the day . . . of your punishment, has come" (Mic. 7:4). So what is the punishment God has visited upon the people, if not an immediate external invasion?

The answer is found in the following words: "Now their confusion is at hand" (Mic. 7:4). In other words, the confused and increasingly miserable state of Jewish society was God's judgment upon his people. This judgment would consist not only of invasion from without but also of decay from within. Their society was unraveling right before them, and Micah reports that God's judgment is at work in this decline.

This is in accord with Romans 1, where Paul describes the typical pattern of man's rebellion against God as involving two main features and having two terrible results. Rebellion takes place as man "did not honor him as God or give thanks to him." As a result, "they became futile in their thinking, and their foolish hearts were darkened" (Rom. 1:21). In rebellion against God, people begin to worship idols—either idols of wood and stone or the more sophisticated idols of pleasure, wealth, and power. God judges this rebellion by giving them "up in the lusts of their hearts to impurity, to the dishonoring of their bodies among themselves" (Rom. 1:24). At the end of history God will judge all of mankind, casting the unrighteous into hell. But while history waits for that end, God frequently judges rebel societies by giving them over to the very sins their wicked hearts crave.

Micah makes no mention of idolatry in this passage, but it is hard to doubt that this perennial problem was increasing in Jerusalem. We know that Hezekiah's successor, Manasseh, whose reign would have begun not long after Micah's death, was the king who led the people into the most debased and offensive idolatry in the history of the Old Testament. In any case, after the people turned their hearts from the Lord, the Lord gave their society over to a most alarming moral decline.

The first manifestation of this decline was in personal relationships: "Put no trust in a neighbor; have no confidence in a friend" (Mic. 7:5). A society that chooses to turn from God must reckon with the consequences. It was not long ago that in most American towns, people would leave the house unlocked and sleep with the doors open; now home security has become a major industry. In our cities, ground-floor windows are protected with iron bars. In societies where depravity has long advanced unchecked, such as Haiti, practically every prosperous home has a surrounding wall to protect against one's neighbors.

But things can get worse. Micah continues: "Guard the doors of your mouth from her who lies in your arms; for the son treats the father with contempt, the daughter rises up against her mother, the daughter-in-law against her mother-in-law; a man's enemies are the men of his own house" (Mic. 7:5–6). After the city turned from God, moral decay would advance so far that a husband dared not tell his secrets to his wife. The household comes to resemble a viper pit: sons mock fathers, daughters raise their hands against their mothers, daughters-in-law feud with mothers-in-law. Micah summarizes this deplorable situation: "a man's enemies are the men of his own house" (Mic. 7:6).

This is the situation mounting in American society as it has deliberately turned from God. The Ten Commandments are considered an unfair intrusion into civil life. Biblical standards are rejected as out of date. Moral restraints in sexual conduct, speech, and public affairs are removed. The result is a chaotic misery in which everyone must fend for himself. The cause is the rejection of humble, obedient faith in the Lord: "This defiant rejection of God's revealed truth is the fundamental reason for the social disintegration we see around us."[4]

Consider the state of marriage today, with the divorce rate now above 50 percent. Christian marriages, while ending in divorce less frequently, can carry on with scarcely less conflict. One Christian couple recounted the scene at a marriage retreat they had attended, with one thousand Christian couples gathered around tables. The conference began with a speaker asking them to look into the eyes of their spouses. Husbands were to gaze at their wives and wives at their husbands, and repeat these words: "You are not my enemy."

---

4. David Prior, *The Message of Joel, Micah & Habakkuk*, The Bible Speaks Today (Downers Grove, Ill.: InterVarsity, 1998), 191.

My friends commented: "You could have cut the air with a knife." Without our hearts turned to the Lord in humble obedience, and without faithful and vigorous use of the means of grace, life can quickly become a violent misery. John Calvin, ever the realist, applies this as a warning to us:

> Now when we reflect on the corruption that dominated Micah's time, let us take heed to ourselves. For his passage is not referring to some savage group of people who had never received instruction, or who were the reprobate of God; they were of Abraham's line, a people who had been chosen from among all the others to be God's inheritance, a people who had been instructed in the Law.... How did such confusion come about? Because they turned aside from God. Therefore, because they despised his doctrine of salvation and had turned aside from his righteous path, God was justified in leaving them in a reprobate state, subject to brutal affections and nothing but cruelty, oblivious to their call. Therefore, let us be fearful lest, because we abuse God's grace ourselves, God should have to make us as equally blind and brutish.[5]

WAITING ON THE LORD

What hope remains for a people in such a deplorable condition—a people like Micah's Jerusalem or America today? Is there hope in a new political leadership? This is hardly likely, for as Micah said of Jerusalem in his day, the entire leadership structure had become a conspiracy of self-serving avarice. Are we to hope in the inherent goodness of humanity, so that people will wake up on their own? Such a hope is vain when we realize that at the root of these problems is our thorough corruption in bondage to sin. So what hope is there?

Micah answers with the word "But." This indicates that there is one place we can turn, one "but" that interrupts the hopeless prospect of doom. Paul made a similar statement in the second chapter of Ephesians, which begins with a hopeless description of mankind dead in sin and bound over in service to Satan and to the passions of the sinful mind and flesh. Paul said of Christians that they had escaped the judgment to which they were bound for only one reason: "*But* God, being rich in mercy, because of the great love with which he loved us, even when we were dead in our trespasses, made us alive together with

5. Calvin, *Sermons on Micah*, 386.

317

Christ—by grace you have been saved" (Eph. 2:4–5; emphasis added). There is only one place to look for help, only one hope for intervention, and that hope is the merciful grace of our God. This is the hope that David took in his lament: "But I trust in you, O LORD; I say, 'You are my God'" (Ps. 31:14). There was hope for Micah in his despairing lament. There is hope for our generation. There is hope for you. But that hope is found only in the Lord.

Micah records three statements that sum up his reliance on the Lord. First, he cries, "As for me, I will look to the LORD" (Mic. 7:7). When the prophet looks at Jerusalem, his heart is embittered, like a hungry man seeking tasty fruit in a barren field. But when he looks to the Lord, he renews his hope. How is this? Because of the grace of the Lord. Because of God's faithfulness to his promises of salvation. Because of God's unchanging character of goodness and love toward his people. Micah's example is paralleled in the book of Isaiah, as that contemporary prophet also looked to the Lord for a future salvation. Isaiah asked, "Have you not known? Have you not heard? The LORD is the everlasting God, the Creator of the ends of the earth. He does not faint or grow weary; his understanding is unsearchable. He gives power to the faint, and to him who has no might he increases strength" (Isa. 40:28–29).

The consistent message of the prophets and apostles sets the agenda for us today. Amid the spiritual decline of our times and the mounting social chaos that can only be seen as God's judgment on our idolatrous culture, let us look again to the Lord. He is ready to save. He is gracious to forgive those who repent. Michael Bentley writes: "Micah turned his eyes away from the things around him, and he looked to God. He knew that, even though the family unit was disintegrating, God remained as firm and stable as he always had been."[6]

Secondly, Micah says, "I will wait for the God of my salvation" (Mic. 7:7). He looks forward to the fulfillment of God's prophecies, especially the promise of a Messiah who will rule in righteousness and "shepherd his flock in the strength of the LORD" (Mic. 5:4), the very Savior whose birth he prophesied in the town of Bethlehem (Mic. 5:2). As we look back on the coming of Jesus Christ, especially to his atoning death on the cross, we see our salvation. Men and women lost in sin may be forgiven, cleansed, and renewed with new life through faith in Jesus Christ. We look forward now to his blessing through

6. Michael Bentley, *Balancing the Books: Micah and Nahum Simply Explained* (Durham: Evangelical Press, 1994), 83.

the gospel, and in the end to his return in glory to vindicate his people and establish God's righteousness on earth.

In addition, those who wait on the Lord "shall renew their strength; they shall mount up with wings like eagles; they shall run and not be weary; they shall walk and not faint" (Isa. 40:31). It is by looking to the Lord and waiting on the Lord's salvation that we, like the prophets, can gain strength in trying times. What is more, as the prophet Habakkuk shows, we can flourish in barren times with a joy that is from the Lord:

> Though the fig tree should not blossom, nor fruit be on the vines, the produce of the olive fail and the fields yield no food, the flock be cut off from the fold and there be no herd in the stalls, yet I will rejoice in the LORD; I will take joy in the God of my salvation. GOD, the LORD, is my strength; he makes my feet like the deer's; he makes me tread on my high places. (Hab. 3:17–19)

Lastly, Micah informs us of his final strategy, one that will not fail: "my God will hear me" (Mic. 7:7). Like Elijah in his despair in the days of Ahab and Jezebel, Micah will draw near to the Lord. He will lift up his heart in fervent prayer. While he waits for God's answer, he knows that God hears and that God's salvation is drawing ever near. Revival always begins with renewed commitment to prayer; indeed, when the Lord opens our hearts anew to prayer, the first sign of a revival is at hand.

Can you enter into this faith of the prophet in such an hour of darkness as he faced? Are you able to look to the Lord, knowing God with such confidence? Can you find peace as you wait for the Lord to deliver you from affliction? Do you find peace in the quiet place of prayer, regardless of the loud clamor of decay and violence around you? If you can, it is only because you can speak in the manner of the prophet. Micah speaks as one who knows God, for he has trusted in God's Word. He speaks of the Lord as "the God of my salvation," and confides that "my God will hear me."

Like Micah, we live in a day when the name of the Lord is so often taken in vain. Leaders in their confusion cry out, "My God!" But, writes David Prior, "For Micah, *my God* meant everything. It summarized his life and his work. It was the most eloquent expression he could apply to the realities of the city in which he was operating."[7]

7. Prior, *The Message of Joel, Micah & Habakkuk*, 192.

If you want to know God like Micah did, and to know that he is your God, the God of your salvation, you need only pick up his Word, read it and believe. There you will meet the Savior God has sent, Jesus Christ. Through faith in him, you will know the God of salvation. God's Word will teach you to look to the Lord, wait for the Lord, and pray with confidence to the Lord. As the Bible declares, "'Everyone who believes in him will not be put to shame.' . . . For 'everyone who calls on the name of the Lord will be saved'" (Rom. 10:11, 13).

31

THE GOSPEL ACCORDING TO MICAH

Micah 7:8–13

*Rejoice not over me, O my enemy; when I fall, I shall rise; when I
sit in darkness, the LORD will be a light to me. (Mic. 7:8)*

O LORD, how many are my foes! Many are rising against me" (Ps.
3:1). "O LORD my God, in you do I take refuge; save me from all
my pursuers" (Ps. 7:1). "Hide me in the shadow of your wings,
from the wicked who do me violence, my deadly enemies who surround
me" (Ps. 17:8–9). These are excerpts from just the first handful of Psalms,
the book of Scripture that most pointedly depicts the prayer life of the
persecuted believer. They show that the life of faith is beset with real and
deadly enemies. While Christians should pray for God to bless those who
abuse us, we nonetheless also imbibe of the Old Testament's fervent desire
for the downfall of the enemies of God and his gospel.

Micah's last chapter provides a choice instance of this biblical theme:
"Rejoice not over me, O my enemy" (Mic. 7:8). How striking it is that in
a passage that might rightly be labeled "the gospel according to Micah," a
prophetic psalm in which he makes his most heartfelt confession of faith,

the context is his reply to the scoffing enemies of God and his people. In these verses, Micah sees the salvation of Israel in terms of their deliverance from the scorn of enemies, and also as the vindication of God through the disgrace of the wicked.

THE CITY BESIEGED

It is not certain when in his ministry Micah preached this message, but there are elements in the text that align well with the invasion of Assyria under Sennacherib, in 701 B.C. Micah's use of feminine nouns and pronouns for Israel and the "enemy" suggests a focus on the city of Jerusalem and the Assyrian capital of Nineveh, since the Hebrew word for *city* is feminine. We are strongly reminded, also, of the taunts hurled by the Assyrian herald before the gates of Jerusalem. The jeer, "Where is the LORD your God?" (Mic. 7:10), is practically a quote from the speech of Sennacherib's emissary, recorded in Isaiah 36:18–20. If Micah is setting his gospel confession in the context of the Assyrian invasion, then it is apparent that he sees salvation as God's deliverance of his people from an enemy siege. Yet there need not be a direct connection with Sennacherib's assault. Bruce Waltke argues, "The prophecy is stated abstractly, never naming the enemy, because it is applicable to the salvation of God's people from any enemy, for that hope rests on God's fidelity to his sworn covenant with Abraham."[1]

That this theme of deliverance from an enemy siege is a primary biblical approach to salvation can be seen at the cross of Jesus Christ. Jesus understood his crucifixion in terms of the prophecy of Psalm 22, which depicts a righteous victim besieged by violent enemies: "For dogs encompass me; a company of evildoers encircles me; they have pierced my hands and feet" (v. 16). This was literally fulfilled as Jesus was besieged by his enemies and wounded by them to the death. Jesus quotes from Psalm 22 in his cry from the cross (Matt. 27:46), and the prophecy of Psalm 22:18 was exactly fulfilled: "they divide my garments among them, and for my clothing they cast lots" (cf. Matt. 27:35).

Since Micah's theme of the city besieged fits Jesus' experience on the cross, we are not surprised to see that the New Testament applies this same model

---

1. Bruce Waltke, *A Commentary on Micah* (Grand Rapids: Eerdmans, 2007), 451.

to the church's deliverance in the second coming of Christ. Paul writes that Jesus will return "to repay with affliction those who afflict you, and to grant relief to you who are afflicted" (2 Thess. 1:6–7). Jesus prophesied that Jerusalem would be "surrounded by armies" (Luke 21:20), and that the fall of the city in A.D. 70 foreshadowed events to occur prior to his second coming (Luke 21:25–28). Jesus will return to the earth to deliver his besieged church and inflict vengeance on his and our enemies (2 Thess. 1:8–9; cf. Matt. 24:3–31).

If Micah presents salvation as God's city rescued from a deadly siege, if this same model defines Christ's own deliverance at the cross and empty tomb, and if the city besieged by enemies describes the church at the return of Christ, then Christians should understand their own salvation in these same terms. The gospel proclaims deliverance from our enemies, including Satan, sin, and death. Micah's gospel is our gospel: God's rescue of his weak and afflicted people in faithfulness to his own covenant promises.

SALVATION FROM THE LORD

Micah's enemies would have included not only the Assyrian invaders but also the scoffing unbelievers inside Jerusalem. He defends himself against their mockery by presenting his hope of salvation from the Lord. Just as Jonah learned in the belly of the great fish that "salvation belongs to the LORD" (Jonah 2:9)—that God saves by his own sovereign will and might—Micah learned the same lesson in his dark hours. Like Jonah in his watery prison, Micah knew that he could do nothing to save himself. He saw no prospect for a change of attitude in sinful Jerusalem. And he saw no mercy in the faces of his enemies. Yet he warns his enemies not to rejoice over his plight. Why? Martin Luther answers: "It is the Lord alone that saves and blesses: and even though the whole mass of all evils should be gathered together in one against a man, still, it is the Lord who saves: salvation and blessing are in his hands."[2]

With his eye on God's grace, Micah sees a great hope through his present and future trials. His enemies have ample reason to scoff, but Micah informs

2. Quoted in Charles H. Spurgeon: *A Treasury of David*, 3 vols. (Peabody, Mass.: Hendrickson, n.d.), 1:32.

them: "when I fall, I shall rise; when I sit in darkness, the LORD will be a light to me" (Mic. 7:8).

Notice that Micah makes no attempt to deny the sad plight of himself and God's people. They had fallen from the glorious height of prior generations of faith. He knows that in the future they will fall altogether, their city destroyed by the agents of God's wrath and the surviving people carried off into exile. They had fallen morally into social decay, and spiritually into idolatry. The prophet pictures God's people as a man sitting in darkness, perhaps in a cell or dungeon, perhaps an allusion to the coming exile. There is no light and no hope, only gloom and despair. But when he turns in faith to the Lord he sees light piercing the darkness: "the LORD will be a light to me." Micah knew God had preserved a faithful remnant among the wicked generation, and he had prophesied a glorious restoration (Mic. 4:6–13; 5:7–9). Perhaps Micah remembered David's words in Psalm 27:1, "The LORD is my light and my salvation; whom shall I fear?" Matthew Henry writes: "In our greatest distresses we shall see no reason to despair of salvation if by faith we eye God as the God of our salvation, who is able to save the weakest upon their humble petition, and willing to save the worst upon their true repentance."[3]

It is to the matter of repentance that Micah next turns. He is concerned that the wicked blaspheme the name of Israel's God because of the state of his people, so Micah hastens to point out that their calamities all result from their own sins: "I will bear the indignation of the LORD because I have sinned against him" (Mic. 7:9). Micah and his people were suffering not because God was absent, but because God in his holiness was most present. Jerusalem's lamentable position is not to the shame of God but to the glory of his holy justice, since Micah says, speaking for the people, "I have sinned against him."

Micah goes on to show us the difference between a true and a false repentance. False repentance involves sorrow not so much for the sin but for its consequences. But Micah exhibits true repentance, saying, "I will bear the indignation of the LORD" (Mic. 7:9). When God punished Cain for the murder of his brother, Abel, Cain complained, "My punishment is greater than I can bear" (Gen. 4:13). But Micah acknowledges that Jerusalem's current

3. Matthew Henry, *Commentary on the Whole Bible*, 6 vols. (Peabody, Mass.: Hendrickson, n.d.), 4:1051.

dismay was not only just, but also bearable in light of the hope of God's grace. He repented in faith, and thus he could bear God's reproach for as long as the Lord saw fit. He knew that the purpose of God's chastisement of his people was ultimately restorative, so he renewed his courage to wait on the Lord.

Repentance is necessary to salvation, since God not only saves us *in* our sin but also *from* our sin. Repentance coupled with faith is certain to receive salvation. Undoubtedly, Micah would have known David's psalm of salvation: "I acknowledged my sin to you, and I did not cover my iniquity; I said, 'I will confess my transgressions to the Lord,' and you forgave the iniquity of my sin" (Ps. 32:5). Micah, writing as a prophet of the Lord, assures us that sincere repentance, looking in faith to God's promise of forgiveness, will result in our salvation. He says that we will find an advocate for ourselves in God ("until he pleads my cause") and a defender from our woes ("and executes judgment for me") (Mic. 7:9).

It was the memory of these words that achieved the gospel restoration of Wang Mingdao, one of the early leaders of the house-church movement in China. In the 1920s and 1930s Wang was one of Beijing's leading preachers, addressing huge crowds until the Japanese invasion in 1937. Despite his refusal to cooperate with the occupiers, Wang avoided arrest. But after the war, he soon ran afoul of the Chinese Communist authorities. He refused to join the Three-Self Patriotic Movement, the government-sponsored Protestant church, which Wang thought to be compromised. For this, he and his wife were arrested in 1955. In his prison, the Communists inserted cellmates who terrified Wang with tales of torture; isolated and weakened, Wang broke. He promised to sign any statement and to preach any message he was told to preach, so the Communists released him and his wife from prison.

After his release, Wang was a spiritually broken man. He willingly attended meetings at which his confession was read and his support of the state church proclaimed. Disgusted with himself, he wandered the streets of Beijing, muttering, "I am Peter, I am Peter," referring to the apostle's denial of Christ. But then suddenly Wang regained his old boldness for Christ. He again refused to cooperate and preached a true faith in Jesus. He explained the change by stating that he had recalled Micah 7:7–9, in which the prophet warns his enemies not to gloat. He saw his sufferings as God's chastisement for his sins and committed himself to wait for the God of his salvation (Mic. 7:7).

He reminded himself and others: "He will bring me out to the light; I shall look upon his vindication" (Mic. 7:9). Desiring only to glorify his gracious God, Wang published a written withdrawal of all his confessions and agreements. He was arrested again and imprisoned for another twenty-two years, during which he provided a strong example that emboldened many other persecuted Christians.[4]

Wang Mingdao had imbibed not merely the words of Micah, but also the prophet's faith and spirit. "He will bring me out to the light," Micah declares. "I shall look upon his vindication" (Mic. 7:9). God's honor was bound up in his salvation, Micah knew, and he fully trusted that God would fulfill his promises and publicly demonstrate his faithfulness to those who call upon his name. This is the same hope that every Christian shares, taking our guilt and shame to the blood of Christ. Remembering that God will not abandon his people, we, like Wang Mingdao, may be emboldened to face persecution and inspired to overcome our own weakness and sin.

Enemies Cast Down

It is with this salvation in mind that Micah warned his enemies not to rejoice over his misery. Dangerous as it is to despise and afflict God's treasured people, how much more so given that God's own honor is bound up in their condition. Micah thus foresees not only his own salvation but also the condemnation of the godless scoffers: "Then my enemy will see, and shame will cover her who said to me, 'Where is the LORD your God?' My eyes will look upon her; now she will be trampled down like the mire of the streets" (Mic. 7:10).

Micah foretells that the first phase of the wicked's judgment will be to "see" the salvation of those they had mocked. This accords perfectly with the teaching of Jesus about the final judgment. Jesus stated that when he "comes in his glory, and all the angels with him, then he will sit on his glorious throne" (Matt. 25:31). The nations will be gathered before Christ the judge, and he will separate them, some for eternal glory and some for eternal condemnation. "He will place the sheep on his right, but the goats on the left. Then the King will say to those on his right, 'Come, you who are blessed

4. Cited from David Aikman, *Jesus in Beijing* (Washington, DC: Regnery, 2003), 47–57.

by my Father, inherit the kingdom prepared for you from the foundation of the world'" (Matt. 25:33–34). Notice that this happens prior to the condemnation of the ungodly; their first judgment is to witness the justification of those whom they had despised in this life.

Even more, those who have trusted Jesus as their Savior, having their sins washed clean in his blood, will be praised for their works of faith in Christ's name. Jesus will recount before the wicked all the good works of the godly—providing food and drink to the needy, welcoming the stranger, clothing the naked, visiting the sick and those in prison. "Truly," Jesus will say to his justified people, "as you did it to one of the least of these my brothers, you did it to me" (Matt. 25:40). With what dismay will the ungodly, who mocked and abused God's people in their weakness, witness the reception of the elect into glory!

The result of this judgment will be their own eternal disgrace: "shame will cover her who said to me, 'Where is the LORD your God?'" (Mic. 7:10). In life, the ungodly boast in the success of their debaucheries, exulting that God has done nothing to punish or thwart them. But how the tables will be turned in the last day, just as it is whenever God visits his church with special blessing. So it was in the resurrection of the Lord Jesus. The Roman soldiers beat him, mockingly dressed Jesus in purple, and crushed a crown of thorns into his skull. While Jesus suffered on the cross, the Jewish leaders jeered: "He trusts in God, let God deliver him now, if he desires him. For he said, 'I am the Son of God'" (Matt. 27:43). When Jesus died, his mockers went away exultant. But on the third day, Jesus was raised from the dead. Paul wrote that Jesus "was declared to be the Son of God in power . . . by his resurrection from the dead" (Rom. 1:4). In the final judgment, the people who scoffed at the crucified Jesus will have the exquisite shame of having their transgressions and sins recounted before his white throne (Matt. 25:41–45).

Third, Micah declares the utter destruction of the enemies of God: "My eyes will look upon her; now she will be trampled down like the mire of the streets" (Mic. 7:10). This indicates that part of God's salvation of his people is to have them behold the ruin of those who had afflicted them. So it was when Moses' generation looked back after their passage of the Red Sea to witness the drowning of Pharaoh and his hosts beneath the waves (Exod. 14:28, 30). Isaiah highlights this very prospect by placing it at the conclusion of his great prophecy. He speaks of the coming of the Lord "in fire and his chariots like the whirlwind" (Isa. 66:15), to rescue his besieged church. "By fire will the Lord enter into judgment, and by his sword, with all flesh; and those slain by the Lord shall be many" (Isa. 66:16). God's people will then behold his glory, amid the glory of the new heavens and the new earth (Isa. 66:18–23). From that vantage point, Isaiah concludes by depicting Christ's church looking out on the eternal sufferings of those who were cast into hell: "And they shall go out and look on the dead bodies of the men who have rebelled against me. For their worm shall not die, their fire shall not be quenched, and they shall be an abhorrence to all flesh" (Isa. 66:24).

Jesus picked up on this language, repeating Isaiah's words about eternal suffering in hell: "their worm does not die and the fire is not quenched" (Mark 9:48). "Depart from me, you cursed," he will declare, "into the eternal fire prepared for the devil and his angels" (Matt. 25:41). If you have never been forgiven your sins, confessing them to God and putting your guilt away at the cross of Jesus Christ, hear Christ's words with dread. Realize that this is your own fate in your present unbelief, trembling before your own just condemnation and punishment in hell. Cast yourself before God, seeking mercy through his provision of the atoning blood of his Son, the only Savior for sinful mankind. Micah, considering from his own context God's just retribution against Assyria's capital and its people, who delighted to trample God's city, wrote: "now she will be trampled down like the mire of the streets" (Mic. 7:10). How can we escape a similar judgment? Only by appealing to God through faith in the blood of his Son Jesus.

The delight of God's people in beholding the sufferings of hell, something we can scarcely imagine now, will be a holy exaltation of God's justice, power, and wrath. It will be the delight of the Song of Moses after the destruction of Pharaoh and his chariots: "I will sing to the Lord, for he has triumphed gloriously; the horse and his rider he has thrown into the sea" (Exod. 15:1). John Calvin concedes that we now find such a celebration hard to conceive, but comments: "We shall therefore be only then capable of this spiritual joy, of which the Prophet speaks, when we shall put off all disordered feelings, and God shall subdue us by his Spirit."[5] It is with the holy and pure mind of Christ that we shall glorify God over the fires of hell.

5. John Calvin, *A Commentary on the Twelve Minor Prophets*, 5 vols. (1559; repr. Edinburgh: Banner of Truth, 1986), 3:382.

Who are our enemies, whose trampling will be celebrated by glorified Christians in heaven? Given Micah's focus, it is impossible to deny that they will include those who afflicted Christians, who opposed the church in this life, and made sport of the Christian gospel. But principal among our enemies, and working behind them all, is the devil. With what joy will we behold the great fall of our tormentor, accuser, and former slave master! The book of Revelation says: "The devil who had deceived them was thrown into the lake of fire and sulfur . . . [and] tormented day and night forever and ever" (Rev. 20:10). Using the figure of Babylon, the song of heaven celebrates the destruction of the entire world system in rebellion against God:

> Hallelujah!
> Salvation and glory and power belong to our God,
>   for his judgments are true and just;
> for he has judged the great prostitute
>   who corrupted the earth with her immorality,
> and has avenged on her the blood of his servants (Rev. 19:1–2).

ON THE DAY OF THE LORD

It is fitting that Micah's gospel hope should conclude with a portrayal of the age of glory after the return of Christ, the vindication of his church, and the judgment of Satan and his rebel world. Micah knows that his city must be judged because of her sins against the Lord. But God has planned a new and greater city, the scale of which boggles the believer's mind: "A day for the building of your walls! In that day the boundary shall be far extended" (Mic. 7:11).

After Jerusalem's fall in 586 B.C., the fervent desire of all devout Jews was the city's restoration, which God granted in 538 B.C. The city was destroyed again by the Romans in A.D. 70, and when the modern nation of Israel recaptured Jerusalem in 1967, many Jews and Christians saw this event as a covenant restoration. But in this present age, God's true city is the Christian church, the people of Israel having forfeited its status by rejecting Jesus the Messiah, so that Jews and Gentiles alike gain their citizenship in God's city only through faith in Christ. The apostle Paul states that while Israel may be seen as the olive tree that God has planted in history, so that salvation is always rooted

329

in God's ancient work among his covenant people, the "branches" of ethnic Israel were "broken off because of their unbelief" (Rom. 11:20). In the age of Christ, the Gentile Christian church has been "grafted in" and now draws saving life from "the nourishing root of the olive tree" (Rom. 11:17); that is, the saving work of God begun in Israel now finds expression in the Christian church. It is not that God has a new covenant people, but rather that the Christian church has been grafted to the one covenant people of God, even as unbelieving Israel was broken off. This is why the apostle Paul, himself an ethnic Jew, could address his Gentile Christian readers as "the Israel of God" (Gal. 6:16). This being said, we return to Micah's vision of the extending of Jersualem's walls and see how marvelously this has been fulfilled in Christ. Waltke comments: "Zion's walls will be expanded to embrace all the elect from the ends of the earth."[6]

Yet such glory as is found in the spiritual blessing of the church today will be far outshone by the glory of God's eternal city in the age to come. The book of Revelation, and the entire Bible, concludes with a vision of the city to come: "the holy city, new Jerusalem, coming down out of heaven from God, prepared as a bride adorned for her husband. And I heard a loud voice from the throne saying, 'Behold, the dwelling place of God is with man. He will dwell with them, and they will be his people, and God himself will be with them as their God'" (Rev. 21:2–3). In the age to come, after the return of Christ, will be the fulfillment of all God's covenant aims and all his salvation promises.

Those who dwell in the glory of the eternal city will be gathered not merely from Jerusalem, but, Micah adds: "In that day they will come to you, from Assyria and the cities of Egypt, and from Egypt to the River, from sea to sea and from mountain to mountain" (Mic. 7:12). The "River" is the Euphrates, the great river of Assyria. Micah sees God drawing people to himself even from the lands of Israel's historic enemies, and in this way he signifies the whole of the earth, "from sea to sea and from mountain to mountain." What a gathering it will be in glory: the redeemed people of God, drawn from every nation, tribe, and tongue, united for worship in the presence of God's glory!

Yet, as we consider the glories of the age to come, and the fulfillment of all our hopes in the Lord, Micah realizes that we need to be reminded of this

---

6. Bruce Waltke, "Micah," in Thomas McComiskey, *An Exegetical and Expository Commentary on the Minor Prophets* (Grand Rapids: Baker, 1993), 756.

present, evil world: "But the earth will be desolate because of its inhabitants, for the fruit of their deeds" (Mic. 7:13). This prophecy refers to the world outside of God's reign. Leslie Allen writes: "For these areas nothing good is promised. Their denizens are to reap the fruit of age-old enmity and exploitation of God's people. As Israel's territory has been the scarred battlefield of successive foreign armies, so by way of compensation their territory is to suffer desolation."[7]

One thing this means is that all the treasures of this world will be destroyed with it. The empires will fall, the buildings will crumble, the piles of gold will evaporate. Paul applies this realization to Christians, urging us to live not for earthly rewards but for the age to come and the spiritual rewards with Christ that will never perish: "For the present form of this world is passing away" (1 Cor. 7:31).

EVERY TEAR WIPED AWAY

It was with this gospel hope that Micah faced the dark times of his own life. He knew that it was because of his own sins and the sins of his people that God's indignation rested on Jerusalem. But he also knew that sin can be confessed, and that by faith in God's promise of salvation in Christ it can be forgiven. Micah knew that when he called upon God, he would find a divine advocate in heaven. Christians know this even better, being told that "Christ Jesus is the one who died—more than that, who was raised—who is at the right hand of God, who indeed is interceding for us" (Rom. 8:34). Micah knew that God would lift him up out of his misery and sin: "He will bring me out to the light" (Mic. 7:9). Thus he did not need to fear his enemies, and he had an answer for the scoffing of the sinful world. Christians, knowing our calling to take this same gospel to everyone, need not hate our enemies, but by loving them in Christ's name we advance the cause of his kingdom and our own salvation.

It is not hard to imagine the light in the prophet's face as he contemplated this gospel of salvation. But imagine how much greater his joy would be if he could read the completed revelation of God in the Bible, a privilege we enjoy. What bitterness Micah experienced as he preached God's Word at the

7. Leslie C. Allen, *The Books of Joel, Obadiah, Jonah, and Micah*, New International Commentary on the Old Testament (Grand Rapids: Eerdmans, 1976), 398.

temple: what joy he would have at the book of Revelation's portrait of the glorified city in which God will eternally dwell with his people! Micah knew that all his labors for Jerusalem had failed, at least in the short run, and that it must suffer destruction. With what rapture, then, would he read Revelation's depiction of the New Jerusalem descending from heaven in its pristine glory! How much suffering he had witnessed, how much sorrow he had known, and how many tears he had shed for God's people. But looking ahead to the world to come, the day he had so boldly predicted, Micah would have received God's answer for all his loss: "He will wipe away every tear from their eyes, and death shall be no more, neither shall there be mourning nor crying nor pain anymore, for the former things have passed away" (Rev. 21:4).

No wonder that the verses following Micah's gospel confession are filled with praise to the glory of God. "Who is a God like you?" he marvels with joy. If we receive the same gospel in faith, looking through perhaps clearer eyes with the completed witness of Scripture and beholding the saving work of Jesus Christ, how these same promises should embolden us to live faithfully in our own dark times, and should transform our present aspect from tears to joy and from lament to praise.

32

PRAYING AND WAITING

Micah 7:14—17

Shepherd your people with your staff,
the flock of your inheritance. (Mic. 7:14)

icah's preaching was over. Like every preacher commissioned by God, he was sent to deliver two messages, which together make up the first half of Micah chapter seven. First, he delivered a message of bad news, God's judgment on sin: "The day of your watchmen, of your punishment, has come" (Mic. 7:4). Second, Micah delivered a gospel message of hope centered on the coming of Christ: "when I fall, I shall rise; when I sit in darkness, the LORD will be a light to me" (Mic. 7:8). Yes, God will judge all sin, but he has provided an advocate to plead the cause of believers (Mic. 7:9), a Savior to gain their forgiveness by the cross. This was Micah's message, and now it had been given.

So what does a preacher do when the sermon is over? What do Christians do when their witness has been given? The answer is found in the remaining verses of Micah chapter 7, in which Micah turns to the Lord in prayer and then worships God for his sovereign grace. Micah's resolve to commit himself to prayer is expressed in the midst of his final sermon: "But as for me, I will

333

look to the LORD; I will wait for the God of my salvation; my God will hear me" (Mic. 7:7). The prayer itself, along with God's reply, is recorded in verses 14–17. Leslie Allen comments:

> The piece forms a worthy climax to the book of Micah. . . . It is a monument to the faith of men who transcended their earthly woes and climbed to a spiritual vantage point. From there they could survey the present in the reassuring light of God's past and future dealings with his covenant people. . . . Here is an earnest of boldness toward God in approaching "the throne of grace to receive mercy and find grace in the form of timely help." (Heb. 4:16)[1]

THE DESIRE OF MICAH'S HEART

I would not be surprised to learn that Micah was a lover of the Psalms. I say this because most scholars classify the concluding section of his book as a psalm of prayer and praise, and because his whole way of thinking is so similar to that of the psalmists. I can imagine Micah exulting over the words of Psalm 37:4, "Delight yourself in the LORD, and he will give you the desires of your heart."

This is exactly what we find in the prayer of Micah 7:14, in which the prophet lays before the Lord the very desire of his heart. "Shepherd your people with your staff," he prays, since they are "the flock of your inheritance" (Mic. 7:14). Micah's longing for the salvation of his wayward people has almost broken his heart, so now he brings his heart before the Lord in prayer.

God as the shepherd of his people is one of the main themes of the Old Testament, and it appears in all three of the salvation messages in the book of Micah (cf. Mic. 2:12; Mic. 5:4–6; and Mic. 7:14). Micah's plea stems in large part from the poor state of Jerusalem's leadership. Starting with the king and working down through the elites, all were devoted to pursuing their own good at the expense of the people. This is why the heart of Micah's prophecy declared the birth of a royal Savior in the town of Bethlehem. In contrast with the weak and corrupt leaders of Micah's day, "He shall stand and shepherd his flock in the strength of the LORD, in the majesty of the name of the LORD his God" (Mic. 5:4).

1. Leslie C. Allen, *The Books of Joel, Obadiah, Jonah, and Micah*, New International Commentary on the Old Testament (Grand Rapids: Eerdmans, 1976), 404.

This looks back on the ancient prophecy of Jacob, Israel's namesake patriarch, who foretold on his deathbed: "The scepter shall not depart from Judah, nor the ruler's staff from between his feet, until tribute comes to him; and to him shall be the obedience of the peoples" (Gen. 49:10). The royal scepter has its origins in the shepherd's rod, employed to defend his people. "Shepherd your people with your staff," Micah prayed, echoing David's famous words, "Your rod and your staff, they comfort me" (Ps. 23:4). Looking forward, how the prophet would have rejoiced to see the royal son of David, God's own Son and our Messiah. Jesus declared, "I am the good shepherd. The good shepherd lays down his life for the sheep" (John 10:11). Therefore, in the light of the completed canon of the entire Bible, we can rightly compare Micah's prayer to the words of the Christian plea: "Come, Lord Jesus!" (Rev. 22:20). For it was in the coming of the Savior Micah had predicted that God would answer the prayer of the prophet's heart.

Micah continues his prayer by setting forth the need of the people, "who dwell alone in a forest in the midst of a garden land; let them graze in Bashan and Gilead as in the days of old" (Mic. 7:14). The word for "forest" is the same term Micah used for "wooded height" (ESV) or "thickets" (NIV) in Micah 3:12. There, the idea was that the temple mount would be in such a state of ruin that it would become like an untended field. Micah returns to this idea to describe the spiritual state of Jerusalem before and especially after God's judgment.

There is a question about the phrase "in the midst of a garden land." Some commentators think this means that while Israel is surrounded by fertile lands, these lands are occupied by its enemies. Jerusalem is hemmed in by increasing poverty while those who beset it enjoy abundance. Other commentators note that the word used for "garden" is *carmel*, which means "orchard." This could be a reference to wooded Mount Carmel by the sea. In this case, the idea may be that Israel, for all its spiritual barrenness, lives a solitary existence, since it is set apart from the world for holiness.

Whatever Micah's precise intent with these words, his overall meaning is clear: God's people long to enjoy the fertile blessings of former days. This is the clear import of the final words of Micah's prayer: "Let them graze in Bashan and Gilead as in the days of old." Bashan and Gilead were choice lands originally possessed by Israel but long since occupied by their enemies. So

Micah prays that in the future God would himself shepherd his people into green pastures, restoring to them the blessings of former times.

Likewise, all Christians should look beyond their present hard times for a salvation that will abound in blessing. Michael Bentley writes: "Believers will not always be living with the trials and testing of this life. There is hope coming, a day when God's people will enjoy the presence and blessings of the Lord forever."[2] Just as Micah longed for the first coming of Christ, Christians join him in looking for Christ's return to bring the fullness of salvation to his people.

A BIBLICAL APPROACH TO PRAYER

It is not incidental that Micah concludes his ministry in prayer. If we will reflect on Micah's prayer, including its source, its content, and its results, we may learn much that will help us in our own prayers.

First, we ask about the source of Micah's prayer: why did the prophet pray? The answer is that he was a realist about the dark depravity of his times. He cared deeply about his generation and the people to whom he sought to minister. This is no cold or formal prayer! "Woe is me!" he began the chapter, frustrated over the spiritual barrenness of Jerusalem. This shows that Micah looked upon the world with honest eyes, gazing through the lens of God's truth. He was not deceived by mere externals. He did not harbor delusions based on the fact that God's temple was in the city, but acknowledged that Israel's covenant privileges only heightened the dreadfulness of their idolatry and sin. He further recognized that God must judge so wicked a city and that Jerusalem's fall was assured, starting with its present moral decay (cf. Mic. 7:1–6).

Micah seems also to have had a sober understanding even of himself. He did not respond to the grave challenges facing him by looking to himself or seeking to devise new techniques of prophetic ministry. Rather, he soberly assessed his sinful world and turned in prayer to God. If we have a similarly sober assessment of our generation, of the moral despair into which Western society has fallen, of the carnal and compromised state of the evangelical church, and of our own feebleness before such forces, we will also respond by devoting ourselves to the ministry of prayer.

2. Michael Bentley, *Balancing the Books: Micah and Nahum Simply Explained* (Durham: Evangelical Press, 1994), 91.

If one source of Micah's prayer was the candid assessment of verses 1–6, a second source was the gospel hope revealed in verses 8–13. Amid the darkness of his times, he looks for God to be his light. Though his ministry seems to have failed, he declares, "when I fall, I shall rise" (Mic. 7:8). Although he knows that God's hand will fall heavy against the city, God has revealed a salvation for the remnant of those who trust in him. We know from the whole of Micah's prophecy that he placed his trust in the coming of a Savior from God to deliver his people. "But you, O Bethlehem Ephrathah," he announced, "from you shall come forth for me one who is to be ruler in Israel" (Mic. 5:2). This was Micah's hope. Whereas Judah's foolish kings cast about for worldly alliances, increasingly becoming like the world in its tactics and idolatrous religion, Micah saw that he must remain faithful to God and his Word, and that God would send a Savior for the remnant of faithful believers, however small it might be.

The gospel is our incentive to pray as well. Many observers have noted the increasing worldliness of many evangelical churches today. Faced with a public that has seemed uninterested in biblical Christianity, church after church has responded by making alliance with worldly sources of power, much as the kings of Jerusalem sought aid from Assyria or Egypt. If worldly people consider biblical worship to be boring, the church has teamed with Hollywood, bringing the glitz and glamour of the entertainment world into the church. If the simple preaching of God's Word has not seemed to win the culture, then churches have taken a page—indeed, whole books—from the business world of marketing by designing the church, its worship, and its ministries according to the results of consumer surveys. One striking result has been the shrinking of prayer in the lives of Christians and churches, if not its complete disappearance. In a book that summed up the lessons of more than three decades of worldwide ministry, James Montgomery Boice commented on the declining place of prayer in evangelical churches:

> It is almost inconceivable to me that something called worship can be held without any significant prayer, but that is precisely what is happening. There is usually a short prayer at the beginning of the service, though even that is fading away. It is being replaced with a chummy greeting to make people feel welcome and at ease. . . . Another prayer that is generally retained is the prayer for the offering. We can understand that, since we know that it takes the intervention of the Almighty God to get self-centered people to give enough money

to keep the church running. But longer prayers—pastoral prayers—are vanishing. . . . How can we say we are worshiping when we do not even pray?[3]

In contrast, a true Christian life will be suffused with prayer. The reason for this is the hope we have through Jesus Christ. The writer of Hebrews reasoned: "Since then we have a great high priest who has passed through the heavens, Jesus, the Son of God, let us hold fast our confession. . . . Let us then with confidence draw near to the throne of grace, that we may receive mercy and find grace to help in time of need" (Heb. 4:14–16). At the heart of our gospel is the finished work of Jesus, who has put away our sins and taken up his ministry in heaven for us. Christ has reconciled us to the faithful God who keeps his promises, the mighty God who rescues his people, and the merciful God who has compassion on his flock. In a situation at least as dark as any we may face today, Micah did not seek worldly allies or strategies but recommitted himself to his covenant Lord in prayer. Likewise, the more we believe the gospel, and the more we understand life through the lens of God's plan for all history, the more energy and time we will devote to looking to the Lord in prayer and then waiting for his salvation.

Having considered the source of Micah's prayer, we should also note its content. It consists of the promises God had already made to him. On what basis, after all, would Micah point to the debauched and idolatrous people of Israel and speak of them to God as "your people . . . the flock of your inheritance" (Mic. 7:14)? The answer is that God had declared this in his Word. In response to the Assyrian siege of Jerusalem, God had told Micah, "I will gather the remnant of Israel; I will set them together like sheep in a fold, like a flock in its pasture" (Mic. 2:12). This was God's promise of a future salvation: he would assemble the scattered sheep of Israel together in a new and stronger fold (cf. Mic. 4:6–7). Micah has set his heart on God's promise, so he utters back to God in prayer what God had spoken to him in his Word. He reminds the Lord that he had made his people his "inheritance"; that is, God had declared that his chosen people were his particular treasure. So Micah calls on God to shepherd his flock unto salvation.

---

3. James Montgomery Boice, *Whatever Happened to the Gospel of Grace?* (Wheaton, Ill.: Crossway, 2001), 178.

This is a pattern we will see repeated in all the great men and women of the Bible. They studied God's Word, gathered the promises God had made, and then repeated these back to God in prayer, asking him to fulfill his Word. If we want our prayers to be strengthened and our hearts to grow more confident in prayer, then we must first be sure what God has promised to do and then bring the promises of Scripture into God's presence with a heart of faith.

This approach to prayer was lived out by Art Matthews and his family, the last missionaries to escape from China after the Communist takeover. They lived in a single room with only a stool for furniture. All contact with outside friends and financial support was cut off. With only a small stove for heat, they often shivered, and their food was reduced to a daily meal of rice cooked over burning manure that Art gathered in the streets. All through this trial the Matthews family trusted God, spoke to him in prayer, and strengthened themselves by his Word. One passage that encouraged them was Jeremiah 17:7–8: "'Blessed is the man who trusts in the LORD, whose trust is the LORD. He is like a tree planted by water, that sends out its roots by the stream, and does not fear when heat comes, for its leaves remain green, and is not anxious in the year of drought.'" When the Matthewses finally were released and returned to America, they were the subject of a biography titled *Green Leaf in Drought Time*, chronicling God's faithfulness in answering their pleas in fulfillment of his Word.[4] Their testimony highlights not only God's great faithfulness to his people in distress, but also the role of prayer in strengthening the faith of suffering believers.

We have considered the source and the content of Micah's prayer, but what about its results? One result was God's answer, provided in verse 15, and the triumphant joy that welled up in Micah's heart. But the ultimate result is found in the final verses of the book, a glorious hymn of praise to the incomparable God of grace. Micah shows us that if we want truly to worship God in the joy of our salvation, then we must devote ourselves to him in prayer. The apostle Paul emphasized this same relationship between prayer and a heart settled before God, urging that when we commit ourselves to God in prayer, "the peace of God, which surpasses all understanding, will guard your hearts and your minds in Christ Jesus" (Phil. 4:7).

4. Isobel Kuhn, *Green Leaf in Drought Time* (Chicago: Moody Press, 1957).

339

THE PRAYER OF FAITH ANSWERED

Few things are more satisfying to believers than answered prayers. Sometimes Christians will find their prayers for understanding answered in the teaching of the Bible. At other times we can see a clear answer from God in the unfolding of his providence. On these occasions, the chief blessing is not merely the help we receive from God but the assurance that God is with us. Micah's prayer received a direct answer that was richly satisfying to the prophet's heart. God told him, "As in the days when you came out of the land of Egypt, I will show them marvelous things" (Mic. 7:15).

The greatest instance of God's saving grace in the Old Testament was Israel's exodus from slavery in Egypt. Whenever God wanted to inspire his people to confidence, he reminded them of these great events. So it is here: God promises Micah that his prayers for salvation will be answered in such a way as can only be compared to the marvelous power displayed by God through Moses. We recall the ten plagues by which God broke the will of mighty Pharaoh, culminating in the death of all the firstborn of Egypt. We are reminded of the crossing of the Red Sea, when the waters parted to allow Israel to pass through, only to close up to destroy Pharaoh and his host. We are reminded further of the cloud of smoke by day and the pillar of fire by night, the manna that fell from heaven, and many other marvelous things God did in leading Israel through the desert. Finally, we are reminded of the crashing walls of the fortress of Jericho when Joshua obeyed God's Word. God points Micah back to these great days. He speaks to this effect, "Do not think that your faith is one that only remembers such mighty things, for I will do more things like it to save my people in days to come."

Again, Micah would find his faith vindicated by reading the New Testament accounts of the coming of Christ. Indeed, the miracles performed by Jesus far exceed the wonders of the exodus, the spiritual salvation to which Jesus brings his people far out-marvels the salvation experienced in the days of Joshua, and the worldwide scope of the church compared with the nation of Israel far better displays the almighty power of God. Bruce Waltke writes: "The exodus that Christ affords his church, bringing them out of a world of sin and judgment and setting them on their heaven-bound journey through the Wilderness, involves far greater 'wonders.' Israel's Passover, the baptism into the Red Sea, whereby they put Egypt behind them and set out for the

Promised land, and the heavenly manna and the water from the rock all typify Christ and his greater salvation (John 6; 7:38–39; 1 Cor. 10:1–4; 2 Cor. 5:17)."[5] If New Testament believers have seen the fulfillment in Christ of all that Micah had prayed for, then we also have a stronger incentive to faith as we await God's answers to our prayers.

BITE THE DUST!

Micah responds to God's brief but wonderful answer to his prayers by lifting his heart to exalt the Lord. Given that his own day saw Israel shamed before the nations, he speaks to the reversal of fortunes and the triumph of God over the wicked: "The nations shall see and be ashamed of all their might; they shall lay their hands on their mouths; their ears shall be deaf" (Mic. 7:16). All the mocking of God that Micah had to endure will then be put to an end. The wicked will be exposed before God's holiness. Israel's enemies will find themselves with nothing to say, trying only to cover their ears in a vain attempt to avoid the reality of their defeat.

In today's terms, Micah's exaltation is the equivalent of a football player spiking the ball after scoring a game-winning touchdown: "They shall lick the dust like a serpent, like the crawling things of the earth; they shall come trembling out of their strongholds; they shall turn in dread to the LORD our God, and they shall be in fear of you" (Mic. 7:17). Micah foresees the fulfillment of God's curse on Satan in the Garden of Eden for his tempting role in the fall of Adam and Eve: "on your belly you shall go, and dust you shall eat all the days of your life" (Gen. 3:14). This is where the popular phrase "bite the dust" comes from, and Micah sees this promise finally coming true. We are reminded of the cringing fear of the demons before the presence of Jesus in the gospels, as well as the book of Revelation's promise of Satan's ultimate defeat in the day of judgment.

An example of how God's enemies meet frustration, even in this present life, is seen in the experience of the French humanist Voltaire, whose writings were so popular during the eighteenth-century Enlightenment. Voltaire was a great mocker of the Bible and Christianity, once writing that in fifty years from his time no one would remember Christianity. "In twenty years," he

---

5. Bruce Waltke, *A Commentary on Micah* (Grand Rapids: Eerdmans, 2007), 460.

said, "Christianity will be no more. My single hand shall destroy the edifice it took twelve apostles to rear." Imagine how threatening this was to the Christians who witnessed the popularity and apparent success of Voltaire's scoffing. Voltaire's contemporaries would have done well to take this page out of Micah's book: "I will wait for the God of my salvation" (Mic. 7:7). For twenty years passed and Christianity remained. Voltaire, however, died, and in death even he remembered Christianity. The doctor who attended him records the bitter frustration of his last words: "I am abandoned by God and man! I will give you half of what I am worth if you will give me six months' life. Then I shall go to hell; and you will go with me. O Christ! O Jesus Christ!" Fifty years after Voltaire's famous boast, the very house from which he assaulted God's church with his pen served as the headquarters of the Geneva Bible Society, from which the church was mass-producing and disseminating Bibles.[6] What a fulfillment, in its own small way, of God's answer to Micah's prayer: "I will show them marvelous things" (Mic. 7:15). What a striking fulfillment of the divine vindication celebrated by the prophet: "They shall come trembling out of their strongholds; they shall turn in dread to the LORD our God, and they shall be in fear of you" (Mic. 7:17). And what a reminder to us of the wisdom of Micah's strategy when faced by dark times: I will pray, and I will wait!

If Micah's triumphant words seem to us to hold a bitter edge, it is because he was more of a realist than we tend to be. Our true enemies are rightly to be hated—namely, Satan, sin, and death. Just as we feel a visceral triumph when cured from a deadly disease, or feel deep satisfaction when a murdering tyrant is brought to justice, Micah rejoices at the humiliating fall of God's enemies. Indeed, the progression of verse 17 is played out over and again under God's holy, providential rule in history, as it will be in the end for all who shake their fists against him: their aims are frustrated, their plans fall to the earth, their strongholds are broken, and unless they confess their sins and seek God's grace, their end is a fearful turning to face the dread of God's wrath. Meanwhile, writes Isaiah in a passage that in many ways parallels the final chapter of his colleague Micah, "They who wait for the LORD shall renew their strength; they shall mount up with wings like eagles; they shall run and not be weary; they shall walk and not faint" (Isa. 40:31).

6. Cited from James M. Boice, *Psalms*, 3 vols. (Grand Rapids: Baker, 1994), 1:101.

THE LORD OUR SHEPHERD

If we reflect on Micah's prayer, its initial fulfillment in the coming of the Lord Jesus Christ, and the promised final fulfillment in the return of Christ to judge the earth, we see a great argument set forth. For those who follow the Lord as sheep to a shepherd, entering his fold through faith in Christ, God promises a salvation that will declare the wonders of his grace. As in the Passover, those who followed the Lord into the desert were spared the penalty of God's wrath and cared for in wonderful ways, but those who refused to submit and follow him felt the full sting of death. So it is for everyone. If we harden our hearts against the Lord we can only end in frustrated defeat, victims of Satan, death, and our own sin. But if we follow the good Shepherd, the Lord Jesus, God will respond to our prayers by displaying marvels of his salvation. The God of Micah is a God to be followed, even through the desert times of our lives, for he promises us a mighty salvation that will give us all the desires of our heart.

33

OUR INCOMPARABLE GOD

Micah 7:18–20

Who is a God like you, pardoning iniquity and passing over trans-
gression for the remnant of his inheritance? (Mic. 7:18)

What's in a name? As the prophet Micah sees things, much in
every way. At numerous points in this book we see the prophet
deriving significant meaning from names. During Sennach-
erib's invasion, Micah took the names of towns and cities as harbingers of
their fate (cf. Mic. 1:10–15). He seems to see his prophecy of Christ's birth
as a fulfillment of the names of Bethlehem (house of bread) and Ephrathah
(bountiful). How appropriate, then, that Micah would conclude his book
with a reference to his own name. The name Micah means "Who is like the
Lord?" As the prophet completes his record he identifies himself with this
testimony, writing: "Who is a God like you . . . ?" (Mic. 7:1).

It is fitting that Micah should conclude his book with this question, which
is really an assertion of God's incomparable glory. The prophet really means,
"There is no one like the Lord, for the God of Israel is greater than all gods!"
Micah not only asserts this claim, but he also goes on in these final verses to
say, "Let me count the ways!" James Montgomery Boice comments: "Micah
rehearses the ways in which the true God is unlike all others. Deliverance by

mighty acts is among those ways. Yet his emphasis is on God's willingness to forgive sin and show mercy, which he concludes is the supreme measure of God's surpassing excellence."[1]

Our Incomparable God

Before we focus on Micah's specific reasons for declaring God's incomparable excellence, it will be profitable to consider the picture of God given throughout the book. When reading the Bible, we should always be concerned to gain a clearer knowledge of God. So as we conclude our studies in Micah, we should ask, "What does Micah reveal to us about God?"

Since so much of Micah describes God's judgment on Israel's sin, our first thoughts should turn to God's *holiness*. The God presented by Micah is a holy God, that is, one who will not abide with sin.

Strictly speaking, God's holiness means that God is set apart from all others. God is in a unique category. He says through Isaiah: "For my thoughts are not your thoughts, neither are your ways my ways, declares the LORD. For as the heavens are higher than the earth, so are my ways higher than your ways and my thoughts than your thoughts" (Isa. 55:8–9). It was because of God's holiness, so integral to his deity, that Moses was required to take off his shoes before the burning bush. J. Gresham Machen writes, "From beginning to end the Bible is concerned to set forth the awful gulf that separates the creature from the Creator."[2] Yet when the Bible speaks of God's holiness, it invariably relates this to his absolute separation from all evil and sin. To quote Geerhardus Vos: "Jehovah's holiness . . . involves not merely that his nature is stainless, empirically free from sin, but means that he is exalted above the possibility of sin—in him, as the absolutely good, evil cannot enter."[3]

We are confronted with this reality all through Micah. The book opens with a scene of frightening cataclysm, with the high places trodden down and the mountains melting in fire (Mic. 1:3–4). Micah explains why: "All this is for the transgression of Jacob and for the sins of the house of Israel" (Mic. 1:5). Most humans think of sin as a slight matter, except perhaps for the sins committed against us. But God, who is the Creator and Lord of heaven and

1. James M. Boice, *The Minor Prophets*, 2 vols. (Grand Rapids: Baker, 1986), 2:357.

2. J. Gresham Machen, *Christianity and Liberalism* (Grand Rapids: Eerdmans, 1923), 62.

3. Geerhardus Vos, *Grace and Glory: Sermons Preached in the Chapel of Princeton Theological Seminary* (Edinburgh: Banner of Truth, 1994), 269.

earth, is grievously offended by all sin. Why? Because he is transcendentally holy. Sin is a gross offense to his person and a stench in his holy nostrils. Even when it is God's own beloved people who give themselves over to sin, God declares his intention to judge it with great severity. "Woe to those who devise wickedness," Micah cries, "and work evil on their beds!" (Mic. 2:1). "Lately my people have risen up as an enemy," God declares (Mic. 2:8). Why? Because they have given themselves over to sin. Our holy God is a just God, so sin will be judged. Our holy God is bitterly, personally opposed to all evil, so his wrath burns against the wicked.

A second attribute of God that Micah highlights is his almighty *power*. We see this, too, in the book's opening verses, which speak not only of God's anger at sin but also of his power in judging it: "I will make Samaria a heap in the open country . . . and I will pour down her stones into the valley and uncover her foundations" (Mic. 1:6). Man's strongest fortress is no match for God's power. No locked door can keep God out and no foundation is solid enough to withstand his stroke. When the Assyrian conqueror Sennacherib besieged God's city and mocked God's name, the Lord struck down a hundred and eighty-five thousand soldiers of the Assyrian army in a single night.

A third attribute of God laid bare in the book of Micah is his *sovereignty*. It is not the king on his throne, the power broker in his mansion, or the general on his stallion who determines the fate of peoples, but only the Lord in his sovereign majesty. This is, in part, a function of his infinite might: God's will reigns supreme in that no other force can hope to thwart him in the least. God is omniscient, knowing even the secret thoughts of the wicked in their bedrooms (Mic. 2:1). While many nations assemble against God's people, Micah points out their folly: "They do not know the thoughts of the LORD; they do not understand his plan" (Mic. 4:12). God employs even the wicked acts of men for his own sovereign purpose: the pagan armies gathered against Jerusalem only because God purposed judgment for his people, and because God summoned them for their own destruction: "He has gathered them as sheaves to the threshing floor," Micah says (Mic. 4:12).

God's absolute sovereignty over all history, including the minutest details of the affairs of men and nations, is best seen in the many and specific prophecies Micah makes regarding the future. Early in his ministry, he foretold that the judgment recently visited upon wicked Samaria was soon coming to wicked Jerusalem (Mic. 1:9). He predicted details of the Assyrian advance prior to the event (Mic. 1:10–16). As the threatened invasion draws near, he prophesies God's deliverance of his people when the enemy comes to the very gate of the city (Mic. 2:12–13). Looking farther into the future, Micah sees the Christian age of the gospel, when people from all over the world will come to God to worship and learn: "Many nations shall come, and say: 'Come, let us go up . . . to the house of the God of Jacob, that he may teach us his ways and that we may walk in his paths'" (Mic. 4:2). Most dramatically, Micah provides one of the most detailed and accurate predictions of the Messiah's birth, nearly 700 years in the future: "But you, O Bethlehem Ephrathah, who are too little to be among the clans of Judah, from you shall come forth for me one who is to be ruler in Israel, whose origin is from old, from ancient days" (Mic. 5:2). How can a prophet dare to speak with such boldness about specific events that have not yet happened, some of which lie many centuries in the future? Because he speaks for a sovereign God, who exercises perfect control over all things, past, present, and into eternity.

INCOMPARABLE GRACE

We might continue this survey of the doctrine of God in the book of Micah, but the prophet himself should be given the last word. We ask, Is there one thing about God that causes Micah to celebrate his incomparable glory? If there is, what is it? The answer, according to these final verses, is that the majesty of the holy, almighty, and sovereign God is seen most wonderfully in his *grace*. "Who is a God like you," Micah marvels, "pardoning iniquity and passing over transgression for the remnant of his inheritance?" (Mic. 7:18). Following Micah's hymn of praise for God's forgiving grace, we observe, first, *what* God forgives; second, *how* God forgives; third, God's *attitude* in forgiving; and, finally, the *finality* of God's forgiveness. In all of these aspects, Micah would have us join with him in wondrous praise for the incomparable grace of God.

First, *what is it that God forgives?* Micah employs three terms to describe the offense that sinners have given to God. First, Micah says that God pardons "iniquity" (Mic. 7:18). This word (Hebrew, *'avon*) refers to our guilt. Our sins have incurred a debt to God's holy justice that must be paid. The second word is "transgression" (Hebrew, *pesha*), which denotes rebellion against God's authority. Whenever we sin we are flouting God's right to govern our lives, and as traitors we deserve to be punished with death. Jesus speaks of this in his parable of the ten minas, in which the rebels insist, "We do not want this man to reign over us" (Luke 19:14). The king rightly responds, "As for these enemies of mine, who did not want me to reign over them, bring them here and slaughter them before me" (Luke 19:27). Third, Micah speaks of "sin" (Hebrew, *chatta'ah*), referring to wickedness or evil. As ruler of creation, God cannot tolerate evil, but must destroy it. All three of these terms—guilt, rebellion, and wickedness—have been ascribed to Micah's Jerusalem, just as they can all be ascribed to us. Judging by the standard of God's perfect law, Paul concludes: "None is righteous, no, not one . . . . no one does good, not even one" (Rom. 3:10, 12).

This was the great problem of Micah's generation: not only enemy armies or inept leadership, but the just wrath of the holy God against their iniquity, transgression, and sin. It was because of their offense against God that Micah's generation suffered such misery and that their immediate future was so dark. It is our great problem, too; just like the Jews of old, we need to be forgiven.

So *how can a holy God ever forgive his people's sin*? Micah's language is vivid and instructive, containing the very heart of the Bible's gospel. First, speaking of our guilt, the prophet says that God displays incomparable grace by "pardoning." The Hebrew word (*nasa'*) literally speaks of God lifting our guilt, taking it away. The Israelite would naturally think of the Day of Atonement ritual, when the high priest would lay his hands on the head of the scapegoat, who was then taken outside the camp and sent far off into the wilderness. Along with the scapegoat, another spotless animal was slain in sacrifice. The meaning was that by the substitutionary death of a God-appointed sacrifice, our guilt is lifted and taken away. Bruce Waltke explains, "God does not wink at sin, but provided the sacrifice of Jesus Christ, the only one who kept his covenant obligations (Rom. 3:21–26) both to bear and to take away sin."[4]

The New Testament applies this teaching directly to the cross of Jesus Christ. Paul writes that God forgave our trespasses: "by canceling the record of debt that stood against us with its legal demands. This he set aside, nailing it to the cross" (Col. 2:14). The theological term for the transfer of our sins

4. Bruce Waltke, *A Commentary on Micah* (Grand Rapids: Eerdmans, 2007), 464.

to Christ is *imputation*. Paul explains this by saying, "For our sake [God] made him to be sin who knew no sin, so that in him we might become the righteousness of God" (2 Cor. 5:21).

With what joy Micah would have witnessed the scene when John the Baptist first identified Jesus as the Messiah, saying, "Behold, the Lamb of God, who takes away the sin of the world!" (John 1:29). This was the same hope of forgiveness foretold by Isaiah in his prophecy of the coming Messiah as the Suffering Servant of the Lord: "All we like sheep have gone astray; we have turned every one to his own way; and the LORD has laid on him the iniquity of us all" (Isa. 53:6). By looking to the cross of Jesus, we who believe can all rejoice to see our sins imputed to Christ and taken away from us forever.

Micah uses a second verb to describe God's gracious response to our rebellion: "passing over" transgression (Mic. 7:18). Because of his compassionate love, God does not demand retribution on his rebellious people, but overlooks their offenses instead. The language here also points to the cross, this time through the events of the Passover. God had determined to punish Egypt for its rebellion, sending his angel of death to strike down all the firstborn of the land. But the Israelites were instructed to place the blood of a Passover lamb on their doorposts; when the angel of death saw the blood, God's wrath passed over the sins of God's people. Paul applies the significance of this event directly to Christians, whose rebellion against God is passed over, "For Christ, our Passover lamb, has been sacrificed" (1 Cor. 5:7). So it is today for those who seek refuge in the blood of Jesus. Micah praises God for "passing over transgression for the remnant of his inheritance" (Mic. 7:18), ultimately, for those who have confessed their sins and believed in the gospel of Christ.

We see why Micah glorifies the incomparable grace of our God. What other god ever spoke of sending his own Son to die on the cross for the sins of his people? What kind of deity responds to our wickedness against him by placing our guilt onto himself? Yet this is exactly what God has done for us. "Who is a God like you?" we marvel. Michael Bentley points out that this is the main difference between Christianity and all other faiths:

> Unlike all other, so-called, deities, our God pardons sin and forgives transgression. This is one of the things that any serious reader of the Gospels notices about Jesus Christ: he often forgave people their sins (e.g., Mark 2:5). He is the

same today. He still shows his wonderful mercy to sinners by forgiving them when they confess their sin, repent of it and turn in faith to him.[5]

Just as marvelous is *God's attitude in forgiving our sins*. Does God forgive begrudgingly, resentfully, or halfheartedly? Micah responds, "He does not retain his anger forever, because he delights in steadfast love" (Mic. 7:18). This is Micah's great hope for his people. Yes, God intended to chastise them for their great sin. But judgment would not last forever, and it would lead to forgiveness and the restoration of blessings. Why? Because of the God that he is! Because of the mercy and compassion in his heart for his people. Micah's hope is in the incomparable God, whose heart is moved by grace.

Micah describes God's heart with the Hebrew word *chesed*, the great Old Testament word for the covenant mercy and love of God. This word is so rich that it can hardly be given a single English translation. It is rendered as "steadfast love" by the English Standard Version; "faithful love" by the Holman Christian Standard Bible; "unchanging love" by the New American Standard Bible; and, perhaps most familiarly, as "mercy" by the King James and New International versions. What is the attitude of God's heart in forgiving our sins? Walter Kaiser writes, "He does not delight in holding a grudge, or in bottling up His anger over our sins."[6] Instead, he delights in tender, loving, mercy for his people.

The Scottish minister Alexander Whyte told of an evening when an older minister came to discuss some pastoral matters. When their business was completed, the old man seemed to linger, not wanting the conversation to end. Finally he asked, seemingly in jest, "Now, sir, have you any word of comfort for an old sinner like me?" Whyte realized that behind the half-smile was a real seriousness and even a deep agony. He wrote later, "It took my breath away. He was an old saint. But he did not know the peace of forgiveness." Whyte walked over and sat beside the older minister, opened his Bible to Micah 7:18 (NKJV) and read, "He delights in showing mercy."

It was on this mercy that Micah relied as well. We can imagine the power of this statement in the prophet's heart as he grasped for hope of Israel's

5. Michael Bentley, *Balancing the Books: Micah and Nahum Simply Explained* (Durham: Evangelical Press, 1994), 92.
6. Walter C. Kaiser Jr., *Micah–Malachi*, The Communicator's Commentary (Dallas: Word, 1992), 91.

forgiveness. In themselves, God's people had nothing to offer to gain their forgiveness. Jerusalem had partaken in the same idolatry that had doomed Samaria. But Micah would have answered, "He delights in showing mercy." Yes, but Jerusalem's leaders were lying awake at night devising new and more wicked schemes of robbing the poor. Nevertheless, "He delights in showing mercy." Corruption had so permeated society that Micah believed no godly people were left. He wrote, "They all lie in wait for blood . . . . Their hands are on what is evil, to do it well" (Mic. 7:2–3). Such wickedness had spread that a man could not even trust his wife or children. How could such depraved people be spared by a holy God? Because "he delights in showing mercy." Micah's hope lay in God's delight in mercy, and there he rested his burdened heart.

This was also Dr. Whyte's answer to the suffering old minister: "He delights in showing mercy." The next morning he received a letter in reply. It read: "Dear friend, I will never doubt Him again. Guilt had hold of me. I was near the gates of Hell, but that word of God comforted me, and I will never doubt Him again. I will never despair again. If the devil casts my sin in my teeth, I will say, 'Yes, it is all true, and you cannot tell the half of it, but I have to deal with the One who delights in showing mercy.'"[7]

Finally, Micah notes *the finality of God's forgiveness*: "He will again have compassion on us; he will tread our iniquities under foot. You will cast all our sins into the depths of the sea" (Mic. 7:19). The word for compassion (Hebrew, *racham*) speaks of tender affection, the way a mother loves a child. God responds to our sins the way a protective parent destroys a snake in the children's playground: "he will tread our iniquities under foot." Kenneth Barker writes, "Sin is pictured as an enemy that God conquers and liberates us from."[8] A. R. Fausset adds, "When God takes away the guilt of sin, that it may not condemn us, He takes away also the power of sin, that it may not rule us."[9] Here is God's answer to the third of our offenses: our guilt he takes away to the cross; our rebellion he covers with Christ's blood; and the corrupting power of evil in our hearts he treads under foot.

7. See Bryan Chapell, *The Promises of Grace: Living in the Grip of God's Love* (Grand Rapids: Baker, 2001), 136–37.

8. Kenneth L. Barker and Waylon Bailey, *Micah, Nahum, Habbakuk, Zephaniah*, The New American Commentary (Nashville: Broadman & Holman, 1999), 134–35.

9. Ibid., 135.

Not only does God tread on our sins, but he "will cast all our sins into the depths of the sea" (Mic. 7:19). Here, the allusion is to the destruction of Pharaoh's chariots in the Red Sea. Just as the Egyptians were prevented by God from catching up to the Israelites so as to destroy them, God will not allow our sins to catch up to us. John Mackay comments, "Just as not one of the entire army of Pharaoh that followed the Israelites into the Red Sea survived (Exod. 14:28), so too the consequences of 'all' their iniquities will be swept away by God."[10] With this in mind, no wonder that Micah echoes the praise the Israelites sang while looking back over the Red Sea:

> Who is like you, O LORD, among the gods? Who is like you, majestic in holiness, awesome in glorious deeds, doing wonders? You stretched out your right hand; the earth swallowed them. You have led in your steadfast love the people whom you have redeemed; you have guided them by your strength to your holy abode. (Exod. 15:11–13)

How important it is to our relationship with God, and to our peace and joy in salvation, that we realize the finality of our forgiveness in Jesus Christ. David Prior points out that in passages like this from Micah, God not only cast our sins into the sea, but he placed a sign on its banks ordering, "No fishing."[11] Another place where we read of the complete removal of our sins is the great new covenant promise made by Jeremiah and echoed in the book of Hebrews. God declares to us: "I will be merciful toward their iniquities, and I will remember their sins no more" (Heb. 8:12). How can an all-knowing God forget that we have sinned against him? Because, in Micah's language, he has lifted our sins and taken them to the cross; he has covered them with the blood of Christ; he has trodden them under his own foot; and he has cast them into the sea of his incomparable grace. Truly, Micah wonders, "Who is a God like you, pardoning iniquity and passing over transgression?" Or as Samuel Davies put it: "Who is a pard'ning God like Thee? / Or who has grace so rich and free?"[12]

---

10. John L. Mackay, *Jonah, Micah, Nahum, Habakkuk and Zephaniah: God's Just Demands*, Focus on the Bible (Ross–shire, UK: Christian Focus, 1998), 137.

11. David Prior, *The Message of Joel, Micah & Habakkuk*, The Bible Speaks Today (Downers Grove, Ill.: InterVarsity, 1998), 201.

12. Samuel Davies, "Great God of Wonders!" 1723–61.

INCOMPARABLE FAITHFULNESS

Can we count on God extending this same grace to us? Will God continue to delight in showing mercy to sinners today? Micah provides the answer in the concluding verse to his book of prophecy, a verse that convinced Micah of God's continuing mercy: "You will show faithfulness to Jacob and steadfast love to Abraham, as you have sworn to our fathers from the days of old" (Mic. 7:20). In other words, God shows mercy to his sinful people because of his incomparable faithfulness to his covenant promises of old in the Bible.

Micah praises God because he will "show faithfulness to Jacob." The word for "faithfulness" is *emet*, which also means "truth." God will be true to Jacob. In Genesis 28:14 God promised Jacob, Israel's namesake patriarch, that his offspring would be "like the dust of the earth," spreading abroad "to the west and to the east and to the north and to the south." How could God fulfill this promise if he annihilated Jacob's descendants because of their sin? Moreover, he promised that "in you and your offspring shall all the families of the earth be blessed." How could Jacob's children bring salvation to all the world if Israel itself fell victim to sin? The answer is that God could not be true to Jacob unless he worked salvation for Jacob's descendants, physical and spiritual, and in faithfulness to the promise God was delighted to show mercy to his people, ultimately by sending his own Son to die for their sins.

God will also show "steadfast love to Abraham." Here is the Hebrew word *chesed* again, which here might be translated best as "merciful, covenant fidelity." Abraham received promises that were even greater than those given to his grandson Jacob. On one occasion, God brought Abraham out under the bright panoply of the sky and said: "'Look toward heaven, and number the stars, if you are able to number them.' Then he said to him, 'So shall your offspring be'" (Gen. 15:5). In all the vast starry host Abraham beheld in that ancient desert sky, one star shone for every sinner who trusts in the Lord Jesus Christ. If you are a Christian, Abraham looked upon a star that represented you. How could God be faithful to Abraham unless you entered into the fullness of the promised salvation?

Micah thus concludes, "as you have sworn to our fathers from the days of old" (Mic. 7:20). All through the Bible, believers read promises of forgiveness and salvation given by God. Those promises now belong to us, who take possession of them by trusting in God's Word. Prominent among them all is the promise of Micah 7:19: "He will again have compassion on us; he will tread our iniquities under foot. You will cast all our sins into the depths of the sea."

The writer of Hebrews said of God's promises, "We have this as a sure and steadfast anchor of the soul" (Heb. 6:19). What other hope do we have but that God will be faithful to his promises of grace? Can we hope that we will win the battle with sin by our own strength? Can we imagine that we can reform our lives so as to make ourselves presentable to the holy God? Neither of these is a realistic hope. God's promises of faithful, covenant, forgiving grace not only assure us of his love for us in Christ, but they also give us the strongest of all incentives to live holy lives to the praise of his incomparable name.

Donald Grey Barnhouse explains how grace motivates us to holiness by telling of a man who was paralyzed by the fear of his sin. During the First World War the man had fallen into bad company, and while living in Paris he became engrossed in sexual sin. After the war, he became a Christian and fell in love with a wonderful Christian girl. But he was afraid to propose marriage to her out of the fear that his past sin would rise up and cause him to betray his marital vows. He came to Barnhouse and asked for advice. Barnhouse told him that if he wanted to marry the girl, he should start trusting her with his heart and tell her the truth about his past.

Barnhouse also told the man of another couple with a similar issue. After they had married, the husband told his wife of his sinful sexual past, and his fears about a future recurrence of those sins. She responded by kissing him and gently saying this:

> John, I want you to understand something. I know my Bible well, and therefore I know the subtlety of sin and the devices of sin working in the human heart. I know you are a thoroughly converted man, John, but I know that you still have an old nature and that you are not yet as fully instructed in the ways of God as you soon will be. The Devil will do all he can to wreck your Christian life, and he will see to it that temptations of every kind will be put in your way. The day might come—please God that it never shall—but the day might come when you will succumb to temptation and fall into sin. Immediately the Devil will tell you that it is no use trying, that you might as well continue on in sin and that above all you are not to tell me because it will hurt me. But, John, I want you to know that here in my arms is your home. When I married

you I married your old nature as well as your new nature. And I want you to know there is full pardon and forgiveness in advance for any evil that may ever come into your life.

Barnhouse finished telling the story, during which the former soldier held his face in his hands. But after the final words, he lifted his eyes and said wonderingly, "My God! If anything could ever keep a man straight, that would be it."[13]

That is it. God delivers us from the power of sin by first assuring us of our complete forgiveness through the blood of Christ. Why would he do this? Because "he delights in steadfast love" (Mic. 7:18). Because of his faithfulness to the promises of the Bible. Because in our salvation by grace alone, the holy, almighty, sovereign God proves the glorious truth of Micah's words of praise: "Who is a God like you, pardoning iniquity and passing over transgression for the remnant of his inheritance?" (Mic. 7:18).

---

13. Donald Grey Barnhouse, quoted in Boice, *The Minor Prophets*, 2:364–65.

Index of Scripture

INDEX OF SUBJECTS AND NAMES

AVAILABLE IN THE REFORMED
EXPOSITORY COMMENTARY SERIES

Esther & Ruth, by Iain M. Duguid
Jonah & Micah, by Richard D. Phillips
Daniel, by Iain M. Duguid
Zechariah, by Richard D. Phillips
The Incarnation in the Gospels, by Daniel M. Doriani,
Philip Graham Ryken, and Richard D. Phillips
Matthew, by Daniel M. Doriani
Luke, by Philip Graham Ryken
Galatians, by Philip Graham Ryken
Ephesians, by Bryan Chapell
1 Timothy, by Philip Graham Ryken
Hebrews, by Richard D. Phillips
James, by Daniel M. Doriani

FORTHCOMING

Acts, by Derek W. H. Thomas
1 Samuel, by Richard D. Phillips
1 Kings, by Philip Graham Ryken
John, by Richard D. Phillips
Philippians, by Dennis E. Johnson